THE
Living Cookbook

YVONNE TURNBULL

BETHANY HOUSE PUBLISHERS
MINNEAPOLIS, MINNESOTA 55438
A Division of Bethany Fellowship, Inc.

All scripture quotations are taken from *The Living Bible*, copyright © 1971 by Tyndale House Publishers, Wheaton, IL. Used by permission.

ACKNOWLEDGEMENTS

A big thank you to my loving husband, Bob, for his help with editing this cookbook. He encouraged me right from the very beginning to the very end. And a special thank you to this *brave* man who tasted and tested all of the recipes, including all my flops!

And a thank you to my mother, Gwen Gourlie, for her wise counsel. She spent one entire Christmas holiday helping me with research.

The Living Cookbook
Copyright © 1981, 1983
Yvonne Turnbull

ISBN 0-87123-318-5

Published by Bethany House Publishers
A Division of Bethany Fellowship, Inc.
6820 Auto Club Road, Minneapolis, MN 55438

Printed in the United States of America

INTRODUCTION

"Hi—I'm Yvonne Turnbull,
Welcome To My Kitchen . . ."

With that opening line I started to welcome the viewers to "The 700 Club" TV show in the early Fall of 1980. My weekly appearances on this popular syndicated TV talk show elicited quite a response. Most of the viewer reaction was to request the recipes of the various dishes I was displaying. Many of them, too, wanted to know when I was going to come out with a cookbook.

Frankly, I had not thought of doing one, but when the requests kept coming in I realized that that would be a natural by-product of the nutrition tips I was presenting on TV and through my seminars across the nation.

I then agonized on what kind of book! I have read so many good cookbooks throughout the years, I hardly knew where to start, or what to say!

Some wise counsel suggested I write a very simple cookbook for my initial publication effort. I could always follow up the first book with an advanced cookbook, plus do a "How To" book for those beginning a new direction into natural, wholesome foods. That made sense to this non-author.

So, here is my initial thrust into the cookbook market! My purpose is to help individuals eat better and enjoy it more by providing delicious, easy to prepare, nutritious foods. The dishes are from scratch, using natural and basic ingredients so you know and have control over exactly what you are eating. Using processed foods does not allow you that control. The little extra amount of time it takes to fix a dish from scratch will end up to be more worthwhile as it will be better tasting, less expensive and more nutritious for you than so-called "convenience foods."

It has been a pleasure to work on this book, and introduce healthy new recipes. I am thankful that all the foods in this book are "poison free."

As I write this I think of two verses in the New Testament of the Holy Bible: Romans 12: 1 & 2—"And so, my dear brothers and sisters, I plead with you to give your bodies to God. Let them be a living sacrifice, holy—the kind He can accept. When you think of what He has done for you, is this too much to ask? Do not copy the behavior and customs of this world, but be a new and different person with a fresh newness in all you do and think. Then you will learn from your own experience how His ways will really satisfy you."

We are to present our bodies as a "living sacrifice—holy and acceptable." We *all* need to strive for good health by eating the natural foods our Lord gave to us.

This book presents many of those God-given foods. Enjoy—and be blessed!

Yvonne Turnbull

CONTENTS

"Haven't you yet learned that your body is the home of the Holy Spirit God gave you, and that he lives within you? Your body does not belong to you. For God has bought you with a great price. So use every part of your body to give glory back to God, because he owns it."

—1 CORINTHIANS 6:19, 20, *TLB*

"It is because you must do everything to the Glory of God, even your eating and drinking."

—1 CORINTHIANS 10:31, *TLB*

CHAPTER 1

YOU MUST START HERE

1. The recipes specify whole grains rather than refined, bleached, enriched products . . . honey and molasses instead of white sugar . . . brown rice instead of white rice . . . cold pressed, unhydrogenated vegetable oils and butter are used in place of margarine and solid shortenings . . . plus wide use of *fresh* vegetables and fruits. Sprouts, yogurt, wheat germ, dried beans and grains are used frequently, too. The reasons for all my substitions can be found in Appendix A.

2. I have not added salt to any of my recipes, as there is too much evidence that indicates it can cause high blood pressure, fluid retention and even attributes to migraine headaches. As a substitute I use kelp, fresh herbs and vegetable seasonings. Through experiments, the absence of salt has shown to have no effect on the result of my recipes.

3. When an item in the list of ingredients is all in capital letters, i.e., "1 cup TOMATO SAUCE," that means the recipe for making Tomato Sauce is included in the book and can be found in the Index.

4. Some recipes will say to use cooked beans or grains. To find out how to cook them go to the grain or bean charts listed in the Index.

5. Vegetable Seasonings—see Appendix A for various listings.

6. When the word *oil* is mentioned, I use a variety of oils. Check in the glossary for different types, any one of which can be used.

7. T. = Tablespoon.

8. tsp. = teaspoon.

CHAPTER 2

APPETIZERS AND MUNCHIES

"Appetizers" and "Munchies" have a definite place in the American diet. However, they usually end up to be highly-processed, full of salt, sugar and white flour. They end up being high in calories but very low in nutrients. I feel they are important foods, so they should be made from all natural ingredients that will *build* the body, rather than food that will tear it down.

When you are entertaining, think of nonsweet snacks. The ingredients should be nutritious. For example—

• Set out platters of fresh raw vegetables and fruits, accompanied by any of the dips listed.

• Bowls of raw and unsalted seeds and nuts, such as cashew, peanuts, walnuts, sunflower seeds, seasame seeds, pumpkin seeds, etc. These make good high-energy munchies. They are also good sources of protein and vitamins B and E.

• Make a buffet of assorted homemade soups and breads.

• Homemade nut butters will assure you of a product free of emulsifiers, sugars and preservatives. For an inexpensive treat, place them on homemade crackers or use as a dip for vegetables.

• Whole Wheat Cream Puffs (see dessert section) filled with chicken salad or other spreads.

• Fresh homemade bread cut into interesting designs, then topped with any of the different spreads you will find located in the sandwich section.

• Nahit is another fun treat for all ages. It is cooked and drained garbanzo beans (chick peas). Just place them in a bowl and serve as you would peanuts.

• A mixture of dried fruit and homemade granola is quite tasty.

Of course you do not have to wait for company to serve these snacks. Have them ready for your family and you'll find they'll reach for these over the greasy potato chips, soda pop, and other junk foods.

Now—enjoy these appetizers and munchies!

HELPFUL HINTS

- For dips or salad dressings calling for yogurt—gently stir in yogurt as the blender blades will kill the friendly bacteria that you want to keep in the yogurt. Plus by beating it, it makes it thin as milk.

- Fresh raw vegetables, seeds and nuts will help add fiber to your diet. They also add a large supply of vitamins, minerals and enzymes.

- Fresh frozen mint and parsley are tasty garnishes that can be directly taken from the freezer and used.

- Dry thin slices of zucchini. Season with kelp and use in place of potato chips.

- Always keep on hand fresh fruit and a selection of cheeses. If company drops in unexpectedly, serve them the fruit and cheese on a platter along with fresh fruit juice.

- To use just a squirt of lemon juice, prick a hole in lemon end with a needle and squirt the juice out. When completed place a toothpick in the hole to seal.

- Wash all fruit and vegetables before using. Use a nontoxic vegetable cleaner and a vegetable brush to remove any pesticide or wax used on the fruits and vegetables.

- Dip your bananas in lemon juice right after they are peeled. They will not turn dark and the faint flavor of lemon really adds quite a bit. The same may be done with apples.

- Keep a toothbrush around the kitchen sink; you will find it useful in cleaning rotary beaters, graters, choppers and similar kitchen utensils.

- To get rid of unpleasant cooking odors—place a small pan of vinegar on top of stove. Add cloves and cinnamon and simmer.

- Shelled nuts and seeds should be stored in a refrigerator or freezer. Because of their high fat content they tend to become rancid if kept too long at room temperature.

- Cook cranberries only until they pop. If cooked longer, they will turn bitter. A slice of apple will remove the bitterness from cooked cranberries. It should be cooked with them.

- Nuts and sunflower or sesame seeds make a good garnish for salads and vegetable dishes.

- To facilitate cracking Brazil nuts, bake at 350° for 15 minutes or freeze them. Then crack open with a hammer.

- A great storage place for all your beverages during a party—the washing machine. Fill with ice and your favorite beverages. Just let ice melt and run through spin cycle to clear it out.

- Freeze unpopped popcorn; you will have fewer "old maids" (unpopped kernels) plus it keeps it fresh.

RELISHES

BEAN RELISH

1 small onion, chopped
3 stalks celery, thinly sliced
2 cups kidney beans, cooked
2 hard cooked eggs, coarsely chopped
2 tsp. Dijon mustard
1 tsp. curry powder

1/2 cup sliced sunchokes
   (Jerusalem artichokes)
1/3 cup chopped parsley
1 tsp. vegetable seasoning
MAYONNAISE

Combine all ingredients adding enough mayonnaise to moisten and bind together. Refrigerate several hours for flavors to blend.

Yield: 3 cups

CARROT RELISH

2 cups diced carrots
1/2 cup diced celery
1/2 small green pepper, finely diced
1 cup mung bean sprouts, chopped
1 onion, diced
1/4 cup water

1/2 tsp. vegetable seasoning
3 T. apple cider vinegar
1 T. oil
1-1/2 tsp. honey
1 tsp. dry mustard
1/2 tsp. mustard seed

Place carrots in steamer and cook until tender, about 6-8 minutes. Drain and put into a bowl with celery, pepper, mung bean sprouts and onion. Put 1/4 cup water into saucepan and add remaining ingredients. Bring to a boil and pour over vegetables. Mix well, cover and chill overnight, stirring once or twice. Add a little more seasoning if needed.

Yield: 6-8 servings

CRANBERRY RELISH

7 cups cranberries, frozen
1 apple, diced
3/4 cup water
1/2 cup honey

1 orange—juice and rind
1 tsp. cinnamon
1/2 cup walnuts

Take the cranberries from the freezer, place in a 2 quart saucepan, add diced apple and water. Cover and simmer until the cranberries stop "popping." Cool before you add honey. Add the juice of the orange and then grate the rind of the orange. Place the rind, cinnamon and walnuts in with other ingredients and mix.

Yield: 4–5 cups

FRESH CORN RELISH

10 ears sweet corn
1/2 cup chopped green peppers
1/4 cup sweet red pepper, diced
1/2 cup chopped onions
1/2 cup chopped celery
1/4 cup honey

2 tsp. dry mustard
1 tsp. vegetable seasoning
1/2 tsp. celery seed
1/4 tsp. turmeric
1 cup water
1-1/3 cups cider vinegar

Combine all ingredients in a saucepan and simmer for 20 minutes. Pack into clean, hot, pint jars, leaving 1" of head space, and making sure vinegar mixture covers vegetables. Adjust lids. Process in boiling water bath, 212°, for 15 minutes.

Yield: 3 pints

DIPS

CHEESE DIP

1 pound grated Cheddar cheese
1 cup SALSA SAUCE

1/2 cup diced chile peppers

Place the cheese, salsa and peppers in the top pot of a double boiler. The water should be hot, but not boiling. Heat until the cheese is melted. Pour into a chafing dish. Serve with cubed WHOLE WHEAT BREAD, PITA BREAD or TORTILLA CHIPS.

Yield: 2 cups

BEAN DIP

2 cups cooked and mashed kidney
beans
2 cups cooked and mashed pinto
beans
3/4 cups water (water that beans
cooked in)
1/4 cup oil
3/4 cup chopped onions

1 jalapeno pepper, chopped
3 tomatoes, peeled
1 clove garlic, minced
2 tsp. chili powder
1 tsp. cumin
1 tsp. kelp
1/4 cup lemon juice
1 cup grated Cheddar cheese

In a large saucepan add the beans, water, oil, onions, pepper, tomatoes, garlic, chili powder, cumin and kelp. Simmer for 1/2 hour. Remove from heat and add lemon juice and cheese. Blend until smooth. Serve with PITA BREAD, homemade CRACKERS or TORTILLA CHIPS.

Yield: 4 cups

FRUIT DIP

1 egg
1 egg yolk
1/2 cup unsweetened pineapple juice

1/4 cup lemon juice
1/2 T. honey

In a double boiler beat the egg and egg yolk slightly. Add the pineapple juice, lemon juice and honey. Cook over hot but not boiling water, stirring constantly until thick. Cool. Dip various fresh fruit into the fruit dip.

Yield: 1 cup

GUACAMOLE

1 large, ripe, avocado
4 tsp. finely chopped onion
1 tsp. finely minced garlic
1/2 tsp. chopped serrano chilies
(optional)

2 T. lemon juice
1/2 tsp. vegetable seasoning
1/4 cup cubed, fresh tomato
3 T. MAYONNAISE

Mash the avocado in a bowl with a fork until smooth or else blend until smooth in a blender. Add all other ingredients except for the mayonnaise. Mix well together. Cover the mixture with a thin layer of mayonnaise which will help prevent it from turning dark. Refrigerate, covered, until ready to serve. Just before serving, stir mayonnaise into mixture. Serve on crisp lettuce leaves as an appetizer; garnished with fresh cherry tomatoes or tomato quarters, celery sticks, cauliflower pieces and TORTILLA CHIPS or LAVOSH.

Yield: Serves 4

HUMMUS DIP

2 cups cooked garbanzo beans
    (chick peas)
1/3 cup TAHINI (sesame seed paste)
1/4 cup lemon juice
2 cloves garlic, crushed

1 T. tamari (soy sauce) optional
1 tsp. vegetable seasoning
Raw vegetables
PITA BREAD, cut into wedges

Place all ingredients, except bread and vegetables in a blender. Blend until a smooth consistency is obtained. This Middle Eastern recipe makes a delicious dip when served with pita bread and vegetables.

Yield: 2 cups

DILL DIP

1 cup plain YOGURT
3 T. finely chopped green onion

1 T. dill weed

Mix all together and chill overnight. Serve with vegetables or SESAME CRISPS.

Yield: 1 cup

VEGETABLE DIP

2/3 cup YOGURT
1/2 cup cottage cheese
2 T. chopped parsley
2 T. chopped chives
2 T. minced onions
1-1/2 T. lemon juice

1/2 tsp. basil
1/2 tsp. thyme
1 small clove garlic, minced
1/2 tsp. powdered kelp
1/4 tsp. dill weed

Mix all together and refrigerate overnight to blend flavor.

Yield: 2 cups

CRAB DIP

8 ounces cream cheese, softened
1 9-ounce can of crab meat, drained
    and flaked
3 T. MAYONNAISE
1 T. milk

2 T. finely chopped onion
1/2 T. horseradish
1 T. chopped parsley
1/3 cup slivered almonds

Combine cheese, crab meat, mayonnaise, milk, onion, horseradish and parsley. Mix well and place in oven-proof dish. Sprinkle almonds on top. Bake at 375° about 25 minutes. Stir lightly before serving. Serve with CRACKERS or vegetables. Can also be served cold.

Yield: 2 cups

TOFU DIP

1 pound TOFU
1 clove garlic, pressed
2 tsp. prepared mustard
1 T. oil
1/2 tsp. dill weed

2½ T. lemon juice
1 T. onion, finely chopped
(green onion)
3 T. tamari (soy sauce)

Purée all ingredients with blender. Serve as dip for CRACKERS, raw vegetables or over a salad.

Yield: 2 cups

APPETIZERS

CHEESE BALL

1 package (8 ounces) cream cheese
1/2 cup grated Cheddar cheese
1/2 tsp. vegetable seasoning
1 cup alfalfa sprouts

1/2 cup wheat sprouts
1 tsp. onions, chopped
1/2 cup chopped walnuts
Wheat germ

Cream together all ingredients except the wheat germ. Form into small balls or one big ball and roll in wheat germ until covered. Chill.

Yield: 20 balls or 1 ball

WHEAT BALLS

1/2 cup cream cheese
1 cup chopped walnuts
1 cup sprouted wheat

1 cup raisins
1/2 cup sesame seeds
Wheat germ

Mix all ingredients together except the wheat germ. Shape into balls and roll in wheat germ. Chill.

Yield: 12 balls

VEGETABLE TRAY

This tray could contain all or some of the following: Carrot sticks, celery sticks, sliced jicima, cherry tomatoes, pickles (beets or cucumbers), red cabbage wedges, sliced raw yams, cauliflower, broccoli flowerets, sliced Jerusalem artichokes, cucumber, zucchini, mushrooms, green onions, green peppers and turnip slices.

STUFFED CELERY

Select stalks of celery having a deep curve. Fill with a mixture made from any of the following:

> PEANUT BUTTER and sesame seeds
> Cream cheese and grated carrots or nuts and raisins
> Plain YOGURT, fruit juice and wheat germ
> Cheddar cheese and walnuts
> COTTAGE CHEESE and chopped cucumbers

Variations: Use the stuffings for dates, prunes and apple halves.

MUSHROOMS A LA GRECQUE

1 pound mushrooms, small
1/2 cup olive oil
1 clove garlic, finely chopped
1/3 cup cider vinegar

1 T. coriander seeds
1 bay leaf
1/2 tsp. thyme
1/4 tsp. kelp

Rinse mushrooms quickly in cold water and drain well. Heat oil in a large skillet and add garlic and all other ingredients, except for the mushrooms. Cover and cook for about 1 minute. Add mushrooms and cook covered for about 7 minutes. Cool. Then place in refrigerator for two days before serving. You can do this with other vegetables such as asparagus, cauliflower, artichoke hearts and zucchini.

Yield: 24 servings

CHEESE STUFFED MUSHROOMS

1½ pounds medium to large fresh
   mushrooms
1 package (8 ounces) cream cheese,
   softened
2/3 cup crumbled Blue cheese

1/4 cup thinly sliced scallions or
   green onions
1/4 cup finely chopped radishes
1/4 cup chopped walnuts

Rinse, pat dry and remove stems from mushrooms (use stems in soups, stews, etc.). Place mushroom caps, hollow-side up, on a platter. In a medium bowl combine cream and blue cheeses; stir until well blended. Mix in scallions, radishes and walnuts; fill mushrooms with mixture. Serve as an appetizer.

Yield: Serves 8

Variation: **Stuffed Cherry Tomatoes**—Slice tops off of 1 pint cherry tomatoes. Scoop out pulp with small melon ball cutter. Add pulp to above cream cheese mixture and proceed to stuff.

SPINACH PÂTÉ

3 pounds fresh spinach, washed
1 T. butter
1/2 cup onion, minced
1/4 pound mushrooms, minced
1 large clove garlic, minced
1 tsp. thyme
3 eggs
1/2 cup milk

1/8 tsp. nutmeg
1 tsp. oregano
1 T. lime juice
1/4 cup fresh parsley, chopped
1/4 cup Parmesan cheese, grated
1/2 cup whole wheat bread crumbs
1/2 tsp. vegetable seasoning
Tomatoes, red peppers,
    hard-cooked eggs for garnish

Heat a large skillet or wok and add the spinach. Cook in its own liquid just until the spinach wilts. Cool under cold water and squeeze out all the moisture. Chop fine. Heat the butter in another skillet and sauté the onion until tender. Add the mushrooms, garlic and thyme and cook, stirring, until the mushrooms are tender. Add this mixture and spinach together in a bowl. Beat the eggs and milk together and stir into the spinach mixture along with the remaining ingredients. Spoon into a buttered loaf pan lined with buttered parchment. Smooth the top and cover with a piece of buttered parchment. Cover pan with foil and bake 45 minutes in a 350° oven, or until firm. Remove from heat and cool. Unmold and serve garnished with tomatoes, red peppers, and hard-cooked eggs. Can also be served with TOMATO SAUCE. You can also freeze this pâté.

Yield: Serves 6

AVOCADO CUCUMBERS

2 cucumbers
1 small avocado
1 grated onion, finely chopped
1 T. of MAYONNAISE

1 T. lemon juice
Vegetable seasoning
6 cherry tomatoes, thinly sliced
1 cup alfalfa sprouts, chopped

Slice peeled cucumber diagonally across, about 1/2" thick. Mash avocado with a fork and whip until creamy. Add onion, mayonnaise, lemon juice and vegetable seasoning. Mix well. Spread cucumber slices with avocado mixture and top with a slice of tomato and sprouts.

Yield: 2 to 3 dozen slices

BITE SIZED PIZZAS

1 loaf of FRENCH BREAD, sliced
2 cups TOMATO SAUCE
1 large tomato, sliced

1 green pepper, sliced
1½ cups shredded Mozzarella cheese
1/2 cup Parmesan cheese

Place slices of french bread on a cookie sheet. Top each slice with tomato sauce, tomato slice, green pepper and the cheeses. Bake at 400° for 10 minutes or until cheese melts.

Yield: 15 pizzas

DEVILED EGGS

8 hard-cooked eggs, cut in half and
   yolks removed
1/4 cup MAYONNAISE
1/2 tsp dry mustard
2 tsp. tamari (soy sauce)

1½ tsp. lemon juice
1/2 tsp. vegetable seasoning
Paprika
Sliced tomatoes

Mash yolks thoroughly with fork. Blend in remaining ingredients except paprika and sliced tomatoes. Fill egg-white halves with yolk mixture; sprinkle with paprika. Arrange in center of platter; surround with tomato slices.

Yield: 16 stuffed eggs

DEVILED EGGS FLORENTINE

6 hard-cooked eggs
1 package (3 ounces) cream cheese,
   softened
1/4 cup fresh spinach, cooked,
   drained and finely chopped
3 T. grated Parmesan cheese

1/8 tsp. nutmeg
1 tsp. vegetable seasoning
Milk to thin
Mushrooms for garnish
Paprika

Cut eggs in half lengthwise. Remove yolks and combine with cream cheese, spinach, Parmesan cheese and seasoning. Thin with milk if desired. Spoon mixture into egg-white halves. Top with sliced or chopped mushrooms. Sprinkle with paprika.

Yield: 12 stuffed eggs

GINGER-MARINATED CHICKEN WINGS

1/3 cup tamari (soy sauce)
1/8 cup honey
1 T. arrowroot powder
2 T. cider vinegar

1 T. finely chopped fresh ginger
1 large clove garlic, minced
1 dozen (about 2 pounds) chicken
   wings

In a bowl, combine tamari, honey, arrowroot, vinegar, ginger and garlic. Arrange wings evenly in the bottom of a shallow dish and pour marinade evenly over top. Cover and chill 1 hour, or up to 4 hours. Remove wings from marinade. Arrange on a broiler pan and set under broiler about 4" from heat source. Cook, turning and basting with the marinade several times, for 15 to 20 minutes, or until done to your liking.

Yield: 12–18 pieces

BEAN BALLS TIDBITS

Ingredients for Balls:

1 cup chopped onion
2 cups cooked pinto beans
1 cup water (water that beans
    were cooked in)
1 cup chopped carrots
2 cups chopped celery
1 cup SALSA SAUCE

1 cup ground whole wheat PITA
    BREAD
1 tsp. garlic powder
1 tsp. onion powder
1/2 tsp. vegetable seasoning
Cracker crumbs, finely ground

Ingredients for Sauce:

1 cup water
3 cups TOMATO SAUCE
1 T. lemon juice
1 T. unsweetened apple juice
1½ tsp. cider vinegar

1 tsp. garlic powder
1 tsp. onion powder
1/4 tsp. ginger
1/4 tsp. cinnamon

Add onion, beans, water, carrots, celery and salsa together in a 2 quart sauce-pan. Cook until the vegetables are tender. Add any additional water that is necessary to keep beans from burning or sticking while cooking. Mash the bean and vegetable mixture. Add ground pita bread (you may use a blender to grind) and seasoning. Mix in enough of the cracker crumbs to firm up mixture so that it will form balls. Roll into small balls (about 1¼" diameter) and bake in a 300° oven for 45 minutes, until brown and crusty. While balls are baking, combine sauce ingredients and simmer 15 minutes. Place the sauce and bean balls into a chafing dish and serve as part of a party buffet.

Yield: Serves 8-10

ARTICHOKE & CHEESE APPETIZER

1 small onion, finely chopped
1 clove garlic, finely minced
Oil
4 eggs
1 can (14 ounces) artichoke hearts
1/4 cup bread crumbs, unseasoned

1/2 pound grated Cheddar cheese
1/2 cup plain YOGURT
2 T. parsley, finely chopped
Tamari (soy sauce)
1 tsp. vegetable seasoning

Sauté onion and garlic in oil, until soft. Beat eggs well in a large bowl. Drain artichokes and dice. Combine with eggs and add cooked onion and garlic, bread crumbs, cheese, yogurt, parsley, seasoning and tamari sauce. Pour mixture into a buttered baking dish, about 7" x 11". Bake for about 30 minutes in a 325° oven. When done, a knife inserted in middle will come out clean. Cool slightly and cut into squares to serve.

Yield: 15 squares

CHEESE & ONION PIE

1 cup milk
3 eggs
1 cup Cheddar cheese, cubed
1 T. arrowroot powder
1 T. oil

1 tsp. vegetable seasoning
1/2 tsp. oregano
2 medium onions, chopped coarsely
2 T. sesame seeds

Place first 7 ingredients in a blender and blend until smooth. Stir in onions and pour into a greased 9" pie pan. Sprinkle with sesame seeds. Bake uncovered at 300° for 50-60 minutes. Cut into wedges and serve either hot or cold.

MUNCHIES

TORTILLA CHIPS

1 dozen 6" CORN TORTILLAS

Heat oven to 400°. Cut each tortilla into 8 wedge-shaped pieces. Spread in single layer on cookie sheets. Bake 7 minutes, or until crispy.

NACHOS

5 cups TORTILLA CHIPS
2 cups grated Cheddar or Monterey
    Jack cheese

1 large tomato, diced
1 small can diced jalapeno chilies

Place all the chips on a heat-proof platter. Sprinkle with the tomato, chilies and cheese. Place the platter in a 350° oven and heat until the cheese melts. Serve at once. Can also be served along with SALSA or GUACAMOLE.

Yield: Serves 3-4

Variation:
Chicken Nachos: Before you add the cheese, pile on 1 cup cooked diced chicken. Place in oven and wait until cheese melts. Place on top shredded lettuce, 3 tablespoons of guacamole and 2 tablespoons plain yogurt.

POPCORN

A big bowl of popcorn is a treat for any age. Here are some exciting additions to the popped popcorn.

Garlic powder
Parmesan cheese
Vegetable seasoning

Cinnamon
ROASTED SOYBEANS and
    peanuts

POPCORN PARTY MIX

2 quarts popped popcorn
1 cup Whole Wheat PRETZEL sticks
1 cup raw mixed nuts, unsalted
1/2 cup sunflower seeds
1/2 cup ROASTED SOY BEANS

1/4 cup butter
1½ T. tamari (soy sauce)
1/2 tsp. garlic powder
1/2 tsp. onion powder
1/2 tsp vegetable seasoning

Melt butter in a small saucepan. Add seasonings. Mix thoroughly. In a large bowl, mix together the first 5 ingredients. Add the butter mixture and toss to mix. Spread into a large baking pan (shallow). Bake at 275° for 45 minutes. Stir 4 or 5 times. Store in a tightly covered container.

Yield: 2 quarts

GET UP AND GO POPCORN MIX

2½ quarts popped popcorn
1/3 cup honey
1/2 cup PEANUT BUTTER
1/2 cup dried milk powder (non-instant)

1 cup toasted coconut
2 T. toasted sesame seeds
1/2 cup raisins

Keep popped popcorn warm. Heat honey; stir in peanut butter and dried milk. Combine popcorn, coconut, sesame seeds and raisins. Pour honey mixture over popped corn while tossing to mix.

Yield: 2½ quarts

ROASTED SOYBEANS

1 cup dried soybeans   3 cups water

Wash soybeans and remove any foreign particles. Add the water to the soybeans and soak overnight in refrigerator. Pour soybeans and liquid they soaked in, into a saucepan. Add more water if needed to keep the beans covered. Bring to a boil, turn down and simmer for at least an hour. Remove from heat and drain liquid (save for soup). Spread soybeans onto a cookie sheet. Bake for a couple of hours in a 250° oven, or until brown and crispy. During the cooking time, stir the soybeans occasionally. Now ready to eat. Great snack—just like peanuts.

Yield: 3 cups

TOASTED PUMPKIN SEEDS

2 cups pumpkin or squash seeds   1½ T. tamari (soy sauce)
1½ T. oil

Separate fiber from pumpkin or squash seeds. Mix all ingredients together and spread onto a cookie sheet. Bake at 300° for 45 to 50 minutes or until crisp and brown; stir occasionally. Cool. Store in dry place. 1 medium pumpkin makes about 2 cups seeds.

Yield: 2 cups

Variation: Add 2 T. grated Parmesan cheese to the mixture.

SEEDS SNACK

1 cup pumpkin seeds
1/4 cup sesame seeds
1½ T. oil
1/2 tsp. cayenne
1 tsp. garlic powder

1 cup sunflower seeds
1 cup peanuts, unsalted
1 T. tamari (soy sauce)
2 tsp. onion powder

Mix all ingredients together in a large bowl. Spread onto a cookie sheet. Bake at 300° for 30 minutes. Stir frequently as it can burn easily. When cool, store in airtight container.

Yield: 3-4 cups

WALNUTS PARMESAN

1/4 cup oil
1 T. ITALIAN HERBS
1 tsp. paprika

3/4 tsp. garlic powder
3 cups walnut halves
1/4 cup grated Parmesan cheese

In a skillet, heat oil over low heat. Stir in seasoning; mix well. Add walnuts and stir until well coated. Spread nuts on a paper-towel lined shallow baking pan. Sprinkle with Parmesan. Bake at 300° 10-15 minutes or until crisp. Store in cool, dry place.

Yield: 3 cups

HOMEMADE PEANUT BUTTER

2 cups raw peanuts, skinned   1/4 cup oil

Spread raw peanuts onto a cookie sheet. Roast in 300° oven for about 20 minutes or until lightly roasted. Stir occasionally so they won't over brown. Cool, then place in blender. Blend about one minute and then gradually add the oil, one tablespoon at a time. Stop blender from time to time and push large pieces of peanuts away from sides of blender with a rubber spatula. Blend peanuts thoroughly. Store in refrigerator.

Yield: 1½ cups

Variations:

Almond Butter: Blanch nuts (2 cups) by covering with boiling water. Let stand for 5 minutes, drain and slip off skins. Place almonds on a cookie sheet and bake at 350° for 10-15 minutes. Place roasted almonds in a blender, add 3 tablespoons of oil and blend until smooth.

Cashew Butter: To roast, bake nuts (2 cups) 10-15 minutes at 350°. Place the cashews in a blender and blend with 5 tablespoons of oil.

CHAPTER 3

SOUPS AND SANDWICHES

"SOUP AND SANDWICHES." We both know they really go well together!

In this chapter I am going to show you quick and easy recipes for a variety of soup and sandwich ideas, and all of them packed full of healthy nutrients. We both know that on a cold winter day a big bowl of hot soup will warm you—and for those hot summer days, an ice cold bowl of soup is equally fitting. Soup making is an excellent way of stretching your food budget by making a little bit go a long way. Regardless of the type of soup—bean, chowder, broth, hot or cold—and whether it is served as an appetizer, main dish or even dessert—a good tasting soup alongside a delicious sandwich is a meal in itself.

Soups provide trace minerals, vitamins, protein, fiber and energy. Soups are low in calories and low in cost. I also *highly* recommend homemade soups over the canned or packaged soups you buy in the stores. The latter soups usually contain large amounts of salt and MSG, plus white flour and sugar, all of which can tear down your body. Homemade soup takes only a short while to fix. You can use the fresh, healthy foods in your kitchen.

Sandwiches should also be nutritious. In this chapter I will present several ideas that if followed will tell you what goes together to mix well, plus recipes for the fillings—all *healthy* for you.

Enjoy!

HELPFUL HINTS

- A good homemade broth is a secret of making any good-tasting soup from scratch.

- Use a light hand when seasoning stock. It should be well-seasoned, but not overpowering. Storage intensifies flavor, so adjust seasoning just before serving.

- Fish stock may flavor plastic freezing containers. You may want to per-manently label several for exclusive "fishy" uses.

- If you use a juicer, save the pulp and use it in making stock.

- Chill stock at least one day before using. You can then skim fat off the top easily.

- Freeze extra stock in one quart container and ice cube trays for later use.

- Do not peel your vegetables as this is where most of your nutrients lie. Just scrub well.

- Vegetables are sautéed in oil or butter first so the flavor of the vegetables is sealed in.

- If you need soup in a hurry, grind the grains and beans in a seed mill or blender and add to soup. They will cook quickly and act as a thickener.

- A blender is a handy gadget to use for making quick soups.

- If your children do not like vegetables, purée them in a blender and add them to the soup. They will not realize they are eating vegetables.

- Use the water in which you have soaked your sprouts and beans as a soup base. The water is full of nutrients that are too good to throw out.

- Use grated carrots and potatoes as thickeners in the soups.

- A light, thin soup is an excellent preface to a meal. It takes the edge off the appetite, and will discourage overeating at the meal.

- Use powdered milk in cream soups as it will improve flavor and nutri-tional value. Just mix up the powder and water to equal the amount of milk stated in the recipe.

- A leaf of lettuce dropped into the soup pot will absorb the grease from the top of the soup. Remove the lettuce after it has served its purpose.

- Another fortifier of nutrients is nutritional yeast. Add 2 tablespoons to a pot of soup.

- Freeze leftover cooked brown rice, bulgur wheat and beans in ice cube trays. When frozen, remove from trays and store in plastic bags. Add a few cubes to thicken and enrich your soups.

- Bean and grain soups are rich sources of protein and can be served frequently. They are also easy on the budget.

- For sandwiches, vary the types of bread used. Use wheat, rye, corn, oat, date, muffins, crackers, sandwich buns, pita.

- Vary the form of the sandwich, plain slices made into doubledeckers or cut into various shapes, or even rolled up.

- Have the sandwich filling plentiful. Make it a good serving.

- To prevent the sandwich from having wilted lettuce, place the lettuce under separate wrap and place on sandwich when ready to eat. A better way is to use sprouts instead of lettuce. You can place sprouts on the sandiwch when you make it as they will not wilt, plus you are getting more vitamins and minerals by eating sprouts instead of lettuce.

- Make sandwiches in bulk, wrap and freeze for up to 3 weeks. Nut butter, cream cheese, bean spread freeze well. Do *not* freeze lettuce, tomatoes, cucumbers or other fresh vegetables; add them later.

- If you have leftover beans, chicken, turkey or bean loaves, tuck them into a taco shell. Top with shredded lettuce, cheese, tomatoes and hot sauce.

GARNISHES FOR SOUPS

They add that something extra to the soup. Add just before serving.

Apples—unpeeled and sliced thin.

Cheese—sprinkle on Parmesan, Swiss or Cheddar cheese.

Crackers and CROUTONS—whole wheat, can be sprinkled with cheese and then added to soup.

Eggs—slice or grate hard-cooked eggs.

Lemon slices—cut very thin and float on top of soup.

Nuts—peanuts, almonds, ROASTED SOYBEANS, cashews.

Parsley—sprigs of parsley or fresh mint.

POPCORN—fresh popped.

Seeds—sunflower, pumpkin or sesame seeds.

SOUR CREAM or YOGURT—add a tablespoon on top.

Sprouts—alfalfa, mung, wheat.

STOCK MAKING

In preparation for stock-making, set aside two containers in your refrigerator. In one container place all your vegetable scraps and vegetables that have gone limp. For example: tough broccoli stems, parsley stems, vegetable peelings, celery and green onion tops, outer leaves of greens, or overripe tomatoes. In another container, store any liquid which is left after cooking vegetables, and even the water that you drain from your sprouts. These liquids are packed full of nutrients. Use these two containers weekly by making vegetable stock.

VEGETABLE STOCK

4 cups vegetables
8 cups liquid
1 bay leaf

1 tsp. each basil, thyme, oregano
1 clove garlic, minced

Add to a large soup pot, vegetable scraps you have been saving plus freshly chopped carrots, celery and onions. All of these vegetables should come to 4 cups. Cover with liquid which is liquid that you have stored plus added water. This mixture should come to 8 cups. Add seasoning. Cover pot and simmer for 1-1½ hours. Strain the stock. Place stock in refrigerator and let sit for a day. The fat will be easier to skim off. Now this stock is ready to be used as the base for vegetable soup or used in recipes that call for vegetable broth.

Yield: 12 cups

CHICKEN STOCK

3 pounds chicken backs or
　1 4-pound stewing chicken
2 sliced carrots
2 large peeled and sliced onions
2 stalks celery and tops

2 sliced leeks (white part only)
4 quarts water
1 bay leaf
1 tsp. each thyme, oregano

Put the chicken in a large kettle, add water and remaining ingredients. Bring to a boil, reduce heat and simmer covered 1 hour. Remove from heat, strain broth and refrigerate both the chicken and broth. When chicken is cool enough, remove the meat from the bones. Let stock sit in refrigerator for one day. The fat will be easier to skim off. Now the stock is ready to use as a base for chicken soup and can also be used in recipes calling for chicken broth. If you do not need all the stock, freeze it.

Yield: 2-3 quarts

Variation:
Turkey Stock: Use a half-bodied turkey carcass in place of the chicken. Add enough water to cover the carcass. Proceed as directed in chicken stock.

FISH STOCK

2 pounds fish heads, tails and bones, washed
5 cups water
1 onion, chopped
1 celery stalk and top, chopped
1 carrot, cut into cubes
2 sprigs of parsley

1 garlic clove, minced
2 T. lemon juice
1 T. cider vinegar
1 bay leaf
1½ tsp. vegetable seasoning
1/2 tsp. oregano
4 peppercorns

Combine all ingredients in a large soup pot. Bring to a boil, reduce heat and simmer for 30 minutes. Lay a cloth in a colander over another pot and strain juice. Refrigerate for a day, then skim off any fat. Use in any recipe calling for fish broth.

Yield: 1 quart

BOUILLON CUBES

2 cups VEGETABLE, CHICKEN or FISH STOCK
1 tsp. vegetable seasoning
1 bay leaf

1/2 tsp. thyme
1 T. fresh chopped parsley
1 T. gelatin
1/4 cup cold water

Add to the stock, the vegetable seasoning, bay leaf, thyme and parsley. Simmer for 2-3 hours. Strain. Soften gelatin in the cold water for 5 minutes. Add the gelatin to the hot stock and stir to dissolve. Add more vegetable seasoning if needed. Pour into a square dish and chill until firm. Cut into small inch-size cubes. Place in a sealed container and store in the refrigerator. One cube is used for each cup of broth desired in a recipe.

HEARTY SOUPS

VEGETABLE SOUP

8 cups VEGETABLE STOCK
5 cups assorted vegetables
1/4 cup chopped fresh parsley
1/3 cup brown rice or whole wheat pasta—cooked
1/3 cup kidney or navy beans, cooked

2 cups fresh, peeled tomatoes, cut up
1 tsp. oregano
1/2 tsp. thyme
1 tsp. vegetable seasoning
Tamari (soy sauce) to taste
Parmesan cheese

For the assorted vegetables you may want to use potatoes, carrots, onions, celery with leaves, cabbage, broccoli, peas and green beans, corn, all cut in different shapes. Don't dice everything. For example, cut green beans and celery in diagonal pieces, carrots and broccoli stalks in thin rounds and potatoes in cubes. Chop cabbage coarsely. Add the vegetables, stock, parsley, rice or pasta, beans, and tomatoes in a large soup pot. Bring to a boil, then turn to simmer and cook for about 45 minutes. Add seasoning and tamari and simmer for another 7 minutes. Serve piping hot topped with Parmesan cheese.

Yield: Serves 6

OLD-FASHIONED MUSHROOM SOUP

6 T. butter
1 pound mushrooms, thinly sliced
2 medium-sized onions, finely chopped
2 cloves garlic, finely chopped
2 carrots, finely chopped
3 stalks celery, finely chopped
3 T. flour
8 cups CHICKEN BROTH (stock)

2 ripe tomatoes, peeled, seeded and chopped
1 cup tomato purée
2 T. tomato paste
3 T. finely chopped parsley
1 T. tamari (soy sauce)
Vegetable seasoning to taste
1 cup SOUR CREAM or plain YOGURT

Heat 4 tablespoons of the butter in a large pot. Sauté the mushrooms for 3 minutes. Remove and reserve the mushrooms. Heat the remaining butter and sauté the remaining vegetables for 5 minutes. Stir in the flour and cook for 2 minutes. Add the chicken broth, half of the reserved mushrooms, the tomatoes, tomato purée and tomato paste. Season with the vegetable seasoning. Bring to a boil. Partially cover the pot, reduce the heat and simmer for 30 minutes. Add the remaining mushrooms, parsley and tamari and simmer for 5 minutes. Ladle the soup into a tureen and top with the sour cream or yogurt.

Yield: 8 servings

FRENCH ONION SOUP

1/2 cup butter
2 T. oil
6 cups white or Bermuda onions, peeled and sliced
1/2 tsp vegetable seasoning
3 T. whole wheat flour
8 cups VEGETABLE STOCK

3-4 T. tamari (soy sauce)
2 cloves garlic, finely chopped
1 bay leaf
8 slices (1½" thick) FRENCH BREAD
3/4 cup grated Parmesan cheese
2½ cups grated Swiss gruyére cheese

Heat the butter and oil in a large kettle or Dutch oven; stir in onions. Cook, covered, over low heat, stirring occasionally, until onions are transparent. Uncover and add vegetable seasoning. Increase heat and continue cooking 15 minutes, until onions are a rich golden brown. Sprinkle flour over onions, then cook and stir a few minutes to cook flour. Add broth, tamari, garlic, and bay leaf. Simmer, partly covered, for 30 minutes. Toast the bread on both sides while the soup is cooking. Pour the hot soup into 8 individual ovenproof casseroles, or a large 10 cup ovenproof casserole. Float the bread on top, sprinkle with the Parmesan cheese and lots of Swiss gruyére. Bake in a 350° oven 10 minutes or until cheese melts and forms a crust.

Yield: 8 servings

MINESTRONE

Has been said to be the national soup of Italy.

1½ cups kidney or navy beans, uncooked
2 quarts water
1 T. olive oil
1 clove garlic, chopped fine
1 onion, sliced fairly thick
1 leek, diced and washed
1 tsp. chopped fresh parsley
1 tsp. chopped basil
2 T. tomato paste

3 tomatoes, peeled and chopped
3 stalks celery, chopped
2 carrots, sliced
1 potato, peeled and diced
1 bunch spinach or chard, chopped
2 zucchinis, cut into rounds
2 tsp. vegetable seasoning
1 cup whole wheat elbow macaroni
Tamari (soy sauce) to taste
PESTO SAUCE

Wash beans and soak in the water overnight. Bring the beans and soaking water to a boil. Cover, turn down heat and simmer the beans for about an hour or until tender. In a saucepan heat the oil and add the garlic, onion, leek, parsley and basil. Brown lightly. Add the tomato paste thinned with a little water and cook 5 minutes. Add the tomatoes, celery, carrots, potato, spinach or chard, zucchini and seasoning. Cook for about 10 minutes. Add this mixture to the beans and water. Add extra water if needed. Simmer for about 20 minutes. Add the macaroni and tamari and simmer for another 15 minutes. Taste and correct seasoning. During the last 2 minutes of cooking, add about 1 tablespoon pesto sauce for each cup of soup.

Yield: 6 servings

Variation:
Soybean Minestrone: In place of the kidney or navy beans, add 2½ cups cooked soybeans.

CHICKEN RICE SOUP

6 cups CHICKEN STOCK
1/2 cup brown rice, raw
1/3 cup onion, diced
2 carrots, cubed
1/3 cup celery, sliced
1/2 cup fresh peas

2 T. oil
1 cup cooked chicken, diced
1 tsp. vegetable seasoning
Tamari (soy sauce) to taste
Chopped fresh parsley for garnish

Heat chicken stock to boiling. Add rice and simmer 40 minutes. Add all the other ingredients, except for the parsley. Simmer for another 20 minutes. When ready to serve sprinkle with chopped parsley.

Yield: serves 6

Variation:
Chicken Barley Soup: In place of the brown rice add 1/2 cup barley.

HEARTY TURKEY VEGETABLE SOUP

4 cups TURKEY STOCK
1/2 cup barley, brown rice, or
   millet (uncooked)
1 tsp. each vegetable seasoning and
   oregano
1 large onion, sliced

1/2 cup chopped fresh parsley
1 cup chopped celery
1 cup sliced carrots
1 cup whole corn, raw
1 cup sliced zucchini
1 cup cubed cooked TURKEY

Combine the stock, barley or other grains, seasoning, onion and parsley in a large soup pot. Bring to a boil; lower heat, cover and simmer 40 minutes. Stir occasionally. Add more stock if necessary. Add celery, carrots; simmer an additional 15 minutes. Add corn, zucchini and turkey and simmer for 7 minutes. Serve right away while still hot.

Yield: Serves 4

LENTIL SOUP

Lentils have a high protein content, potassium and B vitamins. This bean is mentioned quite frequently in the Bible. In fact, as mentioned in Genesis 25: 29–32, Esau sold his birthright to Jacob for a swallow of lentil soup.

2 cups dry lentils, rinsed
6 cups VEGETABLE STOCK
3 T. olive oil
1 large onion, chopped
2 celery stalks and tops, chopped
2 carrots, sliced in circles
1 garlic clove, minced

2 cups stewed tomatoes
1/4 cup lemon juice
2 T. chopped fresh parsley
1/2 tsp. each thyme and tarragon
2 T. tamari (soy sauce)
2/3 cup shredded Swiss cheese

Place lentils in a large soup pot. Add stock and simmer in a covered pot until tender, about 45 minutes. While the lentils are cooking, sauté the onion, celery, carrots and garlic in oil. Sauté for 3 minutes. Add this mixture to the cooked lentils and stock. Also add the tomatoes, lemon juice, parsley, seasoning and tamari. Simmer for about 20–30 minutes or until soup is well-blended. When ready to serve, sprinkle cheese in the bottom of the soup bowl and ladle in the soup. With the addition of cheese, it makes this dish a complete protein.

Yield: Serves 6

Variation:
Lentil-Barley Soup: Add 1/2 cup barley along with all the other ingredients and cook as usual.

SOYBEAN SOUP

2 cups cooked soybeans
1/2 cup bulgur wheat, uncooked
1 large beet
1 carrot
1 potato
7 cups water (water soybeans were
    cooked in)
1/2 cup eggplant, peeled and sliced
1/2 cup chopped celery
1 cup shredded cabbage

2 T. oil
1 onion, chopped
1/3 green pepper
2 T. arrowroot powder
2 cups tomato purée
2 T. parsley, chopped
1/2 bay leaf
1 tsp. vegetable seasoning
2 T. tamari (soy sauce)

Mash beans lightly. Cube or shred beet, carrot and potato. Place in a large pot the beans, bulgur, beet, carrot, potato and water. Bring to a boil, reduce heat to low and simmer for 15 minutes. Add eggplant, celery and cabbage and cook for 10 minutes more. Sauté in oil the onion and pepper until browned lightly. Then add arrowroot. Mix thoroughly and continue cooking 1 to 2 minutes. Add onion mixture, tomato purée, parsley, bay leaf and vegetable seasoning to the soup. Cook for 15 minutes on simmer. Let stand 3 hours before serving to let flavors mingle. When ready to serve, heat until warm and add tamari sauce.

Yield: 6 servings

EIGHT BEAN SOUP

1/4 cup each of kidney beans,
    Great Northern beans, lima beans,
    pinto beans, navy beans, lentils,
    green split peas and garbanzos
8 cups water
1½ cups fresh or stewed tomatoes,
    chopped
1/4 cup chopped onion
1/2 cup chopped green pepper

1/2 cup chopped celery
1/2 cup chopped carrots
1/2 cup chopped fresh parsley
1 minced garlic clove
2 bay leaves
1/4 tsp. each marjoram and thyme
1/2 tsp. each basil and rosemary
2 T. tamari (soy sauce)

Soak the beans overnight in a large pot with the 8 cups of water. In the morning place the beans and any additional water that is needed to make 8 cups, on the stove. Bring to a boil and then turn down heat to low and simmer, covered, until tender, about 1-1½ hours. Add all of the rest of the ingredients (except tamari) and simmer for about 30 minutes. Remove bay leaf and add the tamari just before you are ready to serve.

Yield: Serves 4-5

SPLIT PEA SOUP

5 cups VEGETABLE STOCK or
    water
1 cup split peas (yellow or green)
2 T. oil
1 onion, diced
1 clove garlic, minced
1 stalk celery and top, diced

· 1 carrot, chopped
1 T. chopped fresh parsley
1/2 tsp. thyme
1/2 tsp. savory
1 small bay leaf
2 T. tamari (soy sauce)

Bring the stock or water to a boil. Add the split peas and simmer for 45 minutes. Cook onion, garlic, celery and carrot in oil until soft and translucent, about 5 minutes. Add this mixture, along with the parsley, thyme, savory, and bay leaf to the cooked split peas. Simmer for about 20 minutes. Add the tamari just a few minutes before the soup is finished. Remove the bay leaf before serving.

Yield: Serves 4-6

Variation: After the peas are cooked, place in a blender and blend until smooth. Add the puréed peas back into the soup and cook as usual.

BARLEY STEW

3 T. oil
1 large onion, chopeed
1 garlic clove, minced
1 cup fresh green beans, cut into
    1/2" pieces
1 cup chopped celery
1 cup chopped carrots
2 T. chopped fresh mint
1/4 cup chopped fresh parsley
6 cups VEGETABLE STOCK

1 tsp. vegetable seasoning
2 tsp. dill
1-1/3 cups barley, cooked
1/2 cup dried beans, cooked
    (combine several—Great
    Northern, pinto, baby limas,
    kidney)
3-4 large fresh tomatoes, chopped
2 T. arrowroot powder
1/4 cup water

Sauté the onion and garlic in the oil. Add the green beans, celery and carrots and continue sautéing until the vegetables are tender but crisp. Place in a large pot the sautéed vegetables, mint, parsley, stock, vegetable seasoning and dill. Simmer for 7 minutes. Add the barley, beans and tomatoes. Mix the arrowroot in the water and add this to the pot. Simmer, covered, for about 1/2 hour. Stir occasionally.

Yield: Serves 4-5

CREAM SOUPS

PUMPKIN SOUP

3 T. onion, diced
3 T. oil
2 T. soy flour
4½ cups CHICKEN STOCK
1½ T. arrowroot powder
1/4 cup water
2¼ cups pumpkin purée
1/4 tsp. ginger

1/4 tsp. nutmeg
1/2 tsp. cinnamon
1 cup non-instant dry milk powder
1 cup water
1/2 tsp. vegetable seasoning
3 egg yolks, lightly beaten
Sunflower seeds for garnish

If you are using whole, fresh pumpkins you must prepare them first (see vegetable section). When cooked, run through a blender to purée. Sauté onion in oil until tender. Stir in flour and cook over low heat, stirring constantly. Gradually add the chicken stock, stirring with a wire whisk until mixture is smooth and boils. Mix arrowroot powder with 1/4 cup water and add to mixture. Stir until thickened. Add pumpkin and spices. Transfer all to the top of a double boiler. Combine the milk powder with the 1 cup water in a blender. Add to the soup and heat thoroughly. Add vegetable seasoning. Add some of the hot soup slowly to the beaten egg yolks, stirring constantly. Then add this mixture to the hot soup. Turn heat off and just keep soup warm, but do not cook or else the soup will curdle. Ladle into the soup bowls and garnish with sunflower seeds.

Yield: 8 cups

CHEDDAR CHEESE SOUP

4 T. butter
1/4 cup finely chopped onion
1/2 cup finely chopped green pepper
1/2 cup finely chopped carrot
5 T. whole wheat flour
4 cups CHICKEN BROTH (stock)

3 cups grated sharp Cheddar cheese
(3/4 pound)
2 cups milk
1/4 tsp. vegetable seasoning
1/2 cup CROUTONS
Chopped parsley

In a 3-quart saucepan, cook onion, green pepper and carrot in the butter. Cook until tender, about 10 minutes. Remove from heat; stir in flour, and mix well. Cook one minute, stirring constantly. Gradually stir in broth and cheese; cook, over medium heat and stirring, until cheese has melted. Gradually add milk. Season with vegetable seasoning. Bring just to boiling, but do not boil. Serve with CROUTONS, and sprinkle with the parsley.

Yield: 6–8 servings

TOMATO SOUP

2 cups peeled, chopped ripe tomatoes
    (about 2 tomatoes)
1/4 cup chopped onion
1 small bay leaf
1 clove garlic, minced
1/4 tsp. basil

1/2 tsp. oregano
1 tsp. vegetable seasoning
2 T. butter
2 T. whole wheat flour
1/2 tsp. vegetable seasoning
2 cups milk

In a saucepan combine the tomatoes, onion, bay leaf, garlic, basil, oregano and vegetable seasoning. Bring to a boil, reduce heat and simmer about 10 minutes. Remove the bay leaf. Place mixture into a blender or food processor, cover and process until smooth. Set this mixture aside. In the same saucepan you used for cooking the tomatoes, melt the butter over low heat. Blend in the flour and the vegetable seasoning. Stir with a wooden spoon until no lumps remain. With the saucepan over low heat, add the milk all at once. Stir constantly to distribute the fat-flour misture throughout the total amount of cool milk. Cook over medium heat, stirring constantly in a figure-8 motion so that the sauce is heated evenly throughout. If you beat it it will turn out slick rather than smooth and velvety. Continue cooking until the mixture thickens and bubbles across its entire surface. Cook 2 minutes longer. Slowly add the hot tomato mixture to the white sauce, stirring to blend. Heat through, if necessary. Do not heat mixture too long or allow it to boil as it can curdle. Serve immediately.

Yield: 4 servings

Variation:
Tomato Rice Soup: Add 3/4 cup cooked brown rice to the soup just before it is finished cooking.

POTATO SOUP

5 cups potatoes, peeled and diced
1/2 cup celery, diced
1/3 cup leeks or onions, diced
1/2 cup carrots, diced
1/2 tsp. dill

1/2 tsp. vegetable seasoning
6 cups water
1½ cups milk
1 T. whole wheat flour
Chopped parsley for garnish

In a large saucepan, place the diced potatoes, celery, leeks or onion, carrots, seasoning and water. Place over medium heat and bring to a boil. Cover and turn heat down to low and simmer for 20 minutes or until vegetables are tender. Mix together the milk and flour and then add to the soup mixture. Simmer over low heat about 5 minutes, stirring constantly. Do not boil. Serve garnished with parsley.

Yield: 6 servings

CREAM OF VEGETABLE SOUP

1 cup cooked vegetable, puréed
1/2 cup cooked vegetable, chopped
1 T. oil or butter
3 T. chopped onion
1 garlic clove, minced
1 T. arrowroot powder
1½ cups milk

1 cup VEGETABLE BROTH
(stock)
1 tsp. vegetable seasoning
1/2 tsp. kelp
Additional seasoning
Wheat germ, CROUTONS, parsley
or chopped nuts as a garnish

Heat the butter in a saucepan over low heat. Sauté the onion and garlic until the onion is tender. Stir in arrowroot to form a smooth paste. Gradually stir in the milk and broth and cook until mixture thickens. Cook 1 to 2 minutes longer. Be sure to stir frequently. Steam the vegetables until tender. Place some of the vegetables in a blender and purée—this should come to 1 cup. Chop the other steamed vegetables—this should equal 1/2 cup. Now remove the cream sauce from heat and add seasoning and vegetables, stirring until smooth. Just before serving, reheat but do not boil. Choose garnish you would like.

Yield: 4 servings

Variations:

Cream of Celery Soup: Season with 1 tsp. of rosemary and 1/4 tsp. basil.
Cream of Cauliflower Soup: Season with 1 tsp. dill.
Cream of Carrot Soup: Season with 1 tsp. dill.
Cream of Broccoli Soup: Season with 1 tsp. nutmeg plus add 1 cup shredded
   Cheddar cheese to the cream sauce and stir until melted.
Cream of Asparagus Soup: Season with 1/2 tsp. each basil, marjoram and
   rosemary.

FISH SOUPS

FISH SOUP

8 cups FISH STOCK
1 cup peeled and chopped tomatoes
2 stalks celery, chopped
3 carrots, sliced
4 potatoes, peeled and diced
1 cup beans (of your choice) cooked

1/4 cup lemon juice
2 cups diced raw halibut, cod, or
   other white fish
2 T. arrowroot powder and 1/4 cup
   water
1 tsp. vegetable seasoning
1 T. tamari (soy sauce)

In a large soup pot add the stock, tomatoes, celery, carrots, potatoes, beans, lemon juice and fish. Bring to a boil, reduce heat and simmer for 20 minutes. Mix the arrowroot with the water and add to the soup. Stir until it thickens slightly. Add vegetable seasoning and tamari and simmer for another 10 minutes.

Yield: 6 servings

OYSTER CHOWDER

2 medium sized potatoes, diced
1 carrot, finely chopped
2 stalks celery, chopped
6 T. butter
1-1/3 cups chopped onion
2 pints fresh oysters in liquid or
    2 dozen oysters and 2/3 cup liquid

2 T. whole wheat flour
1 tsp. vegetable seasoning
1/2 tsp. kelp
4 cups milk
2 T. chopped parsley and paprika
    as garnish

In a large saucepan, steam the potatoes, carrot and celery until tender. In a 3 quart saucepan heat butter. Add onion and oysters; cook 3–5 minutes, or until edges begin to curl. Add flour and stir until smooth. To the oyster mixture add the vegetable seasoning, kelp, milk and steamed vegetables. Heat over medium heat, just until bubbles form around edge of pan. Do not boil. Sprinkle with paprika and chopped parsley.

Yield: 4–6 servings

Variations:
Clam Chowder: In place of oysters, add 1 pint shucked fresh clams or 2 cans (10½ ounce size) minced clams plus liquid.
Corn and Clam Chowder: Use the amount of clams specified in the Clam Chowder plus add 1½ cups fresh corn kernels.
Turkey Chowder: In place of the oysters use 2 cups diced cooked turkey. Also add 1 medium-sized tomato, chopped, 1/4 tsp. rosemary and 1/4 tsp. oregano.

MANHATTAN CLAM CHOWDER

36 large chowder clams or 2 cans
    (8 ounces each) minced clams
1/4 cup sweet butter
1 large onion, diced (1 cup)
1½ cups diced potatoes (2 medium-
    sized)
1 cup diced celery
3/4 cup diced carrots (2 medium-
    sized)

1/4 cup diced green pepper
3 T. parsley
1 can (2 pounds, 3 ounces) Italian
    plum tomatoes plus juice
1½ tsp. thyme
1/2 tsp. vegetable seasoning
1/8 tsp. curry powder
1 T. tamari (soy sauce)

Shuck fresh clams; reserve broth; chop clams coarsely. If using canned clams, drain and reserve broth. Broth from clams should measure 2 cups; if not, add water or bottled clam broth. Melt butter in a large saucepan. Sauté onions until lightly browned. Add remaining ingredients and extra water, if needed, to cover vegetables. Bring to a boil, reduce heat, cover and simmer 15 minutes, or just until vegetables are tender. Add fresh or canned clams; turn off heat; cover and let stand 3 minutes. Serve with SESAME CRISPS.

Yield: 6 servings

QUICK SEAFOOD BISQUE

6 cups water
4 medium potatoes, peeled and
    quartered
2 medium onions, coarsely chopped
1 carrot, diced
1/2 bay leaf
1/2 tsp. thyme

1/4 tsp. finely minced garlic
1 tsp. vegetable seasoning
1 cup shopped sea scallops, shrimp,
    lobster or crabmeat
2 egg yolks
1/2 cup heavy cream or YOGURT
Paprika

Bring two cups of water to a boil. Add the potatoes, onion, carrot, bay leaf, thyme, garlic and seasoning and simmer until the vegetables are just tender, about 15 minutes. During the last 5 minutes of cooking add the seafood. Remove the bay leaf and pour the mixture into a blender. Blend until puréed. Return to the saucepan and add the remaining water. Bring to a boil and add any additional seasoning. Turn off the heat and stir in the egg yolks blended with the cream. Serve hot or chill. Garnish with paprika.

Yield: 8 servings

COLD SOUPS

BLACKBERRY SOUP

8 cups blackberries
4 cups water
1/4 cup lemon juice
4 slices of lemon
6 T. honey
2½ T. arrowroot powder

1/4 cup water
1/4 tsp. cinnamon
1/4 tsp. nutmeg
1/8 tsp. cloves, ground
YOGURT

Combine 7 cups of the blackberries with the water, lemon juice, lemons and honey. Simmer for 5 minutes, mashing the berries to get the juice. Strain, pressing the pulp to remove the juice. There should be about 6 cups of juice. Dissolve the arrowroot with the 1/4 cup of water. Place the arrowroot and blackberry juice in a saucepan and heat on low until thickened. Cool. Add the reserved 1 cup of berries and spices and place in refrigerator for 2 hours before serving. When time to serve, serve with a spoonful of yogurt on each serving.

Yield: 8 cups

COLD MELON-PAPAYA SOUP

1 large, ripe cantaloupe	2½ cups orange juice
1 papaya	3 T. lime juice
1/4 tsp. cinnamon	1/2 cup YOGURT
1/4 tsp. nutmeg	Sprig of fresh mint as a garnish

Remove seeds from melon and papaya, peel and cut into cubes. Place melon, papaya and all other ingredients into a blender and purée. Pour mixture into a bowl, cover, and refrigerate at least one hour before serving. Remove from refrigerator and stir before you serve. Serve garnished with sprigs of fresh mint. Good served as a luncheon soup or even as a dessert.

Yield: 4 servings

COLD CURRIED AVOCADO SOUP

2 T. butter	1/2 cup plain YOGURT
2 bunches scallions, finely chopped	1/2 tsp. vegetable seasoning
3 tsp. curry powder	1 T. chopped fresh dillweed
2 medium-sized avocados, peeled	Grated rind and strained juice of
and chopped	1 lemon
8-10 cups CHICKEN BROTH (stock)	Fresh parsley or chives for garnish

Heat the butter in a small skillet. Add the scallions and sauté for 4 minutes, until tender. Add the curry powder and stir for 1 minute to release the flavor. Purée the curried scallions, avocados, 1 cup of broth, yogurt, lemon rind and juice and seasoning in the blender. Transfer the purée into a large serving container, and stir in the remaining chicken broth until a desirable pouring consistency is reached. It will thicken as it stands. Cover and refrigerate for 4 hours. Garnish with fresh herbs and accompany with TORTILLA CHIPS.

Yield: 8 servings

GAZPACHO

This liquid cold soup comes from the country of Spain.

1 cup tomato juice	1 medium chopped cucumber,
3/4 cup VEGETABLE BROTH	peeled
(stock)	1/2 red or green pepper, chopped
1 tsp. tamari (soy sauce)	very fine
1 tsp. vegetable seasoning	2 small green onions, chopped fine
2 T. lemon juice	1 sprig parsley, chopped fine
1 T. cider vinegar	1 clove garlic, minced
4 tsp. olive oil	Bread crumbs and chopped fresh
4 large tomatoes, peeled and chopped	parsley for garnish

Place the first seven ingredients in a blender and blend briefly. Add remaining ingredients; blend with on-and-off motion until vegetables are just chopped. Chill for at least 3 hours. Garnish with the bread crumbs and parsley. A good soup to serve at a luncheon.

Yield: Serves 6

COLD CUCUMBER SOUP

2 T. oil
1 onion, finely chopped
1 clove garlic, minced
3 large cucumbers, peeled and finely
  chopped
2 T. arrowroot powder dissolved in
  3 T. water

2 cups CHICKEN STOCK
1 tsp. vegetable seasoning
3/4 cup plain YOGURT
1 T. fresh dill
1 tsp. grated lemon peel
1/8 tsp. mace

Sauté in oil the onion, garlic and cucumbers for about 5 minutes. Add the arrowroot and mix well. Pour in the chicken stock and vegetable seasoning and bring to a boil. Reduce heat and simmer, covered, until cucumber is tender. Cool. Place cool mixture in blender and purée until smooth. Stir in the yogurt, dill, lemon peel and mace. Chill for several hours.

Yield: 4-6 servings

SANDWICH SECTION

SANDWICH SUGGESTIONS

Following are main ingredients for making delicious sandwiches, plus some sandwich combinations. For example with **Peanut Butter** you would add the line that says "Honey and nuts or wheat germ." With **Cream Cheese** one of the combinations would be the line that says "Pineapple, curry and raisins," and so on.

PEANUT BUTTER or NUT BUTTER

Honey and chopped nuts or wheat germ
Sliced bananas and sesame seeds
Grated carrots and raisins
APPLESAUCE and sliced dates
Cashew, coconut and lime juice
Lemon juice, chopped dates and raisins
Cream cheese and APPLE BUTTER
Sliced peaches, pears or apples

CREAM CHEESE

Cucumbers, mushrooms and sprouts
Pineapple slices, cinnamon and nuts
PEANUT BUTTER and orange juice
Sliced hard-cooked eggs, celery and sprouts
Avocado, shrimp, cucumber and hard-cooked eggs
Pineapple, curry and raisins
Banana, honey, dates or walnuts
Plain—placed on sliced nutbread

JACK, CHEDDAR OR SWISS CHEESE

MUSTARD, hard-cooked eggs, sprouts and pumpkin seeds
EGG SALAD, grated carrots, bean sprouts, sunflower seeds
Avocado, tomato, water chestnuts, sprouts
Avocado, hard-cooked eggs, sprouts

COTTAGE CHEESE

Dried fruit and walnuts
Zucchini, mushrooms and sprouts
Cucumbers, mushrooms, tomato

TAHINI

COTTAGE CHEESE and sprouts on DATE NUT BREAD
Sliced banana, chopped walnuts and sunflower seeds
GARDEN VARIETY and sprouts

OTHERS

Use any bean, grain or nut loaf—top with KETCHUP or MAYONNAISE, a
variety of fresh vegetables and sprouts

TUNA or CHICKEN SALADS—tomato, sprouts and nuts

BREADS TO USE:

FLOUR TORTILLAS/CHAPATI
PITA (Bible) BREAD
Whole grain breads
Whole grain crackers
Nut or date breads

FOOD SUGGESTIONS TO ACCOMPANY SANDWICHES

Fresh vegetables:
   cabbage wedges, carrot and celery curls or sticks, cauliflower flowerets, broccoli, zucchini slices, green pepper strips, cherry tomatoes, radish roses, turnips, jicima and cucumbers

Stuffed celery, apples:
   PEANUT BUTTER, cream cheese, TUNA or EGG SALAD, or any of the spreads listed. Can also be placed on slices of cucumbers, zucchini or rolled in lettuce leaves

Hard-cooked eggs
Chicken or turkey pieces
YOGURT
Soups, chili, stews, chowders
Raisins, dried fruits, nuts, seeds, crunchy coconut, POPCORN
Fresh fruit
Whole grain cookies, cobblers, puddings

FALAFEL

Also called the "Taco from Morocco."

3 cups cooked garbanzo beans (chick peas)	1/4 cup sesame seeds
1/4 cup liquid from cooking beans	1 tsp. vegetable seasoning
1/4 cup wheat germ	1 tsp. cumin
1 small onion, finely chopped	1 tsp. chili powder
2 garlic cloves, minced	1/4 cup lemon juice
4 T. chopped fresh parsley	1/4 tsp. basil
	3/4 cups cracker crumbs or wheat germ

Place the garbanzo beans and liquid into a blender and purée. Place contents in a bowl and add all other ingredients except for the cracker crumbs or wheat germ, but add just enough cracker crumbs or wheat germ so the mixture will hold together. Roll mixture into balls 1½" in diameter. Place balls on a cookie sheet and bake in a 400° oven about 15 minutes, turning to brown evenly. Serve in heated PITA (Bible) BREAD—place 2 or 3 balls in each pocket. Garnish with shredded lettuce, tomato, alfalfa sprouts and pickles. Spoon MUSTARD DRESSING or TAHINI DRESSING over top.

Yield: 20–24 balls

Variation:
Falafel Appetizers: Arrange falafel balls on a platter with tomato wedges, cucumber slices, and celery. Serve with a bowl of Tahini Dressing or Vegetable Dip.

TAHINI (Ground Sesame Seeds)

Sesame seeds furnish the body with a rich source of protein, calcium and unsaturated fats. Used as a butter, salad dressing, dip or dessert topping.

2 cups sesame seeds   1/4 cup oil

Place seeds in a blender or nut grinder and grind to a fine powder. Add oil slowly, blending all the time, until it reaches the consistency of peanut butter.

Yield: 3/4 cup

TAHINI SPREAD

1/3 cup TAHINI   1/4 cup finely chopped nuts
3 T. PEANUT BUTTER

Mix all together. Use on crackers or bread as you would a nut butter.

Yield: 1/2 cup

WHEAT GERM SPREAD

1/4 cup wheat germ   1/4 cup COTTAGE CHEESE or
1/2 cup PEANUT BUTTER   YOGURT
                                           2 T. frozen apple juice concentrate,
                                               unsweetened

Mix all of the ingredients together in a blender. Use as a spread in a sandwich or place on crackers.

Yield: 1 cup

SUNFLOWER SPREAD OR DIP

1½ cups sunflower seeds   1/4 cup PEANUT BUTTER
1 cup walnuts   1/2 tsp. lemon juice
2 T. oil

Place the sunflower seeds and walnuts in the blender and grind until it is very fine. Place this mixture and all the rest of the ingredients in a bowl and mix until smooth. Use as a sandwich spread, stuff celery with it, or use as a vegetable dip.

Yield: 1½ cups

LENTIL-EGG SPREAD

3 hard-cooked eggs
3/4 cup cooked lentils
1/4 cup COTTAGE CHEESE
1 T. onion, chopped

3 T. chopped celery
Season to taste with vegetable
    seasoning and sage

Mash the eggs and lentils together. Add all the other ingredients and mix well. Place on FLOUR TORTILLA, add sprouts and then roll up.

Yield: 1½ cups

GARDEN VARIETY

3/4 cup grated carrot
1/2 cup finely chopped celery
2 T. shredded Cheddar cheese
2 T. MAYONNAISE

1 T. finely chopped green pepper
1 T. tamari (soy sauce)
2 T. chopped peanuts
Vegetable seasoning to taste

Mix all of the ingredients together. Add more mayonnaise if needed.

Yield: Enough for 4 sandwiches

PEANUT BUTTER SPREAD

1/2 cup PEANUT BUTTER
1/4 cup orange juice

1 tsp. grated orange peel
1/3 cup flaked coconut

Mix all together. Can use either plain or crunchy peanut butter.

Yield: 3/4 cup

CHEESE SPREAD

1/4 pound blue cheese, crumbled
6 T. cream cheese
2 T. pineapple juice
2 tsp. tamari (soy sauce)

3 T. diced onion
4 sprigs parsley
1/2 tsp. vegetable seasoning

Place all the ingredients into a blender and blend until mixed.

Yield: Enough for 4 sandwiches

CRANBERRY CREAM CHEESE

6 T. cream cheese
3/4 cup uncooked cranberries,
    chopped
3 T. honey

1/4 cup chopped walnuts
1/2 tsp. grated orange peel
2 tsp. orange juice

Mash cream cheese with a fork. Add all other ingredients and mix well.

Yield: Enough for 4 sandwiches

DATE-NUT SPREAD

1 cup dates, pitted
1/2 cup nuts
1/2 tsp. cinnamon

1/4 cup YOGURT, plain
1/2 cup non-instant dry milk
  powder

Blend all together in a blender. If it is too thin to spread, add more dry milk.

Yield: 3/4 cups

SOYBEAN SPREAD

2 cups cooked soybeans
1 T. oil
2 garlic cloves, minced
1 stalk celery, diced
1 cup finely chopped onion
1 cup fresh chopped parsley

1/2 tsp. oregano
1/4 tsp. basil
1/2 tsp. vegetable seasoning
1 T. tamari (soy sauce)
1/2 cup MAYONNAISE

Mash cooked soybeans when tender with some of the liquid the soybeans were cooked in. Sauté in oil for 3 minutes the garlic, celery, onion, and parsley. Add the sautéed vegetables to the soybeans plus add the oregano, basil, vegetable seasoning, tamari and mayonnaise. Mix well. Now all is ready to spread on the bread and top with sliced tomato, mushrooms and sprouts.

Yield: 2½ cups

SPLIT PEA SPREAD

1 cup cooked green split peas
2 T. MAYONNAISE
2 T. Parmesan cheese

3/4 cup sunflower seeds
1/2 tsp. tamari (soy sauce)
1 T. lemon juice

Mash peas and mix with other ingredients. Spread on bread and top with cucumber, tomato and sprouts.

Yield: 1½ cups

GARBANZO SPECIAL

1½ cups cooked garbanzo beans
  (chick peas)
1/2 cup liquid from cooking beans
3 T. lemon juice
3 scallions, chopped

2 tsp. oil
1 large clove garlic, minced
1/4 cup TAHINI (sesame butter)
1/4 cup chopped fresh parsley
1/2 cup toasted sesame seeds

Combine liquid from beans and lemon juice in blender and purée. Sauté scallions in oil, add garlic and cook until tender but not brown. Combine with beans the remaining ingredients. Spoon into PITA (Bible) BREAD. Top with sprouts, cheese and finely chopped tomato.

Yield: 6-8 servings

CHAPTER 4

SALADS AND
SALAD DRESSINGS

The first salad recorded in history was a fresh green salad combined with vinegar and oil. Now we think of a salad as a combination of many different raw vegetables, fruits, greens or sprouts, served with one of the many different types of salad dressings.

Depending upon the occasion, salads can be light or elaborate. They may be served as the first part of a meal, as the main course, or even as a dessert.

Salads provide a good way to get the green, leafy vegetables and fruits needed in our diets every day. The raw fruits and vegetables are a good source of fiber, contain large amounts of vitamins A and C, plus a wide assortment of minerals. Make sure you include at least one, if not more, salads a day in your diet.

Let your imagination go in creating a salad. You can have as few as two different foods in a salad or as I did once, I combined twenty-eight different foods in one salad. Remember to make your salads appealing to the eye. If it looks good and appetizing you will find a lot of people eager for a taste. Salads are also a good way to introduce new vegetables into the diet, but just add them in small proportions until the family acquires a taste for them.

A good way to serve any leftover vegetables is to marinate them in an oil and vinegar marinade for a few hours and then serve well chilled. Vary the flavor by varying the herbs used in the marinade.

Hope you enjoy the following salads and salad dressing recipes. Plus have fun creating your own combinations.

HELPFUL HINTS

- Leafy vegetables exposed to light at room temperature, lose up to half of their vitamins B and C in a day, so refrigerate them at the first opportunity.

- Drain salad greens well before using to prevent salad dressing from becoming watery.

- Wash greens when you bring them home and then place in a pillowcase. Go outside and whirl it around a few times. A good way to drain the water off the greens.

- Add dressing just before serving to keep greens crisp. For macaroni and potato salads, add dressing one hour or more before serving time.

- Ingredients for a salad should be cold, clean and crisp. Toss lightly together.

- The darker the green leaves are, the richer the source of vitamins and minerals.

- Tear greens rather than cut them with a knife. Besides looking better, it does not do as much damage to the nutrients as cutting does.

- Chill bowl as well as salad greens before making a salad.

- Consider color when combining food in salads. Make sure there is a variety.

- Choose the right salad for the right meal. A light salad is best for a heavy meal. When a salad is used as the main dish for a meal, fish, chicken, beans, eggs, or cheese are best. Fruit and jellied or frozen salads are popular as refreshments for parties.

- Garnishes should be used with care. Garnishes should blend and harmonize in color and flavor with the main part of the salad. Parsley, green and red pepper, radishes, pickles, cheese, hard-cooked eggs, mint or sprouts are often used. It is all right to eat the garnishes as they are full of many nutrients.

- Some different containers to use for salads: Halve zucchini lengthwise into individual boats, scoop out insides and fill with fresh vegetables marinated in oil and vinegar. Hollow out baby eggplants and then fill them up. Place the salad in a scooped-out head of cabbage. Use also tomatoes, green peppers and avocados. Be sure to eat the insides of the vegetables you scoop out.

- If watching weight, forego generous amounts of oil in salad dressings. Use equal amount of oil to vinegar rather than the typical three to one ratio. Or use water in place of some of the oil in the recipe. Another suggestion would be to change to a dressing that has yogurt as the main ingredient.

- Sometimes use salad greens other than lettuce. Have you tried escarole, endive, kale, spinach, dandelion greens, romaine, watercress and Chinese cabbage?

- A measuring teaspoon may be used to make melon balls.

- If lemons are allowed to stand in hot water for five minutes before they are squeezed, they will yield more juice.

- How do you skin a peach? Cover with boiling water and allow to stand for just a few seconds, then the peeling will come off easily.

- Do not wash strawberries until just before you serve them. They spoil quickly if washed and stored. Serve at room temperature as you will get their full flavor.

- The heavier the grapefruits and oranges are the more juice they contain.

- To unmold gelatin salads, run the tip of a knife around the top edge to loosen it and admit air; then invert the mold on a chilled plate. If it does not lift off easily, wet a clean towel in hot water; quickly wrap the hot towel around the mold for a few seconds. Now try to unmold.

- If dips or salad dressings call for yogurt, stir the yogurt in gently. Using the blender or a mixer will make the yogurt soupy, plus the blades kill the friendly bacteria that you want to keep in the yogurt.

- You can refrigerate bananas. The skin turns brown, but the inside is still white. If you have a surplus of them, peel and freeze them. Use in any baking dishes or just eat as a snack. Tastes like ice cream.

- If you have someone in your family who picks certain vegetables out of a salad, just dice them very fine and add to the salad dressing.

KNOW YOUR SALAD GREENS

BOSTON LETTUCE—is also known as "Big Boston" and "Butterhead," and has velvety, spreading leaves that are easily separated, and is available throughout most of the year.

BIBB LETTUCE—or "Limestone Lettuce" is smaller than Boston Lettuce, but has basically the same shape and flavor. Use the whole leaf in a salad. This lettuce gets its name from Jack Bibb, of Frankfort, Kentucky, who introduced it right after the Civil War. It is reaching markets more readily.

HEAD LETTUCE—or "Iceberg Lettuce," or "Simpson Lettuce," is the most familiar of lettuces. It is firm, tight with a compact head. Separated, the leaves make a lettuce cup as a container for potato salad, fruit salad, etc.

LEAF LETTUCE—is a home gardener's favorite. It has a curly edge and is crisp. Has good flavor and grows in large, leafy bunches.

ROMAINE LETTUCE—is more strongly flavored than most lettuces. It has a long head and spoonshape leaves and is crisper than head lettuce. Excellent with avocados.

OAK-LEAF LETTUCE—has deeply notched leaves, making it look like true oak leaves. Delicate flavor.

CURLY ENDIVE—is also known as "Chicory," and has narrow, thin, twisted leaves. It has a slight bitterness and is most often used with grapefruit and orange sections.

BELGIAN ENDIVE—is a member of the chicory and escarole family, and is a straight, pale, slender leaf, six inches or more in length. Can be sliced lengthwise or crosswise into a salad. Some people enjoy eating it as they do celery.

ESCAROLE—tastes like Belgian Endive but not quite as bitter. It resembles chicory but its leaves are broader and not as curly.

SPINACH—is not really a lettuce, but gives interesting taste and color to a tossed green salad.

WATERCRESS—grows along the edges of brooks and springs. It is dark green and leafy with a good "bite" to its taste. Adds color to a tossed green salad, and can be used as a garnish.

GARNISH FOR SALADS

- Quarter or slice hard-cooked eggs.
- Sieve hard-cooked egg yolks or chop the white.
- Slice raw onion, Bermuda or Spanish, paper thin and separate into rings.
- Slice avocados into strips or cubes.
- Cut circles or thin strips of red or green peppers.
- Add sunflower or pumpkin seeds, ROASTED SOYBEANS, or unsweetened coconut shreds.
- Sprinkle with different types of sprouts.
- Add ripe olives or pickles.
- Grated cheese.
- Wheat germ.

SALAD HERBS

3/4 cup Parmesan cheese
1/4 cup dried parsley flakes
1 tsp. garlic powder
1/4 tsp. cayenne
1 tsp. dried, minced onion

1 tsp. crushed basil
1 T. toasted sesame seeds
1 T. toasted sunflower seeds
1 T. toasted rolled oats
1/2 tsp. vegetable seasoning

Mix all together and store in an air-tight bottle in refrigerator. Sprinkle on your salads when you like.

Yield: 1 cup

VEGETABLE SALADS

RAW VEGETABLE SALAD

Make up your own combinations for a salad. Choose from any of the items listed below. You can have as few as 2 items in the salad or as many as you would like to suit your taste.

LETTUCE
Bibb
Boston
Endive
Escarole
Iceberg
Romaine
Butter
Red leaf
Curly leaf

CABBAGE
Red cabbage
Green cabbage
Savory
Chinese cabbage

GREENS
Spinach
Watercress
Beet tops
Mustard greens
Collards
Kale
Swiss chard

VEGETABLES
Avocado
Asparagus
Beets
Broccoli
Carrots
Cauliflower
Celery
Corn
Cucumbers
Jicama
Kohlrobi
Leeks
Mushrooms
Onions
Peas
Peppers
Potatoes
Radishes
Yellow squash
Tomatoes
Zucchini

SPROUTS
Alfalfa
Mung beans
Lentils
Garbanzo
Soybean
Wheat

PROTEIN
Cheese
Hard-cooked eggs
Cooked beans
Sunflower seeds
Sesame seeds
Almonds
Walnuts
Cashews
Peanuts
Chicken
Fish

STUFFED AVOCADO

Red pepper, chopped	Tomato, cut into small pieces
Green onion, chopped	MAYONNAISE
Cucumber, chopped	Vegetable seasoning
Mushrooms or cauliflower buds,	Dill
chopped small	

Toss all of the ingredients (finely chopped) with mayonnaise and the vegetable seasoning and dill. Pile on an avocado half (do not scoop the avocado out) that has been sprinkled with lemon juice. The lemon helps keep it from discoloring.

Another suggestion would be TABOULIE or CRAB SALAD.

STUFFED TOMATO or GREEN PEPPER
Hollow out the tomato or green pepper and fill with the following fillings:
   TABOULIE
   The filling used for the stuffed avocado
   COTTAGE CHEESE mixed with chopped cucumbers, walnuts, onions and
      carrots
   CRAB SALAD
   Any of the sandwich fillings
   Marinated vegetables

AVOCADO-SHRIMP SALAD VINAIGRETTE

3/4 cup olive oil	4 medium or 3 large avocados
2 T. chopped parsley	24-32 shrimp, freshly cooked,
2 T. cider vinegar	shelled, deveined and cooled
1 T. Dijon mustard	1/3 cup sunflower seeds
1 T. capers (optional)	8 lemon slices
1 tsp. vegetable seasoning	3 hard-cooked eggs, halved
Red Leaf lettuce	

Blend thoroughly the oil, parsley, vinegar, mustard, capers and seasoning. Place lettuce on the salad plates. Peel and slice avocados and spoon a little of the dressing over slices. Arrange 3 or 4 slices of avocado and 3 or 4 shrimp over the lettuce. Add additional dressing over all. Sprinkle with sunflower seeds. Garnish with lemon and eggs.

Yield: Serves 8

BEAN SALAD

2 apples peeled
1/4 cup lemon juice
1/2 cup cider vinegar
1 T. red wine vinegar
1/2 cup oil
1 T. frozen apple juice concentrate,
    unsweetened
1/4 cup pickle juice
2 cloves garlic, minced

1/2 tsp. oregano
1/2 tsp. onion powder
1/4 tsp. dill weed
1 tsp. vegetable seasoning
6 cups total of beans—made up of
    cooked garbanzo, kidney, green
    beans and yellow wax beans
1 medium onion, sliced into rings
1 cup celery, diced

Blend apples in blender with lemon juice. Add vinegars, oil, apple concentrate, pickle juice and seasoning. Place the beans, onion, and celery in a large bowl and pour dressing over them. Let stand in refrigerator overnight. The longer it stands the better the flavor.

Yield: 10–12 servings

MACARONI SALAD

4 cups cooked elbow macaroni
1 cup diced carrots
2 cups chopped celery
2 cups diced cucumbers
1 cup fresh green beans, diced

2½ cups chopped fresh tomatoes
1 cup scallions, chopped
1/4 cup fresh chopped parsley
3/4 cup raw peas

Combine all of the ingredients together in a large bowl. Toss with the dressing and place in refrigerator 2 hours before serving.

Dressing:
1 cup COTTAGE CHEESE
1 cup MAYONNAISE
1/2 cup milk
1/2 tsp. vegetable seasoning

1 tsp. dill
1 tsp. Dijon mustard
2 T. lemon juice

Place all of these ingredients into a blender and blend until smooth. Pour over Macaroni Salad.

Yield: 15 servings

ORIENTAL ONION SALAD

1 medium sweet Spanish onion, sliced thin
4 to 6 pineapple rings
1 cup bean sprouts
1 cup small shrimp

1/2 cup sliced water chestnuts
1/2 green pepper, cut into strips
Salad greens
SESAME SEED DRESSING

Separate onion slices into rings. Arrange pineapple rings on lettuce-lined salad plates. Top with bean sprouts, shrimp, water chestnuts, green pepper, and onion rings. Serve with the dressing on the side.   Yield: Serves 4

SALADE NICOISE

Salad greens
8 cold new potatoes, cooked and
  sliced
4 tomatoes, cut into wedges
1 cup diced cooked green beans
1 can (6½ ounce) tuna fish, drained
  and flaked

6 cooked artichoke bottoms
  (hearts)
1 sliced onion
3 hard-cooked eggs, cut into wedges
2 T. dill
FRENCH VINAIGRETTE
DRESSING

Toss lettuce leaves with 2 tablespoons of the dressing. Arrange lettuce on a deep round platter. Arrange the potato slices in a ring on the lettuce. Place the tomatoes and beans in a decorative pattern. Place the flaked tuna in a mound in the center. Sprinkle over the top the artichokes and sliced onions. Place the eggs around the tuna. Sprinkle the salad with dill. Spoon the dressing over the whole salad and serve at once. Can be served on a hot summer evening as the main course.

Yield: 4 servings

FRENCH POTATO SALAD

1½ pounds unpared new potatoes
3/4 cup oil
1/4 cup vinegar
1/8 cup water
2 T. prepared Dijon mustard
2 tsp. dill
1 tsp. celery seed

1/2 tsp. tarragon
1/2 pound leaf spinach, washed and
  dried
1/2 cup chopped celery
1/4 cup chopped green peppers
1/2 cup chopped green onions
Hard-cooked egg halves

Steam potatoes until tender, about 15–20 minutes. While potatoes are cooking, beat oil, vinegar, water, mustard, dill, celery seed and tarragon in a large bowl for the dressing. Arrange spinach leaves in serving bowl. When potatoes are cool enough to handle, slice thin and then toss with dressing in bowl. Stir in celery, peppers and onions. Spoon potatoes into center of spinach leaves in bowl. Garnish with eggs.

Yield: Serves 6

POTATO SALAD

6 medium sized new potatoes
2 stalks celery, diced
1/8 cup diced pickles
2 T. chopped green onions
2 hard-cooked eggs, diced
1/8 cup YOGURT, plain
1/8 cup MAYONNAISE

1 T. pickle juice
1 tsp. horseradish
Dash of dry mustard
1/2 tsp. garlic powder
1/2 tsp. dill weed
1 tsp. vegetable seasoning

Steam the potatoes until semi-soft, but firm. Peel. Dice into bite size when cool enough to handle. In a large mixing bowl add potatoes, celery, pickles, onions and 1 egg. Mix in a separate bowl the yogurt, mayonnaise, pickle juice, horseradish, mustard, garlic, dill and vegetable seasoning. Add this mixture to the potatoes and toss until coated. Slice other egg and place on top of salad.

Yield: Serves 5–6

COLE SLAW

4 cups shredded crisp cabbage,
    1 pound
1/2 cup shredded carrots
1/4 cup minced green pepper
3/4 cup coarsely chopped walnuts
1/2 cup YOGURT, plain
2 T. MAYONNAISE

3/4 tsp. vegetable seasoning
1/2 tsp. garlic powder
1/2 tsp. honey
1 T. vinegar
1 T. lemon juice
Dash of horseradish
Slices of green pepper for garnish

Combine cabbage, carrots, green pepper and walnuts together in a bowl. Blend all of the rest of the ingredients together in a separate bowl, except for the green pepper slices. Add the dressing mixture to the cabbage mixture and toss until coated. Place green pepper slices on top for garnish. Cover and chill thoroughly.

Yield: 6 servings

LENTIL SALAD

2 cups cooked lentils
3 T. vinegar
3 T. oil

1/2 tsp. dill
1/2 tsp. vegetable seasoning
2 T. tamari (soy sauce)

Toss the lentils and all of the rest of the ingredients together. Place in refrigerator and let sit overnight to marinade the lentils. Add to the lentils:

1/2 cup chopped celery
2 T. chopped green pepper
1 cup mung bean sprouts
1 medium onion, chopped

3 T. sunflower seeds
1 tomato, diced
1/2 cup MAYONNAISE (optional)
3 T. chopped parsley

Toss all of the ingredients together gently and serve immediately. Serve on lettuce-lined plates or serve stuffed in tomatoes.

Yield: Serves 5-6

GARBANZO SALAD

2 cups sprouted garbanzos or 2 cups
    cooked garbanzos
1 cup celery, chopped
1/4 cup chopped green onion
1/4 cup finely chopped parsley

1 tomato cut in small pieces
1/4 cup pimiento, chopped for
    garnish
Lettuce, green pepper rings
OIL AND VINEGAR MARINADE

In a large bowl, combine the garbanzo sprouts or beans, celery, onion, parsley and tomato. Pour marinade over mixture and toss lightly. Chill 3 hours before serving. Serve in lettuce-lined bowl, garnish with pimiento and green pepper rings.

Yield: 4-5 servings

TABOULIE

A delicious salad that is a staple in the Middle East.

2 cups bulgur wheat
4 cups boiling water
1/4 cup navy or garbanzo beans,
    cooked and drained
1½ cups minced parsley
1/4 cup mint, minced
3/4 cup minced scallions or green
    onions

2 garlic cloves, minced
3 medium tomatoes, chopped
3/4 cup lemon juice
1/4 cup olive oil
1/2 tsp. vegetable seasoning
1/4 cup cider vinegar

Pour the boiling water over the bulgur and let stand about 1 hour until the wheat is light and fluffy. Drain excess water and shake in a strainer or press with hands to remove as much water as possible. Mix together the bulgur and the rest of the ingredients. Chill for at least 1 hour before serving. Really best, though, if you let it sit for at least 18 hours. Serve on a bed of lettuce.

Yield: Serves 6

BEAN SPROUT SALAD

1½ cups bean sprouts
1 small carrot, grated
1/4 tsp. vegetable seasoning
1 cucumber
2 T. raisins
2 T. tamari (soy sauce)

1½ tsp. oil
1½ tsp. lemon juice
1/4 tsp. dry mustard
1/4 tsp. honey
1 T. toasted sesame seeds
1 thinly sliced hard-cooked egg

Cut peeled cucumber into thin crosswise slices. Rinse raisins in hot water (to plump them); drain well. Combine tamari, oil, lemon juice, mustard and honey. Put bean sprouts, carrots, vegetable seasoning, cucumber and raisins into salad bowl; add dressing and toss lightly. Garnish with sesame seeds and egg.

Yield: Serves 6

MARINATED ZUCCHINI MUSHROOM SALAD

1 zucchini, grated (unpeeled)
2 green onions, chopped
Several large mushrooms, sliced
1/2 bunch parsley, chopped fine

1 tomato, sliced
1/2 cup sunflower seeds
1 Jerusalem artichoke, sliced thin
HERB TOMATO DRESSING

Toss all of the ingredients with the dressing and serve on a bed of sprouts.

Yield: Serves 2

GRATED SALAD

1½ cups grated cabbage
3/4 cup grated carrots
1/4 cup finely chopped broccoli
    stalks
1/2 cup sesame seeds
1 tomato, diced

1/2 avocado, peeled, pitted, and
    cubed (dipped in lemon juice to
    prevent discoloration)
1/2 cup chopped cucumber
1/4 cup chopped green pepper
1/2 cup diced celery
1/4 cup green onions, diced

In a large bowl, combine all of the ingredients together. Toss with a dressing
at the table.

Yield: Serves 8

SUNSHINE SALAD

4 cups mixed greens
1 cup celery, thinly sliced
1 cup zucchini, cut lengthwise in
    half, then thinly sliced
1 cup cucumber, cut lengthwise in
    half, then thinly sliced
1/4 pound mushrooms, thinly sliced
1 large tomato, diced
1/2 cup parsley, coarsely chopped
2 T. pumpkin seeds

2 T. grated Parmesan cheese
1 T. sunflower seeds
1 T. sliced almonds
4 radishes, sliced
1 cup COTTAGE CHEESE
1 cup grated raw beets
1 cup grated carrots
1 cup alfalfa sprouts
Garnishes: lemon slices and parsley

Toss together the first twelve ingredients. Place on four separate plates. Top
each plate with 1/4 cup cottage cheese and surround with 1/4 cup beets, carrots and sprouts. Garnish with lemon slices and parsley sprigs. Serve with
favorite dressing.

Yield: Serves 4

EGG SALAD WITH TOFU

4 hard-cooked eggs, mashed or
    chopped
1/2 cup chopped celery
1/2 cup sunflower seeds
1 cup TOFU, mashed

1/2 cup MAYONNAISE
2 T. lemon juice
1 T. Dijon mustard
1 tsp. curry
1/2 tsp. vegetable seasoning

Mix all ingredients and serve on bed of lettuce or sprouts. Can also use as a
sandwich filling or as a stuffing in a tomato.

Yield: 2-3 servings

TUNA SALAD

1 cup tuna fish (drained)	1/2 cup MAYONNAISE or plain
3/4 cup celery, chopped	YOGURT
1/3 cup green pepper, chopped	1/2 tsp. dill
4 green onions, chopped	1 tsp. vegetable seasoning
1/8 cup diced pickles	1/2 cup chopped walnuts
2 hard-cooked eggs	Sprouts and sliced tomatoes
Juice of one lemon	

Mix tuna, lemon juice, mayonnaise or yogurt, dill and vegetable seasoning. Mix in chopped vegetables, one diced egg and walnuts. Place on bed of sprouts and top with tomatoes and other egg.

Yield: Serves 3-4

SURPRISE TUNA SALAD

3/4 cup oats	1/4 cup YOGURT, plain
1 cup tuna, drained	3 T. chopped green onions
1/2 cup celery, sliced	1/2 tsp. dill
1/2 cup walnuts, chopped	Vegetable seasoning to taste
1/4 cup diced red peppers	1 cup cubed pineapple,
1/2 cup MAYONNAISE	unsweetened

Toast oats in ungreased large shallow baking pan in a 350° oven for about 15 minutes. Cool. Combine oats with remaining ingredients; mix well. Chill. Serve as a salad on lettuce, stuff into a tomato, or use as a sandwich filling.

Yield: 2 cups

CRAB SALAD

This salad does not contain any crab, but in tasting this recipe you would think this is truly a Crab Salad. It is sometimes known as a Mock Crab Salad.

4 cups cooked, drained soybeans	1/2 tsp. kelp
2 dill pickles	1/2 tsp. vegetable seasoning
1 onion	1/4 tsp. dill
1 carrot	2 tsp. prepared MUSTARD
1/3 cup almonds	1/2 cup chopped celery
Dash garlic powder	1/2 cup MAYONNAISE
1/4 cup chopped, green onions	1-2 T. tamari (soy sauce)
2 T. chopped parsley	Lettuce and tomato wedges as
	garnish

In a meat grinder, grind soybeans, pickles, onion, carrot and almonds. Place mixture in a large bowl. Add remaining ingredients and mix well. Consistency should be like tuna salad. Serve on individual lettuce cups, ringed with tomato wedges and topped with your favorite creamy dressing.

Yield: Serves 4-5

CHICKEN-PINEAPPLE SALAD

1 cup diced pineapple (unsweetened)
2 cups cooked chicken, diced
3/4 cup chopped celery
1/2 cup chopped walnuts or cashews
1/4 cup green peppers, diced

1/2 cup cooked brown rice
1/2 cup MAYONNAISE or enough
   to moisten
1 tsp vegetable seasoning
1/2 tsp. dill

Mix all together and refrigerate for 3 hours before serving. Serve on a bed of lettuce or sprouts, or stuff into a tomato.

Yield: Serves 4

FRUIT SALADS

RAW FRUIT SALAD

There are so many wonderful combinations you can put together with the many fresh fruits. They are easy to prepare and so delicious. You can eat the fruits plain or add chopped nuts, dates, raisins, seeds or coconut. You can also add one of the many dressings listed in the "Dressing" section. To serve, place the fruit on a plate lined with lettuce or sprouts and arrange in interesting designs. Or serve in melon and watermelon bowls, grapefruit and orange halves or even in pineapple boats. Here are some suggestions of the different fruits to use to create your salads.

Apple	Mango	Plums	Watermelon
Pineapple	Peach	Nectarine	Cantalope
Papaya	Blueberries	Strawberries	Honeydew
Banana	Cherries	Pear	Grapes

STRAWBERRY SUNDAE SALAD

1 pint strawberries, rinsed, hulled
   and sliced
1/4 cup fresh orange juice
2 tsp. honey (optional)

2 cups COTTAGE CHEESE
1 tsp. grated fresh orange rind
3/4 cup GRANOLA
Salad greens

Combine in a blender 1 cup sliced strawberries, 2 tablespoons orange juice and honey (if sweetener is needed). Cover and process until puréed. Mix cottage cheese with remaining 2 tablespoons orange juice, orange rind and granola. Arrange salad greens on four serving plates, topping each with 1/2 cup cottage cheese mixture and remaining sliced strawberries. Serve with puréed strawberry sauce and sprinkle with additional granola, if desired.

Yield: 4 servings

CARROT-APPLE SALAD

2 cups shredded carrots
3 cups unpeeled apples, chopped
1 cup raisins

1/2 cup sunflower seeds
1/2 cup YOGURT HONEY
DRESSING

Combine carrots, apples, raisins and sunflower seeds with dressing. Stir to blend. Serve on sprouts or lettuce leaf.

Yield: Serves 4

HAWAIIAN FRUIT SALAD

2 cups fresh pineapple, cubed
2-3 bananas, sliced
1-2 papayas, peeled, seeded and cut
   into bite size
2 T. lemon juice (to prevent the
   discoloration of fruits)

2 cups apple, cut in bite size
1/2 cup sliced, pitted dates
1/2 cup walnuts or pecans
1/2 cup unsweetened coconut

Mix all of the ingredients together. Fruit salad is delicious dressed only in its own juice, but you may want to make it into an ambrosia. To do this, add AMBROSIA DRESSING. Serve in lettuce cups or in pineapple boats.

Yield: Serves 6

MOLDED SALADS

PINEAPPLE-ORANGE GELATIN

1 T. unflavored gelatin
1 cup cold water
3 T. honey
1¼ cups pineapple juice
   (unsweetened)
2 T. concentrated orange juice (frozen)

1 cup unsweetened, pineapple
   chunks, drained
2 medium-sized oranges, peeled
   and separated into segments
1/2 cup chopped walnuts
1 banana, sliced

Soften gelatin in cold water. In small saucepan, warm gelatin mixture and honey, just enough to dissolve gelatin and soften honey. Add pineapple juice and frozen undiluted orange juice; cool until almost set. Add pineapple chunks, orange segments, walnuts and sliced bananas; chill until set.

Yield: 4-6 servings

CUCUMBER MOUSSE

1 T. unflavored gelatin
2 T. cold water
1/4 cup boiling water
3/4 cup YOGURT, plain
3/4 cup COTTAGE CHEESE
1/2 cup finely chopped cucumber

1 T. chopped chives
1 T. chopped parsley
1½ tsp. lemon juice
1/4 tsp. dill weed
1/4 tsp. onion powder

Soften gelatin in cold water; let sit 5 minutes. Add boiling water and dissolve gelatin. In blender, combine dissolved gelatin, yogurt and cottage cheese. Blend until smooth, then add cucumber, chives, parsley, lemon juice, dill weed and onion. Pour into 2-3 cup mold. Refrigerate until firm. Great with cold poached salmon.

Yield: Serves 6

LEMON CREAM CHEESE MOLD

1/3 cup cold water
2 T. gelatin, unflavored
2/3 cup boiling water
1/4 cup honey
Juice of one or two lemons
1/2 cup cream (raw)

1/4 cup MAYONNAISE
1 8-ounce package cream cheese, softened
1 cup chopped nuts
2 cups crushed unsweetened pineapple, drained

Soften gelatin in cold water. Dissolve in the boiling water. Stir in honey, and lemon juice. Add cream and mayonnaise. For easier mixing, cube softened cream cheese. Blend into other ingredients. Add nuts and pineapple. Pour into desired mold. Chill overnight.

Yield: Serves 6

BASIC MOLDED FRUIT SALAD

1 T. gelatin, unflavored
1/4 cup cold water
2 cups fruit juice of your choice
1/4 cup YOGURT, plain

1/2 cup COTTAGE CHEESE
1 cup fruit of your choice, cut up
1/2 cup chopped nuts

In this recipe you can use the juice of your choice or you can even combine two different juices together for a new flavor. You do the same with the fruit—choose what you would like, varying with the time of year. Sprinkle the cold water over the gelatin and let sit for 3 minutes until the water is absorbed. Heat the liquid and then pour over the gelatin mixture and stir until dissolved. Let the mixture sit until partially set and then stir in the other ingredients. Pour into a mold and chill until set.

Yield: 4-6 servings

VEGETABLE MOLD

1 T. gelatin, unflavored
1/4 cup water
2 cups TOMATO or V-8 juice
2 tsp. dried broth seasoning
1 T. lemon juice

1 heaping tsp. ascorbic acid crystals
1/2 tsp. vegetable seasoning
1½ cups any combination of vegetables, chopped (onion, peppers, celery, cabbage, carrots)

Melt the gelatin and the water over a low heat. Mix together in a blender, the juice with the broth seasoning, lemon juice, ascorbic acid and vegetable seasoning. Add the gelatin while this is blending. Pour into a mold and refrigerate until the consistency of egg whites. Add the vegetables at this time. Chill until firm. Serve with COTTAGE CHEESE, SOUR CREAM, or homemade MAYONNAISE.

Yield: Serves 8

POTATO SALAD SQUARES

About 2 large new potatoes, cooked
and peeled
3½ T. white wine vinegar
1/3 cup chopped sweet pickle
1 tsp. vegetable seasoning
1/2 tsp. dill
1/3 cup each sliced green onion and
chopped celery

2 T. unflavored gelatin
1½ cups CHICKEN BROTH
1/2 cup MAYONNAISE
1 tsp. Dijon mustard
1/4 cup chopped parsley
Lettuce leaves (optional)
Sliced hard-cooked eggs

Cut enough of the potatoes into 1/2-inch cubes to make 2 cups. Combine 2½ tablespoons of the vinegar, the pickle, vegetable seasoning, dill, onion, and celery. Mix in potatoes and let stand. Meanwhile sprinkle gelatin over the broth; let stand 5 minutes to soften. Stir over direct heat to dissolve, then stir in remaining 1 tablespoon vinegar. Chill until slightly thickened, about 35 minutes. Add mayonnaise and mustard and beat until foamy with a rotary beater. Fold in potato mixture and parsley. Spoon mixture into a 9" square pan. Cover and chill until firm (at least 6 hours or overnight). Cut into 9 squares. Serve on lettuce leaves, if desired, and top with egg slices.

Yield: 9 servings

JELLIED CHEESE SQUARES

1 T. gelatin, unflavored
1/2 cup pineapple juice, unsweetened
1/2 cup onion, finely chopped
1 cup celery, chopped
1/2 cup green ripe olives (optional)
1/2 cup freshly shelled green peas
1 cup pecans, chopped coarsely

1 cup Cheddar or Swiss cheese,
   diced or shredded
1/4 cup parsley, snipped very fine
1 cup MAYONNAISE
1/2 cup whipped cream, raw or
   1/2 cup COTTAGE CHEESE,
   whipped

Soak the gelatin in the juice for about 5 minutes in a small saucepan. Place over low heat and stir until gelatin is dissolved. In large bowl combine all the other ingredients. Add the gelatin mixture and stir until well blended. Pour into a glass baking dish or other mold and chill until time to serve. Cut into squares. Delightful as the main dish of a buffet meal or as part of a make-ahead salad plate.

Yield: 6-8 servings

FROZEN SALADS

FROZEN WALDORF SALAD

1 can (8½ ounce) crushed pineapple,
   unsweetened
2 eggs, slightly beaten
4 T. honey
1/4 cup lemon juice
2½ cups (2 medium sized) diced
   unpared apples

1/2 cup diced celery
1/2 cup coarsely chopped walnuts
1/2 cup unsweetened coconut
   flakes
1/4 cup chopped dates
2/3 cup chilled whipping cream

Drain the pineapple, reserving the syrup. Mix in a saucepan the eggs, honey and lemon juice. Blend in the reserved pineapple syrup. Cook, stirring constantly, until mixture is slightly thickened. Remove from heat; cool. Mix in a bowl the pineapple, apples, celery, walnuts, coconut and dates. Mix the whipping cream in another bowl until soft peaks are formed. Fold the whipped cream into the cooled sauce. Combine with fruit and toss lightly to mix thoroughly. Turn into an 8" square pan and freeze until firm. To serve, cut into squares.

Yield: 9 servings

CRANBERRY FROST SALAD

1 cup fresh or frozen cranberries,
    finely chopped
1/4 cup honey
2 medium oranges
1 8-ounce package cream cheese,
    softened

1 tsp. VANILLA EXTRACT
1 medium apple, finely chopped
1/2 cup chopped dates
1 cup whipping cream
Lettuce

Combine the cranberries and honey; let stand 10 minutes. Meanwhile, peel and section one orange. Finely chop orange sections; set aside. Squeeze remaining orange to make a total of 1/3 cup juice. Beat together the orange juice, the cream cheese, and vanilla until fluffy. Stir in orange sections, cranberries, apple, and dates. Whip cream until soft peaks form. Fold whipped cream into cream cheese mixture. Turn mixture into a 5 cup mold, 8" x 4" x 2" loaf pan, or 8 individual molds. Cover, seal, label, and freeze at least 3 hours or as long as 1 month. Before serving, let stand at room temperature for 10 to 15 minutes to soften slightly. Unmold onto lettuce-lined plate. Garnish with additional orange sections, if desired.

Yield: Serves 8-9

SALAD DRESSINGS

OIL AND VINEGAR MARINADE

1/2 cup oil
1 T. lemon juice
4 T. cider or wine vinegar
1/4 tsp. mustard powder

1/4 tsp. paprika
1 clove garlic, minced
1/4 tsp. each basil, oregano and
    tarragon

Shake all ingredients together in a jar. Use as a marinade with different vegetables and salads.

Yield: 2/3 cups

PESTO VINAIGRETTE DRESSING

6 T. PESTO
1/3 cup red wine vinegar

2/3 cup olive oil
1 clove garlic, minced

Combine all of the ingredients together and shake to blend. Use over mixed greens, over sliced tomatoes; or try as a marinade over mushrooms or lightly cooked vegetables.

Yield: 1-1/3 cups

FRENCH VINAIGRETTE DRESSING

2/3 cup olive oil
1 T. lemon juice
2 T. wine vinegar
2 T. Dijon mustard
1 clove garlic, finely minced

1½ tsp. basil
1 T. fresh parsley, chopped
1 tsp. dill
Vegetable seasoning to taste

Put into a screw-top jar and shake well. Chill well before serving.

Yield: 1 cup

CAESAR DRESSING

1 egg
1/2 cup olive oil
1 cup Parmesan cheese, grated
1/2 cup lemon juice or to taste

1/2 tsp. tamari (soy sauce)
2 cloves of garlic, minced
1 T. anchovy paste (optional)
Cider vinegar

Mix all ingredients together except the vinegar. Add vinegar to taste.

Yield: 1 cup

GREEK SALAD DRESSING

6 T. oil, safflower
6 T. olive oil
2 T. lemon juice
2 T. wine vinegar
2 cloves garlic, minced
1½ T. YOGURT, plain

1 T. Dijon mustard
1/2 tsp. vegetable seasoning
1/4 tsp. sage
1/4 tsp. thyme
1/4 tsp. basil
1/4 tsp. oregano

Combine all ingredients in blender; blend 5 minutes. Store in covered jar in refrigerator.

Yield: 1 cup

POPPY SEED DRESSING

1/4 cup poppy seed
1/4 cup unsweetened pineapple
    juice
1 medium onion, diced

1 tsp. kelp
2 tsp. lemon juice
2 tsp. honey
1/4 cup olive oil

Blend together all ingredients except the oil. Turning blender on to low speed, add the oil very slowly in a steady stream. Stir in a few extra seeds. Chill until ready to serve.

Yield: 1½ cups

SESAME CUCUMBER DRESSING

1 T. green onion, chopped
1/2 cup cucumber, peeled and
   chopped
Juice of one lemon

1/4 cup olive oil
1/4 tsp. vegetable seasoning
1 tsp. tamari (soy sauce)

Blend all ingredients until smooth and adjust seasoning to taste.

Yield: 1 cup

FRENCH DRESSING

3/4 cup olive oil
1/4 cup cider vinegar
2 T. lemon juice
2 T. TOMATO JUICE
1/4 tsp. dry mustard

1/4 tsp. garlic, minced
1 tsp. honey
1/4 tsp. vegetable seasoning
1 tsp. chopped chives
1/2 tsp. oregano

Shake all ingredients together in a bottle. Great on spinach salad.

Yield: 1¼ cups

HERB-TOMATO DRESSING

2 tomatoes, peeled
1 clove garlic, minced
1/4 cup lemon juice
1/4 cup olive oil

1 tsp. kelp
1 tsp. broth seasoning (or to taste)
1/4 tsp. each: basil, oregano,
   thyme, marjoram

Blend all together, except the oil, in a blender. Add oil, with blender at low speed, in a slow steady stream.

Yield: 1½ cups

SESAME SEED DRESSING

1/3 cup juice from unsweetened
   pineapple
1/3 cup oil

3 T. cider vinegar
1 T. tamari (soy sauce)
2 T. toasted sesame seeds

Combine all of the ingredients together. Chill before serving.

Yield: 1 cup

THOUSAND ISLAND DRESSING

1 cup MAYONNAISE
1 T. chopped chives
1/2 green pepper, seeded and finely diced
2 hard-cooked eggs, chopped
2 T. CHILI SAUCE

1 T. lemon juice
1 tsp. honey
1 tsp. vegetable seasoning
1/2 sweet red pepper, seeded and finely diced

Combine all the ingredients until well mixed. Chill before serving.

Yield: 2½ cups

GREEN HERB DRESSING

3/4 cup MAYONNAISE
2/3 cup YOGURT, plain
1 tsp. dill weed
2 T. chopped parsley
2 T. chopped chives

2 tsp. chopped tarragon leaves
1 tsp. thyme
1½ tsp. basil
1/4 tsp. paprika
1/2 tsp. kelp powder

In a small bowl, combine ingredients in order given. Mix together thoroughly. Adjust seasoning. Cover and place in refrigerator several hours or overnight to blend flavors.

Yield: 1½ cups

BLUE CHEESE DRESSING

2 cups plain YOGURT
1/2 tsp garlic powder
1/2 tsp. onion powder

1/2 tsp. vegetable seasoning
1/4 pound blue cheese

Mix ingredients together and crumble the blue cheese into dressing. Let sit a day before using. It allows flavors to mingle.

Yield: 2 cups

HERB-YOGURT DRESSING

2 cups plain YOGURT   3 T. MAYONNAISE
Choice of any combination of the following:
    basil, garlic, kelp, oregano, celery seed, thyme, fresh parsley, fresh dill, onion

Mix all of the ingredients together.

Yield: 2 cups

TAHINI DRESSING

1 cup TAHINI
1/2 cup water
1/4 cup YOGURT, plain

1/4 cup lemon juice
3 cloves fresh garlic, crushed
Vegetable seasoning to taste

Blend all ingredients together in a blender. Use over salads or vegetables.

Yield: 1¾ cups

MUSTARD DRESSING

1 cup plain YOGURT
4 tsp. Dijon mustard

1 tsp. tarragon
1/2 tsp. basil

Combine all ingredients. Chill in refrigerator until ready to serve.

Yield: 1 cup

FRUIT SALAD DRESSING

1 cup YOGURT, plain
1 T. honey

2 T. unsweetened orange juice
2 T. unsweetened pineapple juice

Mix all of the ingredients together.

Yield: 1½ cups

Variations:
Add cinnamon, nutmeg, cloves or VANILLA, almond extract.
1/2 cup coconut, 1/4 cup sesame seeds

AMBROSIA DRESSING

1 cup YOGURT (plain) or
    MAYONNAISE
1/2 cup mashed banana

1/4 cup shredded unsweetened
    coconut
1/2 cup crushed pineapple

Combine all together in a bowl and mix thoroughly. Serve with fruit salad.

Yield: 2 cups

YOGURT-HONEY DRESSING

8 ounces plain YOGURT
2 T. honey

1/4 cup sesame seeds

Blend all of the ingredients together and chill.

Yield: 1 cup

MAYONNAISE

1 T. cider vinegar
1 T. lemon juice
1 egg
1/2 tsp. mustard powder

1/2 tsp. honey
3/4 cup oil
Dash of vegetable seasoning

Place the first 5 ingredients in a blender along with 1/4 cup of oil. Blend until smooth while pouring the other 1/2 cup of oil in blender in a steady stream. Make sure you pour the oil in slowly while the blender is still on. When completed, add the vegetable seasoning.

Yield: 1½ cups

LEMON-DILL MAYONNAISE

1 egg yolk
1 T. lemon juice
1½ tsp. white wine vinegar

1/2 tsp. each honey and dry
   mustard
1/2 cup oil
1/4 tsp. dill weed

Combine in a blender the egg yolk, lemon juice, vinegar, honey and mustard; whirl just until blended. With blender turned on, gradually pour in the oil; blend until smooth. Stir in dill weed; cover and chill.

Yield: 3/4 cup

PESTO MAYONNAISE

1/3 cup PESTO SAUCE
1/4 cup olive oil
1 egg
2 T. lemon juice

1 clove garlic, minced
1/2 cup melted butter
3/4 cup oil (not olive oil)
Vegetable seasoning to taste

In a blender combine the pesto sauce and olive oil; whirl at high speed until smooth. Add the egg, lemon juice and garlic. Whirl until well blended. With blender at high speed slowly pour in the butter and oil. Make sure you pour it in slowly. Add the vegetable seasoning to taste.

Yield: 2 cups

Variations:
Pesto Vegetable Dip—Stir together 1 cup Pesto Mayonnaise and 1/4 cup chopped fresh parsley. Top with 1/4 cup chopped almonds.

Creamy Pesto Dressing—Stir together 1 cup Pesto Mayonnaise and 1 cup plain YOGURT. Add 1 tablespoon lemon juice and 1/3 cup chopped fresh parsley. Serve with chicken or egg salad, mixed greens or as a sauce with cold fish.

SPROUTS

Sprouts are the tiny young shoots that emerge from seeds, beans or grains on the way to becoming mature plants. They are a storehouse of nutrients and you can grow them in your own kitchen. The freshest fresh vegetables you can get.

The sprouted seed has many virtues. Good source of minerals and vitamins A, B, C, E and K. It is a highly digestible protein, a good source of polyunsaturated oil, enzymes, low in calories and a good fiber source.

To give you an example of how the nutritional value increases with sprouting —take soybeans. The vitamin content can increase from 10 percent to even 1,000 percent, depending on the type of seed. The vitamin C content increases 500 percent during the first two days.

Nearly all kinds of seeds, grains, and beans can be sprouted successfully. Some of the different ones are alfalfa, mung bean, lentils, garbanzo beans, rye, barley, sunflower seeds, soybeans, wheat berries, radish and watercress seeds, just to name a few.

Sprouts are an inexpensive way to feed your family, as one pound of seeds, when sprouted, will produce 12 pounds of food in just four days.

HOW TO BUY THE SEEDS

1. Only buy untreated seeds and ones that are sold for growing purposes. The ones for agriculture use have been sprayed with poisonous insecticides.

2. Check seeds for imperfection as the damaged ones can cause others to decay.

3. Seeds can be acquired from health food stores, nurseries, garden shops, or by mail from seed companies.

HOW TO STORE THE SEEDS

Store in a cool, dry, dark place. Keep away from any moisture. Store in glass, metal or plastic containers with a well-fitting lid. Sprout only year-old beans. Older ones may not sprout.

SPROUTING METHODS

1. Place the recommended amount of seed into a *quart jar*, with a wide mouth opening. Fill the jar half full with cool tap water and let soak for at least 12 hours. This is the germination stage. Then cover the opening with a piece of fine nylon netting, or a fine wire mesh, or a double layer of cheesecloth held in place with a mason jar lid or rubber band. You want it so the air and rinsing water can pass through freely but the seeds stay in the jar. Pour off the soaking water, but save the water. It can be used in soups, cooking vegetables or to water plants as it is full of vitamins, minerals and enzymes. Fill the jar again with cool water twice or until the seeds rinse clean, being especially careful at this stage that the force of the tap water stream does not strike the seeds directly and thereby cause them to become damaged. Let the water strike the inside neck of the jar instead of the seeds themselves. Pour rinsing water off slowly so as to spread the seeds one layer thick inside the jar and position the jar on an angle in a low bowl on a shaded windowsill or sink top for good air circulation. Cover with a towel for the first 2 days to allow certain vitamins to develop during the sprouting stage. Rinse 2 to 3 times a day, being watchful that they do not dry out. Remove towel for the last 2 days and you will see the production of chlorophyl in the bright green color of the leaflets.

2. Another method that can be used successfully for the larger beans that need more room, such as garbanzo, soy and kidney, is the soup plate or colander method. Soak the recommended amount of beans in water. Use plenty of water as they more than double in size. The next morning, pour off the liquid and save it. Then rinse the beans and spread them out on the soup plate or colander so that you have only one layer. Now dampen several layers of paper toweling and cover the plate. Slip all of it into a plastic bag in order to retain moisture. Keep in a fairly warm place. Make sure that the paper toweling is always moist. Sprinkle with water a couple of times a day if necessary. Also rinse the beans once or twice a day in order to wash away molds. If placed in a colander it is easier. You simply spray the beans right over the paper two or three times a day and then let the colander sit in the sink to drain.

HOW TO STORE THE SPROUTS

After the sprouts have reached the desired length, place them in a large bowl of water and gently shake, causing hulls to float to the surface. Refrigerate in a firm, airtight container. Keeps a few days to a week depending on how dry they are when stored and how cold the refrigerator is.

HOW TO USE THE SPROUTS

1. Use in salads with lettuce or as a substitute for lettuce.
2. In casseroles—add 1/2 to 1 cup sprouts to your favorite casserole.
3. Use as a garnish in stews and soups.
4. Use in sandwiches.
5. Lightly steam as a vegetable or serve in combination with other vegetables.
6. Place in a blender along with other juices and liquefy.
7. Eat raw as a snack. Garbanzo and wheat sprouts are great this way.
8. Use with scrambled eggs or omelets.
9. Make into a powder or flour for baking or thickening soups and gravies. To dry sprouts, spread on a cookie sheet and place in a 175–200° oven. When dry, place in a blender and grind to a powder. Store in a cool, dark place in an airtight container.
10. Use in most home-baked goods to enhance them. Substitute 1 cup ground sprouts in any recipe for 1/2 cup flour and 1/4 cup liquid.
11. Use in breads to add a special crunchy taste. Add sprouts as late as possible in the mixing process. Do not allow to sit too long as the dough will sour with the sprouts in it.
12. Freeze the sprouts. Use the thawed sprouts in soup, bread or other baked goods as freezing destroys their crispness.

Charts detailing the characteristics, yield, and uses for specific sprouts are included on pages 71 and 72.

GROW YOUR OWN WHEATGRASS

Wheatgrass is sprouted wheat which is vitamin-mineral-enzyme-protein rich. It is a natural detoxifier for your system. Wheatgrass contains more nutrients than any other single grain or seed. It magnifies the vitamin and mineral content, vitamin E by 300 percent; adds enzymes, which help with digestion; and contains plenty of chlorophyll which regenerates the blood.

HOW TO GROW THE WHEATGRASS

Soak wheat seed 12–15 hours. Make it two parts water, one part wheat. Use a baking tray which has sides. Spread onto the baking tray, sand, a light layer of agricultural charcoal, and a layer of top soil. Sprinkle on an even layer of soaked seeds. Cover with wet newspaper and plastic (loosely). Let sit for 3 days in a warm dark place until you can see the sprouts pushing up the paper and plastic. Remove covering and put near a sunny window but do not place in direct sunlight. Harvest when it is 4–6" high, in about 8–15 days. Cut with a scissor near the root. You can then let it come up again. In fact if you keep it moist and fertilize it, you can keep it growing for many months. To use it you can either juice it (use only a small amount, 1/8 cup), chew the blades and spit out the pulp, or chop it up and add to a salad.

LEAFY GREEN SPROUTS: Use them in salads or as a garnish

	Growing time	Harvest size	Yield seed sprout	Taste	Uses
Alfalfa	3 to 5 days	1½ to 2"	1 T. makes 4 cups	crisp, mild, grassy	sandwiches, soups, salads, egg dishes, ground in bread and desserts
Chia	4 to 6 days	1½ to 2"	1 T. makes 2 cups	full-bodied flavor distinctly its own	soup, salads, dips, ground up in breads and pancakes, sandwiches
Garden cress	3 to 5 days	1½ to 2"	1 T. makes 1½ cups	peppery, similar to watercress but milder	Do not cook, but add after item has been removed from heat. Use as a salt substitute –ground and dried.
Mustard	5 to 6 days	1½ to 2"	1 T. makes 2 cups	pleasant bite, similar to mustard greens	salads
Radish	2 to 5 days	1½ to 2"	1 T. makes 2 cups	strong radish flavor gets hot when older or watered infrequently	sandwiches, salads

LARGER WHITE SPROUTS: Use in breads, entrées, salads, soups

	Growing time	Harvest size	Yield seed	sprout	Taste	Uses
Fenugreek	4 to 6 days	2 to 3"	1 cup	makes 12 cups	similar to mung but slightly bitter	add to bland foods, soups, curries, salads
Garbanzo bean	3 days	1/2 to 3/4"	1 cup	makes 5 cups	nutty taste	salads, raw as a snack, soups
Lentil	2 to 4 days	3/4 to 1"	1 cup	makes 6 cups	mildly spicy, fresh vegetable flavor and crunch	salads, steamed with herbs
Mung bean	1 to 5 days (immature) 5 to 7 days (commercial size)	1/4" & up depends on harvest size; 2 to 3"	1 cup	makes 5 cups	pleasant legume flavor, crunchy bland, crunchy	add to favorite Oriental dishes, soups, casseroles, salads, steamed
Rye	2 days	1/4"	1 cup	makes 4 cups	similar to wheat but more subtle flavor, less substantial	good raw as a snack, breads, soups, salads
Soybean	4 to 6 days	1/2 to 1"	1 cup	makes 5 cups	mild flavor	casseroles, salads, stir-fry dishes
Wheat	2 to 3 days	1/4 to 1/2"	1 cup	makes 4 cups	sweet, nutty, chewy, very filling	use in breads, cakes, cookies, soups, salads

SPROUTED WHEAT GOODIES

1 cup raisins
1 cup water
1 cup wheat sprouts, chopped
3/4 cup wheat germ
3/4 cup non-instant dry milk powder
2 tsp. brewer's yeast (optional)
2 tsp. cinnamon
1/4 tsp. each allspice and nutmeg

1/2 cup sunflower seeds
1/4 cup walnuts, chopped
1/4 cup oil
2 T. molasses
2 tsp. VANILLA EXTRACT
1/2 cup raisin water
2 eggs, beaten well

Soak the raisins overnight in 1 cup water. Save the water to use as a sweetener. In a big mixing bowl add the soaked raisins, wheat sprouts, wheat germ, dry milk, yeast, cinnamon, allspice, nutmeg, sunflower seeds and walnuts. Mix well. In a smaller bowl beat together the oil, molasses, vanilla and raisin water. Add this mixture to the dry ingredients and mix thoroughly. Gently fold in the eggs. Bake in 7" x 1" pan lined with wax paper, at 350° for 40–50 minutes. Remove paper and cut promptly.

Yield: 20

SPROUT RELISH

1½ cup bean sprouts, chopped
1/2 cup celery, diced
1½ cups raw beets, grated
1 cup fresh pineapple, diced

1/2 cup pineapple juice,
  unsweetened
1/2 cup chopped walnuts

Mix all of the ingredients together. Goes well with fish or fowl.

Yield: 4 cups

SPROUTED "MEAT BALLS"

2 cups sprouted wheat berries or rye
1 cup walnuts
1 large onion
1½ cups whole wheat bread crumbs

1 tsp. vegetable seasoning
2 T. oil
1 T. tamari (soy sauce)
1 cup milk

Put the sprouted wheat or rye, walnuts and onion through the coarse blade of a meat grinder. Turn into a bowl. Add the crumbs, vegetable seasoning, oil, tamari and milk. Add only enough milk to have the mixture hold together. Form into 1½" balls. Place on a cookie sheet and bake at 400° for 15 minutes or until browned. Serve with spaghetti or rice, topped with tomato sauce or mushroom gravy. Can also serve as an appetizer served along with one of the many dips listed in the Appetizer section.

Yield: 3 dozen

SPROUTS AND NUT PATTIES

2 cups sprouted rye or wheat berries
1 cup nuts
3/4 cup onion, grated
1 cup milk
1 T. soy flour
1 tsp. vegetable seasoning
1/2 tsp. garlic powder

1/4 tsp. kelp
1 sprig fresh parsley
1 egg
1/4 cup carrot, grated
1/4 cup zucchini, grated
1/4 cup grated Cheddar cheese
1½ cups whole wheat bread crumbs

Place the sprouts, nuts, onion, milk, soy flour, vegetable seasoning, garlic, kelp, parsley and egg in a blender. Blend until smooth. Add the carrots, zucchini and cheese and mix well. Stir in enough bread crumbs to make mixture stiff. Shape into patties. Broil on each side until browned.

Yield: Serves 6

SAUTÉED BEAN SPROUTS

3 T. oil
1 leek (white part), chopped
4 cups mung bean, soybean, garbanzo,
   or sprouted wheat berries

1 slice fresh ginger, finely chopped
1 T. tamari (soy sauce)
1/3 cup sliced water chestnuts
1/4 cup sunflower seeds

Heat the oil in a wok or large skillet. Add the leek and sauté for 30 seconds. Add the sprouts and cook for one minute. Add ginger, tamari, water chestnuts and sunflower seeds. Cover and cook for 3-4 minutes. Serve immediately.

Yield: 4-6 servings

CRUNCHY SPROUT SALAD

1 cup alfalfa sprouts
1 cup wheat sprouts
1 cup mung bean sprouts
1 cup sunflower seed sprouts
2 large tomatoes

1/4 cup finely chopped green
   pepper
1/4 cup green onions, chopped
1 large avocado, chopped
POPPY SEED DRESSING

Mix all ingredients together in a large bowl. Toss lightly with the dressing and serve immediately.

Yield: Serves 4-6

CHAPTER 5

VEGETABLES

Vegetables are very important in our diet. They provide fiber and assorted vitamins and minerals. But so often these nutrients are greatly reduced by incorrect storage and cooking. The enemies of vitamins and minerals are light, heat, air and water, so the less exposure to these elements, the better.

You can retain most of the nutrients in vegetables by preparing them in the following manner.

1. Wash vegetables quickly in cold water. Use a vegetable-oil-based, nontoxic cleaner to help remove pesticide residues. Do not soak your vegetables. Many vitamins and minerals are water-soluble, for example vitamins C and B, and these will be leached out into the cooking or soaking water.

2. Chill vegetables quickly. Vegetables contain enzymes that when exposed to light and air will destroy the nutrients in the foods. Chilling inactivates these enzymes. When shopping take a cooler with you and place your vegetables and other perishables in it to help prevent loss of nutrients.

3. Chop or slice the vegetables when you are ready to use them—not half an hour ahead of time. Nutrients are destroyed when the cut surface is exposed to oxygen. If you are going to eat them raw, coat the cut surface with oil to block the exposure to the oxygen.

One of the best ways to eat vegetables is raw, in salads, sandwiches, or used as an appetizer. They contain so many of the valuable vitamins, minerals and fiber needed in the diet. But if you prefer to cook them at times, use one of the following methods that will help insure the retention of a lot of vitamins and minerals.

STEAMING

The air in the pan is replaced by steam, reducing vitamin loss. Use a little stainless steel steamer that fits in any size pan. It is available at any of your variety stores. Place water in the pan, keeping the level 1/4" below the bottom of the steamer. Drop in the basket with the vegetables, cover and bring to a boil. Reduce heat to medium and continue to slow boil. Cook until vegetables are tender.

BAKING

Always place in a preheated oven to help preserve the nutrients. You can bake vegetables such as onions, potatoes and winter squash in their own skins; bake in broths and sauces; or in their own juices in a covered casserole. To conserve energy, bake them when you already have the oven heated for pies, loaves, etc.

SAUTÉING

Use a heavy pan over medium heat. Add a small amount of oil. The oil used seals in flavor and natural juices while at the same time it seals out the air that can destroy the nutrients. Add chopped vegetables and stir until they are coated with oil. Cook until tender. Try a variety of oils such as corn, peanut, soy and sesame as they will add a little extra something to the taste of the vegetables.

STIR-FRY

This method is similar to sautéing, but is done over higher heat for a shorter period of time. Usually done in a wok, or a large skillet. Heat a small amount of oil in the cooking utensil. When very hot, add chopped vegetables, and stir continually until vegetables are done but still crunchy. Takes only a few minutes. When cooking a combination of vegetables, begin with the longest cooking ones, such as onions, and end with the ones that cook the fastest, such as mushrooms.

As early as the book of Genesis in the Holy Bible, vegetables (along with fruits, grains, etc.) are mentioned. The Prophet Daniel considers vegetables more important than meat. Lentils, leeks, onions, garlic and many more vegetables are mentioned in 2nd Samuel, Genesis, Numbers, Isaiah and other books of scripture.

Here are some miscellaneous suggestions when cooking vegetables.

1. When sautéing or stir-frying use a wooden spoon as it will not bruise and tear the vegetables like a metal utensil will.

2. Do not add baking soda to the vegetables as it makes them mushy; but more importantly it destroys valuable vitamins and minerals.

3. Never cook your vegetables ahead of time and then reheat them. You lose a lot of your nutrients this way. Plan your vegetable preparation so it is ready at serving time. Serve leftover vegetables cold as in a salad.

4. When cooking home-frozen vegetables, cook them while they are still frozen. If they thaw and are then cooked they lose a lot of the nutrients and also become watery.

5. Place a clove of garlic or a sliced onion in steaming water to flavor vegetables.

6. Save any water that vegetables have been steamed in and use as stock.

HELPFUL HINTS

- All yellow, orange and dark green vegetables are rich in vitamin A. That includes the root vegetables such as carrots and leaf ones such as spinach.

- Green leaves are a good source of riboflavin, vitamin C and iron, plus calcium.

- When eaten raw, the vegetables are a good source of vitamin C.

- Vegetables are fairly low in calories. It is what you put on them that brings up the calories.

- Vegetables add variety to the meal, so be sure to include them frequently.

- Exposure to direct sunlight softens tomatoes instead of ripening them. Leave tomatoes, stem-up, out of direct sunlight.

- Slice tomatoes with the core to keep juice in (good for sandwiches and salads). Slice against the core when you want the juice to come out.

- Peeling tomatoes. Refrigerate tomatoes and then hold firmly and scrape them with a paring knife from the bottom to the top several times. Prick skin with point of knife and peeling will remove easily.

- Garlic can be stored in freezer. When ready to use, peel and chop before thawing.

- Bake tomatoes, stuffed green peppers, or apples in well-greased muffin pans. They will keep their shape better and be more attractive when served.

- To sweeten garlic-scented finger, rub with lemon or a ripe tomato which you can use later in a salad.

- To remove corn silks, dampen a paper towel and brush downwards on cob. All strands should come off.

- Fresh ginger root keeps well in the freezer. You can grate some of the frozen ginger and then return the rest of the root to the freezer.

- Garlic dishes sometimes taste bitter because the garlic was burned during cooking.

- To keep a whole onion intact when cooking: once peeled, make an X about 1/2" deep at the root end with a small, sharp knife.

- To make onion juice: cut a slice off the onion, then squeeze the larger part of the onion as you would an orange.

- The skins will remain tender if you wrap potatoes in aluminum foil to bake them.

- Test boiled potatoes to see if they're done with a cake tester or a skewer, never a fork. Many holes make them watery.

- Chopping onions without tears: place in freezer or refrigerator before chopping. Then to chop efficiently, cut it in half, sprinkle with lemon juice (also helps prevent tears), and place flat surfaces on your cutting board; cut in thin slices across with chef's knife. Then turn slices around, holding them together, and chop into fine pieces. This method keeps in the juices better.

- To keep parsley fresh, place in a jar or container that has a small amount of water. Place stems into water and place a cover on it. Will stay very fresh.

- One pound of whole pumpkin produces 3/4 cup of cooked pulp.

COMPLIMENTARY HERBS FOR VARIOUS VEGETABLES

	Vegetable	Herbs
1.	Artichokes	Tarragon, parsley, basil
2.	Asparagus	Parsley, chervil, chives, thyme, tarragon
3.	Beans, green	Dill, rosemary, basil, marjoram, parsley, oregano, thyme, savory, chives, chervil
4.	Lima Beans	Parsley, marjoram, dill, chives, thyme, rosemary, savory, basil
5.	Beets	Mint, tarragon, parsley, basil, dill, chives
6.	Broccoli	Sage, parsley, chervil, dill, poppy seeds, oregano, caraway seeds, rosemary, nutmeg
7.	Brussels Sprouts	Nutmeg, chives
8.	Cabbage, red and green	Basil, parsley, bay leaf, dill, tarragon, sage, thyme, oregano, poppy seed, caraway seed, celery seed, sesame seed
9.	Carrots	Mint, parsley, nutmeg, oregano, chives, basil, tarragon
10.	Cauliflower	Caraway seed, nutmeg, savory, rosemary, thyme, basil, parsley, chives, tarragon
11.	Celery	Basil, dill, parsley, chervil, oregano
12.	Celeriac	Parsley

Vegetable	*Herbs*
13. Swiss Chard	Oregano, marjoram, thyme, basil, parsley
14. Corn	Chives, basil, oregano, parsley, celery seed
15. Cucumbers	Chives, celery seed, parsley, dill, basil, mustard seed
16. Eggplant	Tarragon, parsley, thyme, basil, chervil, sage, oregano
17. Greens	Basil, dill, oregano, tarragon, parsley, chives
18. Jerusalem Artichokes	Thyme, marjoram, rosemary, parsley, dill, mustard seed, celery seed
19. Kohlrabi	Basil, dill, parsley
20. Mushrooms	Parsley, chives, tarragon, rosemary, basil, marjoram, thyme
21. Okra	Bay leaf, thyme, parsley, basil, dill, chives
22. Onions	Parsley, chives, thyme, dill, mint, rosemary, cloves, caraway seeds, tarragon
23. Parsnips	Sage, dill, parsley
24. Peas, sweet and sugar	Mint, dill, parsley, marjoram, basil
25. Peppers	Basil, chives, parsley, sage, rosemary, thyme, chervil, marjoram, savory, tarragon, oregano
26. Potatoes	Parsley, rosemary, celery, poppy seeds, caraway seeds, basil, chives, dill, mint
27. Pumpkin	Nutmeg, cloves, cinnamon
28. Salsify or Oyster Plant	Tarragon, parsley
29. Spinach	Chives, tarragon, parsley, basil, dill, oregano
30. Summer Squash	Mint, oregano, parsley, basil, thyme, rosemary, marjoram, chives
31. Sweet Potatoes and Yams	Nutmeg, clove, cinnamon, chives, parsley
32. Winter Squash and Pumpkins	Nutmeg, cinnamon, chives, parsley

Vegetable	*Herbs*
33. Tomatoes	Oregano, basil, bay leaf, mint, parsley, chives, rosemary, dill, thyme
34. Turnips and Rutabagas	Parsley, marjoram, oregano, bay leaf, mint, basil, celery seed

ARTICHOKES

(Contains Vitamins A, B and C, plus assorted minerals)

Buying guide: Compact, firm, heavy globes; green, fresh-looking leaves free from brown blemishes. Best time to buy is March through May.

Storage: Keep cool and moist in a plastic bag in the refrigerator up to 4 days. Can also freeze them whole up to 12 months.

Preparation: Slice off the stem to make the bottom surface flat. Cut 1" off the top leaves, and using a scissor, cut the tips off the remaining leaves.

Basic Cooking: Place in a steamer upright and steam 30–40 minutes. When leaves pull out easily, it is done. Remove and turn over to drain.

Uses: To eat, pull off the leaves and pull the leaf through your teeth. When all the leaves are gone, remove the fuzzy part over the heart and eat the inside or "heart" of the artichoke. Dip the leaves in sauces such as LEMON BUTTER or MAYONNAISE and HOLLANDAISE SAUCE. You can also stuff the artichoke.

Yield: 1 average to large size for each serving.

STUFFING ARTICHOKES

1. Wash the artichoke and, using scissors, cut off the top third of the vegetable.

2. Pull off the tough outside leaves around the bottom. Using the fingers, open the center leaves carefully. Turn the artichoke over on a chopping board or other flat surface and press down firmly at the base to cause the leaves to spread open further.

3. Turn the artichoke right side up and pull the yellow and yellow-white leaves from the center.

4. Sprinkle the center, fuzzy portion of the vegetable with lemon juice to keep it from darkening. Using a soup spoon, carefully scrape and pull the fuzzy and prickly portion from the heart of the artichoke. Make sure all of the choke is removed.

5. Sprinkle the smooth, scraped artichoke bottom with additional lemon juice.

6. Using a sharp, heavy knife, cut off the stem of the artichoke flush with the base. The stem may be peeled and cooked and used in the filling.

7. Stand the vegetable alongside the other artichokes in a steamer pot. Have them fit snugly. You may want to tie a string around them so they can retain their shape.

8. Cook, covered, 20–30 minutes, or until partly tender.

9. Using two spoons, remove the artichokes from the water and turn upside down to drain. When partly cool, fill the centers with stuffing and bake as directed.

MUSHROOM STUFFED ARTICHOKES

4 artichokes

Stuffing:

1/4 cup chopped onions	1/4 cup wheat germ
3-4 mushrooms, chopped	1 clove of garlic, minced
3 T. oilive oil	3 T. chopped fresh parsley
3/4 cup whole wheat bread crumbs	1/2 tsp. vegetable seasoning

Prepare the artichokes per instructions under "Stuffing Artichokes." Prepare the stuffing by sautéing onions and mushrooms in oil until tender. Add bread crumbs, wheat germ, garlic, parsley and seasoning; mix thoroughly. Gently spread open the leaves of each artichoke, spoon stuffing into the center, and push back the leaves. Set artichokes upright in an oiled casserole, brush with a little oil, and cover. Bake at 350° for 20 minutes. Remove cover and bake for another 15 to 20 minutes, or until tender.

Yield: Serves 4

Variation: Add to the above mixture, 1 cup cooked, deveined shrimp.

ASPARAGUS

(Contains Vitamins A and C, phosphorus and calcium)

Buying guide:	Firm stalk with close compact tips. Stalk should be brittle, not woody. Best time to buy is March through June.
Storage:	Keep in refrigerator in an airtight container or crisper for 4 days. Can also be frozen up to 12 months for longer storage.
Preparation:	Break the stalks as far down as they will snap easily and save tough ends for soup stock. Wash thoroughly and scrape off scales.

Basic cooking: Stand stalks in clump tied with a string in bottom half of a double boiler. Add a small amount of water and invert the top half over it. Steam for about 12 minutes. Or sauté them in a small amount of oil for about 8 minutes.

Uses: Serve raw or cooked in salads. Serve with a sauce or dressing such as CHEESE SAUCE and then top with sesame seeds.

Yield: 2 pounds will equal 4 servings.

SPANISH ASPARAGUS

2 pounds asparagus
1/4 cup butter
1 small onion, minced
1 small bay leaf
Vegetable seasoning to taste

3 T. arrowroot powder
2 cups CHICKEN STOCK (broth)
Pinch of nutmeg
2 egg yolks
1 T. lemon juice

Steam the asparagus until tender. In a saucepan heat three tablespoons of the butter, add the onion, bay leaf, vegetable seasoning, and sauté until the onion is tender but not brown. Stir in the arrowroot gradually, add the stock and cook, stirring until thickened. Add the nutmeg. Simmer 5 minutes and strain. Beat the egg yolks until very light and add the lemon juice. Combine with a little of the hot sauce and add the egg mixture to the sauce gradually, while stirring. Cook the mixture over boiling water in a double boiler, or over very low heat, stirring constantly, until thickened. Add the remaining butter. To serve, place the asparagus on toast and pour the sauce over the top.

Yield: 4 servings

BEANS, GREEN

(Contains calcium, phosphorus and Vitamins A and C)

Buying guide: Should be bright and fresh looking, free from blemishes. Pods that are firm, crisp and snap easily when broken. Peak season is May through September.

Storage: Do not store well. Best eaten within a couple of days as they will become limp, tough and dry. Store in a plastic bag unwashed. Can freeze up to 12 months.

Preparation: Wash them and snap off ends rather than cutting them off. Keeps them crisper. Can leave whole or cut into diagonal 1" pieces or into lengthwise strips for French style.

Basic cooking: Steam them for about 3-5 minutes or sauté them in oil for about the same length of time. Do not overcook as they will become very untasty.

Uses: Serve beans raw as a snack or as a salad ingredient. Serve cooked with butter and topped with mushrooms, almonds or water chestnuts. Place in soups and casseroles. Serve also with different sauces.

Yield: 1-1½ pounds for 4 servings

SWISS GREEN BEANS

1½ pounds green beans
2 T. butter
2 T. whole wheat flour
1/4 tsp. oregano

1/2 tsp. grated onion
1 cup YOGURT, plain
1/2 pound Swiss cheese, grated

Crumble Top:

1 cup whole wheat flour
1/2 cup rolled oats

Dill and oregano to taste
3 T. butter, softened

Wash beans, snap off ends and break into 1" pieces. Steam beans until just tender; drain well. Melt butter in saucepan. Stir in flour, oregano and onion and cook 2 minutes. Reduce heat, add yogurt and stir until smooth. Fold in beans and heat gently. Pour into a buttered casserole, sprinkle with cheese. Mix crumble top: Combine the flour, oats and herbs. Work in the soft butter until evenly blended. Scatter crumble top over beans and cheese. Bake at 400° for 20 minutes, or until bubbly and crumbs are nicely browned.

Yield: Serves 8

GREEN BEANS À LA NICOISE

1/2 cup olive oil
1 onion, sliced thin
1 cup plum tomatoes
1/2 green pepper, chopped
1/2 cup chopped celery
1/4 cup water
1/2 tsp. basil
1/4 tsp. marjoram

2 cloves of garlic
1 bay leaf
6 sprigs parsley
1/2 tsp. dried chervil
1 pound green beans, cooked until tender and drained
1/4 cup grated Swiss cheese

In a skillet heat the oil, add the onion and cook until golden brown. Add the tomatoes, green pepper, celery, water, basil and marjoram. Tie the garlic, bay leaf, parsley and chervil in a small cheesecloth bag and add to the vegetables. Simmer, uncovered, about 25 minutes. Add the beans and continue simmering until the beans are hot. Remove the spice bag and serve at once topped with cheese.

Yield: 6 servings

BEANS, LIMA

(Contains iron and Vitamins A and B)

Buying guide:	Dark green, firm pods that are well filled and free from blemishes. The season is from July to November.
Storage:	Unshelled in a moisture-proof container 3–6 days. Can also be frozen.
Preparation:	Cut off rounded edges of the bean and press with your thumb and finger; the pod will open. Rinse and pick out any bad ones.
Basic cooking:	Steam for about 15–20 minutes or until tender. You should cook this bean and not serve it raw as it contains a toxic substance that is destroyed by cooking.
Uses:	Place in soups, casseroles and salads. Serve with sautéed mushrooms and onion and sprinkle with rosemary. Fava, broad and buttered beans are very similar to the lima and can be used in the recipes calling for lima beans.
Yield:	2 pounds will be needed for 4 servings.

LIMA BEAN AND PEANUT ROAST

2½ cups cooked baby limas	1 tsp. dill
1 cup shelled, roasted peanuts	1/2 tsp. fresh parsley, chopped
2 cups mashed potatoes	1/2 tsp. paprika
1/2 cup milk	1 T. finely chopped onion
1 egg, beaten	Butter as needed
1 tsp. vegetable seasoning	TOMATO or CHEESE SAUCE

Chop peanuts finely, reserving 1 tablespoon. Spread a layer of potatoes in the bottom of a greased baking dish. Add a layer of peanuts, then a layer of beans. Repeat until all potatoes, peanuts, and beans are used, ending with a layer of beans. Combine milk, egg, seasoning, herbs and onion, and pour over layered mixture. Dot with butter. Bake uncovered at 350° for 30 minutes. Serve with tomato or cheese sauce, garnished with reserved peanuts.

Yield: Serves 6

BEETS

(Contains Vitamins A and C, calcium, potassium and phosphorus)

Buying guide:	Smooth, firm, free from cracks and blemishes. Sold in bunches. Look to see if the beet tops are fresh looking. Small to medium size are best. Available all year long.

Storage:	Refrigerate in a nonporous container or crisper up to two weeks. Remove leafy tops, but leave 1" of stem and root to preserve tenderness and nutrients. Can, pickle or freeze for long-term storage.
Preparation:	Scrub well. Do not peel so as to prevent "bleeding."
Basic cooking:	Steam 20–30 minutes or until tender.
Uses:	Raw beets are good grated in salads. Or use them cooked in many dishes such as casseroles, soups like Borscht, or they can be served topped with YOGURT and dill.
Yield:	6 medium sized beets will give 3–4 servings.

HARVARD BEETS

3 cups sliced cooked beets
1/4 cup honey
1 T. arrowroot powder
1/2 cup vinegar

2 whole cloves
1/2 cup beet juice
1 T. butter

Combine the honey, arrowroot, vinegar, cloves, and beet juice. Cook, over low heat, stirring until thickened. Add beets and butter, simmer until beets are heated all the way through.

Yield: 4–6 servings

PICKLED BEETS

2 pounds beets
1½ cups cider vinegar
1½ T. dry mustard

1/2 cup honey
2 medium onions, sliced
2 tsp. celery seed

Steam beets until tender, about 30 minutes. Drain, reserving one cup of the cooking water. Slip off the skins and slice. Heat the vinegar and reserved cooking water to a boil. Mix the mustard and honey together. Add to the vinegar and let boil again. Arrange the beets and onions in layers in your storage containers. Add the celery seed and cover with the hot vinegar mixture. Seal, cool and store in the refrigerator. Let stand a few days before using. Will keep for weeks in refrigerator.

Yield: 3 pints

BROCCOLI

(Contains Vitamins A and C, calcium, potassium and B Vitamins)

Buying guide:	Firm, tender stalks with compact clusters. Buds should be dark-green or purple-green, not yellowish (sign of over maturity). Available all year but peak is October through April.

Storage: Should be refrigerated immediately or it will lose its crisp-
                  ness. Store in an airtight container up to 5 days. Can freeze
                  up to 16 months.

Preparation: Remove leaves (good vitamin A source, cook and serve as
                  greens) and cut about 1" off the bottom. If stems are thick,
                  you may want to slit them for faster cooking.

Basic cooking: Steam for about 6-8 minutes. Do not overcook or it will be-
                  come mushy.

Uses: Use raw in salads or as an appetizer with dip. Serve hot with
                  butter, sauces or YOGURT topped with ground nuts or sun-
                  flower seeds. Also good in casseroles and soups.

Yield: 2 pounds will make 4 servings

BROCCOLI POLONAISE

1 large bunch broccoli
2 T. onion, finely chopped
4 T. oil
1 clove garlic, finely chopped
2 T. butter

1 T. chopped fresh parsley
1/2 tsp. dill
2 tsp. lemon juice
3 T. whole wheat bread crumbs
1 hard-cooked egg, finely chopped

Divide broccoli into flowerets, and chop stems. Steam until tender, about
6-7 minutes. Sauté onion in oil for 2 minutes. Add garlic and cook another
minute or two, until onion is soft. Add butter, parsley, dill, lemon juice,
bread crumbs and egg, and mix thoroughly. Blend in broccoli and serve immediately.

Yield: 4-6 servings

GOLDEN BROCCOLI BAKE

1 cup cooked brown rice
2 T. butter
2 T. arrowroot powder
2 tsp. mustard powder
1 tsp. vegetable seasoning

3/4 cup milk
2-3 cups chopped broccoli
2 cups shredded Cheddar cheese
4 eggs, separated

Melt butter in medium-sized saucepan; stir in arrowroot, mustard, and vegetable seasoning. Gradually add milk, stirring until smooth. Add broccoli;
cover and cook, stirring occasionally, until sauce simmers and broccoli is just
lightly cooked. Remove from heat; stir in cheese and cooked rice. Beat egg
whites until stiff peaks form. Beat egg yolks just until blended; stir into rice
mixture. Fold in egg whites. Spoon into ungreased 2 quart casserole or soufflé dish. Bake in 325° oven for 40 to 45 minutes, until golden brown and
firm to the touch. Serve immediately.

Yield: Serves 6

ITALIAN BROCCOLI CASSEROLE

1½ pounds broccoli, cut in bite-size pieces

Sauce:

2 T. butter	2 eggs, beaten
2 T. whole wheat flour	1 tsp. oregano
1 cup milk	2 medium tomatoes, cut up
1/2 tsp. vegetable seasoning	1/4 cup Parmesan cheese, grated
1/2 cup grated Cheddar cheese	

Steam broccoli until barely tender, 5-7 minutes; drain well. Meanwhile, prepare sauce. Melt butter and stir in flour to make a roux (thickening). Add milk and cook, stirring until thickened. Stir in vegetable seasoning and cheese. Add the eggs to the sauce and mix well. Stir in broccoli, oregano and tomatoes. Pour into a 2 quart baking dish and sprinkle with grated Parmesan cheese. Bake, uncovered, in 350° oven for 30 minutes, or until heated all the way through.

Yield: 4-6 servings

BRUSSELS SPROUTS

(Contains iron and is a rich source of Vitamins C and A)

Buying guide: Firm, compact, bright-green leaves free from worm holes and blemishes. Avoid yellow leaves. The season is November through January.

Storage: Store in an airtight container in the refrigerator up to 5 days. Can freeze up to 11 months.

Preparation: Cut off stem end and remove any discolored or wilted leaves. Wash in cold water. Slash stem ends as this allows sprouts to cook more quickly.

Basic cooking: Steam for about 8-10 minutes. Overcooking causes them to have a strong taste.

Uses: Serve marinated in salads. Serve hot topped with butter or your favorite sauce.

Yield: 1 pound will make 4 servings

BRUSSELS SPROUTS CASSEROLE

1½ pounds Brussels sprouts, steamed	1/4 tsp. nutmeg
1 cup tomatoes, stewed	1 cup YOGURT, plain
1/2 cup Cheddar cheese, grated	1/3 cup sunflower seeds

Arrange Brussels sprouts in oiled casserole. Cover with tomatoes. Sprinkle with cheese and nutmeg. Cover. Bake at 350° for 15 minutes. Serve garnished with yogurt and sunflower seeds.

Yield: Serves 6

BRUSSELS SPROUTS IN NUTTY CHEESE SAUCE

4 cups Brussels sprouts

Sauce:

1 T. oil	Dash dry mustard
1 T. whole wheat flour	1/2 tsp. tamari (soy sauce)
1/2 cup grated Cheddar cheese	1/2 cup milk
1/4 tsp. honey	4 T. coarsely chopped walnuts
1/4 tsp. paprika	Chopped chives

Trim the stems off close to the sprouts and remove any discolored leaves. Steam sprouts until tender, about 15 minutes. Sauce: Heat oil in small, heavy saucepan, over low heat. Sprinkle in the flour and blend well. Add the cheese, honey, paprika, mustard and tamari. Stir together well until the cheese is melted, being careful not to scorch. Gradually pour in the milk, continuing to stir constantly until the sauce is thickened. Add the walnuts and mix to blend. Pour sauce over steamed sprouts in serving dish and garnish with chopped chives.

Yield: Serves 4

CABBAGE

(Good source of Vitamin C)

Buying guide: Look for heads that are compact and heavy. Outer leaves should be crisp and deep green or red, depending on the type of cabbage. Avoid yellowing or worm-eaten leaves. Available all year long.

Storage: Place unwashed head in a plastic bag in refrigerator for up to 5–10 days. Do not freeze.

Preparation: Wash, core and cut into wedges, quarters or shred.

Basic cooking: Steam wedges for 10–15 minutes. Shredded steam 3–5 minutes. Overcooking at too high a temperature produces a strong taste. Can also sauté in a little oil for about 5 minutes.

Uses: Serve with sauces, in soups, stuff the leaves, make sauerkraut out of it, although it loses most of its nutritional value this way. Serve with sesame, caraway or poppy seeds. Serve cabbage raw, alone, or along with other greens in a salad.

Yield: 1–1½ pounds will give you 4 servings

HOW TO STUFF CABBAGE

1. Pull off the tough outer leaves from the cabbage and cut out the bottom core of the head with a paring knife. Cook the cabbage in a steamer for about 6 minutes, or until the leaves separate easily. Invert and drain well.

2. Separate the individual leaves and dry them.

3. Place a square of cheesecloth on a flat surface. In the center of it place one of the large cabbage leaves, curly edge up. Insert a smaller cabbage leaf in the first leaf and fill the smaller leaf with one or two tablespoons of the stuffing.

4. Bring the four corners of the cheesecloth together and twist the ends shut. This will shape the stuffed leaves into a compact round.

5. Remove the cheesecloth immediately and arrange the stuffed cabbage in a casserole with the sealed edge of the vegetable down.

6. Continue stuffing the leaves until all have been filled. The same square of cheesecloth may be used repeatedly.

ARMENIAN STUFFING FOR CABBAGE LEAVES

1 large cabbage	1/4 cup chopped nuts
1/2 cup olive oil	1/4 cup tomato paste
2½ cups chopped onion	1/2 cup water
1½ cups celery, chopped	1/4 tsp. allspice
1/2 cup mushroom, chopped	1/4 tsp. cinnamon
1/2 cup cooked brown rice	1/2 tsp. vegetable seasoning
1/2 cup finely chopped fresh parsley	2 cups CHICKEN STOCK (broth)
1/4 cup raisins	TOMATO SAUCE, optional

Prepare the cabbage as instructed in "How to Stuff Cabbage." In a skillet heat the oil, add the onion, celery, mushrooms and cook gently until golden brown. Add rice and cook for about 10 minutes. Stir occasionally. Add the remaining ingredients except the cabbage, stock and tomato sauce and cook 5 minutes longer. Pour the stock into a heavy round casserole. Stuff the cabbage leaves with the rice mixture. Arrange the stuffed leaves in the casserole and weight down with an inverted plate that fits loosely inside the casserole. Add enough chicken stock to reach the rim of the plate and simmer until done, about 30 minutes. If desired, serve topped with a tomato sauce.

Yield: 6 servings

CABBAGE, SWEET AND SOUR

4 cups red or green cabbage, shredded	3 T. honey
3 onions, grated	2 T. oil
Juice of 2 lemons	1 T. caraway seeds
4 tart apples, unpeeled, diced	1/2 cup raisins
1/4 cup apple cider	Pinch of ground allspice and cloves

Blend all ingredients together in a saucepan. Cover. Simmer gently for about 10 minutes.

Yield: Serves 6

CARROTS

(Contain carotene that our bodies use to manufacture Vitamin A)

Buying guide: Firm, clean, smooth, well shaped, with good color. Should be free from bruises and cracks. Available year round.

Storage: Refrigerate in a crisper or in a plastic bag up to 2-3 weeks. Can freeze up to 12 months.

Preparation: Wash thoroughly by scrubbing with a brush. No need to peel as a lot of the nutrients are close to the skin.

Basic cooking: Best eaten raw but can be steamed whole, or cut into lengthwise strips, for 6-8 minutes.

Uses: Use in soups, raw in salads and relish trays, baked in cakes and cookies. Serve hot with butter, sauces, pineapple juice and cinnamon, lemon juice. Grate and add to spaghetti sauce to thicken it.

Yield: 1-1½ pounds for 4 servings

CARROT PUFF

4 large potatoes
6 carrots
3 eggs, separated

1 tsp. each dill and oregano
1/4 tsp. paprika
1/4 cup sesame seeds

Wash, peel and grate potatoes. Scrub and grate carrots. Beat egg yolks until thick and lemon colored. Mix in potatoes and carrots, herbs and sesame seeds. Beat egg whites stiff, then fold into vegetable mixture. Turn into a well-oiled casserole and bake for about 30-40 minutes at 350°.

Yield: Serves 6

BAKED CARROTS

8 carrots, washed and cut into strips
1/2 cup chopped onion
1/2 cup raisins
1 apple, cored and cut into cubes
2 T. honey

2 T. oil
2 T. lemon juice
1/2 tsp. cinnamon
1/4 tsp. cloves
1/2 cup GRANOLA

Place all ingredients in a shallow casserole. Cover tightly. Bake at 375° about 40 minutes, or until tender. If you cut carrot strips thin, less cooking time is required.

Yield: Serves 6

CAULIFLOWER

(Contains Vitamins A and C, calcium and potassium)

Buying guide: Clean, heavy, compact head with white flowerets and green crisp leaves. Avoid heads that have discolorations. Available all year but peak is September through December.

Storage: Refrigerate in an airtight container up to 5 days. After this time the quality deteriorates. Freezes well up to 11 months.

Preparation: Wash and remove outer leaves and part of the core. Cut off any blemishes. If it develops some brownish spots do not throw the head away if it is firm; it still can be used.

Basic cooking: Steam whole or separate into flowerets. Cook 8–12 minutes.

Uses: Serve raw in salads or as an appetizer with a dip. Use in soups, casseroles or steamed with different sauces and topped with sesame or poppy seeds.

Yield: 1 medium sized head will equal 4 servings

CAULIFLOWER POLONAISE

1 large head of cauliflower
1/2 cup whole wheat bread crumbs
2 T. butter

1 hard-cooked egg, chopped
2 tsp. chopped parsley

Steam cauliflower until tender, about 6 minutes. Place in a serving dish and cover lightly with the bread crumbs that have been browned in the butter. Sprinkle with the egg and parsley.

Yield: 4 servings

Variation: Instead of bread crumbs and butter, use roasted soy nuts that have been chopped in the blender. Use 1/2 cup soybeans.

MEXICAN-STYLE CAULIFLOWER

1 medium head of cauliflower,
    separated into flowerets
1½ cups TOMATO SAUCE
2 T. chopped parsley
1/8 tsp. cloves

1/4 tsp. cinnamon
2 T. chopped olives
3 T. grated Cheddar cheese
2 T. fine bread crumbs
1 T. olive oil

Steam the flowerets for about 6–7 minutes. Drain. Mix the tomato sauce, parsley, spices, and olives together. Pour a little of the sauce into a heatproof 1 quart baking dish, add cauliflower and cover with remaining sauce. Sprinkle with the cheese, crumbs and oil and bake until brown (a few minutes).

Yield: 4–5 servings

BUTTER TOPPED CAULIFLOWER

1 medium sized head of cauliflower	1 T. chopped fresh parsley
3 T. butter	1 T. chopped fresh dill
1 T. chopped fresh chives	Vegetable seasoning to taste

Clean and wash cauliflower. Leave two rows of leaves surrounding the head. Steam cauliflower until just tender, 6-8 minutes. Place on a serving platter. Melt the butter and blend in the herbs. Pour this mixture over the cauliflower. Serve at once.

Yield: 4-6 servings

SWISS CAULIFLOWER

1 medium head of cauliflower	Pinch of thyme and rosemary
2 to 3 stalks celery, with leaves	1 T. chopped fresh parsley
2 T. butter	1/4 pound Swiss cheese, grated
1 clove garlic, minced	

Separate cauliflower into flowerets. Slice celery. Steam both vegetables together until almost tender, 5-8 minutes. Drain. Melt butter in a large skillet. Sauté garlic, add steamed vegetables and sauté lightly for 5 minutes. Stir in herb, parsley and blend together well. In a small but deep baking dish, layer vegetables and cheese, ending with cheese. Bake at 350° 15-20 minutes, until cheese is melted.

Yield: 4 servings

CELERY

(Contains potassium, Vitamins A and B plus sodium)

Buying guide:	Crisp, thick stalks that snap easily. Buy stalks with many green leaves as they can be used in casseroles and soups for flavor. Available all year round.
Storage:	Store in a vegetable crisper for about 7 days. Does not freeze well.
Preparation:	Trim off root end and discolored or damaged leaves. Scrub well.
Basic cooking:	Best eaten raw, but can be steamed for about 6 minutes.
Uses:	Use whole, chopped or sliced. Place in soups, stews, casseroles. Use raw in salads, as an appetizer with a dip or stuffed with one of the many spreads listed in the "Sandwich" section.
Yield:	2 cups equals 4 servings

BAKED CELERY RING

1 bunch celery
1/4 cup butter
1 cup chopped onion
1/2 cup diced green pepper
3 eggs, lightly beaten

1/2 cup milk
1 cup whole wheat bread crumbs
1/4 cup chopped parsley
1/2 tsp. dill
1¼ cups finely chopped peanuts
(unsalted)

Separate celery into stalks. Trim off leaves. Slice celery to make 4 cups. Heat butter in skillet. Add onion, green pepper and celery. Sauté until celery is crisp-tender, about 3 minutes. Set aside to cool. Generously grease a 6-cup ring mold. Trace a ring of waxed paper the size of the bottom of the mold. Press into bottom and grease; set mold aside. In a large bowl combine eggs, milk, bread crumbs, parsley, dill and peanuts; stir in celery mixture. Spoon into wax-paper lined pan; press down and smooth top. Bake in preheated 350° oven for 30 minutes or until firm. Loosen with spatula and unmold onto serving dish.

Yield: 4-6 servings

CELERIAC

Celeriac is a root crop that can be substituted in recipes that call for cooked celery.

Storage: Store in a cool, dry area.

Preparation: Peel and slice.

Basic cooking: Steam until tender, about 8 minutes.

Uses: Use raw, shredded in salads. Serve hot with a cream sauce. Can be used in place of celery in recipes.

Yield: 1½ pounds will furnish 4 servings

CORN
(Contains Vitamins A and C and some phosphorus)

Buying guide: Buy corn with the husks still left on as the flavor and nutritional value rapidly deteriorate when unhusked. Green husks, with silk ends free from decay. The kernels should be plump and milky. Available year round but peak season is May through September.

Storage: Store unhusked ears in a plastic bag in the coldest part of the refrigerator up to 4 days. Can be frozen in its husk for 12 months.

Preparation: Remove husks, wash and remove silks.

Basic cooking: Steam until tender, about 3-5 minutes. Can also bake in husk for 30 minutes at 400°.

Uses: Serve on cob with butter, in casseroles, soups, puddings and in combination with other vegetables. Great raw in a salad as it adds a special sweetness.

Yield: 1 ear per person

CORN PUDDING

2½ cups uncooked corn, scraped from the cob
4 eggs, lightly beaten
2 cups milk
1/4 cup green pepper

1/4 cup onion
2 T. oil
1 tsp. vegetable seasoning
1 T. honey
3/4 cup Cheddar cheese, grated

Combine all of the ingredients together, except the cheese. Pour into an oiled 8" casserole dish. Place in a pan with boiling water 1/4" deep. Bake at 350° for 45 minutes or until set. Cool 5 minutes before serving.

Yield: Serves 4

MEXICAN CORN

1/2 cup chopped green pepper
1/2 cup chopped sweet, red pepper
2 T. chopped onion
1 tsp. chopped chili peppers
3 T. oil

3 cups fresh corn kernels
2 T. chopped parsley
1/2 tsp. vegetable seasoning
1 medium tomato, chopped

In a large skillet, sauté green pepper, red pepper, onion and chili pepper in the oil for 5 minutes. Add corn and continue sautéing for 8 minutes. Add parsley, vegetable seasoning and tomato and cook for another 3-5 minutes.

Yield: Serves 6

CUCUMBER

(Low in calories. Mostly water but does have Vitamins A and C)

Buying guide: Look for unwaxed cucumbers if available. Should have an even shape and good green color. Whitish streaks are charac-teristic of the cucumber. It should not be real big as that means it is over mature. Available all year long.

Storage: Wrap in plastic bag and can be stored up to 11 days. If longer storage is necessary, best if pickled.

Preparation: Do not peel or slice until ready to use.

Uses: Raw in salads, sandwiches or as appetizer garnish. Marinate in vinegar and dill.

Yield: 2 medium size ones will serve 4

EGGPLANT

(High in carbohydrates, but low in calories)

Buying guide:	Firm, heavy and free from blemishes. Should have a shiny, smooth purple skin. Available all year long.
Storage:	Store for 1 week in a cool, dry place; does not need to be refrigerated. Can be frozen up to 12 months.
Preparation:	Peel as the skin may contain wax and chemical residue. Remove stem and top before cooking.
Basic cooking:	Bake for 10 minutes or steam for 6–7 minutes.
Uses:	Can be halved, diced, cubed, sliced; baked, steamed, stuffed, broiled, breaded or sautéed; served alone or in a casserole. Can be combined with cheeses, tomatoes, onions, garlic and herbs.
Yield:	1 pound will give 4 servings

STUFFED EGGPLANT

3 small eggplants (about 1 pound each)
1 medium sized green pepper, chopped
1 medium onion, chopped
1 clove garlic, minced
3 T. oil
1½ cups cooked brown rice

2 cups stewed tomatoes, plus liquid
1 tsp. vegetable seasoning
1 tsp. basil
1/2 tsp. lemon juice
1/2 tsp. oregano
1/4 tsp. kelp
1/4 cup Parmesan cheese, grated
3 T. sunflower seeds

Cut eggplant in half. Scoop out pulp to within 3/4" of skin. Dice pulp. Do this for all of the eggplants and the pulp should measure 4 cups at least. Place eggplant pulp, green pepper, onion and garlic in a skillet and sauté with oil for about 6 minutes. Stir periodically. Add to the eggplant mixture the rice, tomatoes and juice, vegetable seasoning, basil, lemon juice, oregano and kelp. Break up tomatoes with fork. Heat to boiling and then reduce heat, cover and simmer for 10 minutes. Put eggplant shells into ungreased shallow baking pan; spoon mixture into shells. Sprinkle with Parmesan cheese and sunflower seeds. Bake in a 350° oven for 30 minutes or until tender.

Yield: 4–6 servings

BAKED EGGPLANT SLICES

2 medium eggplants
Oil
1/4 tsp. basil

2 small onions, grated
3 T. chopped fresh parsley
1¼ cups shredded Cheddar cheese

Leave the skin on the eggplant and slice into rounds 1/2" thick. Brush both sides with oil. Arrange eggplant slices on a baking sheet. Sprinkle with basil and onions. Bake at 350° for 20 minutes, 10 minutes on each side. Sprinkle with the fresh parsley and cheese and run under broiler to melt cheese.

Yield: Serves 6

GREENS
(Contain Vitamins A and B, calcium, and iron)

Buying guide: Young, tender, crisp leaves. Free from blemishes and a good green color. Available all year round.

Preparation: Sort leaves, discard discolored leaves, wash thoroughly, drain, blot dry.

Storage: Store in refrigerator 4-6 days.

Basic cooking: Are best when served in a fresh, crisp salad or can be placed in a pan with only the water that clings to them when washed. Cover and steam for 5 minutes until wilted. Serve with butter and fresh herbs.

Uses: Beet greens—treat like spinach, tender leaves for salad, older leaves best steamed.
Collard—large amount of calcium. Use in salad or steam.
Dandelion—use with SOUR CREAM and chives or a cooked dressing.
Endive and Escarole—can be bitter, so best mixed with other greens.
Kale—best used cooked as its texture is too coarse for salads.
Mustard—can be used either raw or cooked.
Sorrel—usually used in soups and salads.
Spinach—use in soufflés, quiches, or just plain with butter, lemon juice, vinegar and hard-cooked eggs. Serve raw as a salad.
Swiss chard—strong flavor, so best used cooked.
Turnip—use as you would collards or mustard greens.
Watercress—use in soups and salads. A pungent flavor.

SPINACH RING

1/2 tsp. lemon juice
1 pound spinach leaves, cooked and
   finely chopped (2 cups)
3 T. butter
1 T. chopped onion

3 T. whole wheat flour
1 cup milk
3 eggs, separated
Dash of nutmeg
Vegetable seasoning to taste

Add the lemon juice to the finely chopped spinach. In a large skillet, melt the butter and sauté the onion until golden. Blend in the flour and slowly add the milk. Cook, stirring, until smooth and thickened. Reduce the heat to low. Beat the egg yolks and stir a little of the heated mixture into them. Add to the hot mixture and cook one minute. Add the spinach, nutmeg and seasoning to taste. Remove the mixture from the heat. Beat the egg whites until stiff and fold into the mixture. Turn into a buttered 1 quart ring mold and set mold in a pan of hot water. Bake at 300° for about 25 minutes or until it is set. Unmold onto serving dish and fill center with creamed vegetables or chicken.

Yield: 4 servings

SCALLOPED CHARD AND POTATOES

1 bunch (about 1 pound) Swiss chard
4 medium-sized (1½ to 2 pounds)
   baking potatoes
1/2 cup melted butter
3 eggs, slightly beaten

1/4 cup milk
1½ tsp. garlic powder
1/2 tsp. vegetable seasoning
2 T. minced onion
1/2 cup grated Parmesan cheese
3 T. sesame seeds

Wash chard and pat dry. Cut stems out of each leaf; slice stems into 1/4" pieces and place in a large bowl. Stack leaves and cut across in 1/2" strips; add to stems. Scrub potatoes and slice into 1/8" slices (6-7 cups); set aside about 1½ cups to go on top of the casserole. Add the rést of the potatoes to the chard in the bowl. Use about 3 tablespoons of the butter to grease a shallow 2 quart baking dish. Add remaining butter to chard mixture, stir, and set aside. In a small bowl, combine eggs, milk, garlic, vegetable seasoning, onion, and 1/4 cup of the Parmesan cheese. Stir all of this into the chard mixture. Pour mixture into baking dish and arrange remaining potato slices in a layer over the top. Sprinkle on remaining cheese and sesame seeds. Cover with foil and bake at 375° for about 1 hour or until potatoes are tender.

Yield: 6 servings

JERUSALEM ARTICHOKE (SUNCHOKE)

This artichoke is not related to the globe artichoke. It is a member of the sunflower family. It does not contain any starch, is low in calories and sodium, and contains vitamin B and potassium.

Buying guide:	Firm and free from cracks and blemishes. It is a potato like tuber.
Storage:	Keep in a cool, moist place or it will dry out.
Preparation:	Scrub but no need to peel.
Basic cooking:	Steam for 10–12 minutes.
Uses:	Serve hot with butter and sauces. Place in soups, stews and casseroles. Use as you would potatoes, baked, broiled, mashed or sautéed. Serve raw in salads, but it is best marinated as it discolors when exposed to air.
Yield:	1 pound equals 4 servings

JICAMA

A root vegetable that is sweet.

Buying guide:	Should be firm without any blemishes or cracks.
Storage:	Refrigerate up to a week.
Preparation:	Peel and slice into whatever shapes you would like.
Basic cooking:	Can be sautéed for just a few minutes.
Uses:	Best eaten raw in salads and used on relish trays. Can be sautéed with Chinese vegetables.
Yield:	1 medium size will furnish 4 servings

KOHLRABI

Common in Chinese cuisine. It has a milk, sweet, turnip-like flavor. Rich in calcium and vitamin C.

Buying guide:	Should be no larger than 2" in diameter or it will be tough and bitter.
Storage:	Store in refrigerator for a few days.
Preparation:	Wash, peel and slice if used raw. Just wash if it is to be steamed.
Basic cooking:	Steam until tender, about 8 minutes.
Uses:	In Chinese cooking, slice or dice and use like bamboo shoots in soups and stir-fry dishes. Use raw in salads or relish trays. Can be cooked in its skin, peeled and mashed with butter like a turnip.

LEEKS

The taste is similar to that of onion, only milder and sweeter.

Buying guide: Should have an even green color and be crisp and firm.

Preparation: Cut lengthwise for easier cleaning. Take off outside layer of bulb.

Basic cooking: Sauté in butter for about 4-5 minutes.

Uses: Use to flavor soups, stews, casseroles or in other vegetable combinations. Sautéed served with a sauce or top with breadcrumbs. Slice up raw in a salad.

Yield: 1 pound will equal 4 servings

MUSHROOMS

(Low in calories and contain Vitamin B)

Buying guide: Choose small to medium sized ones unless you are stuffing them. Should be light in color, not damp or brown looking. The cap should be closed around the stem so you do not see the gills.

Storage: Refrigerate in a plastic bag for a couple of days.

Preparation: Wash gently or wipe with a damp cloth. Do not soak. Trim stem ends when ready to use mushrooms.

Basic cooking: Sauté in butter for about 7 minutes.

Uses: Use all parts of the mushroom. Serve hot with other vegetables, in casseroles, in soups, stuffings or by itself with oregano, garlic and tamari (soy sauce). Use raw or marinate for salads.

Yield: 1 pound will furnish 4-6 servings

BROILED WALNUT STUFFED MUSHROOMS

1 pound medium to large mushrooms
4 T. butter
3/4 cup chopped onions
1 clove garlic, minced
1/4 cup celery, finely diced

1/2 cup whole wheat bread crumbs
1/4 cup chopped walnuts
1/4 tsp. vegetable seasoning
Tamari (soy sauce)

Rinse and pat dry mushrooms. Remove stems reserving both caps and stems. Chop stems to make 1 cup. In a medium skillet melt 1 tablespoon of the butter and add the chopped stems, onions, garlic and celery. Cook and stir until moisture has evaporated, 3-4 minutes. Remove from heat and stir in bread crumbs, walnuts, seasoning and tamari. Place mushroom caps hollowside down on a baking sheet. In a small saucepan melt the remaining butter. Brush each cap lightly with the butter. Broil 5" from heat source, until barely tender, about 2 minutes. Remove from broiler. Turn mushroom caps hollowside up. Spoon mushroom-onion mixture into caps. Drizzle remaining butter over tops. Broil until tops are lightly browned, about 2 minutes. Serve at once. A good party pleaser. You could make the stuffing ahead of time and then just before the guests arrive, stuff the mushrooms and pop them into the oven.

Yield: Serves 8

OKRA

(Contains Vitamins A and C, calcium, phosphorus and iron)

Popular ingredient in "gumbo."

Buying guide: Tips should bend easily with slight pressure if fresh. Choose ones that are only 2½" long. Peak season is June through September.

Storage: Best used as soon as picked as pods toughen with storage. Store in a cool, well-ventilated place and keep moist.

Preparation: Wash and remove stem ends.

Basic cooking: Dip in egg and cracker crumbs and sauté until tender.

Uses: The gluey sap is used as thickener in soups and stews. Serve as vegetable with a vinaigrette.

Yield: 1 pound equals 4 servings

FRIED OKRA

1 pound okra, sliced in 1/4" rounds
2 eggs, slightly beaten
1/2 tsp. vegetable seasoning
1/8 tsp. kelp
3/4 cup cornmeal or cracker crumbs

2 T. each wheat germ and sesame seeds
2 T. oil
TOMATO SAUCE

Combine the eggs, vegetable seasoning and kelp together in a bowl. In another bowl combine the cornmeal or cracker crumbs, wheat germ and sesame seeds. Dip okra in the eggs and then roll in the cornmeal mixture. Place in the 2 tablespoons (hot) oil and cook until tender and golden brown, 12–15 minutes. Serve with tomato sauce poured all over the cooked okra.

Yield: 4–6 servings

ONIONS

(Contain Vitamins A and C)

Buying guide: Firm, dry skins, free of soft spots. Should be free of sprouts. Available all year round.

Storage: Keep in a cool, dry place up to a month. Put a few in the refrigerator before you slice or chop so you can reduce the "tears."

Preparation: Peel and slice or leave whole.

Basic cooking: Sauté in butter or oil for just a few minutes.

Uses: Adds flavoring to many dishes—casseroles, soups, stuffings or sauces. Be careful not to overcook onions; it breaks the sulfur down and smells bad. The Spanish and Bermuda onions are sweet and can be served raw in a salad.

BAKED ONIONS

4 medium sized onions

Remove only the outer, loosest layers of skin. Place whole onions in a baking dish and then into a 400° oven. Bake for 40 minutes, until inside is tender and outer skin is crispy.

Yield: 4 servings

ONIONS AU GRATIN

8 medium onions, sliced
1/2 cup sliced celery
1/4 cup oil
1/2 cup grated Parmesan cheese

1/3 cup grated Cheddar cheese
1/4 cup sunflower seeds
Paprika

Sauté onion slices and celery in oil for about 10-15 minutes. Place in a baking dish and sprinkle with the cheeses. Broil under heat until the cheese melts. Sprinkle on sunflower seeds and paprika.

Yield: 6 servings

PARSNIPS

Parsnips look like carrots but are white in color. Good source of minerals.

Buying guide: Small to medium in size. Smooth, firm, well shaped and free from blemishes. Season is September to May.

Storage: Can be refrigerated for a week or two. Can store longer if kept in a root cellar. Can also be frozen.

Preparation: Scrub them well, leave whole or cut into slices.

Basic cooking: Can be steamed for about 10 minutes. Can also sauté them. They discolor easily so should be cooked unpeeled.

Uses: Serve mashed with YOGURT, parsley and caraway seeds.

Yield: 1½ pounds equal 4 servings

PEAS

(Contain Vitamins A and B)

Buying guide: Bright green, free from yellow or bruises. Should have a velvety feel and the pods should be full but not swollen. Peak time is May through July.

Storage: Unwashed in plastic bag; do not shell until ready to use. Can freeze up to 12 months.

Preparation: Shell peas and wash.

Basic cooking: Steam 6-7 minutes.

Uses: Eat raw in salads, serve as a vegetable with butter and dill. Use in casseroles, soups and in combination with other vegetables.

Yield: 1 pound equals 1 cup shelled

PEPPERS
(Good source of Vitamins A and C)

Red peppers have a higher content of vitamins. Red and green peppers are sweet whereas chili peppers, jalapenos and cayenne peppers are hot varieties.

Buying guide: Firm, bright peppers with strong color. Heavy for their size with thick walls, not flimsy ones. Available year round.

Storage: Keep in an airtight container in refrigerator up to 5 days. If the core and seeds are removed they will last longer. Freezes well.

Preparation: Wash, remove the core, seeds and membranes. Cut into whatever sizes you wish.

Basic cooking: Sauté for about 5 minutes.

Uses: Good raw in salads or as an appetizer. Use in casseroles, soups and Mexican dishes. Stuff and bake.

STUFFED GREEN PEPPER

6 medium-sized green peppers

Filling:

3½ cups SPAGHETTI SAUCE
1½ cups assorted vegetables (corn, lima beans, string beans, peas, carrots)

1 cup coarsely chopped tomatoes
3/4 cup cooked brown rice or bulgur wheat
1/2 cup chopped walnuts
1¾ cups shredded Cheddar cheese

Remove tops from 6 green peppers; scoop out seeds and membranes. Parboil until just tender, about 10 minutes. Drain. Prepare filling: Combine 1 cup sauce with the rice or bulgur wheat, walnuts and 1½ cups of cheese. Reserve remaining sauce and cheese. Fill each pepper with the filling mixture. Pour reserved sauce into buttered 11" x 7" shallow baking dish. Set in filled peppers. Bake at 350° for 20 minutes or until hot and bubbly. Remove from heat and sprinkle on the remaining 1/4 cup cheese. Return to oven to melt cheese. Serve with some of the sauce poured over each serving.

Yield: 6 servings

POTATOES
(Contain Vitamin C and potassium)

Buying guide: Firm, smooth, free of eyes and sprouting. Do not eat potatoes that have turned green. Available year round.

Storage: In a cool, dark, well-ventilated area; they need to breathe. Do not refrigerate.

Preparation: Scrub potatoes and remove any bad spots. You can peel before cooking if you would like, but this is not necessary when steaming potatoes.

Basic cooking: Bake in the skin for about 1 hour. Steam, peeled or unpeeled, for 15-20 minutes.

Uses: Baked, steamed, mashed. Add to many other dishes such as casseroles, soups, vegetable dishes. Top with whipped COTTAGE CHEESE, parsley, dill, YOGURT, or a number of different sauces.

Yield: 1 pound equals 4 servings

POTATO CASSEROLE

6-7 cups sliced new potatoes
1/3 cup butter, melted
1 garlic clove, minced
1 medium onion, sliced thinly

1 cup Swiss cheese, grated
1 cup Mozzarella cheese, grated
1 cup chopped fresh parsley

Peel potatoes and slice in thin circles. Place in cold water in which a squeeze of lemon juice has been added. This will prevent them from turning brown while you prepare the other ingredients. Melt butter and garlic together. To prepare, place a layer of potatoes on the bottom of a 2 quart casserole dish. Next place a layer of sliced onions on top of the potatoes. Pour some of the butter over the onions. Then sprinkle on some parsley and then a layer of cheese (use a mixture of both of the cheeses). Repeat this layering process at least three times, until all of the items are used up, ending with a layer of cheese. Cover the casserole and bake in a 400° oven for 30 minutes. Remove cover and continue cooking for 30 minutes at 350°.

Yield: Serves 6

BAKED POTATO SKINS

1 T. melted butter
1/3 cup plain YOGURT
1/4 tsp. basil

1/8 tsp. vegetable seasoning
4 baked potatoes
Sesame seeds

Combine the butter, yogurt, basil and vegetable seasoning together. Cut the potatoes in half lengthwise. Leaving about 1/4" potato next to the skin, scoop the potato centers out. Use the centers for mashed potatoes. Brush the insides of the potato skins with the yogurt mixture. Sprinkle with sesame seeds. Bake at 375° for 25 minutes or until crunchy and brown.

Yield: 4 servings

TWICE BAKED POTATOES

4 baked potatoes
1/4 cup milk
2 T. grated Parmesan cheese
1/3 cup grated Jack or Cheddar
   cheese

2 T. chopped green onions
1/2 tsp. vegetable seasoning
1/4 tsp. dill
3-4 T. butter
Paprika

Scrub potatoes well, pat dry, then rub skins with 1 tablespoon butter and prick with a fork. Bake potatoes at 350° for 1 hour. When finished cut a thin slice off the top of each potato. Carefully scoop out the pulp, leaving about 1/4" shell. Set shells aside. Mash potatoes with all of the ingredients listed. Mix well. Mound potato mixture into shells and arrange in a baking dish and sprinkle lightly with paprika. Bake at 350° for about 20 minutes.

Yield: 4 servings

Variation:
Turkey Supreme: Follow instructions for stuffing the potatoes in the above recipe. To cook the turkey filling place 3 T. oil in a skillet and blend in 2 T. whole wheat flour and 1 tsp. vegetable seasoning. Stir in 3/4 cup TURKEY STOCK and stir until thickened. Then add 2 cups chopped cooked turkey, 1/4 cup chopped celery and 1/2 cup grated Cheddar cheese. Mix all together. Place a mound of this mixture on top of each stuffed potato. Bake at 350° for 30 minutes. If you have any filling left over just freeze and use some other time.

HOT POTATO AND BROCCOLI VINAIGRETTE

4 medium new potatoes (about
   1-1/3 pounds), peeled and cut
   into 1" cubes
1 bunch broccoli (1-1½ pounds),
   trimmed and broken into small
   bunches
1/2 cup oil

1/4 cup cider vinegar
1 clove garlic, finely minced
1½ tsp. vegetable seasoning
1 tsp. basil
1/8 tsp. liquid hot pepper sauce
2 green onions, sliced
Cherry tomatoes

In a saucepan over medium heat, steam potatoes until just tender, 10-15 minutes. In another saucepan over medium heat, steam broccoli, covered, steaming it for about 6-8 minutes. Drain thoroughly and keep hot. In a small saucepan combine remaining ingredients except tomatoes. Bring just to boiling over medium heat, stirring. Arrange hot potatoes and broccoli in serving dish; pour hot vinegar mixture over and toss gently. Garnish with cherry tomatoes.

Yield: Serves 4-6

PUMPKIN

(High in Vitamin A)

Buying guide: Firm heavy pumpkins with a bright orange skin.

Storage: Store in a cool, dark, dry place up to 4 months. Can freeze up to 12 months.

Preparation: Wash well. Halve or quarter and scrape out seeds (toast the seeds for a snack) and strings.

Basic cooking: Bake halves or wedges. Place in an oiled dish and bake at 325° for about 1 hour or until tender. Steam halves or wedges—place rind side up in steamer for 30–45 minutes.

Uses: Use in desserts, soups, bread, baked with butter and seasoning. Can go into soups, casseroles and stuffings.

BAKED PUMPKIN RING

3 pounds pumpkin
1 small onion, minced
2/3 cup celery, finely diced
3 T. oil
1 cup whole wheat bread crumbs

3 eggs, beaten
1/4 cup milk
1/4 tsp. allspice
Vegetable seasoning to taste

Cut the pumpkin into chunks. Remove the seeds and stringy portion. Steam until tender and then scoop pulp from the rind. There should be about 2½ cups of pulp. Sauté the onion and celery in the oil until onion is tender. Stir in bread crumbs. Place the eggs, milk, allspice and seasoning and pumpkin pulp in a blender and blend until smooth. Add the sautéed mixture to the pumpkin mixture. Turn into a greased mold, set into a pan of water and bake at 350° for 45 minutes or until set. Turn out on a serving dish and fill the center with peas, onions or mushrooms.

Yield: 6 servings

PUMPKIN BUTTER

4 cups cooked pumpkin purée
3/4 cup honey
2 T. unsulfured molasses
1 T. cinnamon

1/2 tsp. cloves, ground
1/4 tsp. each nutmeg and ginger
Juice of 1 lemon

Combine all ingredients in a heavy saucepan. Cook over low heat for about 1 hour, stirring often. Taste and adjust spices. Pour boiling butter into hot, sterilized canning jars and seal immediately. You can just make a small amount to keep in the refrigerator to use for toast, muffins and pancakes.

Yield: Approximately 4 cups

RHUBARB

(Contains Vitamins A and C, calcium and iron)

Storage: Wrap in plastic bag and refrigerate up to 5 days. Freezes well or can be stored as a juice or sauce.

Preparation: Wash stalks well and cut off tops.

Basic cooking: Cut the stalks into 1" pieces and stew them in a small amount of apple juice. Can be steamed or baked until tender.

Uses: Use in pies, preserves, sauces for desserts, in beverages or as a relish for grain or game dishes.

Yield: 1 pound will give you 3 or 4 servings

BAKED SPICED RHUBARB

2 pounds rhubarb, cut in 1" pieces
1 cup raisins
1 cinnamon stick

4 whole cloves
1/2 cup pineapple juice, unsweetened

Place rhubarb in a 2 quart casserole dish. Add all the rest of the ingredients. Cover and bake at 375° for 20 minutes. Baste frequently with the juice in the pan. You want the rhubarb tender, but not mushy. Remove from oven and let cool. Serve plain or top with YOGURT and sunflower seeds.

Yield: Serves 6

TURNIPS AND RUTABAGAS

(Contain Vitamins C and A, iron, niacin and riboflavin)

Turnips have white flesh and purple shading at the top. Rutabagas are yellow fleshed, large-sized cousins of the turnip.

Buying guide: Turnips that are small to medium size. Need to be firm, smooth, free from blemishes and with few bruises.
Rutabagas should be heavy for their size, firm and free from deep cuts. Peak season for both is October through March.

Storage: In a cool, well-ventilated area. Can keep up to 30 days.

Preparation: Scrub well and remove top and root. Keep whole or else slice.

Basic cooking: Steam for 15–20 minutes or place in oven and bake.

Uses: Use in soups and stews. Good raw in salads, or serve mashed or baked as a potato.

Yield: 2 pounds equals 4 servings

TURNIPS AND CHEESE DISH

2 cups steamed turnips, diced
1 cup COTTAGE CHEESE
1 cup plain YOGURT
1 cup grated Cheddar cheese
1 T. minced fresh parsley
1/2 cup grated carrot

1/2 cup chopped onion
2 eggs, beaten
1 clove garlic, minced
1/2 tsp. vegetable seasoning
1 tsp. marjoram
1 tsp. basil

Mix all of the ingredients together. Pour into a buttered casserole dish and bake at 350° for 40 minutes.

Yield: 4-6 servings

SALSIFY

(Contains calcium, phosphorus and iron)

Also called Oyster Plant. Tastes much like oysters.

Storage: Roots discolor and shrivel quickly, so get them refrigerated right away. Can keep up to 2-3 days.

Preparation: Scrub and keep whole.

Basic cooking: Should be cooked unpeeled, otherwise it will discolor. Steam for about 10 minutes.

Uses: Use with a HOLLANDAISE SAUCE or use in a soup. Can be used like parsnips.

Yield: 2 roots will equal one average size serving

SALSIFY WITH PARSLEY AND GARLIC

1 pound salsify, cut into 1/2" cubes
2 T. butter
1 clove garlic, minced

2 T. chopped fresh parsley
1/2 tsp. vegetable seasoning
1/4 tsp. kelp

Steam the salsify until tender, about 10 minutes. Melt butter in a skillet and add garlic and parsley. Sauté for about 2 minutes. Add salsify and seasoning to the skillet and simmer 2 minutes. Serve immediately.

Yield: 4 servings

SQUASH, SUMMER

(High in Vitamin A)

Buying guide: Heavy for size, free from blemishes. Look for thin, tender skin.

Storage: Keep in a plastic bag in refrigerator up to one week. Can freeze the zucchini in cooked casseroles, purées or if grated.

Preparation:	Wash, trim off the ends, cut or slice as recipe directs.
Basic cooking:	Steam 6-8 minutes.
Uses:	Raw in salads, as an appetizer with a dip, used in soups, casseroles, stuffed as a main dish, served with other vegetables or even added to desserts.
Kinds:	Crookneck: yellow in color, great raw Straightneck: yellow in color, placed in salads Zucchini: dark green, raw or steamed Scallopini: green or white, bake or steam Patty Pan: white in color, bake or steam
Yield:	2 squash for one serving

ZUCCHINI CASSEROLE

1 T. oil	2 cups TOMATO SAUCE
1 clove garlic, minced	1/2 cup grated Jack cheese
1/2 cup diced onions	1/4 cup grated Swiss cheese
6 cups thinly sliced zucchini	

Place oil and garlic in a fry pan and stir until garlic is browned. Add onions and zucchini, cook until vegetables are coated with oil and lightly cooked. Mix in the tomato sauce and place in a 2 quart casserole dish. Cover and place in a 350° oven for 20 minutes. Remove from oven and sprinkle on cheese. Place cover on casserole and let sit for 2 minutes, until cheese melts.

Yield: 8 servings

CRUNCHY ZUCCHINI SLICES

2 medium-sized zucchini	1 tsp. oregano
1 egg, slightly beaten	1/2 tsp. vegetable seasoning
1/4 cup milk	1/4 tsp. garlic powder
1/4 cup wheat germ	2 T. oil
2 T. whole wheat flour	Mozzarella cheese

Thinly slice zucchini. Combine the egg and milk. Combine together the wheat germ, flour, oregano, vegetable seasoning and garlic. Dip the zucchini slices into the egg mixture and then roll in the wheat germ mixture. Sauté in the oil until tender, about 5-8 minutes. Top with the cheese and run under broiler briefly, to melt cheese.

Yield: 4-6 servings

SQUASH CASSEROLE

4 cups thinly sliced zucchini,
scallop, banana, crookneck or
other summer squash
2 tomatoes, sliced
1 onion, thinly sliced and separated
into rings

3 T. chopped fresh parsley
1 tsp. marjoram
2 cups CHEESE SAUCE
Parmesan cheese

Fill the baking dish with alternate layers of squash and tomato and onion. Sprinkle each layer with parsley and marjoram. Cook the cheese sauce and pour over the casserole, top with the Parmesan cheese. Bake at 350° for 20-25 minutes, until squash is tender.

Yield: 4 servings

Variation:
Instead of the cheese sauce, pour 1/2 cup melted butter in which 3 T. of tamari sauce and 1 clove garlic, minced have been added.

SQUASH, WINTER

(High in Vitamin A. Carotene content increased during storage.)

Buying guide: Heavy for size, free from blemishes and bruises. Hard rind. Season is October through December.

Storage: In a cool, dry place. If moisture occurs, it can bring on mold. Store for 4-6 months this way. Freezes well.

Preparation: Wash well. Halve or quarter, scoop out seeds (roast for a snack) and strings.

Basic cooking: Bake for 1 hour in an oiled casserole dish or steam the pieces for about 20-30 minutes.

Uses: In pies, bread, or served alone with butter, honey and spices.

Kinds: Acorn: dark green with deep ridges
Butternut: dull tan and looks like an elongated pear
Buttercup: turban-shaped and dark green
Hubbard: weighs up to 15 pounds. Can substitute for pumpkin in pie recipes.
Spaghetti: Can be used in place of spaghetti.

Yield: 3 pounds equal 4 servings

SPAGHETTI SQUASH

The Dieter's Pasta. Cut squash in half, remove the seeds. Bake cut side down in baking pan containing a small amount of water. Bake at 350° for 45 minutes. After cooking pull strands free with a fork. Looks just like spaghetti but with only a fraction of the calories. Can use in place of spaghetti in recipes or just serve topped with butter and herbs.

SQUASH SOUFFLÉ

1/3 cup butter	1 T. unsulfured molasses
1/4 cup chopped onion	2½ cups mashed, cooked acorn or
1/3 cup whole wheat flour	hubbard squash
1/2 tsp. cinnamon	1/4 cup apple juice, unsweetened
1/4 tsp. nutmeg	6 eggs, separated
1 cup milk	3/4 tsp. cream of tartar
2 T. honey	

Butter bottom and sides of 12" x 7" x 2" baking dish. In a medium saucepan cook onion in 1/3 cup butter over medium heat until tender, but not brown. Blend in flour, cinnamon and nutmeg. Cook, stirring constantly until mixture is smooth and bubbly. Stir in milk all at once. Add honey and molasses. Stirring constantly, cook until mixture boils and thickens. Remove from heat. Blend in squash and apple juice. In a small mixing bowl beat egg yolks slightly. Blend small amount of hot squash mixture into egg yolk mixture. Stir egg yolk into squash mixture. Beat egg whites and cream of tartar until stiff but not dry. Gently but thoroughly fold egg whites into the squash mixture. Pour into prepared dish and gently smooth surface. Bake at 350° until puffy, delicately browned (and soufflé shakes slightly when oven rack is gently moved back and forth), 40–45 minutes. Serve immediately.

Yield: 6 servings

SWEET POTATOES AND YAMS
(Contain Vitamins A and C)

Buying guide:	Firm, plump, free from soft spots or blemishes. Buy only a small amount as they are highly perishable. Yams have skins that are white to reddish. Flesh is light orange. Sweets have skins that are pale to deep yellow. Flesh is deep orange.
Storage:	Store at room temperature in a cool, dry place—not in the refrigerator. Also do not stack one on top of another, as that causes quick spoilage.
Preparation:	Scrub thoroughly but no need to peel.
Basic cooking:	Bake at 350° for about 1 hour.
Uses:	Grated raw in salads. Serve as you would any other potato: baked, mashed, in soups, and in stews. Top with honey and cinnamon.
Yield:	1 medium size equals one serving

STUFFED BAKED YAMS

4 medium yams
3/4 cup shredded Cheddar cheese
1/4 cup milk

2½ T. melted butter
3/4 tsp. vegetable seasoning
Paprika

Bake yams at 400° for 15 minutes. Lower temperature to 375° and bake for 45 minutes or until tender. Cut lengthwise and scoop out center leaving some in the shell. Beat the yam centers with 1/2 cup cheese, milk, butter and seasoning. Fill shells with the mixture and top with remaining cheese. Sprinkle with paprika. Place under broiler until lightly browned and cheese is melted.

Yield: 4 servings

Variation:
Stuffed Baked Sweet Potatoes: Use sweet potatoes in place of the yams.

YAM CASSEROLE

5 large yams
4 T. butter
3 T. molasses, unsulfured
1¼ cups unsweetened chunk
pineapple (drained)

1/4 tsp. nutmeg
3/4 cup GRANOLA or CRUMBLY
TOPPING

Scrub yams and pierce with a fork. Bake at 400° for about 1 hour, until they feel soft to the touch. Peel and cut into medium-sized chunks. Heat in a saucepan, butter, molasses, chunked pineapple, and nutmeg. Heat until butter is melted. Stir into yams and coat well. Place into a 2 quart casserole dish. Sprinkle with granola or crumbly topping. Bake 30–40 minutes in a 325° oven.

Yield: Serves 6

TOMATOES
(Contain Vitamins C and A)

Buying guide: Look for firm, plump tomatoes which have good color. Should not have any blemishes on them. Also look for a tomato that smells like a tomato as they will be vine-ripened tomatoes as opposed to tomatoes that have been gassed to ripen them on their way to the market. Peak season is June through September.

Storage: In refrigerator up to 5 days.

Preparation: If used raw, core and slice just before using. If cooking, may need to be peeled first.

Basic cooking: Follow instructions on the recipe you are using.

Uses: Hot with vegetables, stuffed, added to soups, stews and casseroles. Serve cold in salads, relishes, dressings, juice and as a garnish.

Yield: 1 pound will make 3 servings

STUFFED TOMATOES

4 large tomatoes
1 tsp. vegetable seasoning
1/2 cup chopped celery
2 T. finely chopped onion

1/2 green pepper, seeded and finely chopped
1/4 cup wheat germ
1½ cups puréed soy beans

Cut a slice from top of each tomato, remove soft center and place in a bowl. Sprinkle with seasoning inside each tomato case. Combine celery, onion, pepper, wheat germ and puréed soy beans with tomato pulp. Mix together thoroughly. Fill tomato case with mixture and place in a greased shallow ovenproof casserole. Cook in a 350° oven for 20–30 minutes or until tender.

Yield: Serves 4

BROILED TOMATOES

3 medium sized tomatoes
2 tsp. prepared MUSTARD
1/4 cup whole wheat bread crumbs
1/2 cup grated Cheddar cheese

2 tsp. wheat germ
1 T. fresh parsley, minced
Parmesan cheese, grated

Slice the tomatoes in half. Spread each half with the mustard. Mix together the bread crumbs, cheese, wheat germ and parsley. Sprinkle some of the mixture on each tomato half. Top with Parmesan cheese and then place on a baking sheet. Put the baking sheet into the oven set on broil and heat for about 5 minutes, until the cheese is bubbly and brown. Serve immediately.

Yield: 4–6 servings

TOMATO RELISH

2 pounds firm, ripe tomatoes
1 green pepper
1 cucumber
1/4 cup oil
1/3 cup wine vinegar
3 T. minced onion

1 tsp. vegetable seasoning
1/2 tsp. crushed fresh mint
1/2 tsp. basil
1/2 tsp. honey
1/4 tsp. dry mustard

Core and cut tomatoes and pepper into small wedges. Pare and cut cucumber into thin slices. Combine remaining ingredients; pour over vegetables in salad bowl. Toss lightly; cover and chill at least 1 hour before serving.

Yield: 6–8 servings

MIXED VEGETABLE DISHES

VEGETABLE NORMANDY

2 cups coarsely cut broccoli, carrots, and cauliflower

Sauce:

1/4 cup butter
2 T. milk
1/2 tsp. dry mustard
1/2 tsp vegetable seasoning
6 T. water

1 T. whole wheat flour
1/4 tsp. paprika
1/4 cup grated Cheddar cheese
Dash tamari (soy sauce)
1 tsp. lemon juice

Steam vegetables until just tender. While vegetables are cooking, prepare the sauce. Melt butter. Combine all remaining ingredients in a small bowl and blend thoroughly; slowly add melted butter to the bowl while continuing to blend. Pour into a saucepan and heat, stirring, until thickened. Pour over cooked vegetables.

Yield: 4 servings

RATATOUILLE

1/3 cup olive oil
2 cloves garlic, minced
1 large onion, sliced into thick rings
4 medium zucchini, sliced
1/4 pound mushrooms, sliced
1 green or red pepper, seeds removed
    and cut into rings

1 medium eggplant, peeled and
    diced
4 firm tomatoes, quartered
1/4 cup fresh chopped parsley
1/2 tsp. oregano
2 tsp. basil
1 tsp. vegetable seasoning
1/4 cup grated Parmesan cheese

Heat the oil in a Dutch oven and sauté garlic and onion until onions are limp. Add zucchini, mushrooms and pepper and sauté a few minutes longer. Remove from heat and add the eggplant and tomatoes, parsley, oregano, basil and vegetable seasoning. Mix well. Pour into a casserole dish and sprinkle with Parmesan cheese. Bake at 350° for 30 minutes or until vegetables are tender. Serve at once. Can also be served cold along with dark bread and cheese.

Yield: 8 servings

VEGETABLE MÉLANGE

4 carrots, thinly sliced
4 parsnips, pared and thinly sliced
4 turnips, pared and thinly sliced
2 yellow onions, peeled and sliced
2 medium zucchini, unpared and
 sliced
1/2 head cabbage, cored and
 shredded

1 large potato, peeled and thinly
 sliced
1-2/3 cups CHICKEN STOCK
 (broth)
2 garlic cloves, minced
1 tsp. basil
1 tsp. thyme
Parmesan cheese

Combine vegetables and remaining ingredients, except for the cheese, in a buttered 4 quart casserole. Cover and bake at 375° for 40 minutes or until vegetables are tender. Serve hot with Parmesan cheese sprinkled over the top.

Yield: 8 servings

GARDEN SCRAMBLE

2 T. oil
1 large clove garlic, minced
1 cup broccoli flowerets, cut in
 1/2" slices
1 cup cauliflower flowerets, cut in
 1/2" slices
3 T. water

1/2 cup carrots, cut diagonally in
 1/2" slices
1/2 red bell pepper, cut in 1/2"
 strips
Vegetable seasoning to taste
1 T. tamari (soy sauce)
Cashews for garnish

Place wok over high heat. When wok is hot, add 1 tablespoon of the oil. When oil is hot, add garlic; stir-fry for 30 seconds. Add broccoli and cauliflower and stir-fry for 1 minute. Add 2 tablespoons of the water; cover and cook, stirring frequently, for about 3 minutes. Remove vegetables from wok and set aside. Add remaining 1 tablespoon oil to wok. When oil is hot, add carrots and red pepper. Stir-fry for 1 minute. Add remaining 1 tablespoon water and tamari; cover and cook, stirring occasionally, for about 2 minutes or until vegetables are tender-crisp. Return broccoli and cauliflower to wok and stir-fry to heat through (about 1 minute). Add seasoning and garnish with cashews.

Yield: 2–3 servings

MAIN DISHES

CHAPTER 6

What can you say about main dishes other than they are usually the main part of our meals, with other foods acting as accompaniments. In this chapter you will find recipes for fish, poultry and vegetarian meals. You will find the recipes prepared in many new and different ways. You will also find some very old favorite dishes revised using more nutritional ingredients. Enjoy.

HELPFUL HINTS

- Fish is low in calories, good source of protein, trace minerals, and vitamin D. The fat is high in polyunsaturated factors (that is good).

- Buy fish that is fresh when possible. If you do not live near a fish source, get frozen fish that has been quickly frozen and shipped. Will be fresher than fresh fish shipped to your area.

- Lean fish is good for a low-fat diet.

- A menu of baked or broiled fish with a delicious vegetable dish can equal many meat dishes.

- How to avoid fish odors: It is not the fish you smell, it is the fat or oil in which it has been cooked. Do not let the oil get to the smoking stage.

- Never defrost a fish at room temperature. It will cause the fish to spoil.

- Best way to test the fish for doneness is with a fork rather than the clock. Probe it with a fork in the thickest part and if it flakes easily it is done.

- Figure 15 minutes per inch of thickness if you need a time gauge.

- Overcooking is one reason most people do not enjoy fish. It will make the fish tough and dry.

- If fish smells on your hand, take a lemon and rub it in.

- Iodine is necessary for good health, and fish is rich in it.

- To keep raw fish fillets fresh and odorless, rinse them with fresh lemon juice and water, dry thoroughly, wrap and refrigerate.

- Serve your fish with one of the many sauces or butters listed in the "Sauce" section.

- Lemon or lime juice rubbed over fish before broiling or baking enhances the flavor.

- Your fish dealer can be helpful in introducing you to lesser-known fish that may be more flavorful and cheaper than the popular varieties.

- Cooked flaked fish can be used in spreads for crackers or breads. Mix with YOGURT and herbs and serve.

- Leftovers: Use in a salad, cold with a sauce, or in a sandwich. Mix 1 cup fish with 1 diced cooked potato. Add 4 eggs, milk and seasoning and cook as an omelet.

- Ask your fish dealer for the heads and bones and take home to make stock from them.

- The most economical way to buy chicken is whole, rather than cut up.

- Do not buy chicken on Monday as it may have been in the market all weekend.

- The white part of the turkey has less calories than the dark meat.

- Let any large size turkey rest after it cooks, about 20 minutes. It will then be easier to cut.

- After coating chicken with a coating such as flour or wheat germ, let sit for 1 hour in the refrigerator. The coating will adhere better.

- Turkey legs dry out easily. To prevent this, cover with 3 layers of cheesecloth soaked in melted butter. Baste the turkey right through the cheesecloth.

- Does a tiny blood clot or pink flesh indicate fowl is insufficiently cooked? No. Slight pinkness of the meat or miniature clots are perfectly normal.

- Freeze pizzas without the vegetables on them. Remove from freezer, add the vegetables, then pop them into the oven.

- Shape your bean loaves or patties into hot dog shape and place in a hot dog bun and decorate with condiments of your choice.

GARNISHES FOR MAIN DISHES

Carrots—Thin rounds, curls and sticks.
Celery—Small whole stalks with leaves, curls, and stuffed.
Cheese—Coarse shreds, strips, small flat shapes.
Chives—minced.
COTTAGE CHEESE—Small portions in cucumber boats, tomato or beet cups.
Cream Cheese—Shaped into balls or sticks, rolled in finely chopped parsley, chives, nuts.
Cucumbers, raw—Thin, green-bordered slices, notched slices, or hollowed-out boats filled with other foods.
Dates—Stuffed with cream cheese, pineapple, chopped nuts.
Eggs, hard-cooked—Wedges, rings, slices, stuffed halves.

Endive, curly—Sprigs.
Fruit—Slices, halves, some larger ones used as cups to hold other foods.
Lemon—Thin slices or wedges, cups to hold other ingredients.
Lettuce—Bibb, curly, red leaf.
Mushrooms—Caps or slices.
Olives—Chopped, stuffed, slivers.
Onions—Raw rings, small whole, fresh green onions.
Parsley—Sprigs, chopped.
Pepper, red or green—Finely chopped, narrow strips, rings, stuffed.
Prunes—Stuffed with cheese, PEANUT BUTTER, nuts.
Radishes—Fans or roses.
Tomato—Sliced, wedges, hollowed-out cups filled with other foods.
Watercress—Sprigs.

FISH

PURCHASING FRESH FISH

Fresh fish is usually sold in either the whole or drawn form, or as dressed fish, steaks, or fillets. Some pointers on what to look for when buying the fish:

1. Eyes: bright, clean and bulging

2. Gills: reddish-pink, no discoloration

3. Scales: shiny, tight to the skin without slime

4. Flesh: firm and elastic and when you press it, it should spring back

5. Odor: *Fresh* fish does not have an odor

PURCHASING FROZEN FISH

1. Should be solidly frozen.

2. Wrapped in moisture-proof, vapor-proof material with little or no air-space in the package.

3. Packages should be kept below the freezer line in open freezer cases.

4. Check for freezer burn—an uneven, dry, white appearance on flesh.

MARKET FORMS OF FISH

Whole or round fish are marketed just as they come from the water. Before cooking, the entrails, scales, head, fins and tail are removed.

Drawn fish have had the entrails removed. Before they are cooked the scales, head, fins and tail are removed.

Dressed or pan-dressed fish are scaled and entrails have been removed. Smaller fish, 1 pound or less, are called pan-dressed. Have head and tails left on. Larger, dressed fish have the heads removed.

Steaks are made by cutting a large dressed fish across the backbone in 1"-1¼" intervals.

Fillets are the sides of dressed fish cut lengthwise away from the backbone, and are usually practically boneless.

Butterfly fillets are the two sides or fillets of the fish held together by the uncut belly skin. Used in outdoor cooking. Bones and scales are sometimes left on.

HOW MUCH TO PURCHASE

Whole or drawn fish — 1 pound per person
Dressed fish — 1/2 pound per person
Steaks or fillets — 1/3 pound per person

STORING FISH

Storing fresh fish: To preserve their natural freshness and flavor, they should be kept under refrigeration in the coldest part of the refrigerator. Store in a moisture-proof and vapor-proof wrapping. Best used within 2 days.

Storing frozen fish: After your purchase, take fish home right away and place in your freezer. Keep in original packaging. Store in freezer that maintains 0°. If fish thaws before you get it home, do not refreeze as it loses considerable amount of quality. If you have fresh fish and want to freeze it, place it in freezer bags and make sure you get all the air out of it before you seal it; otherwise it will dry the fish out.

Thawing frozen fish: Place package in refrigerator and allow 18 to 24 hours for a 1-pound package to thaw. If in a hurry, place the package under cold running water, allowing 1 to 2 hours for a 1-pound package to thaw.

TYPES OF FISH

Listed are some of the different types of fish available and whether or not they are fat or lean.

Lean—Abalone, bluefish, cod, crappie, flounder, grouper, haddock, hake, halibut, mullet, ocean perch, pike, red snapper, sea bass, sole, turbot.

Fat—Butterfish, mackerel, porgie, salmon, sea herring, striped bass, tuna.

BAKED FISH

1½ pounds fish fillets or steaks
(fresh or frozen)
1 tomato, diced
1/2 cup TOMATO SAUCE
1/4 cup water
1 T. lemon juice
1/4 cup diced celery
1/4 cup chopped green pepper

4 T. minced onion
1/4 cup sliced fresh mushrooms
1/4 tsp. thyme
1/4 tsp. vegetable seasoning
3/4 cup whole wheat bread crumbs
1/4 cup Parmesan cheese
Chopped fresh parsley as garnish

Place fish in a shallow baking dish. Place diced tomato over fish. Combine tomato sauce, water, lemon juice, celery, green peppers, onion, mushrooms, thyme and vegetable seasoning in a saucepan. Bring to a boil; reduce heat and let simmer 5 minutes. Pour over fish. Sprinkle with breadcrumbs and Parmesan cheese. Cover and bake in 350° oven 15-20 minutes, or until fish flakes when tested with a fork. Top with chopped parsley.

Yield: 4 servings

POACHED FISH

2 pounds fish (steaks or fillets)
1/2 cup VEGETABLE STOCK
1 tsp. vegetable seasoning
2 T. lemon juice

1 onion, sliced
1 parsley sprig
1 bay leaf
6 peppercorns

Place fish in a baking dish. Add all other ingredients and cover. Bake in a 400° oven for 10-20 minutes or until fish flakes when tested with a fork. Drain fish. Serve with a favorite sauce such as DILL SAUCE. Or, use poached fish for salads, casseroles, creamed dishes, or as a sandwich filling.

Yield: 4 servings

BROILED FISH

2 pounds fish, fillets or steaks
Vegetable seasoning

Oil

Place fish on preheated broiler pan and brush with oil. Place 3-4" under broiler and broil 3-5 minutes, or until slightly browned. Baste with oil and turn carefully. Brush other side with oil and broil 3-5 minutes or until fish flakes easily when tested with fork. Thin fillets need not be turned during broiling.

Yield: 4 servings

Variation:
Lemon Garlic Broiled Fish: Combine 1/4 cup melted butter, 2 T. lemon juice, 1/8 tsp. garlic powder and 2 tsp. chopped fresh parsley. Brush over fish as it broils.

OVEN FRIED FISH

1 pound fish fillets or steaks,
   fresh or frozen
1/3 cup whole wheat bread crumbs
3 T. sesame seeds
2 T. Parmesan cheese

1 tsp. vegetable seasoning
1/4 tsp. each garlic powder,
   oregano and marjoram
1 egg, beaten
1/4 cup oil

Thaw fish if frozen. Mix together the bread crumbs, sesame seeds, Parmesan cheese, vegetable seasoning and herbs. Combine in a separate bowl the egg and oil. Dip the fish in the egg mixture and then roll in the bread crumbs. Spread the fish out in a single layer to dry for about 5 minutes before cooking. Arrange fish in a well-greased shallow baking pan, dot with butter. Place pan near top of a 500° oven. Bake for 5-10 minutes or until flakes separate easily when gently probed with tines of a fork.

Yield: Serves 2-4

FISH WITH MUSHROOM LEMON SAUCE

1/4 cup butter
2 cups mushrooms, sliced
1/4 cup sliced green onions
2 T. arrowroot powder
1/2 tsp. oregano
1/2 tsp. vegetable seasoning

1 tsp. fresh parsley, chopped
1 tsp. grated lemon peel
1 cup milk
2 pounds fish (turbot or other
   mild flavored fish)

Place butter, mushrooms and onions in a pan and cook until butter melts. Stir in arrowroot, oregano, seasoning, parsley, lemon peel and milk, stirring until well mixed. Cook until mixture boils. Stir well. Add fish and spoon sauce over fish. Cook until fish flakes, about 10 minutes.

Yield: Serves 4

SALMON LOAF

2/3 pound canned salmon
2 T. lemon juice
1/4 cup chopped green pepper
1 medium onion, diced
1/2 cup chopped celery
1/4 cup chopped fresh parsley
1/2 cup ground sunflower seeds

1/2 cup wheat germ
3/4 cup whole wheat cracker crumbs
2/3 tsp. vegetable seasoning
1/2 tsp. dill weed
1/2 cup milk
1/4 cup liquid from fish
2 eggs (beaten)

Mix all ingredients together. Pack into a greased loaf pan. Bake for 1 hour at 325°, or until firm.

Yield: Serves 4

FISH AND VEGETABLE STIR-FRY

1/2-3/4 pound flounder or other fish
1 egg white
1½ T. arrowroot powder
2 medium zucchini, unpeeled
1/2 pound mushrooms
1/4 pound snow peas
6 scallions

1 celery stalk
1 red pepper sliced
3 T. water
1 T. tamari (soy sauce)
1 tsp. sesame oil
Oil for cooking
1/2 cup nuts—cashew, almonds

Cut fillets into 1½" squares. Put egg white and 1 tablespoon arrowroot in a bowl and beat until smooth and a little fluffy. Add fish and mix with hands to coat all surfaces. Set aside at least 15 minutes. Prepare vegetables. Cut zucchini into matchstick pieces. Slice mushrooms. Leave snow peas whole. Trim scallions of most of the green tops and halve white bottoms lengthwise. Cut celery in thin slices. Slice red peppers into small sizes. In a small bowl, prepare glaze by stirring together 1/2 tablespoon arrowroot, water, soy sauce and oil. Set aside. Pour oil in a wok to film the bottom generously. Once oil is hot, lift fish pieces from bowl and place in oil. Fry about 1 minute. Transfer to a dish. Add a little more oil and when hot, stir-fry all vegetables until lightly browned. Cover and steam vegetables for about 1 minute. They must remain crisp and crunchy. Remove cover and return fish and nuts to pan. Pour in glaze mixture and stir until sauce thickens, about 1 minute.

Yield: Serves 4

BAKED STUFFED FISH

4-6 pound fish (red snapper,
   striped bass or salmon) cleaned
   and ready for stuffing

5 cups BREAD STUFFING
1/3 cup GARLIC BUTTER, melted
Lemon wedges and parsley as
   garnish

Spoon stuffing into fish cavity loosely. Close the cavity with wooden toothpick or string. Place fish in a greased baking dish. Bake fish at 375° approximately 15 minutes per inch of thickness. Baste several times with the garlic butter. Fish is done when flakes separate easily when gently probed with tines of fork. Remove to preheated serving platter, garnish with lemon wedges and parsley, and pour juices from baking dish over it.

Yield: Serves 6-8

Variation:
Baked Stuffed Fish Steaks or Fillets: Use 2 steaks or 2 fillets, weighing 1 pound each. Place 1 fillet or steak in greased pan and top with 1½ cups bread stuffing. Top with other fillet or steak and fasten with skewers. Brush top with melted garlic butter. Bake at 350° 30-40 minutes.

FISH-VEGETABLE CASSEROLE

3 new potatoes, cooked, sliced
2 pounds fresh fish fillets, raw
1 cup tomatoes, sliced
1/2 cup celery and tops, chopped
1/2 cup green pepper, chopped
1 onion, sliced
1/2 cup sliced zucchini

1/4 cup soy grits, soaked in
1/2 cup stock
1/2 tsp. each thyme, basil
1/2 tsp. garlic, minced
1 T. arrowroot powder
1/2 cup whole wheat bread crumbs

Arrange potatoes at bottom of oiled casserole. Place fish on top. Cover with tomatoes, celery, pepper, onions and zucchini. Blend together remaining ingredients, except for bread crumbs, and pour over top. Sprinkle with bread crumbs. Cover and bake for 20 minutes at 350°.

Yield: Serves 6

TURBOT FLORENTINE

4 turbot fillets
1/2 cup chopped spinach
1 T. grated onions
1/2 cup chopped mushrooms
1/2 cup walnuts

1/4 tsp. vegetable seasoning
1/4 tsp. nutmeg
2 T. melted butter
Juice of 1 lemon

Spread fillet flat. Combine spinach, onions, mushrooms, walnuts, seasoning and nutmeg. Spread in a thin layer over each of the fillets. Roll up and fasten with toothpicks. Place on a buttered baking pan. Combine melted butter and lemon juice, brushing over tops of fish rolls. Bake uncovered in a 350° oven for 10 minutes or until it flakes.

Yield: Serves 4

STUFFED ROLLED FLOUNDER

1 pound flounder fillets
1 T. oil
4 T. finely chopped onions
1/3 cup chopped raw spinach
1/4 cup mushrooms, chopped finely
4 T. finely chopped parsley
1 tsp. oregano
4 T. shredded Cheddar cheese

1/2 cup cooked brown rice
1 cup puréed tomatoes
2 T. wheat germ
1/4 cup whole wheat bread crumbs
1/8 cup Parmesan cheese
2 T. sesame seeds
Fresh parsley and lemon slices as garnish

Brush fillets with oil. Combine onion, spinach, mushrooms, parsley and oregano. Place on top of fillets and top with cheese. Place the rice on top of cheese. Roll each fillet up, starting with the narrow end. Fasten with toothpicks and place side by side in an oiled baking dish. Pour puréed tomatoes over rolls and sprinkle with mixture of wheat germ, bread crumbs, cheese and sesame seeds. Bake 30 minutes at 350°. Remove toothpicks. Place on platter with parsley and lemon slices.

Yield: Serves 4

CRUNCHY TUNA CASSEROLE

13 ounce can flaked tuna
4 cups chopped spinach, fresh
2 cups chopped broccoli
1/2 cup green pepper, diced
1 cup celery, sliced
1 cup sliced carrots
1/4 cup water
1½ cups sliced fresh mushrooms
2 T. butter

3 T. whole wheat flour
1 cup milk
1/2 tsp. each dill and oregano
1/4 tsp. nutmeg
1/2 cup chopped cashew or walnuts
4 T. wheat germ
3 T. bran
2 T. sesame seeds
2 T. grated Parmesan cheese

Drain the tuna. Combine the spinach, broccoli, green pepper, celery and carrots with 1/4 cup water in a skillet. Cook, covered, for about 2 minutes. Remove the vegetables but save the liquid. Combine the vegetables with the tuna and mushrooms. Set aside. In a saucepan, melt the butter, stir in flour until blended. Combine the water from the vegetables with the milk. That should come to 1½ cups. Add this mixture gradually to the saucepan and cook until thickens. Add dill, oregano, nutmeg and nuts. Fold the sauce into the vegetables and tuna. Pour into a 2 quart baking dish. Top with the mixture of wheat germ, bran, sesame seeds and Parmesan cheese. Bake at 350° for 30 minutes.

Yield: Serves 4-6

AVOCADO TUNA JELLIED LOAF

1 T. unflavored gelatin
1/4 cup cold water
1 cup boiling water
3 T. lemon juice
1/2 tsp. vegetable seasoning
1/4 cup shredded Cheddar cheese
1/2 cup chopped celery
1/2 cup chopped green pepper
3 T. green onion, diced
1 7-ounce can tuna, drained and
  flaked

1/2 cup walnuts, chopped
1 T. unflavored gelatin
1/4 cup cold water
1/2 cup boiling water
3 T. lemon juice
1 tsp. honey
1/2 cup MAYONNAISE
1/4 cup YOGURT
1/4 tsp. vegetable seasoning
2 cups mashed avocado

This loaf has two layers that are made separately and then put together. Soften the gelatin in the cold water. Then add the boiling water to dissolve the gelatin. Add to this the lemon juice, seasoning, cheese, celery, green pepper, onion, tuna and walnuts and mix. Pour this mixture into a 9" loaf pan. Refrigerate until firm. To make the other loaf, sprinkle the other tablespoon of gelatin in the cold water. Add the boiling water to it to help dissolve the gelatin. Add all the rest of the ingredients and mix well. Pour this mixture over the firm tuna mixture and refrigerate until firm. When ready to serve, turn out onto a bed of salad greens.

Yield: 8 servings

TUNA BURGERS

2 cans (6½ ounce each) chunk tuna
1/2 cup finely chopped celery
1/4 cup finely chopped green pepper
1/3-1/2 cup MAYONNAISE
3 T. chopped green onion

2 T. tamari (soy sauce)
3 T. chopped fresh parsley
1/4 cup sunflower seeds
1/2 cup fine bread crumbs or
  rolled oats

Drain and flake the tuna. To the tuna, add the celery, green pepper, mayonnaise, onion, tamari, parsley and sunflower seeds. Mix all together. Shape into 5 patties and roll in the bread crumbs or rolled oats. In a skillet heat a small amount of oil—just enough to lightly coat the surface. Add patties and cook for about 5 minutes, turning to brown each side. Serve on HONEY WHEAT BUNS and decorate as you would hamburgers.

Yield: 5 burgers

CHICKEN TERMINOLOGY

Broiler or broil-fryer: Chicken about 9 weeks old, weighing 1½ to 3½ pounds. Tender and has flexible breastbone cartilage. Of all chickens sold, 70-80 percent are broiler-fryers.

Roaster: Tender chicken about 12 weeks old. Weighs 3½ to 5 pounds.

Stewing chicken: Mature female chicken, less tender than roasters.

BUYING AND STORAGE

How much to buy per serving:

1/2 of one 1½ pound broiler per serving
3/4 pound for frying
3/4 pound for roasting
3/4 pound for stewing

If you bought your fresh poultry in a plastic wrapping, leave it in the plastic when you get it home. It will keep several days. It can be frozen up to 12 months.

If you buy a frozen chicken, keep frozen until 24 hours before cooking. Leave it on your refrigerator shelf overnight. Or if you need it thawed faster, run it under cold running water for 1 or 2 hours.

SWEET-SOUR CHICKEN

3 pound frying chicken, cut up
1 can (20 ounces) unsweetened
    pineapple chunks and juice
4 T. cider vinegar
1 T. tamari (soy sauce)
1/2 tsp. dry mustard

1 tsp. vegetable seasoning
1/8 tsp. ginger
1 medium-sized green pepper
1 medium-sized red pepper
1 T. arrowroot powder
2 T. cold water

Place chicken in a shallow baking dish. Surround with the drained pineapple chunks. In a bowl, combine unsweetened pineapple juice, vinegar, tamari, mustard, vegetable seasoning and ginger. Mix together and then pour over chicken. Place in 350° oven, uncovered, for 40 minutes. Baste frequently. Cut green and red peppers into strips and add to chicken after it has baked for 40 minutes. Also combine arrowroot with the water and stir into liquid in baking dish. Bake for another 15 minutes until sauce thickens. Serve immediately over rice or bulgur wheat.

Yield: 4-6 servings

GRANOLA CHICKEN BAKE

8 chicken thighs (about 1½ pounds)
2 cups water
1½ tsp. vegetable seasoning
6 peppercorns
1/2 pound fresh broccoli
1 cup celery

4 eggs
1-1/3 cups milk
1½ cups grated Swiss cheese
1/2 tsp. thyme
1/2 tsp. tarragon
1 cup GRANOLA

Combine chicken, water, 1 teaspoon vegetable seasoning and peppercorns. Cover and bring to boil. Boil gently 30 minutes or until tender. Remove chicken from broth. Cool enough to handle then remove skin and bones. Cut chicken into cubes. Trim coarse stalks from broccoli and slice. Chop celery into thick slices. Beat eggs with milk. Mix in cheese, herbs and remaining 1/2 teaspoon vegetable seasoning. Place chicken, broccoli and celery in a 2 quart casserole dish. Cover with half the milk/cheese mixture. Sprinkle half of the granola over the sauce. Repeat layers of sauce and granola. Bake at 375° for about 15-18 minutes. Do not overbake.

Yield: 4 servings

CHICKEN CACCIATORE

An Italian dish that is one of my favorites.

3 pound frying chicken, cut up
1/4 cup olive oil
2 cloves garlic, thinly sliced
1/2 cup whole wheat flour
1/2 tsp. each oregano and tarragon
1 tsp. vegetable seasoning

1/4 tsp. kelp
2 eggs, lightly beaten
1/4 cup milk
1 T. chopped fresh parsley
1/2 cup Parmesan cheese

Sauce:

1 T. oil
2 large onions, finely cut
1 green pepper, diced
1 cup celery, diced
1/2 pound mushrooms, sliced
3½ cups stewed tomatoes

1 cup TOMATO SAUCE
1/4 tsp. thyme
1/4 tsp. oregano
1 bay leaf, crumbled
1/2 tsp. allspice
1 tsp. chopped fresh parsley

Heat oil and garlic in a large skillet until garlic is browned. Meanwhile, prepare the chicken by removing the skin and rinsing with water. Place the flour, oregano, tarragon, vegetable seasoning, and kelp together in a paper bag. Mix together the eggs, milk and parsley. Place the Parmesan cheese in a bowl. Take 2 or 3 pieces at a time and place in the paper bag. Shake to coat the chicken. Then dip the pieces in the milk and egg mixture and roll in the Parmesan cheese. Do this until all pieces are coated. Place in the skillet and brown on all sides—about 15 minutes. While chicken is browning, make the sauce. Sauté in oil the onion, green pepper, celery and mushrooms until the onion is tender. Add all the other ingredients and simmer for about 10 minutes. Pour the sauce over the chicken and simmer, uncovered, about 30–40 minutes. Can be served plain, over spaghetti, or with POLENTA. If served with polenta, spoon the sauce and chicken over it.

Yield: Serves 4

SESAME BAKED CHICKEN

1 egg, lightly beaten
1/2 cup milk
1/2 cup whole wheat flour
1 tsp. vegetable seasoning
1/2 tsp. each oregano and tarragon

1 tsp. garlic powder
4 T. sesame seeds
1 frying chicken, cut into serving pieces
(3 pounds)
1/2 cup melted butter

Beat the egg and milk together. Combine the flour, vegetable seasoning, oregano, tarragon, garlic powder and sesame seeds in a paper bag. Remove the skin from the chicken. Dip the chicken pieces in the egg mixture and then shake in the paper bag to coat it with flour. Place the chicken pieces skin side up in a baking dish. Pour melted butter over and bake for about an hour at 350°.

Yield: Serves 4

CHICKEN WITH CASHEWS

1/2 pound chicken
2 T. oil
2 T. fresh ginger, sliced
1½ cups sliced celery
1 cup thinly sliced carrots
1/2 cup snow peas
1 cup diced bok choy
1/2 cup water chestnuts, sliced

1 cup mushrooms, sliced
3 cups CHICKEN STOCK
1/2 tsp. vegetable seasoning
1 T. tamari (soy sauce)
2 T. arrowroot powder
1/4 cup water
1/2 cup whole cashews

Cut chicken into strips 1/4" thick, 1/2" wide and 1½" long. In a wok, over medium high heat, sauté the ginger in oil. Remove the ginger and the chicken strips and cook until no longer pink. About 5 minutes. Push chicken to the side and add the vegetables in the order given and cook for 2 minutes. Add chicken stock and bring to a boil. Cover and steam 1–2 minutes. Add the vegetable seasoning, tamari and arrowroot that has been dissolved in 1/4 cup water. Stir until mixture is thickened. Add cashews and stir a couple of times. Serve immediately over brown rice or fried noodles.

Yield: Serves 4

CHICKEN AND FRESH VEGETABLES

1 small head cauliflower
2 large ripe tomatoes, sliced
2 medium carrots, sliced thinly
1 zucchini, cubed
1 large onion, thinly sliced
1 cup brown rice, cooked
3 T. chopped fresh parsley

1 T. basil
1 tsp. vegetable seasoning
1/3 cup CHICKEN STOCK
2 cloves garlic, minced
1 lemon, freshly squeezed
2 whole chicken breasts, split

Break cauliflower into flowerets. Combine the cauliflower, tomatoes, carrots, zucchini, and onion together. In a 2 quart shallow baking dish, place the brown rice layered on the bottom. On top of that place all of the vegetables. Sprinkle with 1 tablespoon parsley, 2 teaspoon basil, and 1/2 teaspoon vegetable seasoning. Pour chicken stock over vegetables. Make a paste of remaining 2 tablespoons parsley, 1 teaspoon basil, 1/2 teaspoon vegetable seasoning, garlic and lemon juice. Chop parsley and garlic finely and mix with lemon juice, basil and vegetable seasoning in a small bowl with the back of the spoon. Spread paste between skin and flesh of each chicken breast. Place chicken over vegetables in the baking dish; cover with foil. Bake in 350° oven for 1 hour, until chicken is tender and vegetables are crisp-tender. Baste chicken occasionally with juices during baking.

Yield: 4 servings

CHICKEN AND NOODLE FRICASSEE

3 pound roasting chicken, cut up
2 T. oil
2 celery stalks, cut up
1 tsp. ITALIAN HERBS
1¼ tsp vegetable seasoning
1 tsp. sage
2 cups water or CHICKEN STOCK
2 large carrots, halved lengthwise

2 medium new potatoes (1 pound),
    pared and quartered
2 medium onions, quartered
8 ounces wide whole wheat noodles
2-3 T. arrowroot powder
1/4 cup water
Chopped fresh parsley

Remove the skin from the chicken. In a 6-quart Dutch oven, sauté chicken in oil until golden brown. Add celery, Italian herbs, vegetable seasoning and sage. Sauté, stirring, 3 minutes. Add 2 cups water; bring to boiling; reduce heat and simmer, covered, 30 minutes. Add carrots; cook 10 minutes. Add potato and onion; simmer, covered, until tender—about 15 minutes. Meanwhile cook noodles. Drain. Stir arrowroot into the 1/4 cup of water to dissolve. Remove 1/2 cup hot chicken broth and stir into the arrowroot mixture. Gently stir this into the Dutch oven. Stir until thickened. Fold in noodles and simmer, uncovered, 5 minutes. Remove to a serving dish. Sprinkle with parsley.

Yield: 6 servings

CHICKEN PIE

6 cups cooked chicken, cut in large
    pieces
3 T. oil
1 clove garlic, minced
1 large onion, chopped
1/2 pound mushrooms, sliced
1 cup sliced carrots
6 cups CHICKEN STOCK (broth)

1/2 tsp. each sage, rosemary and
    thyme
5 T. arrowroot powder
1/3 cup water
1 cup chopped celery
1 cup fresh peas
1 medium zucchini, sliced 1/4"
    thick
FLAKY PIE CRUST recipe

In a 5-quart Dutch oven, sauté the garlic, onion, mushrooms, and carrots in oil. Cook, stirring until onion is limp. Stir in the stock and seasoning. Heat to simmering. Meanwhile, blend the arrowroot and water together. When broth just begins to simmer, stir in arrowroot mixture. Cook until mixture thickens. Add more arrowroot if needed to thicken. Stir in the celery, peas, zucchini and chicken. Stir together and make sure all vegetables are coated with sauce. Remove from heat. Roll one half of the dough out and place the bottom crust in a 9" pie pan. Pour in chicken and vegetable filling and place on top crust. Place in a 350° oven and cook until crust is brown, about 20 minutes. Remove from oven and let sit 10 minutes before serving.

Yield: Serves 6

Variation:
Turkey Pie: Use cooked turkey in place of the chicken.

TURKEY

ROAST TURKEY

Thawing a Turkey

Thaw in the refrigerator in the original wrapping.

```
 4-8  pounds  —  1½ to 2 days
 8-12 pounds  —  2 days
12-16 pounds  —  2-3 days
16-24 pounds  —  3-4 days
```

Quick Method:

Best method is to thaw in refrigerator but if you need it thawed in a hurry, keep turkey in its original wrapping and place in the sink and cover with cold water. Change water frequently. Allow 1/2 hour per pound of turkey. Never let the bird sit at room temperature as it could become a breeding ground for bacteria.

Preparing the Turkey

Free legs and tail from tucked position. Remove neck and giblets. Rinse the turkey and pat dry with paper towels. Now prepare the stuffing. DO NOT stuff the turkey until just before it is to be cooked. If you do, you have a greater chance of bacteria breeding in the uncooked turkey and stuffing. Allow about 3/4 cup stuffing per pound of turkey for those that weigh up to 13 or 14 pounds. For larger birds (16 pounds or more) allow about 1/2 cup per pound. Fill the neck cavity lightly with stuffing; fasten neck skin to the back skewers and lace shut with cord. Leave legs free to allow heat penetration to the thigh joint. Tie wings to body with cord.

If you are not going to stuff the bird, or even if you do, try this mixture.

3 cloves of crushed garlic
Juice of 3 lemons
6 T. of tomato paste

2 tsp. poultry seasoning (sage, thyme, marjoram)
2 tsp. each of kelp and paprika

Mix all together and rub one half of the mixture inside the turkey cavity. The other half will be rubbed on the outer turkey skin later.

Cooking the Turkey

A way to assure yourself of very moist white and dark meat is to cook the turkey half of the time breast side down and half of the time breast side up. Place the turkey with breast side down on a rack in a shallow roasting pan. Rub oil and the remaining spice mixture all over the skin of the turkey. By rubbing the oil on the turkey, it will keep all of the juices within the turkey itself. Insert a meat thermometer into the thigh muscle. Make sure the tip does not touch the bone or you will not get a correct temperature reading. When meat is about half done, remove from oven, and with your hands (protected by paper towels) turn bird over onto its back. Continue cooking.

Timetable for Roasting Turkey

Roasting will be done in a 325° oven as roasting it in a slow oven will preserve more moisture and juices. It also does the least violence to the many nutrients in the turkey meat.

Weight	Approximate Roasting Time
6 to 8 pounds	3 to 3½ hours
8 to 12 pounds	3½ to 4½ hours
12 to 16 pounds	4½ to 5½ hours
16 to 20 pounds	5½ to 6½ hours
20 to 24 pounds	6½ to 7 hours
24 and over	Approx. 21 minutes a pound at 300°

Test for Doneness

1. When done, the meat thermometer should register 185°.

2. The drumstick should move easily when jiggled and thigh meat should be soft when pinched.

3. Pierce the thigh of the bird with the tip of a small sharp knife. Juices should be a clear yellow. If still pink, roast a little longer.

4. When done, remove to a platter and let it rest for one-half hour so it will be easier to carve.

Factors that May Affect Cooking Times and Results

1. If temperature of turkey is warmer or colder than refrigerator temperature, roasting time will be shorter or longer than shown on schedule.

2. If turkey is not stuffed, reduce cooking time up to 1 hour.

3. If the oven door is open frequently, the roasting time will be longer.

TURKEY PUFF

Crust:

3/4 cup water
6 T. butter
3/4 cup whole wheat flour
3 eggs

1/2-1 tsp. dry mustard
1/2 tsp. vegetable seasoning
2/3 cup grated Swiss cheese
1 tsp. prepared stone-ground
  mustard

In a small heavy saucepan, bring water and butter to a boil. Add flour all at once. Cook, beating hard with a wooden spoon, until ingredients are blended and mixture leaves sides of pan. Remove pan from the heat and beat in one egg at a time. Beat well after each addition. Mix in dry mustard, vegetable seasoning, and cheese. Butter a 9" pie pan well. Using two-thirds of the dough, line bottom and sides of pan. Use back of spoon to do this. Bring dough well up on the sides of the pan. Spread the prepared mustard over bottom crust. Spoon filling into crust.

Filling:

1 onion, diced
1 celery stalk, sliced
1 cup sliced mushrooms
1 tomato, diced
1/2 cup chopped carrots
1 clove garlic, minced
2 T. butter
1 T. whole wheat flour

1/2 cup CHICKEN or TURKEY
  STOCK
2 cups cooked diced turkey
2 T. Parmesan cheese
1/2 tsp. poultry seasoning
1/2 tsp. oregano
1/4 tsp. vegetable seasoning

Sauté onion, celery, mushrooms, tomato, carrots, and garlic in butter until onion is golden. Add flour and blend, cooking about 1 minute. Add stock and cook until thickened. Stir in turkey, cheese and herbs. Remove from heat and pour into pie crust. Using remaining dough, form teaspoon sized puffs around top of filling. Bake at 375° for 40 minutes, until puffed and well browned.

Yield: Serves 4-6

TURKEY DIVAN

1 pound broccoli	1 T. tamari (soy sauce)
1½ cups sliced zucchini	1/2 tsp. oregano
2 T. butter	Vegetable seasoning to taste
4 T. whole wheat flour	1½ cups cooked brown rice
2 cups TURKEY STOCK	8 slices cooked turkey—1/4" thick
1/2 cup plain YOGURT	6 T. grated Parmesan cheese

Steam the broccoli and zucchini just until tender. Keep hot. Melt butter in a saucepan, add flour and blend thoroughly. Gradually add the turkey stock and cook until the sauce is thick—stir frequently. Remove from heat and fold in yogurt. Add tamari, oregano and vegetable seasoning to taste. Place the brown rice on the bottom of a shallow casserole and top with steamed broccoli and zucchini. Pour half of the sauce over the top. Arrange sliced turkey over the sauce-covered vegetables. Add 4 tablespoons Parmesan cheese to the remaining sauce and pour over the turkey. Sprinkle with the additional cheese and place dish under the broiler until lightly browned. Serve immediately.

Yield: 4 servings

Variation:
Chicken Divan: Use chicken in place of turkey in the recipe.

TURKEY TOSTADA

4 CORN TORTILLAS	1/4 cup diced avocado
1 cup GUACAMOLE	4 T. SOUR CREAM
1½ cups cooked and sliced turkey	1 cup SALSA sauce
2 cups shredded lettuce or alfalfa	4 lettuce leaves
sprouts	8 ounces sliced pineapple
1 tomato, diced	8 slices melon
1 red onion, thinly sliced	4 hot yellow peppers

Place the corn tortillas on a griddle that has been wiped with oil. Cook tortillas until they become soft. Then place the tortillas on four separate plates. Top tortillas with guacamole, turkey, lettuce or sprout, tomato, onion, diced avocado and sour cream. Layer in that order. Serve with salsa sauce poured over top. Garnish plate with lettuce, pineapple, melon and hot peppers.

Yield: Serves 4

STUFFINGS

BREAD STUFFING

12 cups whole wheat bread crumbs
1/2 cup butter
1½ cups celery, chopped
1¼ cups onions, chopped
2¼ cups CHICKEN or TURKEY BROTH
2 eggs, beaten lightly

1 cup fresh parsley, chopped
2-3 large apples, chopped
1½ cups walnuts or pecans, chopped coarsely
3 tsp. each thyme, marjoram, sage, savory

Sauté the celery and onion in butter. Place all of the rest of the ingredients into a large bowl—bread crumbs, broth, eggs, parsley, apples, nuts, and herbs. Add the celery and onion mixture to the large bowl and mix well. Lightly spoon this mixture into the neck and body cavities of the bird. It will expand so do not over stuff. Bake according to the time set out for the bird. If you would like it as a casserole, spoon into a greased 2½ quart casserole dish. Bake covered in 350° oven for 30-40 minutes. For a crispy topping, remove top the last 5 minutes.

Yield: Stuffs a 16-18 pound bird or 12 servings

Variations:

Chestnut Stuffing: Boil unshelled chestnuts 15 minutes; drain, shell, and cut off brown skin while hot. Substitute 2 cups of chestnuts for 2 cups of bread crumbs.

Oyster Stuffing: Add 2 cups chopped or whole oysters and liquid.

Corn Stuffing: Add 3 cups fresh corn kernels or 3 cups creamed corn plus 1/3 cup chopped green peppers.

Pineapple Stuffing: Add 3 cups pineapple chunks.

MUSHROOM STUFFING

1/2 pound mushrooms, chopped
1 cup grated carrots
1 cup diced celery
3/4 cup onion, diced
1 cup walnuts, chopped
1/2 cup green pepper, diced

1/2 cup non-instant dry milk powder
1 T. chopped fresh parsley
1/2 tsp. marjoram
1/4 tsp. sage
1/4 tsp. kelp
1/2 tsp. vegetable seasoning

In a medium saucepan, combine all of the ingredients together. Place over a low heat and stir until a liquid from the vegetables appears—about 5 minutes. Cover and simmer 12 minutes; stir occasionally. Serve hot with fowl or fish dishes, or use as a stuffing in a bird.

Yield: 3 cups

BRAZIL NUT–MUSHROOM STUFFING

1/2 cup butter
1/2 pound mushrooms, finely
   chopped
1/2 cup diced celery
1/2 cup chopped Brazil nuts
1/4 cup chopped onion
1/2 tsp. rosemary

1/2 tsp. sage
1/4 tsp. thyme
1/4 tsp. basil
3 cups whole wheat bread crumbs
1 cup cooked barley
2 T. chopped fresh parsley
1/3 cup VEGETABLE STOCK

Melt the butter in a large skillet; add the mushrooms, celery, nuts and onion. Sprinkle with the herbs and cook about 10 minutes, stirring occasionally. Add the bread crumbs, barley, parsley and stock. Toss to combine. Add more stock if needed. Can be used to stuff vegetables as well as poultry.

Yield: 6 servings

CORNBREAD DRESSING

5 cups crumbled CORNBREAD
1 cup whole wheat bread crumbs
1/2 cup butter, melted
1½ cups chopped celery
1 cup chopped onion
1/4 cup chopped fresh parsley
1/2 cup sliced mushrooms

1/2 tsp. each thyme, marjoram
   and sage
1 tsp. vegetable seasoning
1/2 tsp. savory
1/4 tsp. kelp
1 egg
3/4 cup walnuts
3/4 cup CHICKEN STOCK

Heat 1/4 cup butter in medium skillet. Add celery, onion, parsley and mushrooms. Sauté, stirring, until celery and onion are tender—about 5 minutes. Add this mixture to the crumbled cornbread, bread crumbs, seasoning, herbs, egg, and walnuts; mix well. Add just enough stock to dampen the mixture; it should be moist. With hands, lightly form mixture into balls, using about 1/2 cup for each. Arrange in greased shallow baking dish. Brush with rest of butter; bake, covered, for 30 minutes. Remove cover and bake 15 minutes longer, or until browned on top.

Yield: 10 servings

FRUIT STUFFING

2 cups whole wheat bread crumbs
1/2 cup diced fresh oranges
1/2 cup diced apple
1/2 cup celery, chopped
1/4 cup raisins

1/4 cup sunflower seeds
1/4 cup chopped pecans
1/2 tsp. vegetable seasoning
1/4 tsp. nutmeg

In a large mixing bowl, combine all ingredients. Cover and let stand 1 hour. Stir before using.

Yield: 5 cups

RICE DRESSING

4 cups cooked brown rice
1 cup onions, diced
1/2 cup butter, melted
1 cup celery, diced
1/2 tsp. sage
1/2 tsp. marjoram

1/2 tsp. oregano
1/4 cup chopped fresh parsley
1/3 cup TURKEY or CHICKEN
   BROTH
1/2 cup pecans

Mix all of the ingredients together and place into a 1½ quart casserole dish. Bake for 30 minutes at 350°. Or this dressing can be used to stuff the cavity of a turkey.

Yield: 5 cups

Variation:
Barley Dressing: Replace 4 cups cooked barley for brown rice.

VEGETARIAN

VEGETABLE STROGANOFF

2 cups steamed vegetables
2 T. oil
1 T. butter
1 large onion, sliced thin
1/2 cup mushrooms, sliced
3 T. whole wheat flour

1 cup CHICKEN or VEGETABLE
   STOCK
1 tsp. Dijon mustard
1 tsp. vegetable seasoning
2 tsp. tamari (soy sauce)
1 cup plain YOGURT

Steam a variety of vegetables, such as zucchini, cauliflower, broccoli, peas, celery and tomatoes, until tender. Heat oil and butter together in a skillet and sauté the onion and mushroom until onion is translucent. Add flour and stir until flour is browned. Add stock gradually, stirring all the time. Add mustard, vegetable seasoning and tamari and mix well. Simmer, stirring until sauce thickens. Add steamed vegetables and mix. Remove from heat and stir in the yogurt. Serve over cooked bulgur wheat or brown rice.

Yield: Serves 4

TURNBULL'S PIZZA

Crust:

1 T. dry active yeast	1/2 tsp. kelp
1 cup warm water	1 T. oil
1 tsp. honey	3 cups whole wheat flour
1/2 tsp. oregano	

2 cups SPAGHETTI SAUCE
Condiments—use some or all of the following items:

diced olives	chopped or sliced onions
sliced green peppers	sliced mushrooms
shredded zucchini	tomatoes, sliced
kidney or soybeans, cooked	

3 cups Mozarella cheese
1 cup Parmesan cheese

To assemble the crust, dissolve the yeast in warm water and honey. Let it sit for 5 minutes. Add the oregano, kelp and oil. Add the flour until you have enough to make a stiff dough. Turn onto a lightly floured board and knead until smooth and elastic, about 7 minutes. Place in a greased bowl, turning to grease top. Cover, and place in a warm place until double in bulk, about 1 hour. Punch dough down. Roll into a circle and fit into a lightly greased and floured (with cornmeal) 12" pizza pan. This will make a thick crust. If a thinner crust is desired, just roll thin and you will be able to cover two 12" pizza pans. Pinch up around the edges. Pour the sauce over entire crust and then top with any of the condiments listed. Add the Mozzarella and Parmesan cheese on top of the condiments. Bake at 350° for about 20 minutes, until crust is brown.

Yield: 1 pizza

SUKIYAKI

1 T. oil	1 cup sliced bok choy
1 large onion, chopped	6 fresh mushrooms, sliced
1 cup sliced celery	1/4 cup water chestnuts, sliced
1/2 cup sliced red pepper	8 ounces TOFU
1/2 cup CHICKEN or VEGETABLE STOCK	1 T. arrowroot powder plus 1/4 cup water
1 T. tamari (soy sauce)	1/2 cup bean sprouts
1 cup shredded Chinese cabbage	

Heat the oil in a wok and add the onion, celery and pepper. Sauté until onion is tender. Add the stock and tamari and mix in well. Add the cabbage, bok choy, mushrooms, water chestnuts and tofu. Cover and steam for about 5 minutes. Mix the arrowroot in the water and add to the wok. Stir until thickened. Add the bean sprouts and cover for about 30 seconds. Remove from heat and serve over brown rice.

Yield: Serves 4

CHILI CON CARNE

2 T. oil
2 stalks celery, chopped
1/4 cup green pepper, chopped
1 small diced green chili pepper
1/2 cup chopped onion
2 cloves garlic, minced
4 cups fresh tomatoes, puréed
2 cups TOMATO SAUCE

Dash cayenne
1½ tsp. cumin
1½ tsp. chili powder
1 T. tamari (soy sauce)
1/2 cup tomato paste
1 cup lentils, cooked
4 cups kidney beans, cooked

Sauté the celery, green pepper, chili pepper, onion and garlic in oil. Add the sautéed mixture and all the rest of the ingredients together in a large pot. Simmer for about 1 hour. Let sit for 1 day so the flavors will really mingle. Goes well with hot CORN BREAD.

Yield: 5–6 servings

STEW

5 peeled, cubed new potatoes (large)
3 large carrots, sliced
3 celery stalks, diced
1/2 of a medium-sized onion, diced
2 cups cooked soybeans
1½ cups cooked kidney beans
2-3 tomatoes, chopped
1 cup TOMATO SAUCE

3 cups liquid (can use liquid beans
  are cooked in)
1 clove garlic, minced
1 bay leaf
1 tsp. fine herbs
1 tsp. vegetable seasoning
1/3 cup flour
1 cup water
1½ T. tamari (soy sauce)

Place the first thirteen items in a big soup kettle. Heat to boil for 1 minute and then turn down and simmer for 30 minutes. Add the flour to the 1 cup of water and mix well. Then add this mixture to the pot of stew. Stir until the liquid thickens; you may even have to add more flour. Simmer another 10–15 minutes. Add tamari just before serving.

Yield: Serves 8

BARLEY SAUTÉ

1 cup chopped onion
2 cloves garlic, chopped
2 T. butter
1 T. oil
4 cups cooked barley
1 small eggplant, cut into 1/2" cubes

2 small zucchini, sliced
1 tsp. oregano
Pinch of cayenne pepper
2 cups stewed tomatoes, plus juice
1/4 pound Jack or Mozzarella
  cheese, grated

In a large skillet, sauté the onion and garlic in the butter-oil mixture. When translucent, add the barley. Sauté 2 minutes longer, then add the eggplant and zucchini. Make sure all the vegetables are coated. Sprinkle on oregano and cayenne pepper. Add the tomatoes and their juice and simmer only until the vegetables are just tender. Stir in grated cheese or you can sprinkle it on the top and place it under the broiler until it melts.

Yield: Serves 4

CASSEROLES AND PIES

RECYCLED CASSEROLE

2 cups brown rice, bulgur or wheat noodles, cooked
1 cup beans, cooked (soybeans, kidney beans, or garbanzo beans)
3 cups chopped vegetables
    Any combination of the following or other vegetables:
    Onions, red or green peppers, carrots, celery, mushrooms, broccoli,
    peas, cauliflower, asparagus

3 eggs
1 cup milk
2/3 cup shredded Cheddar cheese
1/4 cup Parmesan cheese
1 tsp. vegetable seasoning

1/2 tsp. oregano
1/2 tsp. thyme
Sliced tomatoes
Parmesan cheese

Combine the rice, beans and chopped vegetables in a large bowl. In another bowl mix together the eggs, milk, cheeses and herbs. Pour this mixture over the vegetables, rice and beans and mix well. Place into a 2 quart casserole dish. Place tomatoes on top and sprinkle with Parmesan cheese. Bake at 350° for 40 minutes, until all is warmed.

Yield: Serves 5

RICE VEGETABLE CASSEROLE WITH SALSA

1 bunch broccoli (1 pound)
1 small head cauliflower (1 pound)
2 medium-sized crookneck squash
   or zucchini
1/4 cup sliced celery
1/4 pound mushroom, sliced
3 cups cooked brown rice
1/4 cup shredded carrot

1/4 cup chopped green onions
1/2 tsp. tamari (soy sauce)
1 cup SALSA sauce
20 cherry tomatoes, cut in half
1 cup grated Jack cheese
1 cup grated Cheddar cheese
1/4 cup sunflower seeds

Break the broccoli into bite-size flowerets leaving some of the stem. Break the cauliflower into bite-size flowerets. Cut squash into 1/2" thick slices. Combine the broccoli, cauliflower, squash and celery in a saucepan with a steamer. Steam for about 8 minutes, until vegetables are just tender. Remove from heat and stir in the mushrooms. Add carrots, green onions and tamari to the rice. Spread the rice mixture evenly in a shallow 2 quart casserole. Spoon salsa over the rice and then top with the steamed vegetables and cherry tomatoes. Combine the two cheeses and sprinkle over the vegetables. Bake at 350° for 15-20 minutes or until heated throughout. Sprinkle with sunflower seeds and serve immediately. If you want to make it ahead of time, compile the casserole then cover and place in the refrigerator until you are ready to bake.

Yield: 6 servings

BEAN CASSEROLE

2 cups cooked soybeans, garbanzo
   or lentils
1 T. oil
2 large green onions
1/2 cup chopped celery
1/3 cup chopped green or red pepper
12 mushrooms, sliced
1/4 cup cashews, raw

1 tsp. vegetable seasoning
1/4 tsp. thyme
1/4 tsp. marjoram
1 cup TOMATO JUICE
1 egg, well beaten
3/4 cup grated Jack cheese
4 slices of tomatoes

Sauté the onions, celery, pepper, mushrooms and cashews in the oil until the onion is tender. Add this mixture to the cooked beans. Then mix in the vegetable seasoning, thyme, marjoram, tomato juice and egg. Mix well. Pour this mixture into a casserole dish and sprinkle with the cheese. Place sliced tomatoes on top of the casserole. Cover casserole and bake until firm 30-40 minutes at 350°. Uncover for the last 10 minutes to brown cheese and make top crisp.

Yield: Serves 4

CUSTARD-TOPPED VEGETABLE CASSEROLE

1 large eggplant (1½ pounds)
5 T. oil
2 large onions, chopped
2 cloves garlic, minced
1 tsp. each cinnamon, basil and
   vegetable seasoning
1/4 tsp. kelp

3 pounds tomatoes, seeded and
   chopped
2 carrots, chopped
1/2 cup chopped parsley
1/2 cup water
3 medium zucchini, 1/4" thick
2 cups cooked brown rice
1 cup coarsely chopped walnuts

Custard Topping:

1/4 cup butter
1/4 cup whole wheat flour
2½ cups milk

4 eggs
1/4 tsp. ground nutmeg
3/4 cup grated Parmesan cheese

Cut eggplant into 1/2" thick slices. Pour 3 tablespoons of oil in a bowl. Dip the eggplant in oil and then place on a baking sheet. Bake in a 400° oven for 20 minutes, until well browned. Meanwhile, sauté the onions and garlic in the remaining 2 tablespoons of oil. Add the cinnamon, basil, vegetable seasoning, kelp, tomatoes, carrots, parsley and water. Simmer, uncovered, for about 25 minutes. Stir often. Add the zucchini, cover and cook for 5 minutes. Arrange the baked eggplant in the bottom of a 9" x 13" baking pan. Top with the rice, then the vegetable sauce, then the nuts. Pour the custard topping over all of it. Bake, uncovered, in a 350° oven for 50 minutes. Let stand 15 minutes before serving. To make the topping: Melt the butter in a pan and stir in the flour. Cook until bubbly. Gradually stir in the milk and cook, stirring, until it thickens. Beat 4 eggs with the nutmeg and gradually stir in 1 cup of the hot mixture, then stir into the remaining sauce. Return to heat and cook for 1 minute. Remove from heat and stir in cheese. Now ready to use.

Yield: 8 servings

ZUCCHINI CASSEROLE

1 cup brown rice
2½ cups water
1 tsp. oil
4 medium zucchini, sliced
4 cups grated Jack cheese
3 medium tomatoes, sliced
2 cups SOUR CREAM or YOGURT

1/2 cup green chiles, chopped
1 T. parsley
2 T. green pepper, diced
2 T. green onion, diced
1 tsp. oregano
1 tsp garlic powder
1/2 tsp. kelp

Boil the water and then add the rice and oil slowly so the boil will not go down. Reduce heat to low, cover and cook for 40-45 minutes. Spread cooked rice in a baking dish. Cover rice with zucchini, 2 cups of the cheese and a layer of sliced tomatoes. Mix sour cream or yogurt with all of the remaining ingredients. Pour this mixture over the tomatoes. Top with the remaining 2 cups of cheese. Bake 30 minutes at 350°.

Yield: Serves 6

MOUSSAKA

2 eggplants (1 pound each), washed and dried
1/2 cup butter, melted
2 T. oil
1 cup finely chopped onion
1 clove garlic, minced
2 cups coarsely grated zucchini

3 stalks celery, chopped fine
2 tomatoes, diced
1/2 tsp. oregano
1 tsp. basil
1/2 tsp. vegetable seasoning
2 cups TOMATO SAUCE

Cream sauce:

2 T. butter
2 T. whole wheat flour
1/2 tsp. vegetable seasoning
2 cups milk
2 eggs, beaten

2 T. Cheddar cheese
1/2 cup grated Parmesan cheese
1/2 cup grated Cheddar cheese
2 T. whole wheat bread crumbs

Halve unpared eggplant lengthwise; slice crosswise, 1/2" thick. Place on a cookie sheet and brush lightly with melted butter. Broil, 4" from heat, 4 minutes per side, or until golden. While that is cooking, place the oil in a saucepan and add the onion and garlic and stir until brown, about 7 minutes. Add the zucchini, celery, tomatoes, oregano, basil, seasoning and tomato sauce. Bring to boiling, reduce heat and simmer, uncovered, 15-20 minutes. Make the cream sauce by melting the butter in a medium saucepan. Remove from heat and stir in the flour and seasoning. Add milk gradually. Return to burner and bring to boiling, stirring until mixture is thickened. Remove from heat. Add some of the hot mixture into the eggs and mix. Then pour the eggs and cheese into the saucepan; mix well. To assemble the casserole layer half of the eggplants on the bottom of 12" x 7" baking dish, overlapping slightly. Sprinkle with 2 tablespoons each grated Parmesan and Cheddar cheeses. Stir bread crumbs into the vegetable mixture and spoon this over the eggplant in the casserole. Then sprinkle with 2 tablespoons each Parmesan and Cheddar cheeses. Layer rest of eggplant slices, overlapping, as before. Pour cream sauce over all. Sprinkle top with remaining cheese. Bake at 350° for 35-40 minutes, or until golden brown and top is set. Cool slightly to serve. Cut in squares.

Yield: 12 servings

EGGPLANT PARMESAN

3 cups brown rice, cooked
5 cups SPAGHETTI SAUCE
1 medium-sized eggplant, peeled
2 eggs, beaten
3 T. water
1/4 cup whole wheat flour
1/4 cup wheat germ

1/4 cup Parmesan cheese
2 T. sesame seeds
1/2 tsp. garlic powder
1/2 tsp. oregano
1/2 tsp vegetable seasoning
1½ cups grated Mozzarella cheese
3 T. Parmesan cheese

Mix 2 cups of the sauce with the brown rice and then layer in the bottom of a 9" x 13" baking pan. Slice the eggplant into 1/4" thick pieces. In one bowl mix the eggs and water together. In another bowl mix together the flour, wheat germ, Parmesan, sesame seeds, garlic, oregano and seasoning. Take the eggplant slices and dip first in the egg bowl and then dip in the other bowl so both sides are coated. Layer the slices of eggplant over the rice in the baking dish. Sprinkle on top of the eggplant 1 cup of Mozzarella cheese. Pour the other 3 cups of sauce over the eggplant mixture. Bake for 40 minutes at 350°. Remove from the oven and sprinkle on top the rest of the Mozzarella cheese and Parmesan cheese. Bake until the cheese is melted.

Yield: 8-10 servings

DEEP DISH VEGETABLE PIE

1 recipe for FLAKY PIE CRUST
3½ cups vegetables: Choose from any of the following:
    broccoli, shredded cabbage, carrots, cauliflower, zucchini, tomatoes,
    green pepper

1/2 cup chopped celery
1/4 cup chopped parsley
1/2 cup cooked soybeans
1/2 cup mushrooms, sliced
3 T. chopped onions
1/4 cup oil
1/4 cup whole wheat flour

2 cups VEGETABLE STOCK
1/2 tsp. basil
1/2 tsp. thyme
1/4 tsp. garlic powder
1/2 tsp. oregano
1 egg, beaten
1/4 cup grated Cheddar cheese

Cut all the vegetables into bite sizes. Place in a large bowl along with the celery, parsley, soybeans, mushrooms and onions. Roll the pie crust out and place in a 1 quart pie pan. Now turn vegetable mixture into the pie shell. Place the oil in a saucepan and stir in flour. Heat until browned and bubbly. Gradually add stock, basil, thyme, garlic and oregano. Stir over low heat until mixture thickens. Place 1/4 cup of the hot sauce in a cup with the egg; beat together. Then add this mixture to the hot sauce. Cook for another minute. Pour sauce over vegetables and mix in. Sprinkle with cheese and then make a lattice or top crust with the remaining dough. Bake at 350° for 45 minutes.

Yield: 6 servings

BROCCOLI CHEESE PIE

1 recipe for RICE CRUST
1 medium onion, chopped
1 garlic clove, minced
1/2 cup chopped celery
1 T. oil
2½ cups broccoli flowerets and stems
1 cup grated Cheddar cheese
1 cup milk

2 eggs, beaten
1/2 tsp. vegetable seasoning
1/4 tsp. dry mustard
1/2 tsp. oregano
1/2 tsp. thyme
1/4 cup chopped nuts
3 T. wheat germ
2 T. Parmesan cheese

Sauté the onion, garlic and celery in the oil until the onion is tender. Spread the sautéed vegetables over the bottom of the rice crust. Place the broccoli pieces over this and sprinkle the cheese over the broccoli. Combine in a small bowl the milk, eggs, vegetable seasoning, mustard, oregano and thyme. Pour this mixture into the pie pan. Mix together the chopped nuts, wheat germ and Parmesan cheese and sprinkle over the top of the pie. Bake at 350° for 45 minutes or until it is firm.

Yield: 4-6 servings

LOAVES AND PATTIES

THREE BEAN LOAF

2 cups cooked garbanzo beans
2 cups cooked kidney beans
1 cup fresh green beans, cooked and
    chopped
1/2 cup mushrooms, chopped
1 cup chopped celery
1 medium-sized onion, chopped
1 T. tamari (soy sauce)

1/2 cup pecans, very finely
    chopped
1 T. paprika
1/4 tsp. vegetable seasoning
1 egg
1 T. oil
3 T. wheat germ
1 cup TOMATO SAUCE

Combine garbanzo and kidney beans in a large bowl; mash well. Add green beans, mushrooms, celery, onion, tamari, pecans, paprika, vegetable seasoning, egg, oil, wheat germ and 3 tablespoons of the tomato sauce. Stir until well blended. Spoon mixture into a loaf pan. Bake in 375° oven for 50 minutes. Allow to cool slightly before slicing. Heat remaining tomato sauce and pour over the loaf.

Yield: 6 servings

LENTIL LOAF

2 cups lentils, cooked
1 small onion, chopped
2 stalks celery, chopped
1 small green pepper, diced
1 clove garlic, minced
3/4 cup bulgur wheat, cooked
3/4 cup walnuts or sunflower seeds
1 cup chopped carrots

2 eggs
1/2 tsp. kelp
1/4 tsp. oregano
1 tsp. sage
1/2 tsp. marjoram
1 cup TOMATO SAUCE
1 T. oil
1 cup whole wheat bread crumbs
1/2 cup wheat germ

In a large bowl place all of the ingredients. Mix with a wooden spoon until all ingredients are mixed well. Pour into an oiled 1 quart loaf pan. Bake at 350° for 45-50 minutes. Serve with additional tomato sauce poured on top. If you want to freeze the loaves, bake at 350° for 30 minutes. Cool slightly; cover with foil and freeze. To reheat: defrost halfway and bake at 350° for 30 minutes.

Yield: 1 loaf pan

SOYBEAN LOAF

1 cup cooked soybeans, puréed
3/4 cup coarsely grated cooked
    soybeans
1 cup cooked bulgur wheat
1 cup grated carrots
1/2 cup chopped onions
1/3 cup diced green pepper
3/4 cup chopped celery
3 T. fresh chopped parsley

1 T. sesame seeds
1/3 cup TOMATO SAUCE
1/3 cup milk
2 eggs, slightly beaten
2 T. tamari (soy sauce)
1 tsp. fine herbs
1 tsp. vegetable seasoning
TOMATO SAUCE

To make the 1 cup of puréed soybeans, place cooked soybeans in a blender and add a little water and blend until the soybeans are puréed (consistency of mashed bananas). Remove from the blender and place in a big bowl. Now add more cooked soybeans and blend until coarsely ground. Add these soybeans along with all the other ingredients into the large bowl. Stir until well blended. Pour into a 9" loaf pan. It will not be real firm at this point but will firm up during the cooking process. Bake at 350° for 50 minutes. Take it from oven and let it sit for 10 minutes before serving. Serve topped with TOMATO SAUCE.

Yield: Serves 6

OAT-ZUCCHINI LOAF

3 T. oil
1/2 cup chopped onion
1 clove garlic, minced
1/2 cup chopped celery
1/4 cup green pepper, chopped
2 cups uncooked rolled oats
3 cups grated zucchini

1/2 cup shredded Cheddar cheese
1/2 cup wheat germ
2 eggs, beaten
1/2 cup sunflower seeds
1/4 tsp. nutmeg
1 tsp. vegetable seasoning

Sauté the onion and garlic in the oil until tender. Combine with all the other ingredients and mix well. Press into a greased loaf pan and bake at 350° for 30–40 minutes.

Yield: Serves 6

VEGETARIAN BURGERS

3/4 cup bulgur wheat
1½ cups rolled oats
1/2 cup raw wheat germ
2½ cups water
1 small bell pepper, diced
1 onion chopped

1 or 2 eggs
1 tsp. garlic powder
1 tsp. vegetable seasoning
1½ tsp. sage
1 tsp. oregano
1/4 tsp. paprika

Soak together in a bowl: bulgur, rolled oats and wheat germ with the water for 3 hours or overnight. Add all other ingredients, mix well. Shape and fry as burger patties in a small amount of oil. Or you can cook like ground beef for use in spaghett and other dishes calling for ground beef.

Yield: 5 burgers

LENTIL BURGERS

1 cup dried lentils
1/2 cup brown rice, uncooked
3 cups water
1 cup whole wheat bread crumbs
1/2 cup wheat germ
1 medium onion, chopped (1/2 cup)
2 stalks celery, chopped

1/4 cup diced green pepper
1/2 tsp. celery seed
1/2 tsp. oregano
1 tsp. vegetable seasoning
Wheat germ
3 T. oil

Combine lentils, rice and water in a medium-size saucepan. Bring to a boil; lower heat; cover and simmer about 45 minutes, until beans and rice are tender. Remove from heat; let stand 10 minutes, then mash well with any liquid remaining in pan. Stir in bread crumbs, wheat germ, onion, celery, green pepper, celery seed, oregano and vegetable seasoning. Shape into patties (1/3 cup each); sprinkle with wheat germ; turn and coat other side. Heat oil in large skillet; sauté patties until brown on both sides, about 10 minutes. Serve in PITA BREAD with sprouts and tomato slices.

Yield: 10 burgers

CARROT PATTIES

1/2 onion, finely chopped
1/2 cup chopped mushrooms
1/2 cup chopped celery
2 T. oil
1 cup raw grated carrots
1/3 cup ground (in blender)
  sunflower seeds

1/4 cup chopped walnuts
1 egg, well beaten
1 T. chopped fresh parsley
1 tsp. dill
1 tsp. vegetable seasoning
Dash of garlic powder
Wheat germ

Sauté the onion, mushrooms and celery in the oil until the onion is tender. Combine the sautéed vegetables and all the rest of the ingredients, except for the wheat germ, in a large bowl. Add only enough wheat germ to hold patties together. Shape into patties. Place in a fry pan with a small amount of oil and sauté until lightly browned. Can be served with TOMATO SAUCE.

Yield: Serves 4

TOFU DISHES

TOFU VEGETABLES CASSEROLE

1 medium-sized eggplant (1 pound)
1 pound zucchini, about 4 of them
1 pound TOFU, drained
1/4 cup oil
2 T. tamari (soy sauce)

1½ T. honey
2 large tomatoes, sliced
3 cups TOMATO SAUCE
3 cups shredded Mozzarella cheese

Cut eggplant lengthwise into 1/2" thick slices. Cut zucchini in slanting slices about 1/4" thick. Slice tofu into little cubes. Brush eggplant slices on both sides with about 2 tablespoons of the oil. Arrange the slices in a single layer in a shallow baking dish. Bake eggplant in a 425° oven for 20 minutes or until tender. Meanwhile combine the tamari and honey together in a small bowl. Heat a skillet with the remaining oil over medium heat. Add tofu slices and cook, turning once, until lightly browned. Pour the tamari and honey mixture into pan. When sauce bubbles, carefully turn tofu to coat both sides. Remove pan from heat. Place half of the eggplant in a well-greased 9" x 13" baking pan, then layer half of the zucchini slices over eggplant. Place over top of this 1 tomato, sliced. Spread 3/4 cup of the tomato sauce over top. Arrange all tofu strips in the casserole and cover with 1½ cups of cheese; spread over another 3/4 cup of sauce. Top with a layer of remaining eggplant, zucchini slices and other tomato, sliced. Spread with remaining tomato sauce. Refrigerate if made ahead. Bake for 40 minutes in a 350° oven. Remove from oven and sprinkle remaining mozzarella cheese over top. Place back in oven and cook for 10 minutes.

Yield: 8 servings

SWEET AND SOUR TOFU AND VEGIES

1 T. arrowroot powder and 2 T. water
2/3 cups pineapple chunks with unsweetened juice
1/4 cup water
1 T. cider vinegar
1/4 tsp. vegetable seasoning
1 T. honey
2 T. tamari (soy sauce)

1/4-1/2 tsp. ginger, ground
2 T. oil
1 medium onion, chopped
1 large carrot, sliced thinly
3/4 pound TOFU, cut into chunks
1 green pepper, chopped
2 celery stalks, sliced at a diagonal
1 cup broccoli flowerets
1/8 cup raw cashews

Dissolve the arrowroot powder in the water, add 1/4 cup pineapple juice, 1/4 cup water, vinegar, vegetable seasoning, honey, tamari and ginger. Set aside. Heat the oil in a wok or large skillet over high heat. Add the onion and stir until strong onion smell starts to go away. Then add carrot and stir a few times. Add tofu and cook until lightly browned. Then add green pepper, celery, and broccoli and cook for about 1 minute. Reduce heat to medium and cook, covered, until carrots are partly softened, about 4 minutes. Remove cover and add pineapple chunks and the arrowroot/pineapple juice mixture. Cook for about 4 minutes, stirring frequently, until the mixture thickens. Sprinkle with cashew and serve over brown rice or noodles.

Yield: Serves 4

TOFUBURGERS

1 cup bulgur wheat
2 cups water
1 pound TOFU
2 eggs, beaten
1 medium onion, finely minced
1/2 green pepper, chopped
1 celery stalk, chopped
1/2 cup Cheddar cheese

2 T. tamari (soy sauce)
1½ tsp. basil
1/2 tsp. oregano
3/4 tsp. garlic powder
2 T. Parmesan cheese
1½-2½ cups whole wheat flour
Wheat germ

Bring water to a boil, add bulgur, simmer with lid ajar for 15 minutes or until all water is absorbed. Meanwhile, mash tofu with eggs in a large bowl, add remaining ingredients except bulgur wheat, flour and wheat germ. Mix well. Mix cooked bulgur with tofu mixture and stir until cool enough to handle. Add enough flour to form patties—they will be a little sticky. Form into patties about 1/2"-3/4" thick. Roll in wheat germ and either bake in a 350° oven for 30 minutes or fry in oil until brown on both sides.

Yield: 15 burgers

MEXICAN DISHES

CHALUPAS

1 T. oil
1 medium onion, chopped
1 cup TOMATO SAUCE
6 T. SALSA sauce
3 cups cooked, diced chicken
2½ cups pinto beans, mashed in a
    blender with 2 T. SALSA added
1 large clove garlic, minced

2 cups shredded Cheddar cheese
6 CORN TORTILLAS
GUACAMOLE
2 large tomatoes, diced
Shredded lettuce
Alfalfa sprouts
1 large onion, diced
1 cup SOUR CREAM or YOGURT
1/3 cup sunflower seeds

Sauté onion in the oil until golden brown. Add tomato sauce and 4 table-spoons salsa sauce. Simmer, uncovered, stirring often until slightly thickened (about 5 minutes). Add chicken, cover and set aside. In a baking dish combine beans, garlic, 2 tablespoons salsa and 1 cup shredded cheese. Mix well. Place uncovered beans in the oven. Pour chicken mixture into another baking dish and place this also into oven uncovered. Bake at 350° for 30 minutes. Drop tortillas one at a time onto a skillet with a small amount of oil, until softened. Remove and drain, wrap in foil to keep pliable. When ready to serve, spread tortillas with beans, guacamole and chicken mixture. Add tomatoes, shredded lettuce, sprouts, the remaining 1 cup of cheese, onion and sour cream or yogurt. Sprinkle on sunflower seeds. Serve with an extra dish of salsa on the side.

Yield: Serves 6

CHILI RELLENO CASSEROLE

2 cups coarsely crushed TORTILLA
    CHIPS
8-10 whole green chili peppers,
    split and seeded
2½ cups shredded Jack cheese
1 large avocado, diced

3 T. diced onion
6 eggs, beaten
1/2 cup milk
1/2 tsp. cumin
1/4 tsp. chili powder
1/2 tsp. vegetable seasoning

Grease a 7" x 11" baking dish. Place 1 cup of the tortilla chips on the bottom of the baking dish. Place the chili peppers on top of the chips, then 1½ cups of cheese over the chili peppers, the avocado over this, and sprinkle the onion over the avocado. Mix together the eggs, milk, cumin, chili powder and vegetable seasoning. Pour this mixture over the ingredients in the baking dish. Top with the other cup of chips and remaining cheese. Bake at 350° for 30 minutes.

Yield: Serves 4

BURRITOS

Filling:

2 cups cooked kidney beans, mashed
2 cups cooked pinto beans, mashed
1 large, finely grated carrot
1 stalk celery, finely chopped
1 medium onion, finely chopped
1 garlic clove, minced
2 chopped green chili peppers

1 tsp. cumin
1/4 tsp. kelp
1 tsp. chili powder
1/8 tsp. thyme
1 tsp. vegetable seasoning
Dash of cayenne
TOMATO JUICE

12 FLOUR TORTILLAS
Condiments:
Grated Cheddar cheese
Thinly sliced tomatoes
Thinly sliced onion

SALSA sauce
GUACAMOLE

Place all of the filling ingredients in a large skillet and simmer gently for 20 minutes. Stir frequently and add enough tomato juice to keep the mixture from sticking. When it is finished cooking it should have a pasty consistency. While the beans are cooking, place the tortillas in a skillet with a small amount of oil. Cook until tortillas become soft and pliable. Place cooked bean mixture in the center of each tortilla and add the condiments of your choice. Roll the tortillas up snugly and serve with a bowl of salsa sauce.

Yield: Serves 4-6

Variation:

Instead of rolling the tortillas up, leave them flat and just top it all off with alfalfa sprouts.

MEATLESS TACO

12 CORN TORTILLAS

Oil

Filling:

2 T. oil
1 cup green onions, chopped
3 small zucchini, diced small
1/2 green pepper, chopped

1 cup fresh mushrooms, sliced
1/4 cup chopped walnuts or sunflower
  seeds
1/4 cup ENCHILADA SAUCE

Topping:

2 cups Jack or Cheddar cheese
1 ripe avocado, diced

2 cups alfalfa sprouts
SOUR CREAM or plain YOGURT

Fry tortillas in a small amount of oil, one at a time, over medium high heat. It should be about 1½ minutes per side. Using tongs, bend in half during the last few seconds of frying to form a pocket shape. Hold desired shape with tongs until crisp. Remove and drain. If you want a softer taco shell, fry only 10 seconds on each side. Now start the filling, by sautéing in oil the onion, zucchini, green pepper, mushrooms and walnuts. Add the sauce and cook for about 4 minutes. Spoon the hot vegetable mixture into each shell and top with cheese, avocado, sprouts and a spoonful of sour cream or yogurt.

Yield: 12 tacos

TAMALE BEAN PIE

Filling:

1 T. oil	2 tsp. chili powder
1 medium onion, chopped	1 tsp. cumin
1 clove garlic, minced	1/2 tsp. vegetable seasoning
1/2 cup chopped green pepper	2 T. sliced black olives
2 cups stewed tomatoes, plus juice	2 cups cooked pinto beans
1½ cups kernel corn	

Crust:

3/4 cup stone-ground cornmeal	2 eggs, beaten lightly
2½ cups milk	1 cup grated Jack cheese
1 T. oil	

To make filling, heat oil in a large skillet. Sauté the onion, garlic and green pepper for a few minutes. Add all the rest of the ingredients except for the beans. Simmer, uncovered, stirring occasionally to break up the tomatoes, for 10–15 minutes. Add the beans and continue to simmer while making the crust. To make the crust, combine the cornmeal and 1/2 cup of milk and let sit for a few minutes. Bring the remaining milk and oil to a boil. Slowly add the cornmeal mixture, stirring constantly, and simmer until thick. Remove from heat and quickly stir in beaten eggs until they are well blended. Also add 3/4 cup of the cheese and mix until the cheese is melted. Spoon half of the crust mixture into the bottom of a greased 10" square baking dish. Cover with the filling mixture and then spoon on the remaining crust mixture and spread to cover. Sprinkle with the remaining cheese. Bake in a 350° oven for 40 minutes. The crust will stay soft like cornmeal mush.

Yield: Serves 6

ENCHILADA CASSEROLE

5 FLOUR TORTILLAS	1 cup chopped celery
3-3/4 cups ENCHILADA SAUCE	1/4 cup chopped green pepper
2 cups cooked brown rice	2 cups grated Cheddar cheese
3 cups REFRIED BEANS	

Place a small amount of oil in a skillet and add tortillas, one at a time. Cook on both sides until soft. Combine 1 cup of sauce with the rice and mix well. Place the rice in the bottom of a 2 quart rectangular baking dish. Place in the center of each tortilla, the bean mixture, then spoon some sauce over it. Add celery, green pepper, and some grated cheese. Roll up and place seam side down on top of the rice in the baking dish. After you have all five tortillas lined in the dish, pour the rest of the sauce over all of it. Top with the remaining cheese. Cover with foil and bake at 350° for 30 minutes.

Yield: Serves 6

BEANS AND PASTA

CHAPTER 7

Legumes (beans, peas and lentils) are the best buy for your money. They average 30 to 40 cents a pound, and each pound can give you up to 10 servings. They furnish you with variety in your meals as there are 25 different legumes and so many different combinations, whereas there are only four to five types of meats. Most legumes contain 20–30% protein. Soybeans have an even higher percentage. They also contain B vitamins, calcium, phosphorus, magnesium and iron. They are a good source of fiber, which helps keep the foods moving through your system. Meat is not able to do that properly because it lacks the fiber.

The dried legumes can be stored without refrigeration for long-term storage. If stored properly they can be stored up to 10 years. Once cooked they can keep in the refrigerator up to 10 days. You can even freeze the cooked beans. Just drain the liquid and place them in plastic bags. When you remove from the freezer they are ready to pop into soups, salads and main dishes.

What to do with the legumes:

1. Serve as an accompaniment with a main dish. Add sautéed onion, garlic and mushrooms and season with Italian or Mexican herbs and tomatoes.

2. Serve cold—marinated in oil and vinegar and use as a salad.

3. Add to soups for a protein packed meal.

4. Use as a main course in a meal as a casserole, loaf or burger.

As I mentioned, legumes are a very good source of protein, but they are an "incomplete" protein. Protein is made up of 22 amino acids. Eight of the amino acids can not be manufactured by the body so you have to get them in the foods you eat. You have to get them at the same time and in the proper balance so your body can manufacture protein properly. If an amino acid is lacking, or too low, it is called an "incomplete" protein.

Complete proteins are fish, meat, chicken, eggs and dairy products, plus soybeans. Incomplete proteins are legumes, grains, nuts and seeds. You can combine a complete and an incomplete protein to get the proper proportions of amino acids that are needed in your body. An example would be macaroni and cheese. Or you can combine two incomplete ones to get a complete protein—such as peanut better and whole wheat bread.

Following is a chart that will help you match up the different foods that will go together to give you a complete protein. For further details on this subject and correct proportions, see the book *Diet for a Small Planet* by Frances Moore Lappé.

COMBINATION CHART

Wheat	and	Milk
Wheat	and	Beans
Wheat	and	Rice
Wheat	and	Sesame Seeds
Rice	and	Beans
Rice	and	Wheat
Rice	and	Milk
Rice	and	Sesame Seeds
Beans	and	Rice
Beans	and	Wheat
Beans	and	Milk
Beans	and	Sesame Seeds
Beans	and	Corn
Corn	and	Soy Products
Corn	and	Beans
Corn	and	Milk
Potato	and	Milk
Peanuts	and	Milk
Peanuts	and	Sunflower Seeds

HELPFUL HINTS

- Add a tablespoon of oil to the cooking water. This will reduce boilovers and will also help soften beans quickly.

- Do beans give you gas? Try this method of cooking the beans: Presoak the beans for at least 3 hours. Throw the soaking water away. Add boiling water to cover and cook for at least 30 minutes. Discard this water. Add fresh water and continue cooking for the required period of time. This will rid the beans of trisaccharides which is what causes the gas, although you may lose some vitamins and minerals using this method.

- 1½ cups of dried beans will serve six people.

- Most of the dried beans increase in volume and double their size.

- Enhance the flavor of the beans by adding onions, garlic and herbs to the cooking water.

- When you soak the beans overnight, be sure to refrigerate otherwise they will ferment.

- Make up a big batch of beans and freeze. Thaw quickly by placing the container in hot water. Use as you would any freshly cooked beans.

- When cooking bean flakes, the skins from the flakes may rise to the top; just stir them back in.

- Mashing beans is a lot easier when the beans are hot.

- To purée the beans, place hot beans in a blender and add a little cooking water and blend.

- One cup cooked soybeans yields just about 1 cup soybean purée or pulp.

- Add one cup cooked and mashed soybeans to your ground beef loaf and use as an inexpensive meat extender.

- Freezing soybeans after soaking will lessen cooking time.

- Use any leftover beans in salads, bean patties or loaves, in soups or make a sandwich spread out of them.

- Pasta is nutritious as well as delicious. Make your own pasta by using any of the whole grain.

- When making your own pasta, make up an extra batch and freeze the dough. When you want some fresh pasta, thaw and roll it out.

- Homemade pasta does not take as long to cook as prepackaged pasta. Usually cooks in just minutes.

- Do not add too much sauce or cheese to the pasta. Add just enough to coat the pasta, otherwise you will end up with soupy pasta.

- Add 1 tablespoon oil to the pasta cooking water. Will help prevent it from foaming over.

- When pasta is through cooking, drain and run cold water over it. Then add a little oil to keep it separated.

- Homemade noodles have a shorter storage life than store bought ones. Do not store for more than a few weeks.

- If you want to make a protein pasta, substitute one cup soy flour for one cup whole wheat flour in your recipe.

TIMETABLE FOR COOKING BEANS

(1 cup dried beans will equal 2½–3 cups cooked beans)

	Beans	Regular Cooking Water (cups)	Time	Pressure Cooker Water (cups)	Time
1 cup	Black beans	4	1½ hours	3	30 minutes
1 cup	Black-eyed peas	3	1 hour	2½	30 minutes
1 cup	Garbanzos (chickpeas)	4	3 hours	3	45 minutes
1 cup	Great Northern	4	1½ hours	3	30 minutes
1 cup	Kidney beans	3	1 hour	2½	25 minutes
1 cup	Lentils	3	45 minutes	2½	10 minutes
1 cup	Limas	2	1½ hours	2	20 minutes
1 cup	Navy beans	3	1½ hours	2½	25 minutes
1 cup	Pinto beans	3	1½ hours	2½	30 minutes
1 cup	Red beans	3	1½ hours	2½	30 minutes
1 cup	Soybeans	4	2-3 hours	3	45 minutes
1 cup	Split peas	3	45 minutes	2½	15 minutes
1 cup	Soy grits	2	4-6 minutes	Do not cook in a pressure cooker	
1 cup	Bean flakes	2	45 minutes to 1 hour	Do not cook in a pressure cooker	

Notes: Black beans and soybeans tend to foam up and clog the pressure cooker's vent. Should be cooked over a very low heat.

No need to soak beans if you are going to cook them in a pressure cooker.

Do not fill pressure cooker more than 3/4 full when cooking beans.

Lentils, split peas and pinto beans do not need to be presoaked when using the traditional method of cooking.

TRADITIONAL METHOD:

Wash beans and remove pebbles or bad beans. Soak beans overnight or for at least 8 hours. In the morning, bring soaking water to a boil, add 1 tablespoon oil and slowly add the beans. Reduce heat and simmer beans partially covered for required time. Make sure beans are covered with water during the entire cooking period.

SHORT-CUT METHOD:

Instead of soaking overnight, bring the beans and water to a boil. Cover and remove from the heat. Let sit at least an hour. After this period of time, cook using the regular cooking schedule.

BLACK BEANS (Black Turtle Beans)

Used in South American and Mediterranean dishes. High in B vitamins, calcium and potassium. Nourishing, filling and full of flavor. You can use these hearty beans in salads, stews, casseroles and side dishes, and, of course, for that old-time favorite, Black Bean Soup.

BEANS AND RICE CON QUESO

1½ cups raw brown rice
1/2 cup black beans or black-eyed peas
3 cloves garlic, minced
1 large onion, chopped
2 T. oil

1/2 pound COTTAGE CHEESE thinned with 1/4 cup milk
3½ cups chredded Jack cheese
4 green chili peppers, seeded and chopped

Separately cook brown rice and beans until tender. Combine in a large bowl and set aside. Sauté the garlic and onion in the oil for 2 minutes. Mix together the rice-bean mixture, garlic, onion and chili pepper. Combine the cottage cheese with 3 cups of the Jack cheese. Layer these two mixtures in a greased, shallow 12-cup casserole dish. End with the rice-bean mixture. Bake in a 350° oven for 30 minutes. Remove at this time and sprinkle with the remaining 1/2 cup of cheese. Place back in oven for 3 minutes.

Yield: Serves 6

BLACK-EYED PEAS (Cow Peas)

They are a small, oval-shaped bean that are creamy in color with a black spot on them. Originated in Asia and have become popular in many other countries. Probably best known in Southern cookery here in the U.S. Use in stews, soups and part of a main dish.

GARBANZO BEANS (Chick Peas)

A traditional food in the Middle East, especially for the dishes HUMMUS and FALAFEL. Packed with protein, minerals and vitamins. Has a nut-like flavor that makes it great just as a snack by itself (NAHIT). Or, serve as a main dish, marinated in salads and in vegetable recipes.

GARBANZO CASSEROLE

1 onion, chopped
2 cloves garlic
2 T. oil
4 medium-sized carrots, sliced
2 celery stalks, chopped
2 cups cabbage
2 cups cooked garbanzo beans

2 cups cooked kidney beans
2 cups stewed tomatoes, plus juice
1½ tsp. vegetable seasoning
1/2 tsp. basil
1 tsp. thyme
1/4 tsp. cayenne
2 T. tamari (soy sauce)

In a large Dutch oven, sauté the onion and garlic in oil until golden. Add the carrots, celery and cabbage and cook for 5 minutes. Add the remaining ingredients and stir to combine. Cover with the lid and bake at 350° for 1 hour.

Yield: Serves 8

GREAT NORTHERN BEANS

They are a large white bean, and an excellent source of protein—twice as much as cereal grains—and iron and thiamine. Try them in your favorite baked bean dish or experiment with adding them to soups, salads and casseroles.

KIDNEY BEANS

They are red and shaped like a kidney. An outstanding source of vitamin B_1. They are also a good source of vitamin A and are high in beneficial minerals. Used frequently in Mexican cooking. Place in salads, soups like CHILI, and makes a tasty vegetable dish.

KIDNEY BEAN SALAD

2 cups cooked kidney beans
1/2 cup sliced celery
1/2 cup coarsely chopped walnuts
2 T. chopped onion
1/8 cup MAYONNAISE

1/8 cup YOGURT, plain
1 T. frozen apple juice concentrate, unsweetened
1 cup diced, unpeeled apples
1/3 cup diced Cheddar cheese

Combine the beans, celery, walnuts, onion, mayonnaise, yogurt and apple juice. Mix well. Cover and chill. Stir in apples and cheese. Serve in a lettuce-lined bowl.

Yield: Serves 8

LENTILS

Lentils are an ancient food that is widely used in the Middle East and South America. In the Bible Esau sold his birthright to Jacob for some lentil stew (Genesis 25:34). They are disc-shaped and flat. Most nutritious of all legumes except for the soybean. High levels of protein and carbohydrates, an outstanding source of vitamins B and A. Serve as a base for one-meal dishes. Makes tasty soups and stews, loaves and patties. The lentil does not need soaking before cooking, plus it cooks in a short time.

CHEESE AND LENTIL MANICOTTI

2/3 cup dried lentils
2 cups water
1½ tsp. vegetable seasoning
1 bay leaf
1/4 tsp. kelp
1/4 tsp. sage
1/4 tsp. marjoram

1/4 tsp. thyme
2½ cups COTTAGE CHEESE
1/4 cup Parmesan cheese
1/4 cup fresh parsley, chopped
2 cups SPAGHETTI SAUCE
1 (3.75 ounce) package manicotti
   noodles

In a saucepan, mix lentils, water, vegetable seasoning, bay leaf, kelp, sage, marjoram, and thyme. Heat to boiling. Reduce heat, and simmer about 20 minutes until lentils are tender. Remove from heat. Stir in the cottage cheese, Parmesan and parsley. Place 1/2 cup of the spaghetti sauce in the bottom of a 13" x 9" baking dish. Fill each manicotti noodle with cottage cheese mixture. Arrange in baking dish. Stir in the rest of the spaghetti sauce into remaining cottage cheese mixture. Pour over manicotti. Bake at 375° for 50-60 minutes, until tender.

Yield: Serves 4

LIMA BEANS

This is the bean with the delicate flavor. Like all beans, it is one of the best sources of protein. Better use of this protein is achieved by combining grains and limas in the same meal. There are large and baby limas.

NAVY BEANS

This is the classic "baked bean." Excellent for hearty soups, as an extender for other foods, and in traditional bean recipes.

BAKED BEANS

1 pound Navy beans
2 quarts water
2 T. oil
1 onion, chopped
1 clove garlic, minced
1 cup grated carrots
1/2 cup chopped celery
1 tsp. dry mustard

1 tsp. vegetable seasoning
1/4 cup molasses, unsulfured
1 T. cider vinegar
1/4 cup TOMATO SAUCE
1/4 tsp. allspice
1 T. tamari (soy sauce)
Bean liquid to cover all ingredients

Soak the beans overnight in the 2 quarts of water. Cook the soaked beans until tender, in the same soaking liquid. Sauté the onion, garlic, carrots and celery in the oil until the onion is tender. Combine in a 2 quart casserole dish the drained cooked beans, the sautéed vegetables, and all the rest of the ingredients. Cover and bake in a 300° oven for 2-3 hours. Add more liquid if necessary. Uncover during the last half of the baking time.

Yield: Serves 6-8

PEAS

Peas come in two different colors—green and yellow. The green ones have a more distinct flavor than the yellow ones. They are an excellent source of low cost protein. Also rich in A and B vitamins and high in beneficial trace minerals—calcium, phosphorus, potassium and iron.

Whole Green Peas:—Serve just plain with butter, place in delicious vegetable dishes, and use in soups and stews. Have to be soaked before cooking.

Split Peas:—Try serving as a vegetable, in stews, dips and great for your SPLIT PEA SOUP.

SPLIT PEA AND ALMOND ROAST

1 cup cooked split peas
1 cup diced celery
1/2 cup diced green pepper
1 cup raw chopped almonds
1 cup oatmeal, cooked
1 tsp. vegetable seasoning

1 cup water
1 T. onion, minced
2 T. butter
1/2 tsp. each basil and dill
1 T. tamari (soy sauce)

Combine all the ingredients together and mix well. Pour into a casserole dish and bake at 350° for 1 hour.

Yield: Serves 4-6

PINTO BEANS

A relative of the kidney bean, but it is beige-colored with speckles. This bean has a 22% protein level and is rich in iron and trace minerals. Used in the same recipes you would use kidney beans. This has been a popular bean for ranch-style cooking. Your family will enjoy pinto beans in chili, burritos and refried beans.

REFRIED BEANS (Frijoles)

1½ cups cooked kidney beans
1½ cups cooked pinto beans
1 large onion, chopped
1 clove garlic, minced
1/2 cup green pepper, diced

1/4 cup SALSA sauce
1/2 tsp. cumin
1/2 tsp. chili powder
Dash cayenne
1/4 cup grated Cheddar cheese

Heat oil in a skillet and add onion, garlic and green pepper. Sauté for a few minutes. Add the beans, salsa, cumin, chili powder and cayenne. While cooking, mash the beans with the back of your spoon. Cook for 10 minutes stirring occasionally. If too dry, add a little of the bean liquid so beans will not burn. Remove from heat and add cheese. When cheese is melted you can serve this as a side dish or use in tostadas and other Mexican dishes.

Yield: 3 cups

SOYBEANS

This is nature's super bean with protein levels close to 40%. Compared to other beans, soybeans contain more high-quality protein, small amounts of sugars and no starch. High in calcium, B vitamins, vitamins A, D, and E, the unsaturated fatty acids and lecithin. A 3½-ounce serving of cooked soybeans has about 130 calories and costs only pennies. The bean can be used throughout your daily diet in side dishes, loaves, soups, stews and salads. There are many forms the soybean can take, and the following list will acquaint you with some of those forms.

Green Soybean: Use them as you would limas; put very young ones in raw salads, or steam them with herbs.

Soybean Oil: Use for salads, cooking and baking.

Soy Flour: Made from beans that have been cooked and then dried before they are ground. It has a nut-like taste. It will help boost the nutritive value of your baking recipes. Has almost no starch, so it can not be used as thickening. Also has no gluten, so do not replace more than 2 tablespoons per cup of flour in recipes that call for yeast. For recipes that do not contain the yeast you can replace up to 1/4 cup of soy flour per cup. It browns more quickly so lower baking temperature 25°.

Soy Sauce: Made from the whole soybean, wheat, salt and well water that has been fermented for 12-18 months. The all-natural soy sauce is imported from Japan. Also called tamari and shoyu. Used to season vegetables, soups, gravies and sauces.

Soy Grits: Crushed raw soybeans. Can be used in place of nuts in bakery items, add to stews as a thickener, in loaves to help bind the ingredients, and as an ingredient in granola.

Soy Flakes: Made by a process that cooks and compresses the whole bean to flakes. Can be added to anything from desserts to casseroles. Cooking time is less than the dried bean. Usually cooks in 45 minutes to 1 hour.

Lecithin: This food supplement is made from the soybean. It works to help control cholesterol build-up.

Soy Milk: Use as you would regular milk. If allergic to cow's milk try substituting soy milk in your diet.

Tofu: Also called soybean curd. Has a texture similar to cream cheese. It is made from soybean milk with a solidifier added such as vinegar or lemon juice. Used for centuries in Oriental cooking. A very good source of low-cost protein. It is low in calories (4 ounces is 88 calories) and saturated fats, and is entirely free of cholesterol. High in iron, phosphorus, B vitamins and vitamin E. When fresh it is rather tasteless, but when prepared properly it is delicious. It can be served chilled topped with tamari and green onions, stir-fried with vegetables, made into a dip, salad dressings, used in place of cottage cheese, as a sandwich spread, burger and even pancakes. The ways to use tofu are unlimited. Throughout the book you will find recipes containing tofu. Check the Index. You can find this inexpensive food in grocery stores, health food stores and Oriental food stores. Always keep the tofu covered with water. Change the water daily and you should be able to keep it refrigerated for 7-10 days. If you would like to make it yourself, the following is a recipe for homemade tofu:

HOMEMADE TOFU

1 quart SOY MILK   1 cup lemon juice or cider vinegar

Bring soybean milk to a boil in a large pot, reduce heat and simmer for 7 minutes. Let cool until temperature of milk drops to 180°. Add the lemon juice or vinegar and stir. Let sit undisturbed for 15 minutes. It will curdle in that time. Pour into a cheesecloth bag. Discard the liquid. Dip the bag into cold water several times to wash away the excess acid. Place the bag in a colander and allow to drain for 1 hour. Press out remaining liquid from tofu by placing a plate on top of it and pressing. Refrigerate until mold is firm enough to cut. Wrap in cheesecloth, place in a bowl, cover with cold water and refrigerate. Now it is ready to use in your favorite recipe.

SOY MILK

1 pound dried soybeans   4 quarts water

Wash the dry soybeans and soak in 2 quarts cold water overnight. Discard the water. Place the soybeans into a blender and grind until fine. Place the ground beans into a cheesecloth bag and place in a pan containing 2 quarts lukewarm water. Using your hands, work pulp all around thoroughly for at least 10 minutes. Wring the bag out over the pan and then remove the soybean pulp. The liquid left is soy milk. Bring the milk to a boil, reduce heat and simmer for 15 minutes, stirring frequently. Cool and place in refrigerator.

SOFTENED SOY GRITS

To be used in loaves or patties, chili, stuffings or wherever you want a meal extender.

1 cup boiling VEGETABLE STOCK   1 cup uncooked soy grits

Soak the grits in the stock until all moisture is absorbed. Cool and store in a covered jar in the refrigerator. Add 1/4 cup to omelets, scrambled eggs, or soufflés. 1/2 cup to loaves and patties. Do not presoak if used in desserts.

SOY GRITS CROQUETTES

1 T. oil   1/2 tsp. vegetable seasoning
2 cups cooked soy grits   1 T. tamari (soy sauce)
1 cup cooked brown rice   1/2 tsp. oregano
5 T. minced onion   1 egg, beaten
1/3 cup chopped celery   1/2 cup whole wheat bread crumbs
1 tomato, diced

Brown the grits, rice, onion and celery in the oil, about 3 minutes. Add the tomato, seasoning, tamari and oregano to the mixture. Dip in beaten egg and then roll in the bread crumbs. Place in shallow greased pan and bake at 350° for about 30 minutes or until brown. Serve with gravy or TOMATO SAUCE.

Yield: Serves 6

BAKED SOYBEANS

4 cups soybeans, cooked   1/4 cup chopped green pepper
1 cup water soybeans were cooked in   1 tsp. dry mustard
1 onion, chopped fine   1 tsp. curry powder
1 cup tomato purée   1 tsp. garlic powder
3 T. molasses, unsulfured   1/4 cup fresh parsley, chopped

Combine all of the ingredients together thoroughly. Turn into a casserole dish. Cover and bake at 350° for 1½ hours.

Yield: Serves 6

SOYBEAN SALAD

2 cups cooked soybeans
1½ cups cooked lima beans
1 medium celery stalk, sliced
3 green onions, diced

12 cherry tomatoes, cut in half
4 hard-cooked eggs, diced
3 T. chopped fresh parsley

Dressing:

1 cup YOGURT, plain
1/2 cup buttermilk
1/4 cup crumbled blue cheese

1 tsp. dill
1 tsp. dry mustard
Vegetable seasoning to taste

Mix all of the salad ingredients together in a large bowl. To make the dressing, mix all of the ingredients together and then pour over the salad. Mix well and chill for 2 hours. Serve on alfalfa sprouts.

Yield: 6-8 servings

SOYBEAN CASSEROLE

2 cups soybeans, cooked
2 cups corn kernels, uncooked
1/4 cup grated Cheddar cheese
2 cups stewed tomatoes
1/2 cup chopped celery
1/4 cup VEGETABLE STOCK
2 T. tomato paste

3 T. oil
1 bay leaf
3 T. fresh chopped parsley
1/2 tsp. thyme
1/4 tsp. oregano
1/3 cup GRANOLA

Layer the soybeans, corn, cheese, tomatoes and celery in a casserole dish. Alternate the layers and repeat until all ingredients are used. Mix the stock, tomato paste, oil, bay leaf, parsley, thyme and oregano together. Pour this mixture over the casserole. Sprinkle the granola on the top. Bake at 350° for 30 minutes.

Yield: Serves 6

SOYBEAN PATTIES

2 cups cooked soybeans, mashed
1 cup rolled oats, uncooked
3/4 cup cooked brown rice
4 T. chopped onion
2 eggs, beaten
1 stalk celery, diced
4 T. chopped fresh parsley

2 T. TOMATO SAUCE
1 T. tamari (soy sauce)
1/4 tsp. each sage and marjoram
1 tsp. vegetable seasoning
2 T. sesame seeds
Wheat germ

Add all of the ingredients together except for the wheat germ. Add wheat germ to the mixture if it is too moist to hold together. Form into patties and roll in wheat germ. Place on a baking sheet and bake at 350° for 35 minutes.

Yield: 4 servings

PASTA

WHOLE WHEAT PASTA

4 cups whole wheat flour   1/3-1/2 cup water
4 large eggs

Mound flour on a work surface or in a large bowl and make a deep well in the center. Break eggs into well. Beat eggs lightly and stir in half of the water. Using a circular motion, begin to draw flour from the sides of the well. Add 2 tablespoons more water and continue mixing until all flour is moistened. Add more water, a tablespoon at a time if necessary. Use your hands to finish mixing when dough becomes stiff. Pat into a ball and knead a few times to help flour absorb liquid. Turn the dough onto a lightly floured board and knead dough until smooth and nonsticky, 5-7 minutes. Cover with wax paper and let rest for 30 minutes. Divide dough into four equal parts, then roll and cut 1 portion at a time. **To roll and cut by hand:** On a lightly floured surface, roll one portion out into a rectangle, about 1/16'' thick. After it is rolled out, let rest and dry, turning once, until dough has the feel and flexibility of soft leather. Dry for about 5 minutes; if dried too long dough will become brittle. Roll the dough up jelly roll fashion, then cut into the different widths depending on what noodle you want. **To dry noodles** as they are cut, sprinkle with flour if sticky, and hang them over a wood pole or lay them on a waxed paper surface. Let dry for 30 minutes. If you do not want to cook the noodles as soon as you make them, store the dried noodles in a plastic bag in the refrigerator for a couple of days. Or you can place them in the freezer up to 2 months.

To cook the noodles: Bring water to a boil, add about 1 tablespoon oil so they will not stick together. Add pasta and cook only 2-3 minutes for the smaller ones and 5-6 minutes for the larger noodles. The noodles should be *al dente* (firm to the bite). Keep them under the texture you want because noodles will continue to cook during the process of draining. If used right away, lift them out with a twirling motion with a long handled fork or slotted spoon. Let drip for a second and place on serving plate. Doing it this way will prevent pasta from becoming dry. If not going to be used right away, rinse in cold water as you drain pasta and toss with a little oil.

Size of noodles

Soup noodles: sliver thin   Fettuccine: 1/4'' wide
Spaghetti: 1/8'' wide   Lasagne: 2½'' and 4-6'' length
Stroganoff: 1/4'' wide

Variation:
Spinach Noodles: 1½ cups cooked fresh spinach that has been squeezed dry and chopped fine to equal 1/2 cup. Follow instructions for whole wheat pasta except stir the minced spinach in with the eggs and omit the water. Cooking time is about 2-3 minutes.

LASAGNE

3-4 cups SPAGHETTI SAUCE
12 whole wheat lasagne noodles
1/2 pound spinach, washed and
   chopped
1 cup COTTAGE CHEESE
1 egg

3 T. chopped fresh parsley
1 tsp. vegetable seasoning
3/4 cup Parmesan cheese, grated
1¾ cups Mozzarella, grated
3/4 cup Jack cheese, grated

Prepare sauce as directed per instructions from recipe. Meanwhile, cook noodles in water (with 1 tsp. of oil added) for about 10 minutes or until tender. Drain well. In a bowl combine the spinach, cottage cheese, egg, parsley, vegetable seasoning and 1/4 cup Parmesan cheese. In another bowl, combine the rest of the Parmesan cheese, Mozzarella and Jack. To assemble, spoon 3 tablespoons of the sauce into the bottom of a 9" x 13" baking pan. Cover the sauce with 4 of the noodles, then half of the cottage cheese mixture, a third of the mixed grated cheeses, and a third of the sauce. Make a second layer using another 4 noodles, the rest of the cottage cheese mixture, another third of the grated cheese, and another third of the sauce. Cover with the last 4 noodles and top with the rest of the sauce and grated cheese. Bake in a 350° oven for 40 minutes. Let stand for 15 minutes before cutting into squares.

Yield: 8-10 servings

FETTUCCINE ALFREDO

1 pound fettuccine noodles or
   spaghetti
1/2 cup butter

3/4 cup cream or milk
2 cups Parmesan cheese, grated
Vegetable seasoning and kelp to
   taste

Cook the fettuccine in boiling water until just tender. While the noodles are cooking, melt the butter in a saucepan over low heat. Add the cream or milk and cook just until warm. Drain the noodles and place in a bowl. Pour the butter and cream mixture over the noodles and begin tossing to mix. Add the cheese, seasoning and kelp and toss to mix all of these ingredients.

Yield: Serves 6

Variations:

Turkey or Chicken Fettuccine: Sauté 1/4 pound of sliced mushrooms and 3 tablespoons chopped onions in 1 tablespoon of oil. Add this mixture to the Fettuccine Alfredo. Also mix in 3 cups of cooked, cubed turkey or chicken. Pour all of this into a casserole dish and bake at 350° for 20 minutes.

Spinach Fettuccine: Follow the same recipe as the Turkey Fettuccine but in place of the turkey use 1 pound spinach, steamed and chopped.

Vegetable Fettuccine: To the Fettuccine Alfredo add 3 cups chopped vegetables. The types of vegetables are up to you. Place in a casserole and bake for 20 minutes at 350°.

SPAGHETTI SALAD

1 pound whole wheat spaghetti
1 T. oil
1½ pounds Mozzarella cheese
(6 cups), shredded
6 tomatoes, chopped
3 bunches watercress, finely chopped

2 garlic cloves, finely minced
1½ pounds fresh pea pods
2 cups fresh green peas
Vegetable seasoning to taste
Freshly grated Parmesan cheese

Cook spaghetti in large pot of boiling water with the oil until *al dente*. Drain well. Return to pot, add mozzarella and toss until cheese melts. Cheese will be gummy and will be in clumps but will break up as other ingredients are added. Cook over low heat 15 minutes. Remove from heat, add remaining ingredients except for the Parmesan cheese. Toss gently but thoroughly (using hands if necessary). Serve at room temperature. Pass bowl of Parmesan cheese separately.

Yield: 12 servings

NOODLING AROUND

8 ounces (4 cups) egg noodles
3 T. butter
1/2 cup sliced celery
3 T. whole wheat flour
2 cups milk
1/2 cup grated Muenster cheese
1/2 cup grated Cheddar cheese

1/4 tsp. vegetable seasoning
1/4 tsp. dry mustard
1/2 tsp. tamari (soy sauce)
1½ cups hot cooked broccoli
1/2 cup hot cooked corn
1/2 cup hot cooked carrots

Cook the noodles until tender and then drain. Melt butter in a saucepan; sauté celery until crisp tender. Blend in flour; stir in milk. Cook over medium heat, stirring constantly, until sauce boils. Add cheeses, vegetable seasoning, mustard and tamari. Cook and stir until cheese melts. Combine the noodles and vegetables. Pour CHEESE SAUCE over it all and mix well.

Yield: Serves 4

SPAGHETTI PIE

6 ounces whole wheat spaghetti
2 T. butter
1/3 cup grated Parmesan cheese
2 eggs, well beaten
2 cups SPAGHETTI SAUCE
3/4 cup chopped celery

2 cups sliced zucchini
1 cup COTTAGE CHEESE
1/4 cup fresh chopped parsley
3 T. Parmesan cheese
1/2 tsp. vegetable seasoning
1/2 cup shredded Mozzarella cheese

Cook spaghetti until it is tender but firm to the bite. Drain. Combine hot pasta with the butter, stirring until butter is melted. Add the Parmesan cheese and eggs. Toss to combine. Place spaghetti mixture in buttered 10" pie plate. Shape into a crust. Add to the prepared spaghetti sauce, the celery and zucchini. Mix together in a small bowl the cottage cheese, parsley, 3 tablespoons Parmesan cheese and vegetable seasoning. To assemble, spread the cottage cheese mixture over the bottom of the crust. Fill center with the tomato vegetable sauce. Bake 20 minutes at 350°. Remove from oven and sprinkle the Mozzarella cheese on top. Return to oven just until cheese melts, about 5 minutes. Serve immediately.

Yield: 6 servings

SPAGHETTI WITH BROCCOLI, TOMATOES AND WALNUTS

1 pound thin spaghetti or linguine
1/2 cup coarsely chopped walnuts
1/4 cup butter
2 T. oil
1 pint cherry tomatoes, stems
  removed
1 large clove garlic, minced

1/2 tsp. vegetable seasoning
1 tsp. basil
1 medium-sized bunch broccoli,
  cut into 1" pieces (about 6 cups),
  steamed
1/2-1 cup CHICKEN STOCK
1/2 cup grated Parmesan cheese
1/4 cup chopped fresh parsley

Start cooking pasta in boiling water. Toast walnuts 5 minutes in a 350° oven. Melt 2 tablespoons of the butter and all of the oil over medium heat in a skillet. Add the tomatoes and cook, stirring often, 5 minutes. Tomatoes should be tender, but still hold their shape. Stir in the garlic, vegetable seasoning and basil and cook 2 minutes longer. Remove from heat; cover and keep warm. Now drain the pasta. Return the pasta to the pot it was cooking in and add the broccoli and the remaining 2 tablespoons of butter. Toss to coat with butter. Add tomatoes, 1/2 cup of the stock, the cheese and parsley and toss to blend. Add more stock only if mixture seems dry. Place on the individual serving plates and sprinkle the walnuts on top. May add more Parmesan if desired.

Yield: 4 servings

VEGETABLE CARBONARA

2 T. oil
1/2 pound mushrooms, sliced
1 large onion, chopped
2 cloves garlic, minced
2 tsp. basil
1/2 tsp. vegetable seasoning
1 pound whole wheat noodles or
   spaghetti

1 cup lightly packed chopped
   parsley
1 raw carrot or zucchini, coarsely
   grated
2 cups fresh raw peas
1/4 cup melted butter
6 eggs, beaten
1½ cups grated Parmesan cheese

Sauté the mushrooms, onion and garlic in the oil until limp. Add basil and vegetable seasoning; keep warm. Cook the noodles until tender. Drain well. Top with the mushroom mixture, parsley, carrot or zucchini, and peas. Mix the melted butter into the noodles and vegetables and quickly blend by lifting pasta with two long forks. At once, pour in the eggs and continue to mix, quickly lifting and mixing the pasta to coat well with the eggs. Sprinkle in the cheese and mix again. Serve immediately.

Yield: 8 servings

STUFFED MACARONI SHELLS

1 package extra large shell macaroni
   (whole wheat or vegetable)
1/2 cup wheat germ
1/4 cup bran
2 cups COTTAGE CHEESE
1 cup grated Jack cheese
1/2 cup sesame seeds

6 T. milk
2 tsp. basil
1 tsp. tarragon
1/3 cup minced parsley
1/2 tsp. vegetable seasoning
2 cups TOMATO SAUCE
Grated Parmesan cheese

Cook shells in boiling water until tender, about 10 minutes. Drain and rinse in cold water. In a bowl mix together the wheat germ, bran, cottage cheese, Jack cheese, sesame seeds, milk, basil, tarragon, parsley and seasoning. Fill shells with this mixture. Pour half of the tomato sauce in the bottom of a 2 quart casserole dish. Place shells in the casserole on top of the sauce. Pour remaining sauce over the top. Sprinkle with Parmesan cheese. Bake at 375° for 20 minutes.

Yield: Serves 8

LINGUINE WITH CREAMY ZUCCHINI SAUCE

1 pound linguine or macaroni,
  whole wheat
1/3 cup oil
3 large cloves garlic, minced
2 cups Mozzarella cheese, shredded
1/2 cup freshly grated Parmesan cheese

1 pound fresh zucchini, scrubbed
  and coarsely grated
  (about 3 cups)
1/2 cup chopped fresh parsley
1/2 tsp. vegetable seasoning
1/4 tsp. kelp

Cook the linguine or macaroni until tender and then drain. Heat in a large saucepan the oil and garlic. Cook for 30 seconds. Add the cooked pasta and toss to coat with oil and garlic. Add cheeses and toss again. Add remaining ingredients and continue to toss over moderate heat until cheese and moisture from zucchini coat pasta with a light sauce. Serve immediately with additional cheese, if desired.

Yield: 4 servings

GRAINS AND CEREALS

CHAPTER 8

Grains and cereals have been the main source of food for many people throughout the world for centuries. In the U.S. we are familiar with rice, but it is white rice which has been stripped of its wheat germ and bran which contain all the essential vitamins and minerals. It is essentially a mass of carbohydrates. Try brown rice; it is tastier than white rice plus it contains all the vital nutrients that God gave us to sustain life.

The sugar-laden packaged cereals have also been stripped of nutrients. Producers say they are enriched, but they have been stripped of many of the nutrients, and only a small fraction have been replaced. Most of the fiber is removed during processing, and sugar and fats are added. Children eating these cereals become accustomed to heavy sweetening on their foods.

Cereal grains in their natural state have the much-needed fiber and also contain the vital vitamins and minerals that are needed in our diet. There are many tasty and nutritious grains and cereals available for your use. In this chapter different ones are described and ideas are given for preparing them. Experiment and see what grains and cereals you and your family prefer.

HELPFUL HINTS

- When you have leftover cereal add 1 cup to bread dough before kneading.
- Add vegetables and herbs, then shape into patties and broil.
- Make cereals into pudding.
- Freshly ground cereals should be stored in the refrigerator or freezer as they can spoil if left at room temperature more than 10 days.
- Sprinkle cooked grains with nuts, sunflower or sesame seeds.
- Add assorted chopped vegetables and cook along with the grains.

- To add extra protein, top the cooked grains with yogurt.

- Toppings for cooked cereals:

  | granola | fresh fruit | chopped nuts | yogurt |
  | seeds | raisins and dates | cinnamon and nutmeg | wheat germ |

- Try combining different grains. You end up with some interesting flavors.

- To keep cereals from getting wormy, place a couple of bay leaves in the container.

- When cooking your grains or cereals, make an extra batch (especially rice) and freeze. It will help in those hurried times when you do not have the time to wait for the grains or cereals to cook. Defrost and use as recipe calls for.

- Use bulgur wheat in place of brown rice in your recipe when you are hurried for time. Bulgur only takes 10–15 minutes to cook, whereas brown rice takes 40 minutes.

- Make sure nuts and grains are chewed well; it is better for your digestion.

- Save your leftover grains from dinner for breakfast. Serve with fresh juice, seed and nuts mixed in to give a real special treat.

- Tape the instructions for cooking grains and cereals in their containers. If someone other than yourself is using them they will know how to cook them without any measurement mistakes—plus fewer questions for you.

- Too much stirring makes the grain gummy. Stir only as suggested.

- Serve bulgur, millet, cornmeal or buckwheat dishes in place of potatoes.

- A blend of oat and soy flours makes a delicious coating for chicken.

- A combination of barley flour and oat flour makes a delicious pie crust.

COOKING GRAINS

	Grain	Water	Cooking Time	Yield
1 cup	Barley	4 cups	1 hour	4 cups
1 cup	Buckwheat	2 cups	15 minutes	2½ cups
1 cup	Bulgur	2 cups	20 minutes	2½ cups
1 cup	Cornmeal	3½-4 cups	30 minutes	2 cups
1 cup	Millet	4 cups	45 minutes	4 cups
1 cup	Oats	3 cups	15 minutes	2 cups
1 cup	Brown rice	2½ cups	45 minutes	3 cups
1 cup	Wild rice	3 cups	1½-2 hours	4 cups
1 cup	Rye	3 cups	1 hour	4 cups
1 cup	Triticale	3 cups	1 hour	4 cups
1 cup	Whole wheat berries	3 cups	1-2 hours	3 cups

1. Wash grains before you cook them.

2. Try sautéeing them first in a little oil until grains are brown. Add water and cook as directed.

3. Double boilers work well for cooking grains. Pressure cookers can also be used for whole grains but not for ones that have been broken up as they can get in the heat vents.

4. In the grinder you can coarsely grind the grains into "grits." It cuts their cooking time. Can also add an interesting texture to breads and burgers.

5. Can grind the grains, except for bulgur and wild rice, into "flours." Need to use a flour grinder for this.

6. Can buy grain "flakes." They cook in a shorter period of time than the whole grain.

BARLEY

A favorite with ancient civilizations. It is mentioned in the Bible 32 times. In John 6:9-11 the young boy gives the Lord five barley loaves and two small fish. This sweet, nutty flavored grain lacks gluten which must be added for baking. (For baking, one part barley to five parts wheat flour.) Puts new flavor appeal in soups, casseroles, pilaf, and puddings. Can serve as a substitute for rice and millet in recipes. High in minerals and protein.

COOKED BARLEY

1 cup barley   4 cups water

Bring the 4 cups of water to a boil. Slowly stir in barley and stir until it returns to a boil. Turn heat down, cover and cook for 1 hour. Can grind to a flour and mix with water or milk for a porridge. Serve cooked barley with dried fruit, raisins, honey or grated orange rind.

Yield: 4 cups

BARLEY-RICE PILAF

2 T. oil
1 medium onion, finely chopped
1 cup sliced fresh mushrooms
1 cup chopped celery
1 cup barley, uncooked
1/2 cup raw brown rice

5 cups boiling water or stock
1/2 cup chopped dried apricots
1/3 cup chopped almonds
1/3 cup raisins
1 tsp. cinnamon

In a large skillet, heat the oil and sauté the onion, mushrooms and celery. Sauté until the onion is transparent. Remove to another dish. Sauté in the same pan, the barley and rice. Do not allow it to burn or brown, just cook for about 3 minutes. Add the boiling water or stock to the barley and rice. Add also the sautéed vegetables and remaining ingredients. Cover and simmer on low heat for about 1 hour. Stir mixture carefully and then replace lid and allow to stand 15 minutes before you serve it. Serve as a side dish or as a stuffing.

Yield: Serves 4-6

BARLEY LOAF

1 cup cooked barley
1 cup cooked millet
1/2 cup cooked oatmeal
1/2 cup ground sunflower seeds
1/2 cup water
1/4 cup sesame seeds
1 T. chopped fresh parsley

1 T. onion powder
2 T. PEANUT BUTTER
1/2 tsp. celery seed
1/4 tsp. thyme
1 T. tamari (soy sauce)
1/2 tsp. vegetable seasoning

Mix all of the ingredients together. Spoon mixture into a greased loaf pan and bake for 1 hour at 350°. Remove from oven and let sit for 15 minutes before serving. Great served with TOMATO SAUCE over top.

Yield: Serves 4

BUCKWHEAT

Also called groats and kasha. Was very popular a hundred years ago. Today used mostly for buckwheat cakes. This breakfast treat is high-quality protein with fewer calories than wheat, corn or rice. Can also be used as a side dish for a casserole, added to soups, or ground into flour for bread.

BUCKWHEAT GROATS (KASHA)

1 cup buckwheat groats
1 egg, beaten

2 cups boiling water

Place the groats in a skillet and stir in beaten egg, stirring constantly over a medium high heat. After each grain is separate and dry add boiling water. Reduce heat, cover tightly and steam 30 minutes. Serve with butter.

Yield: 2½ cups

KASHA AND MUSHROOMS

1/2 cup uncooked kasha (buckwheat)
1 egg, beaten
1 cup CHICKEN STOCK or water
1/4 tsp. kelp
1/4 tsp. vegetable seasoning
1/8 tsp. thyme

1/2 cup diced onion
1/2 cup diced celery
1 T. oil
1/2 cup sliced mushrooms
1/2 cup cooked whole wheat
   macaroni

Combine the egg and the kasha well to coat all the grains. Heat a skillet and brown the kasha until each kernel is separated. Bring the stock or water to a boil and add to kasha along with the seasoning. Cook very slowly until all the liquid is absorbed and the kasha is fluffy. In another skillet sauté the onions and celery in the oil. Add the sliced mushrooms and continue to sauté for about 6 minutes. In another pot, cook the macaroni. When the kasha is cooked, add all three mixtures together. Can be served as a side dish or as a main dish topped with YOGURT and sunflower seeds.

Yield: Serves 4

KASHA PATTIES

1 T. oil
1/2 onion, finely chopped
1/2 cup chopped celery
1 garlic clove, minced

2 cups cooked kasha (buckwheat)
1 egg
3 T. chopped sunflower seeds

Sauté lightly the onion, celery and garlic in the oil. Add this sautéed mixture to the kasha, egg and sunflower seeds. Form into patties and sauté on a hot griddle until both sides are browned. Serve with MUSHROOM GRAVY or in PITA (Bible) BREAD as a sandwich.

Yield: Serves 4-6

BULGUR WHEAT

Bulgur or cracked wheat is a staple of many Eastern countries. Made from precooked and dried wheat that is coarsely cracked, it's rich in iron, calcium, B vitamins and protein. In the supermarket it is known as Ala. Other spellings for it are: bulghur, bulgor, bulgar, bulger and boulgur. Use the same way as you would brown rice, but it does not take as long to cook. Use in soups, casseroles, and in salads.

COOKED BULGUR

1 cup bulgur wheat
2 tsp. oil

2 cups VEGETABLE STOCK or
water

Sauté bulgur in oil until grains are browned. Add stock or water and bring to a boil. Reduce heat, cover and simmer for 15 minutes.

Yield: 2½ cups

Variation:
To serve as a breakfast cereal, add honey, raisins, sunflower seeds and milk.

BULGUR PUDDING

2 cups cooked bulgur
2 eggs, beaten
2 cups milk

1/8 cup unsweetened frozen apple
juice concentrate
3/4 cup chopped dates
1/2 cup chopped walnuts

Mix all of the ingredients together and pour into a 1½ quart casserole dish. Cover and bake at 325° for 1 hour.

Yield: 6 servings

BULGUR PILAF

2 medium carrots, chopped
1 clove garlic, minced
1 small onion, diced
1 medium green pepper, chopped
2½ cups sliced mushrooms
1/2 cup chopped cashews or walnuts
2 stalks celery, chopped
3 T. oil

2½ cups VEGETABLE or CHICKEN
STOCK (broth)
2 T. sesame seeds
1 T. wheat germ
1 tsp. vegetable seasoning
1/4 tsp. kelp
1/2 tsp. thyme
2 tsp. chopped fresh parsley
1 cup uncooked bulgur wheat

Sauté the first seven ingredients in the oil for about 3 minutes. Add broth, other ingredients and seasoning. Stir in bulgur, cover and simmer for 15 minutes or until all the liquid is gone.

Yield: Serves 4

Variation:
Rice Pilaf: Just replace 1 cup raw brown rice for the bulgur wheat and cook for 45 minutes.

CORNMEAL

Used as the basis for cornbread, tortillas, polenta, hominy grits and johnny cake. Cornmeal is high in vitamins A and B plus phosphorus. When cornmeal is substituted for whole wheat, use 3/4 cup cornmeal to replace 1 cup of whole wheat flour in a recipe.

CORNMEAL MUSH

1 cup cornmeal   3½-4 cups water or milk

Bring water or milk to a boil in a saucepan. Meanwhile, mix cornmeal with just enough water to form a paste. When water boils, add the paste. Mix in well with a whisk. Cook for 45 minutes. Serve with honey and raisins.

Yield: 2 cups

BAKED POLENTA

Polenta is a coarse cornmeal that is a staple in northern Italy. Use as you would a side dish. Goes well with Italian and Mexican dishes.

3 cups water or VEGETABLE
STOCK
2 cloves garlic, minced
Dash of kelp
1 cup yellow cornmeal

1/4 cup finely chopped fresh
parsley
1/4 cup butter, melted
1/3 cup grated Parmesan cheese

In a large saucepan add the water or stock, garlic and kelp. Bring to a boil; then reduce heat and slowly add the cornmeal. Cook, stirring, for 5-7 minutes or until very thick. Remove from heat and spread evenly over a buttered cookie sheet to 1/2" thickness. Cool completely. To bake, cut cooled polenta into 2" squares, then cut the squares in half diagonally to form triangles. Lift out triangles and arrange on an ungreased cookie sheet. Drizzle melted butter over top and sprinkle with the cheese. Bake at 400° for 10 minutes. Serve hot. Can also use Jack cheese in place of the Parmesan.

Yield: 4-6 servings

MILLET

A most versatile light flavored grain. Can be used as a substitute for rice or in combination with rice. Try it as a side dish, cereal, in soups, casseroles, breads, puddings and even in desserts. Good source of lecithin, calcium and protein. May taste a little bland to you at first so you may have to spice it up.

MILLET PORRIDGE

1/2 cup millet   2 cups water

Bring water to a boil, add millet and bring back to a boil. Reduce heat to low, cover and simmer for 40 minutes. Add honey, cinnamon, raisins, bananas or chopped apples.

Yield: 2 cups

MILLET SOUFFLÉ

1¾ cups cooked millet   2/3 cup milk
1/2 tsp. vegetable seasoning   3/4 cup grated Cheddar cheese
3 egg yolks, beaten   3 egg whites, stiffly beaten

Mix the millet, vegetable seasoning, egg yolks, milk and 1/2 cup cheese. Fold in the egg whites and sprinkle the 1/4 cup of cheese on top. Pour into a greased soufflé dish or a baking dish and sprinkle with remaining cheese. Place dish in another container that contains hot water. Bake at 350° for about 20 minutes or until set.

Yield: Serves 4-5

MILLET DESSERT

2 cups millet cooked   1/2 cup raisins or dates
1 cup milk   1/2 cup sunflower seeds
3 eggs, beaten   1 tsp. cinnamon
3 T. molasses, unsulfured   Nutmeg

Blend millet, milk, eggs, molasses, raisins or dates, sunflower seeds and cinnamon together. Pour mixture into six oiled custard cups. Sprinkle tops with nutmeg. Bake at 350° for 1/2 hour or until firmly set. Serve hot or cold with milk or cream.

Yield: Serves 6

OATS

Steel-cut oats have to cook a little longer than rolled oats. Serve as hot oatmeal or bake in cookies. This versatile grain is popular in granola. Provides a chewy, sweet flavor to yeast breads. Can also be ground in a blender to make oat flour that adds sweetness to your baked goods. Can contain up to 15% protein plus vitamin B and iron.

OAT PORRIDGE

1/2 cup oats   1 cup water or milk

Pour oats slowly into boiling water. Reduce heat, cover and simmer for 15 minutes. Add more water if necessary. Serve with honey, cinnamon, raisins and chopped apples.

Yield: 2 cups

BROWN RICE

Brown rice has not been stripped of its nutrients like white rice. It contains plenty of vitamins B and E. Long Brown Rice has a nutty flavor and is appealing to all tastes. It is best for salads, curries, entrées and side dishes. Short Brown Rice can be used interchangeably with long brown rice. Usually selected for dishes requiring a creamy consistency such as puddings and stuffing. Can be ground into flour and used in cakes, cookies and breads.

2½ cups water, broth or tomato   1 cup brown rice
   juice   1 tsp. oil

Place water in a saucepan and bring to a boil. Add the oil, which prevents boiling over, and the rice. Pour the rice slowly into the water so the water does not stop boiling. This little trick will prevent sticky rice. Turn heat to low, cover and simmer for 45 minutes. Do not remove the lid until the end of the cooking time. Remove from the heat at the end of 45 minutes and let sit for a few minutes. For a nutty flavor stir the dry rice in a dry saucepan over medium heat until lightly toasted.

Yield: 3 cups

Variations:
1. Top cooked rice with nuts (walnuts are great) and sesame or sunflower seeds.
2. Add diced vegetables and cook along with the rice.
3. Stir into rice (after cooking) YOGURT, cinnamon, ginger and raisins.
4. Add TOMATO SAUCE and a number of different types of cooked beans to the cooked rice.

BAKED RICE

2 cups cooked brown rice   1 T. lemon juice
1 cup raisins   1/8 cup molasses or unsweetened
1/2 cup sunflower seeds   frozen apple juice concentrate
1½ cups milk   1/2 tsp each nutmeg and cinnamon

Mix all together and pour into a deep casserole dish. Cover and bake 45 minutes at 325°.

Yield: 6 servings

RICE TOMATO BAKE

1/4 cup sesame oil
1½ cups chopped onions
1 cup diced green pepper
1 cup chopped mushrooms
2 cups raw brown rice
3½ cups water
1 tsp. vegetable seasoning
1 tsp. oregano

1 tsp. basil
2/3 cup sesame seeds, ground in
   blender
2 eggs, beaten
3 tomatoes, cut into 1/2" slices
Sprigs of fresh parsley
1 tomato, cut into chunks

Heat the oil in a saucepan and add chopped onions, green pepper, and mushroom. Sauté until they are slightly tender. Add the raw rice and continue to sauté until the whole mixture is golden. Add the 3½ cups water, vegetable seasoning, oregano and basil. Stir, cover, and cook until the rice is tender. While the rice cooks, stir the ground sesame seed in a flat dish. Dip the tomato slices in the beaten eggs, then into the sesame meal, coating both sides well. Fry slices in oil until tomatoes are cooked through. Remove from heat. Arrange rice on a serving platter. Place the sesame-browned tomatoes over the rice. Top with fresh tomato chunks and parsley. Serve hot.

Yield: 6 servings

FRIED RICE

2-3 T. oil
1 clove garlic, minced
1/4 cup onions, diced
1/4 cup green pepper, diced
1/4 cup sliced water chestnuts
1/4 cup celery, diced

3 cups cooked brown rice
1/2 cup cooked green peas
2 T. chopped fresh parsley
3 eggs, beaten slightly
1/4 cup mung bean sprouts
Tamari (soy sauce) to taste

Sauté garlic, onions, green pepper, water chestnuts and celery in 2 tablespoons oil until tender. Remove from pan. Add the remaining 1 tablespoon of oil to the pan and then sauté the rice in it. Add sautéed vegetables, peas, parsley and eggs. Stir for 2 or 3 minutes or until eggs are set but not dry or brown. Add bean sprouts. Season with tamari and serve immediately.

Yield: 6-8 servings

PINEAPPLE RICE

3 cups cooked rice, hot
1 cup shredded Cheddar cheese
1 20-ounce can crushed pineapple,
   unsweetened
1 cup raw peas
1/2 cup chopped celery

1/2 cup chopped green onions
1/4 cup chopped red or green
   pepper
1/2 tsp. vegetable seasoning
1/8 tsp. tarragon
1/8 tsp. garlic, minced

Add the cheese to the hot rice and stir until it melts. Drain the pineapple and add the pineapple along with the peas, celery, onion, pepper, vegetable seasoning, tarragon and garlic to the rice mixture. Mix lightly. Serve warm.

Yield: 4 servings

Variation:
Add a 5-ounce can of shrimp (drained) or 1 cup chopped chicken to the rice.

SPANISH RICE

1/4 cup celery, chopped
1/4 cup green pepper, chopped
1/4 cup sliced mushrooms
1/4 cup onion, chopped
1 T. oil
1/4 cup TOMATO SAUCE

Cayenne pepper to taste
1 garlic clove, minced
1 large tomato, cut up
1 tsp. vegetable seasoning
2 cups cooked brown rice
1/2 cup sliced almonds

In a skillet, sauté the celery, green pepper, mushrooms and onion in the oil. Sauté until golden brown. Warm the tomato sauce, adding the cayenne, garlic, tomato and vegetable seasoning. Combine all of the ingredients, except for the almonds, with the cooked rice. Mix well and place into a casserole dish. Bake at 350° for 15 minutes. Remove from oven and sprinkle with almonds just before serving.

Yield: 2 cups

WILD RICE

Wild rice is really not a rice, but the seed of a grass. It grows in the marshlands and is very expensive. It is high in protein, phosphorus and potassium. Use as a side dish and in stuffing, but be sure to wash it several times before cooking.

1 cup wild rice   3 cups water

Bring the water to a boil and then slowly add the wild rice. Reduce heat, cover, and simmer for 1½ hours or longer.

Yield: 4 cups

RYE

Wholesome high-stamina European favorite for flour, grits or meal. Delicious, sweet, heavy taste. Use in rye, pumpernickel and black breads as a flour. Rye is popular for breakfast cereals, breads and pancakes. Has a 12% protein level with especially low gluten content. For this reason you need to add whole wheat flour to bread recipes using rye flour so it will rise.

RYE PORRIDGE

1 cup rye berries   3 cups water

Bring the water to a boil and then add the rye slowly. Reduce heat, cover, and simmer for 1 hour. Serve with fruit and apple juice.

Yield: 4 cups

RYE MIXTURE DISH

3 cups cooked rye   1/2 cup chopped almonds
1/4 cup butter   2 T. tamari (soy sauce)
2 cups onion, chopped   1½ tsp. garlic powder
1 cup celery, chopped fine   1 tsp. each rosemary, oregano and
1/4 cup diced green pepper   thyme
1 tomato, diced   1/2 tsp vegetable seasoning
1/2 cup sunflower seeds   1 cup SOUR CREAM or YOGURT

In a skillet, melt butter and add onion, celery, green pepper, tomato, sunflower seeds and almonds. Sauté until onion is transparent. Add rye, seasoning and sour cream or yogurt. Mix well and serve immediately.

Yield: 8-10 servings

TRITICALE

A new hybrid that blends the best of the wheat and rye. It combines the amino acids and ruggedness of rye with the high digestible protein level of wheat. Makes hearty bread and baked goods when ground into a flour. Mix in recipe with whole wheat flour for flavor and taste variety. Use whole or in-flakes for a cereal. Can also be used in place of rice or potatoes.

TRITICALE CEREAL

1 cup triticale   3 cups water

Bring the water to a boil and then add triticale. Reduce heat and cover. Simmer for 1 hour until tender.

Yield: 4 cups

WHOLE WHEAT (WHEAT BERRIES)

You will usually see the two main varieties—hard red spring wheat and hard red winter wheat—when shopping. The spring wheat is high in fiber but low in gluten, so it is made into pastry flour and used in cakes, cookies and pastries. The winter wheat is higher in protein than the spring. It is also higher in gluten and is better in bread baking. As opposed to white flour it contains the germ and bran which is where you find the vitamins B and E. Grind and make into flour that can be used in all dessert and breadmakings or any place else flour is needed. The whole berry is good as a cereal, in casseroles or good sprouted.

WHOLE WHEAT BERRIES

2 cups whole wheat berries   6 cups water or broth

Soak wheat overnight; save the water for your soup broth. Bring the water to a boil and slowly add the berries. Lower heat, cover and simmer for 1–2 hours. Serve with butter, honey or tamari (soy sauce). Will be chewier than rice. Leftovers can be added to soups, salads or kneaded into bread dough.

Yield: 4 cups

CRISPY WHEAT BERRIES

4 cups whole wheat berries   12 cups boiling water

Place wheat berries in a container, add the boiling water, cover and let sit overnight. Drain water (save for making stock) and spread the wheat onto a cookie sheet. Place in a 300° oven for 10–15 minutes or until brown and crispy. Great as a snack by just eating out of hand. Try sprinkling on top of your favorite salad.

Yield: 10 cups

CREAM OF WHEAT CEREAL

1 cup ground wheat   3 cups water

Toast grain first and then put into a grinder and grind. Bring the water to a boil and add cereal. Return to a boil, reduce the heat, cover and simmer for about 1 hour. Stir occasionally. Serve topped with honey, fruit or nuts.

Yield: 3 cups

Variation:
Cream of Rice: Substitute the same amount of rice for the wheat. Cook as directed.

WHEAT GERM

Wheat germ is considered the heart of the wheat kernel. In making white flour this germ is removed. It is high in protein and especially vitamins B and E. Can spoil easily, turn rancid, so it is important to find out how old your wheat germ is before you buy it. If it is over 3 weeks old it could be spoiled. Fresh wheat germ should have a sweet smell. Make sure you keep the wheat germ refrigerated.

USES FOR WHEAT GERM

Use it in pancakes, bread, cookies or cake recipes. Can add up to 1/3 cup; increase liquid in recipe to adjust for addition.

Use it as a breakfast cereal with milk and fresh fruit.

Add to GRANOLA or other cereals.

Use as a topping on fresh fruit, casseroles or eggs.

Add to juices or MILK SHAKES and SMOOTHIES.

Roll patties or burgers in it and then bake them.

WHEAT GERM BREADING MIX

2/3 cup cornmeal
2/3 cup wheat germ
2/3 cup rye flour

1/3 cup sesame seeds
2 tsp. vegetable seasoning

Combine all of the ingredients together and place in a storage container to be stored in the refrigerator. Use as a breading on patties, chicken or fish.

Yield: 2-1/3 cups

THREE GRAIN CEREAL MIX

3/4 cup rye flakes
3/4 cup wheat flakes
1 cup rolled oat flakes
1 cup raw wheat germ

1/2 cup unprocessed bran
1/4 cup Brewer's yeast
1 tsp. each nutmeg and cinnamon

In a plastic bag, combine all of the ingredients. Shake the bag to combine thoroughly. Seal and store until you want to make a hot cereal.

Yield: 3½ cups–8 servings

To cook Three Grain Cereal: For 2 servings, bring 1½ cups water or 1 cup apple juice and 1/2 cup water to a boil. Sprinkle in 3/4 cup cereal; add 1/4 cup chopped dates or raisins, if you wish. When water comes to a boil again, reduce heat, cover, and simmer for 10 to 12 minutes. Serve with honey and topped with nuts.

FOUR GRAIN CEREAL MIX

3/4 cup barley flakes
3/4 cup triticale flakes
3/4 cup rye flakes

3/4 cup wheat flakes
1/4 cup sesame seeds
1/2 cup unprocessed bran

Combine all of the ingredients together in a plastic bag. Shake to combine thoroughly and seal.

Yield: 4 cups–8 servings

To cook Four Grain Cereal. For 2 servings, bring 2 cups of water to a boil, then add 1/4 cup chopped dried pineapple or apple. Sprinkle in 1 cup of the cereal mix. Bring back to a boil, reduce heat, cover and simmer for 8-10 minutes.

COLD CEREALS

GRANOLA

A quick and easy cereal to make. Supplies you with protein, vitamins E and B. Make a large batch and store it in refrigerator until needed. You can vary your granola recipe by adding or substracting items from it. Let your imagination go!

3 cups oat flakes
1/2 cup wheat flakes
1/2 cup bran
1/2 cup wheat germ
1/2 cup sunflower seeds
1/3 cup sesame seeds

1/2 cup non-instant dry milk
  powder
1/2 tsp. nutmeg
1 tsp. cinnamon
3/4 cup raisins (added after baking)

Mix all of the ingredients together in a large bowl, except for the raisins which are added after baking. Heat in a saucepan over low heat the following ingredients:

2/3 cup oil
1/3 cup honey

1/4 cup molasses, unsulfured
1 T. VANILLA EXTRACT

Pour the above heated ingredients over the dry ingredients and stir well. Spread the mixture onto a cookie sheet and bake at 300° for 1 hour. Stir occasionally. Cool and store in a refrigerator, freezer or in a cool, dry place.

Yield: 6 cups

USES FOR GRANOLA

Add to cookie or cake dough.

Use as a pie crust or add it to your favorite quick bread.

Eat it as a cereal or top other cereals with it.

Eat it out of hand as a snack.

Top fresh fruit, ice cream, puddings, casseroles and vegetables with it.

Stir into YOGURT.

FIVE GRAIN GRANOLA

3 cups oat flakes
1/2 cup wheat flakes
1/2 cup barley flakes
1/3 cup triticale flakes
1/2 cup rye flakes
1/2 cup bran
1/2 cup wheat germ
3/4 cup unsweetened coconut
1/2 cup sunflower seeds

1/3 cup sesame seeds
3/4 cup nuts, almonds, walnuts, cashews
1/2 cup dried milk
1 cup raisins or dried fruits (added after baking)
1/2 tsp. nutmeg
1 T. cinnamon

Mix all of the ingredients together in a large bowl. Heat in a saucepan over low heat the following ingredients:

2/3 cup oil
1/2 cup honey

1/4 cup molasses, unsulfured
1 T. VANILLA EXTRACT

Pour the above ingredients over the dry ingredients and stir well. Spread onto a cookie sheet and bake at 300° for 1 hour, stirring occasionally. Cool and store in refrigerator, freezer or in a cool, dry place.

Yield: 8-9 cups

Variation:
Peanut Butter Granola: Decrease oil to 1/2 cup. Add 1/2 cup PEANUT BUTTER.

CAROB GRANOLA

1 cup oats
2 cups wheat germ
1 cup wheat flakes
1 cup rye flakes
1/2 cup bran
1/2 cup chopped dates
1/2 cup carob powder

1/2 cup walnut pieces
1/2 cup chopped almonds
2½ cups dried milk, in the
    powdered form
1/4 cup sunflower seeds
1/4 cup soy grits

Combine all of the dry ingredients together in a large bowl. Now mix together the following:

1/2 cup honey
2 T. blackstrap molasses

1/4 cup oil
1 T. VANILLA EXTRACT

Pour the liquid ingredients over the dry ingredients and stir until well mixed. Bake for 1½ hours at 225°, stirring constantly. Bake longer for drier, crunchier granola. Great dessert.

Yield: 8 cups

BREAKFAST CRUNCH

1/4 cup rolled oats
1/4 cup wheat flakes
1/4 cup rye flakes
2 T. raw wheat germ
2 T. bran
3 T. pumpkin seeds

3 T. sesame seeds
3 T. sunflower seeds
2 T. chopped almonds or walnuts
1 apple, cubed
1 banana, sliced
YOGURT

Place 1/2 of each of the wheat, rye and oats in a blender and grind until cornmeal consistency. Place this mixture and other half of rolled oats, wheat and rye flakes and all the rest of the ingredients into a bowl. Mix all together. Place in individual serving bowls. Fill with apple juice or milk. Place a spoonful of plain yogurt on top.

Yield: 3 cups

Variations: Add dates or raisins. Use orange juice.

HOMEMADE GRAPE NUTS

3 cups graham or whole wheat flour   2 cups buttermilk
1/2 cup wheat germ   1 tsp. soda
1/4 cup molasses, unsulfured

Place all of the ingredients into a large bowl and beat until smooth. Spread dough on two large greased cookie sheets. Bake 25-30 minutes at 350°. While warm, whirl in blender until crumbly. Crisp in 250° oven for 20 minutes.

Yield: 2 pounds

BREADS

One of the most delightful smells in the kitchen is
that of Homemade Bread!

Bread provides a very good source of nutrition, is
relatively easy to make and costs only half of what
you would pay in a store.

CHAPTER 9

Commercial breads are mostly made of white
flour that is practically devoid of nutrients, and contains many preservatives
and additives.

Homemade breads should use freshly ground whole grain flours that contain
the bran and germ, which have the vitamins and minerals. Bread also contains
the protein and fiber that is so needed in our diet, and can actually be more
satisfying than a sweet dessert. Homemade bread is also a thoughtful gift to
give a friend.

Many people have shared with me that baking bread brings them a deep,
inner satisfaction, and that it takes very little time, once you master the art.
I will explain all of the "How To's" in this chapter.

Following is a collection of recipes for various breads that will feature different textures and flavors. You'll have fun experimenting with these recipes
and your family will enjoy healthy breads that will leave them wanting
more. Have fun and *don't* get discouraged the first time you try to bake
bread. I am glad I didn't—even though my first attempt ended in a culinary
disaster. Now I bake these many breads and enjoy the time I spend with the
Lord while doing so, and the thankful response of my family!

HELPFUL HINTS

- If your bread does not turn out like you expected, do not throw it away.
  Use it for making croutons, bread crumbs or slice thin and dry in an oven
  at low temperature and you can make it into a toasted cracker. Leftovers
  can be used the same way.

- To make bread crumbs: Dry the bread first in an oven and then place between two layers of waxed paper and roll a rolling pin over it. Or, you can place it in a blender and blend until broken up. Store in the freezer until needed.

- Use bread crumbs in loaves, stuffings, casseroles, patties and bread doughs.

- Cornmeal is best used in bread baking when combined with other flours. It should be yellow undegerminated cornmeal.

- For rye bread, use a combination of rye and wheat to give it a light texture.

- If you're converting a recipe from one using white flour to one using whole wheat, follow these pointers: For each cup of white flour substitute with only 3/4 cup whole wheat. If it calls for 3 tablespoons oil in the recipe, use only 2 tablespoons. To substitute oil for butter in the recipe use it in the same quantities. You may have to add more liquid for whole wheat bread. For sweeteners use half as much as they use for white sugar.

- Use regular whole wheat flour in making yeast breads as the flour has more gluten than the whole wheat pastry flour. Use the pastry in dessert making when not using yeast.

- If you have problems getting the whole grain bread to rise, use a little extra yeast.

- If you are not home during a day of bread baking let the dough rise in the refrigerator; then when you come home, just punch it and shape it into loaves and let it rise once before baking.

- When you purchase bread at the store make sure the flour states that it is from 100% whole wheat. If it does not it may be from white flour (wheat flour is how it is stated on the package) or it may be white flour with caramel color added.

- Try grinding your own flour to get the freshest bread possible. It is not that hard to do. You just need a flour grinder that will do the job in a few minutes.

- In the recipes you can substitute date sugar for the honey or molasses.

- Grease pans well as whole grains are more prone to stick to the pan.

- Grease pans with butter rather than oil. Bread tends to stick to the oil.

- There is a slight variance in the amount of flour needed for bread recipes. Flour differences depend on brands, types, and weather. Always start with slightly less flour than the recipe calls for. Then add as needed. This difference will show up more in yeast breads as compared to quick breads.

- To thaw frozen bread, place in brown paper bag and put into a 325° oven for 5 minutes to thaw completely.

- If it is inconvenient to shape the bread after the first rising, simply punch it down and let it rise again.

- If the bread over-rises in the pans, remove, knead and reshape. Allow it to rise again.

- Some days are so hectic and the need for bread so immediate that you may need to skip the first rising period entirely. Allow the dough to rest 20 minutes after kneading, then shape into loaves and rise in the pan. Texture will not be as fine though.

- If there is high humidity, the dough will require 1 cup more flour.

- The addition of 1/4 teaspoon of ginger to the yeast and water seems to enhance the yeast action. Plus it adds a good flavor.

- Using dry milk in bread recipes is easy and economical. The proportion of milk to water is 1/3 cup to 2/3 cup. You can just add it to the flour and the appropriate amount of water added as the liquid.

- Keep a plastic bag handy while kneading. When the telephone rings, slip your hands into the bag. This will prevent a sticky and floured telephone.

- Never use the same board to knead and slice bread on that you use to cut meat. The bacteria from the meat juices may contaminate your bread.

- Crackers freeze well. Good for snacks, garnish for soups and salads.

- Rolls can be reheated by placing them in a paper bag, sprinkle with water, fold top over and place in a 400° oven for 10 minutes.

- Quick breads are improved by resting the dough for 15 minutes before placing it in the oven. Allow the bread to rise a little, but not enough to keep the top from cracking during the baking period.

- In making homemade crackers, cut into diamonds or squares. You can even use a cookie cutter for a variance of shapes.

- When using yeast in quick breads, omit baking powder and dissolve 2 tablespoons of dry yeast in some liquid and proceed as directed by the recipe.

- For making any types of bread, the ingredients should be at room temperature.

- The aluminum used in baking powder is toxic to your body. In quick breads that call for baking powder, use low sodium baking powder. You can find it in your local health food stores or you can make it yourself (see "Specialty" section).

- Never use more than 1 teaspoon baking powder to every 1 cup flour in muffins, rolls or bread recipes. They will not turn out lighter by using more.

- Get your children and husband involved in baking bread. It is a fun family project.

- Quick breads can have many protein fortifiers added to them such as wheat germ, dry milk powder, seeds and nuts.

- Quick breads will store up to 4-5 days at room temperature. You can freeze the bread up to 2-3 months.

- Use glass pans rather than aluminum ones as the aluminum can get into your food through the cookware.

- When cooking popovers do not open the door before the end of the cooking time; otherwise they will collapse.

- If muffins get stale, dry thoroughly and add to cookie crumbs to be used as a topping on desserts and cakes.

- For easy removal of muffins from the cookware, oil the tins with soy lecithin spread. That is available at your local health food stores.

- Do not over mix muffins or they will turn out heavy and grainy with an uneven texture.

- Stir a quick bread only until moistened. If over mixed the bread will be tough and heavy.

- If allergic to wheat flour, here are a few suggestions as to what you can use. Choose one substitute, or combine several to replace each cup of wheat flour:

1 cup corn flour	7/8 cup rice flour
3/4 cup coarse cornmeal	1 cup soy flour plus 1/4 cup potato
1 cup fine cornmeal	flour
5/8 cup potato flour	

If your favorite recipe using wheat flour has less than 2 cups wheat flour, add one extra egg to the recipe. You may have to increase the amount of baking powder to make up for the lack of gluten in the substitute flour.

TIPS FOR YEAST BREAD BAKERS

INGREDIENTS

Yeast

It is the leavening for the bread. It is a living plant that thrives on the sugar in the dough. In growing, yeast forms the gas that makes the bread light. Its action is continuous and needs a framework capable of holding the gas over a period of time. That is provided by the gluten in the flour. Kneading the dough develops this gluten.

Dry active yeast will stay fresh for months (up to 6 months) in a cool, dry place. After opening a jar of active dry yeast be sure to replace the lid tightly and store in the refrigerator. One package of yeast equals only 2 teaspoons of yeast, not 1 tablespoon as so commonly thought. Also 1 ounce of yeast equals 3 tablespoons of dry granules.

Flour

Whole wheat flour is used as it contains gluten which is needed to get the bread to rise. The amount and quality of the gluten varies with different flours. The type of wheat and where it is grown all influence the amount of gluten. Another factor that affects the use of your flour is the moisture content. It varies with each bag of flour and so the water-to-flour ratio may have to be adjusted. When substituting whole wheat for white flour in your favorite bread recipe use 3/4 cup whole wheat to every cup of white flour. Different flours may be added along with whole wheat by adding a cup or two. Try using rye, oat, rice, barley and millet.

Liquid

The usual liquids for making breads and rolls are milk, water, and water in which potatoes have been cooked. For the milk you can use whole or skim, or even dry milk powder. The liquid in which you dissolve the yeast must be warm (105-115°). Liquid that is too cold will slow down the yeast action. Water that is too hot will kill the yeast. If you are using the method of adding the yeast to the dry ingredients and then adding the warm liquid, the water should be between 120-130°. For best results use water for dissolving the dry yeast. If the recipe calls for liquid other than water, substitute 1/4 cup of warm water for 1/4 cup of the other liquid. For example, if the recipe calls for a cup of milk, dissolve the dry yeast in 1/4 cup warm water first, then add 3/4 cup warm milk. Water makes breads crusty. Milk gives them a soft crust and are not as coarse as the water breads. In adapting your favorite white bread recipe for whole wheat, you may have to add more liquid.

Sweeteners

Adding a sweetener to the yeast and liquid will help hasten the action of the yeast. Make sure the sweetener is warm so as not to retard the action. You can use honey (mild flavor) or molasses in your breads. The more sweetener in the recipe, the browner the crust. Honey retains moisture and helps preserve the freshness of the loaf. When substituting honey or molasses for the white sugar in your recipes, use only half as much honey and molasses as white sugar.

Shortening

It is not necessary to use shortening in the recipe, but you can if you like. It helps make the bread tender and gives it a softer crust. It also helps to ensure the quality. Use oil in place of solid fats to cut down on saturated fats. If your favorite recipes use 3 tablespoons, use only 2 tablespoons when changing to a whole wheat bread. If you are just substituting oil for butter, keep it the same proportion.

Eggs

Eggs add flavor and improve the structure so that breads can be richer a more nutritious. They also add color and help make the crumb fine and the crust tender.

PROCEDURE

Kneading

When all the ingredients have been combined, the next step is to knead the dough. This step is necessary to develop the gluten that gives the bread its structure that results in a fine even texture, with a smooth rounded top. The way to knead is to turn the dough onto a lightly floured board. With floured hands, pick up the dough. Fold dough over toward you, then push it down and away from you, with the heel of your hand. Give dough a quarter turn; repeat kneading, developing a rocking rhythm. Continue this until dough becomes smooth and elastic, about 7-10 minutes. Be sure not to knead too much flour into the dough. Also never put flour on top of the dough you are kneading. Put it on the table and then knead the dough on top of it. Do not overknead—it injures the baking quality of gluten and you will end up with poor texture and volume.

Rising

After kneading, place dough to rise in a greased bowl (use oil) twice the size of the dough. Turn the dough once to coat the entire surface of the dough with the oil. Cover with a clean dish towel or cheesecloth and place in a warm (about 85°) draft-free place. The location is very important because if it is too warm it may kill the yeast or it ends up with a yeasty taste and smell. If it is in a draft it will not rise properly. One of the best places is in an oven which has been turned on to 200° for 5 minutes and then turned off. A pan of hot water may be placed on the lower shelf and the bowl placed above it on another shelf. This first rising will probably take about 1½-2 hours. To test for the proper amount of rising, poke a finger 1/2" into the dough. If the imprint remains when your finger is removed then it is done. If it rises too long it will turn out coarse. If it does not rise long enough, it will be as heavy as a brick.

Punching Dough Down

After dough has doubled in size you need to punch your fist into the risen dough and you will find it will collapse. It forces gas out of the dough. Remove from the bowl and allow to sit and rest for 10 minutes before shaping.

Shaping

If the recipe calls for the dough to make more than one loaf, then divide dough into the number of loaves it is to make. Then take each portion and flatten into a 9" x 7" rectangle. Fold over each end to the center, overlapping ends a little. Pinch overlap to seal. Place the loaf seam-down in a well-greased pan. Any bread recipe can be made into rolls. The baking time will just be shorter. Oil top of loaf and cover again. Put in another warm place until the dough rises to the top of the pan and center is rounded above pan. The rising time will be a little shorter than before.

Baking

Bake in center of oven, leaving a few inches between pans. Do not place more than 2 loaves on one shelf. If the bread is browning too quickly, cover the top loosely with foil. Test for doneness by tapping the loaf with your knuckles. It will have a hollow sound when done. Remove from the pans immediately after baking and cool on a rack. For a soft crust brush loaf with butter as soon as it comes out of the oven. For a glazed crust, brush with milk or egg white before baking.

Storage

Wrap in plastic and keep at room temperature for only a few days. Because it does not contain any preservatives it will spoil fast. Do not put it in the refrigerator as that will quickly dry it out. The best way to store it is to freeze it. Make sure it is properly wrapped in moisture-vaporproof packaging. Can keep up to 3-4 months.

Reheating

Place bread in a brown paper bag and add a few drops of water. Put in oven for only a few minutes. Or, you can wrap it in foil and place in the oven.

BREAD FAILURES AND WHY

Porous bread—

1. Over rising
2. Cooking at too low a temperature

Crust dark and blisters—

1. Under rising
2. Shaping and molding of the bread was poor

Dough does not rise—

1. Over kneading
2. Yeast too old
3. Yeast was killed by using too hot a liquid
4. Yeast was not activated by using too cold a liquid
5. Oven could have been too hot

Uneven baking—
1. Using old dark pans
2. Putting too much dough in pan
3. Crowding the loaves on the oven shelf
4. Too high a cooking temperature

Volume too great—
1. Dough was allowed to rise too long
2. Oven temperature too cool

Bread has holes throughout—
1. Excessive amount of dusting flour

Bread has a yeast smell—
1. Too warm during rising
2. Allowed to rise too long

WHOLE WHEAT BREAD

1 T. honey
2 T. dry active yeast
1/4 cup warm water (105-115°)
1/2 cup oil
1/4 cup molasses, unsulfured
2¾ cups water

3 eggs
8 cups whole wheat flour (can also use 3/4 whole wheat and 1/4 of a mixture of any other whole grain flours)

Place the honey, yeast and warm water in a bowl. Let it sit for 5 minutes to dissolve. Add the oil, molasses, water, eggs and 4 cups of the flour. Blend well with a wooden spoon. Mix in more flour, adding only enough to give a stiff dough. Turn dough out onto a lightly floured board. Knead until smooth and elastic, about 7 minutes. Place in a greased bowl and turn to oil all sides. Cover with a cloth and let rise in a warm place until doubled in size. Punch dough down and divide into thirds and shape into loaves. Place in oiled loaf pans and cover and let double again in size. Bake at 375° for 25 minutes. Remove from pan immediately and let cool. Before it is shaped into a loaf you can add up to 1 cup of any of the following: chopped nuts, sunflower seeds, sesame seeds or wheat germ.

Yield: 3 loaves

Variation: Knead into the dough, raisins, nuts, dates or seeds.

This dough can also be frozen by following these instructions:

To Freeze Dough: Place the dough in the loaf pans and before the second rising wrap well and place in the freezer. Best used within 3 weeks but can keep for 4 weeks.

To Bake Frozen Dough: Remove from the freezer and place in a 225° oven for 40 minutes or until the bread has risen. Once it has risen turn the temperature up to 375° and bake for 40 minutes. Remove from pan and cool.

WHEAT GERM YOGURT BREAD

8-9 cups whole wheat flour
3/4 cup non-instant dry milk
   powder
1 tsp. kelp
1 T. active dry yeast
2¾ cups water

1 cup plain YOGURT
1/4 cup honey
2 T. butter
1 cup wheat germ
1 egg, beaten
Wheat germ

In a large bowl mix 3½ cups flour, dry milk, kelp and dry yeast. Combine water, yogurt, honey and butter in a saucepan. Heat over low heat until liquids are very warm (120-130°). The butter need not melt. Gradually add to the dry ingredients. Beat 2 minutes at medium speed of mixer, scraping bowl occasionally. Add 1 cup flour. Beat at high speed 2 minutes. Stir in 1 cup wheat germ and enough additional flour to make a stiff dough. Turn out onto a lightly floured board and knead until smooth and elastic, about 8-10 minutes. Place in a greased bowl, turning to grease top. Cover and let rise in warm place until double in bulk, about 1 hour. Punch dough down and divide in half. Divide each half into 3 equal pieces. Shape each piece into a 16" rope. Braid 3 ropes together; pinch ends to seal. Place on a greased baking sheet. Repeat with remaining ropes. Cover and let rise in a warm place for about 1 hour. Brush top with beaten egg and sprinkle with wheat germ. Bake at 350° for 35 minutes. Remove from baking sheet and cool on racks.

Yield: 2 loaves

SPROUTED WHEAT BREAD

2 T. yeast
1/4 cup warm water (105-115°)
2¼ cups milk
1/4 cup honey

3 T. oil
1 tsp. kelp
5-6 cups whole wheat flour
2 cups wheat sprout, ground

Soften yeast in the warm water for about 5 minutes. Scald milk and cool to lukewarm. Add the milk, yeast mixture, honey, oil and kelp to a large bowl. Mix well. Gradually add 3 cups flour and beat until elastic. Cover dough and let rise until double in size. Stir down and add remaining flour and the sprouts. Knead dough until smooth and elastic, 8-10 minutes. Place in a greased bowl and turn to coat all sides. Cover and let rise in a warm place until double in size. Punch down and shape into 2 loaves. Place in loaf pans and let rise again. Bake at 375° for 25 minutes.

Yield: 2 loaves

BANANA ANADAMA DATE BREAD

1½ cups whole wheat flour
3/4 cup cornmeal
1/2 tsp. kelp
1/2 tsp. soda
1 T. active dry yeast
2½ T. oil
1/3 cup molasses, unsulfured

1 cup plus 2 T. very warm water
(120-130°)
2¾-3¾ cups whole wheat flour
1/2 cup mashed ripe banana
1 cup diced pitted dates
1 tsp. cornmeal

In a large bowl, mix together the whole wheat flour, cornmeal, kelp, soda and yeast. Stir in oil, molasses, and water; beat at medium speed for 2 minutes. Add 1/4 cup of the whole wheat flour and beat at high speed for 2 minutes. With a heavy-duty mixer or spoon, stir in the banana and enough of the whole wheat flour (about 2½ cups) to make a stiff dough. Turn dough out onto a floured board and knead until smooth, adding flour as necessary to prevent sticking. Knead the dates into dough, a portion at a time. Turn dough over in a greased bowl to grease top. Cover and let rise in a warm place until doubled, about 1½ hours. Grease a 9'' pie pan and sprinkle with the 1 teaspoon cornmeal. Punch down dough, knead a few times, then shape it into a smooth ball. Place in the pan, cover with a towel, and let rise in a warm place until almost doubled, about 45 minutes. Bake in a 375° oven until browned, 35-40 minutes. Turn out of pan onto a wire rack to cool.

Yield: 1 loaf

OATMEAL-HONEY BREAD

1 cup rolled oats, uncooked
2 cups boiling water
2 T. active dry yeast
1/3 cup warm milk
1/4 cup honey

1/4 cup oil
1/2 cup non-instant dry milk
powder
2 tsp. kelp
6½ cups whole wheat flour

Combine the oats and boiling water and allow the mixture to stand for 30 minutes. Soften the yeast in the milk. When the yeast mixture bubbles, add the oats mixture and then the honey, oil, milk powder, and kelp. Then add enough whole wheat flour to make a moderately stiff dough. Turn dough out onto a lightly floured board and knead until it is smooth and elastic. Place in a greased bowl. Brush top with oil. Let rise until double in bulk. Punch down, and knead again. Shape into 2 loaves and place in 2 greased bread pans. Let rise for 10 minutes. Bake at 325° for 50-60 minutes.

Yield: 2 loaves

FRENCH BREAD

1/4 cup warm water (about 110°)
1 T. active dry yeast
2 T. honey

2 cups water, warm
5-6 cups whole wheat flour
1/3 cup wheat germ

Place the yeast in the 1/4 cup of warm water to dissolve, about 5 minutes. In another bowl combine the honey and 2 cups of water. Add the yeast mixture. Add 3 cups of the flour and all of the wheat germ. Stir well. Add extra flour only until it forms a stiff dough. Place on a floured board and knead until smooth and elastic, about 10 minutes. Place in a bowl, cover and let rise until double in size. Punch down and shape into 2 loaves. It really works best if you have special pans to bake the bread in as it has a tendency to spread and flatten out, but if you do not, place on a cookie sheet. Cover loaves and let rise again until double in size. Score the top with diagonal cuts 2" apart. Bake at 350° for 25 minutes. Sprinkle water on the top while it is baking. Do this a couple of times. This will give it a chewy crust.

Yield: 2 loaves

RYE BREAD

3 T. active dry yeast
1 cup warm water (105-115°)
1 T. honey
1/2 cup dark molasses
1/2 cup boiling water
2 T. oil

2 T. caraway seed
1 tsp. kelp
1/2 cup wheat germ
2¾ cups rye flour
2½-2¾ cups whole wheat flour

Dissolve the yeast in warm water along with the honey. In a large bowl combine molasses, boiling water, oil, caraway seed, and kelp, stirring until all is mixed. Cool to lukewarm (110-115°). Stir in yeast and wheat germ. Stir in all the rye flour and as much of the whole wheat as you can mix in with a spoon. Turn out onto a lightly floured surface. Knead in enough remaining flour to make a moderately stiff dough that is smooth and elastic. Shape dough into a ball. Place in greased bowl, turning once to grease surface. Cover; let rise until double in size (about 1½ hours). Punch dough down and divide in half. Cover; and let rest 10 minutes. Shape into loaves. Place in 2 greased pans. Cover and let rise until almost double (about 1 hour). Brush loaves with water and take a sharp knife and gently score tops of loaves diagonally at 3" intervals. Bake in 350° oven for 45 minutes. Remove from pans; cool on wire rack.

Yield: 2 loaves

HERB BREAD

1½ cups water
1 cup COTTAGE CHEESE
1/4 cup honey
3 T. oil
6-6½ cups whole wheat flour

2 T. active dry yeast
1 egg
2 tsp. dill
3 T. chopped onion
2 T. chopped fresh parsley

Heat first four ingredients in a medium saucepan, until very warm (110-120°). Combine warm liquid, 3 cups of flour and the remaining ingredients in a large bowl. Beat 2 minutes. By hand stir in remaining flour to make a stiff dough. Knead dough until it is smooth and elastic, about 5 minutes. Place in a greased bowl and turn over to grease all sides. Cover and let rise in a warm place until double in size. Punch down and divide into 2 balls. Shape into 2 loaves and place in 2 greased loaf pans. Let rise again until double in size. Bake 40-50 minutes in 350° oven.

Yield: 2 loaves

DILL-ONION BREAD

1 T. active dry yeast
1/2 cup warm water (105-115°)
1 beaten egg
1/2 cup COTTAGE CHEESE
1/3 cup finely chopped onion
1 T. butter, melted
2 cups whole wheat flour

1/3 cup whole bran cereal
1/2 cup wheat germ
1 T. honey
1 T. dillseed
1 tsp. kelp
1/4 tsp. baking soda

Soften yeast in warm water. Combine egg, cottage cheese, onion, and butter; mix well. In another bowl stir together the flour, cereal, wheat germ, honey, dill, kelp and soda. Add cottage cheese and yeast mixtures, stirring well. Cover and let rise until double in size, about 1 hour. Stir dough down. Knead on a lightly floured surface 1 minute. With greased hands pat in a well-greased 9" round baking pan. Cover; let rise until double in size, about 1 hour. Score top in diamond pattern. Bake 40 minutes at 350°. Remove from dish and cool on rack.

Yield: 1 loaf

PUMPERNICKEL BREAD

3/4 cup cornmeal
1½ cups cold water
1½ cups boiling water
1 tsp. kelp
2 T. molasses, unsulfured
2 T. oil
2 T. active dry yeast

1/4 cup lukewarm water
(110-115°)
2 cups mashed potatoes
1 T. caraway seed
3½ cups rye flour
4¼ cups whole wheat flour
1 egg white, lightly beaten

Mix the cornmeal with the cold water in a saucepan. Slowly pour in the boiling water and cook the cornmeal to make a mush. Combine the kelp, molasses and oil, set aside. Dissolve the yeast in the lukewarm water. Add the mashed potatoes and blend until smooth. Combine yeast-potato mixture with cool cornmeal mush. Stir until smooth, then add caraway seeds. In a large mixing bowl mix the flours together, then make a well in the center. Pour the liquid mixture into well and work flour into it. Knead gently until the dough is stiff. Turn out onto a lightly floured board and continue kneading until dough is smooth and elastic. Place in a greased bowl and turn to coat all sides. Cover and set in a warm place until double in size, about 1½ hours. Punch down and divide into 2 equal parts. Shape into round loaves or into standard bread shape. Cover and let rise until double in size again. Before baking, brush top of loaves with the egg white. Bake at 375° for 1 hour, or until loaves sound hollow when tapped.

Yield: 2 loaves

TRITICALE YEAST BREAD

1 T. active dry yeast
1/2 cup warm water (105-115°)
2 T. honey
2 T. non-instant dry milk powder
1 tsp. kelp

2¼ cups whole wheat flour
1¼ cups triticale flour
1/4 tsp. ginger
1/2 cup warm water
1 T. melted butter or oil

Dissolve the yeast in the warm water along with the honey. Add 1 cup whole wheat flour, kelp, milk powder and ginger and beat until smooth. Add remaining ingredients and beat with a wooden spoon until a stiff dough forms. Turn out onto a lightly floured board and knead for 10-15 minutes. Place smooth dough into a greased bowl, turn to coat all sides, and cover. Let rise in a warm place until doubled in size. That will take about 1 hour. Punch dough down and shape into a loaf. Place in a greased loaf pan and let rise one more time until double in size. Bake for 30 minutes at 375°.

Yield: 1 loaf

Variation:
Triticale Sprout Bread: Add 1 cup chopped triticale sprouts to the dough while you are kneading it.

BRAIDED SWEET BREAD

1 T. active dry yeast
1/4 cup warm water (110-115°)
1/2 cup warm milk (110-115°)
2 T. honey
1/4 cup butter
1½ tsp. kelp

1/2 tsp. ground cardamon
2 eggs
1 tsp. grated lemon peel
3½ cups whole wheat flour
Choice of fillings

In a large bowl dissolve the yeast in the water. Blend in the milk, honey, butter, kelp, cardamon, eggs and lemon peel. Beat with a mixer until mixed. Add 2 cups flour, 1 cup at a time. Then beat on medium speed for 3 minutes; scrape bowl often. With a wooden spoon, beat in enough remaining flour to form a soft dough. Turn dough out on a lightly floured board and knead until smooth, 5-10 minutes. Turn dough over in a greased bowl, cover, and let rise in a warm place until doubled in size, about 1½ hours. Punch dough down and turn out on a floured board. Roll dough into a 9" x 30" rectangle. Sprinkle the filling over the dough to within 1" of the edge. Starting with a long side, roll dough up tightly. Moisten edge with water; pinch firmly to seal. With a flour-coated knife, cut roll lengthwise in half. Carefully turn so cut sides are up. Loosely braid ropes, keeping cut sides up. Move to greased and floured baking sheet. Shape into a 10" circle; pinch ends together firmly. Let rise in a warm place, uncovered, until puffy looking, about 45-60 minutes. Bake at 375° until nicely browned, about 20 minutes. While hot, drizzle with glaze.

Glaze: Combine in a saucepan 1/3 cup honey, 1/3 cup water, 2 teaspoons lemon juice and heat for just a few minutes. Pour over the cooked bread.

Fillings:

Date Almond Filling:

1/4 cup butter
1/4 cup whole wheat flour
2 T. honey
2/3 cup chopped almonds

1/4 cup each raisins and chopped
    dates
1/2 tsp. grated lemon peel
3/4 tsp. almond flavoring

Beat the butter, flour and honey together until smooth. Add the rest of the ingredients and mix.

Apple Raisin Filling:

1/4 cup butter
1/4 cup whole wheat flour
2 T. honey
1/2 tsp. each cinnamon, nutmeg,
    and anise

1 tsp. grated lemon peel
3 cups finely chopped apples
3/4 cup chopped walnuts
1/2 cup raisins

Beat the butter, flour, honey and spices together until smooth. Add all the other ingredients and mix well.

Yield: 1 large wreath

QUICK BREADS

DATE NUT BREAD

1 cup dates
1/2 cup nuts (walnuts are good)
1 cup boiling water
1/4 cup sunflower seeds
1/2 cup raisins
2 T. unsulfured molasses

1 tsp. soda
2 T. butter
1 egg
1 cup whole wheat pastry flour
3/4 cup wheat germ

Chop dates and nuts coarsely. In a large bowl pour boiling water over the dates, nuts, seeds, raisins, molasses, soda, and butter. Stir to dissolve the butter. Let cool to room temperature. Stir in egg. Add the flour and wheat germ. Stir only until moistened. Do not over stir. Pour into a greased 8" x 4" loaf pan. Bake for 50-60 minutes in a 350° oven. Serve as a breakfast or dessert bread. Can top it with cream cheese or COTTAGE CHEESE.

Yield: 1 loaf

PUMPKIN NUT BREAD

1 cup pumpkin, cooked and mashed
1/3 cup honey
1/4 cup unsulfured molasses
1/2 cup milk
2 eggs
1/4 cup softened butter
2 cups whole wheat flour

2 tsp. BAKING POWDER
1/2 tsp. soda
1 tsp. cinnamon
1/2 tsp. nutmeg
1/4 tsp. ginger
1 cup raisins or chopped dates
3/4 cup nuts

Mix together with a mixer the pumpkin, honey, molasses, milk, eggs and butter. Make sure they are well combined. In a separate bowl combine the flour, baking powder, soda, cinnamon, nutmeg, ginger, raisins and nuts. Mix well. Add the dry ingredients to the liquid ones and mix only until the batter is moistened. Pour into a greased 9" loaf pan. Bake at 350° for 45-50 minutes.

Yield: 1 loaf

NO RAISE OLD FASHION BREAD

2 cups graham flour
1 cup whole wheat flour
2 cups milk plus 1-1/3 T. vinegar

1/2 cup honey
2 tsp. soda

Mix the two flours together. In another bowl mix milk and vinegar together, let sit for 5 minutes. Add honey to the milk and mix well. After that add soda to the milk mixture. Pour the milk mixture into the flour mixture and mix until moist. Pour into a well-greased loaf pan (9"). Bake for 45 minutes at 350°. When completed take out of oven and butter top of loaf. Let cool before slicing.

Yield: 1 loaf

MOLASSES BREAD

3 cups whole wheat flour
1 cup buttermilk
1 tsp. baking soda

1 cup raisins
1 cup walnuts, chopped
3/4 cup molasses, blackstrap

Mix all of the ingredients together in a large bowl until well blended. Pour into a greased loaf pan (9") and bake at 350° for 1 hour.

Yield: 1 loaf

BANANA BREAD

2½ cups whole wheat pastry flour
2 tsp. BAKING POWDER
1/4 tsp. soda
1/4 tsp. each nutmeg, cinnamon,
   cloves and ginger
1/4 cup molasses, unsulfured
1/3 cup honey
1/2 cup butter

1/8 cup oil
2 eggs, slightly beaten
1/4 cup buttermilk
1 cup ripe mashed bananas (about
   3 medium)
1/2 cup chopped nuts
1 cup chopped dates

In a large bowl mix together flour, baking powder, soda and spices. Melt the butter in a saucepan over low heat. Cool until room temperature. In a separate bowl mix together cooled butter, honey, molasses, oil, eggs, and buttermilk. Add to the flour mixture and mix only until moist. Stir in bananas, nuts and dates. Pour into a greased loaf pan. Bake 45 minutes at 350°. Best if you let it sit for a day before serving.

Yield: 1 loaf

SPOON BREAD

3 cups milk
1 cup cornmeal
1 T. butter

3 eggs, separated
3 tsp. BAKING POWDER
1 T. honey

Stir cornmeal into 2 cups milk and place in a saucepan on the stove. Bring the milk and cornmeal to a boil, making a mush. Remove from heat and add butter. Stir until butter melts. Add the rest of the milk, beaten egg yolks, baking powder and honey. Fold in stiffly beaten egg whites. Pour into a greased 2 quart baking dish. Bake at 350° for 30 minutes or until brown. Serve with honey and butter. Can be served in place of cornbread. Try it as a breakfast bread.

Yield: Serves 4

SPICY ZUCCHINI PINEAPPLE BREAD

3 eggs
1 cup oil
1/2 cup honey
1/4 cup molasses, unsulfured
1 tsp. VANILLA EXTRACT
2 cups shredded peeled zucchini

1 8-ounce can well-drained crushed
  pineapple (unsweetened)
3 cups whole wheat flour
2 tsp. soda
1 tsp. BAKING POWDER
1 tsp. each cinnamon and nutmeg

Mix together in a bowl the eggs, oil, honey, molasses and vanilla. Stir into the mixture the zucchini and pineapple. Mix together in a separate bowl the flour, soda, baking powder and spices. Add the flour mixture to the other mixture and stir only enough to moisten the ingredients. Pour into 2 greased loaf pans. Bake at 350° for 50 minutes.

Yield: 2 loaves

Variation:
You can add nuts, raisins, sunflower seeds, or sesame seeds.

PAPAYA BREAD

1/3 cup honey
1/2 cup butter
2 eggs
1 cup mashed papaya
1/4 cup chopped walnuts
1/2 cup raisins

1½ cups whole wheat flour
1/4 tsp. BAKING POWDER
1/2 tsp. cinnamon
1/2 tsp. allspice
1/2 tsp. ginger
1 tsp. baking soda

Cream honey and butter until light. Add eggs and beat until fluffy. Add papaya, nuts and raisins. Mix well. Add all of the dry ingredients to the mixture. Stir only until dry ingredients are moist. Pour into a paperlined greased loaf pan (9"). Bake at 325° for 50 minutes.

Yield: 1 loaf

ALL SEASON BREAD

3¼ cups whole wheat flour
1 tsp. soda
1½ tsp. BAKING POWDER
2 tsp. cinnamon
1 cup chopped nuts
3 eggs

3/4 cup honey
1 cup oil
1 tsp. VANILLA EXTRACT
2 cups prepared fruit or vegetable
(directions follow)

Stir together the flour, soda, baking powder, cinnamon and nuts; set aside. In a medium-sized bowl, lightly beat the eggs with a wire whip. Add the honey and oil and stir until blended. Stir in the vanilla and your choice of fruit or vegetables. Add the flour mixture all at once and stir just until moist. Divide batter between 2 greased loaf pans. Bake bread in a 350° oven for 50 minutes. Let stand 10 minutes, then turn out onto a wire rack. Let loaves sit a day before you slice them. Refrigerate up to a week, or freeze for longer storage.

Yield: 2 loaves

Variations:

Orange Bread: Grate 1 tablespoon orange peel. Then peel and finely chop 4 large oranges. The pulp should equal about 2 cups. Combine the pulp and peel; add to the bread mix.

Apple Bread: Peel, core, and shred 3 or 4 medium-size apples to make 2 cups total. The apples should be tart ones. Stir 1 teaspoon lemon juice into apples and add to batter.

Tomato Bread: Peel 3 or 4 medium-sized tomatoes. Cut each in half and squeeze gently to remove seed pockets. Finely chop the firm pulp to make 2 cups total. Add this to the batter.

CRANBERRY NUT BREAD

2 cups whole wheat flour
1½ tsp. BAKING POWDER
1/2 tsp. soda
1/2 cup honey
1/2 cup butter
3/4 cup orange juice

1 T. grated orange rind
1 egg, well beaten
3/4 cup chopped walnuts
1/2 cup sunflower seeds
*1 or 2 cups fresh or frozen cranber-
ries, coarsely chopped

Mix together in a large bowl the whole wheat flour, baking powder and soda. Cut in honey and butter until mixture resembles coarse cornmeal. Combine orange juice and grated rind with well beaten egg. Pour all at once into dry ingredients, mixing just enough to moisten. Carefully fold in walnuts, sunflower seeds and cranberries. Pour into a greased 9" loaf pan. Spread corners and sides slightly higher than center. Bake in a 350° oven for 1 hour. Cool and let sit overnight before slicing.

*If using frozen cranberries, do not thaw first. Chop up in frozen state.

Yield: 1 loaf

RHUBARB BREAD

3/4 cup honey
1/2 cup oil
1 egg
1 T. baking soda
1 cup buttermilk
2¼ cups whole wheat flour

1/4 cup soy flour
1½ cups diced rhubarb
1 tsp. VANILLA EXTRACT
1/2 cup chopped walnuts
1/3 cup sunflower seeds

Topping:

1/2 cup date sugar
1 tsp. cinnamon

1½ T. butter

In a large mixing bowl beat together the honey and oil. Add the egg and continue to mix well. Dissolve the soda in the buttermilk and set aside. Add the flour to the oil, honey, egg combination alternating with the buttermilk. Stir in the rhubarb, vanilla, walnuts and sunflower seeds. Pour into 2 greased loaf pans. Combine the topping ingredients together and sprinkle over top of unbaked bread. Bake at 325° for 50 minutes.

Yield: 2 loaves

BOSTON BROWN BREAD

1 cup cornmeal
1 cup rye flour
1 cup whole wheat flour
1½ tsp. BAKING POWDER
1/2 tsp. baking soda

3/4 cup molasses, unsulfured
2 cups buttermilk
1 cup raisins, dusted with flour
1/2 cup sunflower seeds

In a mixing bowl, stir together the cornmeal, rye, whole wheat, baking powder, and soda. Combine molasses and buttermilk; add to dry ingredients all at once. Stir in the raisins and sunflower seeds. Stir just enough to moisten thoroughly. Divide batter between two well-greased 1 pound coffee cans or three 20-ounce cans. Fill cans to two-thirds full. Cover the cans with foil (can use crumpled foil or a jar lid). Set the cans in a large pot on top of a rack. Fill the pot with boiling water to halfway up on the cans. Cover the pot and let the bread steam on very low heat for 2 hours. Let cans cool 20 minutes before removing from cans. Keeps well wrapped in foil and refrigerated.

Yield: 2 1-pound loaves

ROLLS AND CRACKERS

HONEY WHEAT BUNS

1 cup bulgur wheat or cracked wheat
1 cup boiling water
2-3 T. active dry yeast
1/4 cup warm water (about 110°)
1/3 cup honey

2 T. oil
1½ cups small curd COTTAGE
   CHEESE
3 eggs
5½ cups whole wheat flour (about)

In a large bowl, stir together the wheat and boiling water; let cool to luke-warm. Dissolve yeast in the warm water and stir into the wheat. Also add the honey, oil, cottage cheese and eggs; mix well. Gradually add 3 cups of the flour, beating well after each addition. Add enough of the remaining flour to form a stiff dough. Turn dough out onto a floured board and knead briefly as you shape the dough into a smooth ball. Place in a greased bowl, cover and let rise in a warm place until double in size. Punch dough down and divide into 20 equal pieces. Shape each piece into a smooth ball by kneading briefly on the floured board. Place the balls on a cookie sheet and flatten slightly. Let rise again until puffy and double in size. Bake at 350° for 12-15 minutes.

Yield: 20 buns

Variation:
Hamburger Buns: Use the same recipe but only divide into 10 pieces. Shape the buns the same as above. When ready to go into the oven, sprinkle the tops with sesame seeds. Bake as usual.

WHEAT ROLLS

3/4 cup boiling water
1/2 cup butter
1/8 cup honey
1 T. molasses, unsulfured
1 T. active dry yeast

1/2 cup lukewarm water
   (110-115°)
1 egg
3½ cups whole wheat flour
Melted butter

Pour boiling water over butter and stir to melt. Add honey and molasses and cool. Add yeast to 1/2 cup water and stir to dissolve, then add to cooled but-ter mixture. Add egg and stir in flour, stirring until dough forms a soft ball. Rub dough with some oil, cover and refrigerate for at least three hours. You can refrigerate as long as three days. When ready to use, roll dough into 1½" balls and place in greased 9" round pan with sides of rolls touching. Brush with melted butter, cover and let rise until double in bulk, about 1½ hours. Bake at 350° for 20-25 minutes.

Yield: 2 dozen

SHAPES FOR ROLLS

Bowknots: Roll the dough under your palms to 1/2" thickness. Cut these into pieces about 6" long and 1/2" wide. Tie each piece into a single knot.

Braids: Roll the dough and cut it the same as for bowknots. Press the top ends of three strips together, braid the strips, and press the bottom ends together.

Cloverleafs: Roll small pieces of dough into balls, between your palms. They should be about 1½" in size. Place 3 balls in each well of greased muffin pan or place balls in a 9" round pan with sides of balls touching.

Crescents: Use only part of the dough at a time. Roll into a 9" round 1/4" thick. Cut the round into pie-shaped wedges (about 10-12 of them). Brush with melted butter. Roll up, beginning at the wide end. Press the tip of the wedge gently so that the rolled roll does not open. Curve each roll into a crescent.

Fan tans: Roll a piece of dough into a very thin rectangular sheet. Brush it with melted butter, and cut into strips about 1" wide. Pile 6 strips, one on top of another. Cut into 1½" long pieces, and place on end, in the wells of greased muffin tins.

Parker House: Roll dough to 1/4"-1/2" thickness and cut into 2" rounds. Using the dull edge of a knife blade, crease through the center of each circle. Fold the dough over, and press the edges together.

WHOLE WHEAT BATTER ROLLS

1 T. active dry yeast	1 tsp. ITALIAN HERBS
1¼ cups warm water (105-115°)	2 T. oil
3 cups whole wheat flour	1 T. honey
1 tsp. kelp	1 T. molasses, unsulfured

In a large bowl dissolve the yeast in the warm water. When it is dissolved add to it 1 cup flour, kelp, Italian herbs, oil, honey, and molasses; beat well. Stir in the rest of the flour to make a stiff dough. Cover; let rise 30 minutes. Punch dough down. Reserve about 1/2 cup batter. Spoon remaining batter into greased muffin cups, filling 2/3 full. Spoon an additional teaspoon of the reserved batter atop batter in each muffin cup to make a topknot. Bake at 375° for 10-15 minutes. Cool on a wire rack. Brush tops with melted butter if desired.

Yield 16 rolls

WHOLE WHEAT BISCUITS

2 cups whole wheat flour
4 tsp. BAKING POWDER
1/3 cup butter

3/4 cup milk
1/4 cup sesame seeds

Mix flour and baking powder together in a bowl. Cut butter into flour and baking powder. Make a well in the center and pour in milk. Stir quickly with a fork. If mixture is too dry, add a little more milk to form a dough moist enough to gather into a ball. Turn dough out onto lightly floured surface and knead for 1 minute. Roll dough out from center to 3/4" thick. Cut with a biscuit cutter and sprinkle with sesame seeds. Place on cookie sheet and bake at 350° for 20 minutes. To make DROP BISCUITS add 1/4 cup more milk. Do not knead or roll out. Drop by tablespoon and sprinkle with sesame seeds. Bake the same as for whole wheat biscuits.

Yield: 1 dozen

Variations:

Cheese Biscuits: Cut 1/2 cup Cheddar cheese into the flour mixture along with the butter.

Herbed Biscuits: Add 2 tablespoons dill and 1 tablespoon chopped parsley to the flour mixture before the butter is added.

Poppy Biscuits: Add 1 cup poppy seeds to the dough.

POPOVERS

3 eggs
1 cup whole wheat flour
1 T. oil

1 cup milk
Oil

Heat oven to 350°. Grease aluminum popover or muffin pans with 2 tsp. oil in each cup. Set aside. If glass or earthenware cups are used, place on a baking sheet in the oven to heat. Remove and grease just before filling. Add all ingredients together and beat until smooth. Pour in batter, almost to the top of the cup. Bake at 350° for 40-45 minutes. Do not peek or they will fall. Serve warm or store airtight and reheat. You can add spices to the dough—cinnamon, nutmeg, dill or rosemary.

Yield: 1 dozen

Variation:
Cheese Popovers: Add 1/2 cup grated Parmesan cheese.

WHOLE WHEAT SOFT PRETZELS

1 T. active dry yeast
1 tsp. date sugar
1¼ cups warm water (105-115°)
1 tsp. kelp

3-3½ cups whole wheat flour
Butter
4 tsp. soda
Sesame seeds

Dissolve the yeast and date sugar in 1/4 cup warm water and allow to double in bulk. This only takes a few minutes. Combine the flour and kelp in a large mixing bowl. Add the remaining 1 cup of water and the yeast mixture and mix well. Add enough additional flour to make a stiff dough if necessary. Knead the dough for about 10 minutes. Form the dough into a ball and coat with butter. Place the dough into a greased bowl and cover with a towel. Allow to rise until double in size, about 1½ hours. Divide the dough into 12 pieces. Roll each piece with your hands to form a rope about 20" long and 1/4" in diameter. Shape each rope into a pretzel shape. Wet your fingers to pinch the pretzel together firmly. Put 4 cups water in a large pan, add the baking soda and bring to a boil. Carefully lower each pretzel into the boiling water and boil for 1 minute or until the pretzel floats to the top. Remove the pretzel from the water with a spatula and place on plate to drain. After all the water has drained off, carefully place the pretzel on a greased baking sheet. Sprinkle with sesame seeds. Bake at 350° for 25 minutes or until a golden brown. These pretzels are best served warm.

Yield: 24 pretzels

Variation:
Crisp Pretzels: Prepare and shape the dough into thin sticks or twists as described above, but do not boil. Place on greased cookie sheet, brush with 1 egg yolk, beaten with 2 tablespoons milk, and sprinkle with sesame seeds. Let rise until almost doubled in bulk, about 25 minutes. Bake as directed above.

CHEESE WAFERS

1/2 cup butter
3/4 cup whole wheat pastry flour
1 cup Cheddar cheese, finely grated

1/3 cup walnuts, finely chopped
1/4 tsp. cayenne pepper

Mix flour and butter together with mixer. Add cheese, nuts and pepper. Form into a ball and refrigerate until firm. Roll into balls and flatten with your hand. Bake at 350° for 8 minutes. Great with CHEESE BUTTER.

Yield: 3 dozen

SESAME CRISP CRACKERS

1 cup whole wheat flour	1/4 cup oil
1/2 cup whole wheat pastry flour	1 T. honey
1/4 cup soy flour	1/2 cup water
1/4 cup sesame seeds	

Stir flours and sesame seeds together. Pour in oil and honey and blend well. Add enough water to the dough to make it of pie dough consistency. Gather the dough into a ball, then roll out to 1/8" thick. Cut into cracker shapes and place on an unoiled baking sheet. Bake at 350° for 7 minutes, until crisp and golden.

Yield: 6 dozen

WHOLE WHEAT SODA CRACKERS

2 cups whole wheat flour	1/2 cup buttermilk
1/2 tsp. baking soda	1 egg, beaten
1/4 cup butter	Sesame seeds

Mix together the flour and soda. Add butter, softened and cut into bits, and blend the mixture until it resembles cornmeal. Pour the buttermilk and egg into the flour mixture and toss until the liquid is well incorporated. Turn the dough onto a lightly floured board and knead for 5 minutes. Roll out half the dough into a rectangle 1/8" thick. You want it quite thin. Transfer it to buttered baking sheet. Cut dough into 2" squares. Prick it with a fork, sprinkle with sesame seeds and bake at 400° for 10-12 minutes. Break the squares apart and transfer to a rack to cool. Prepare and bake the remaining dough. Store in an airtight container.

Yield 3-4 dozen

GRAHAM CRACKERS

2¼ cups whole wheat flour
3/4 cups whole wheat pastry flour
1 tsp. BAKING POWDER
1/2 cup butter
1/3 cup honey

1/8 cup molasses, unsulfured
1 tsp. VANILLA EXTRACT
1 tsp. cinnamon
1/2 cup milk

In a bowl combine the two flours and baking powder. In another bowl cream together the butter, honey, molasses, vanilla and cinnamon. Cream until fluffy. Add flour mixture and milk alternately to the creamed mixture. Mix well after each addition. Chill for several hours. Divide dough in half. Rechill one portion while rolling out other half. Roll on a lightly floured board to 1/8" thickness. If dough becomes too soft while working with it, rechill. Using a knife or pastry wheel, cut dough into 3" squares. Prick each square 3 times with a fork. Do this with the other half of the dough. Bake at 325° for about 30 minutes. Cool and store in an airtight container.

Yield: 40 crackers

Variation:
Graham Cracker Treats:

1/3 cup honey
1/2 cup butter
1/2 tsp. VANILLA EXTRACT
1/4 tsp. cinnamon

3/4 cup chopped walnuts
1/3 cup sesame seeds
20 graham crackers

In a saucepan heat together the honey and butter. Bring to a boil over medium heat stirring constantly. Stir and boil gently for 5 minutes. Remove from heat and stir in the vanilla, cinnamon, nuts and seeds. Drizzle mixture quickly over the graham crackers and spread evenly.

LAVOSH

3-3½ cups whole wheat flour
1/4 cup butter
1 cup milk

1 egg
Milk
Sesame seeds

Cut butter into flour until it resembles cornmeal. Add milk and egg and mix well. Knead the dough for a few minutes on a lightly floured board. Place in a covered bowl in refrigerator for at least 1/2 hour. Break off a small piece from the dough and roll out until thin. Place on greased cookie sheet. Coat lightly with milk and sprinkle with sesame seeds. Bake for 10 minutes at 350°.

Yield: About 4-5 batches

SOURDOUGH

American colonists brought crocks of sourdough to America with them. When covered wagons moved westward, sourdough was aboard and it was guarded jealously. Sourdough became legendary with the California Gold Rush of 1849. The Sourdough "starter" was passed from neighbor to neighbor and was a common leaven in the days before packaged yeast became available. San Francisco is famous for its sourdough bread. Today more and more homemakers are taking it into their own kitchens.

A little sourdough goes a long way. By adding flour and warm water to the sourdough starter you can make pancakes, breads, rolls and cakes. Just save a cup of sourdough from each batch and you will be able to keep your starter going for years.

Sourdough is a form of yeast reacting to all the same conditions other yeasts do. But it is slower and needs more warmth for a longer period of time.

SOURDOUGH STARTER

A good starter has a strong, sour milk odor. The smell is part of the aging process. The starter will stay fresh by using it regularly. If it is not going to be used for several weeks, freeze or dry it so it will not spoil. In the dried form the yeast goes into a spore stage, and it can stay inert for a long time.

Keep the sourdough, once made, in the refrigerator. Storing at room temperature invites the growth of undesirable bacteria and molds. It is not harmful, but not desirable. Storing at cold temperatures is important because the starter is not a sterile yeast culture. The cold does not harm the yeast. It just reduces its reproduction rate.

Temperature is a very important factor in helping your starter become sour and bubbly. You should keep it at a temperature of 80-100°. Some spots to keep it warm would be on top of your water heater, refrigerator, near a gas range burner or pilot light. Or, in an electric range 2½" below the inside light. Heat oven for a few minutes so it is warmer than the air outside the oven, then turn it off. Place starter by light and close door. Come up with your own spot, but do not put it out in the sun as it will get too hot.

SOURDOUGH STARTER RECIPE

1 cup skim or low fat milk
3 T. plain YOGURT (unflavored)

1 cup whole wheat flour

Begin with a dry, sterile, 1½ quart jar, made of glass, plastic or pottery. Do not use metal as a chemical reaction kills the starter's leavening action. Heat the milk to 90-100°. Remove from heat and add 3 tablespoons of yogurt. Warm the outside of the jar by running it under hot water a few times. Then pour milk mixture into the container. Cap tightly and let stand in a warm place (80-100°). After 18-20 hours, the starter should be the consistency of yogurt. If a clear liquid rises to the top, just stir it back into the mixture. If the liquid is pink, discard starter and begin again.

After curd has formed, stir in one cup flour; blend until smooth. Cover tightly and set in a warm place (80-100°) until mixture becomes bubbly and sour smelling. This will take 2-5 days. Again if a clear liquid rises to the top, stir it back in. If a pink liquid rises, discard all but 1/4 cup. Take the 1/4 cup and add 1 cup warm milk (90-100°) and 1 cup flour. Blend until smooth. Cover tightly and return to a warm place until it bubbles and smells sour. When mixture is completed, cover tightly and store in the refrigerator. Now the starter is ready to use in your recipes. You should use your starter every 10 days or it will develop a strong taste.

NOW YOU ARE READY TO USE THE STARTER IN A RECIPE

The traditional batter should be prepared the evening before you want to use it in your recipes.

1 cup SOURDOUGH STARTER
2 cups warm water

2 cups whole wheat flour

Place the starter in a large mixing bowl (do not use a metal one—it will kill the starter) and add the milk and flour. Mix thoroughly. The mixture will be thick and lumpy. Cover the bowl and let it sit in a warm place overnight (10-12 hours). It should bubble. In the morning return 1 cup of this mixture to the storage jar and use the rest of the mixture in your recipes. This batter is considered a starter in the recipes. If you are going to use it for pancakes or waffles, you will need to make an extra big batch of batter. To use in a recipe just measure out the amount called for and use as directed.

HINTS

If your starter does not seem as bubbly after continued use, sprinkle with a small amount of dry yeast and mix well. This is also recommended if thawed frozen starter does not resume its bubbly appearance. If clear liquid forms on top of mixture, simply stir down and continue to use as needed. To add sourdough to your favorite yeast recipes, there are a few guidelines to follow. Until you are used to working with it, it is best you add or keep the yeast in the recipes. You can add up to 1 cup starter to most yeast doughs if you first reduce the total amount of liquid by 1/4 to 1/2 cup. You will probably need to use all the flour called for in the recipe or even a little more.

WHOLE WHEAT SOURDOUGH BREAD

1 cup SOURDOUGH STARTER	1 tsp. kelp
1½ cups water	1/2 cup oil
4 T. honey	6 cups whole wheat flour

In a large mixing bowl, beat starter, 1 cup water, honey, kelp, oil and 1½ cups flour until smooth, using an electric mixer. Add in rest of water and beat in as much whole wheat flour as mixer can handle. Mixture will be soft and sticky. Turn out onto floured surface and knead about 5 minutes. Knead just enough flour into dough to make it soft. The dough, after it is kneaded, will feel plump. Place in an oiled bowl, turn to grease all sides, and cover and let rise until double in size. That will take about 3 hours. When dough is doubled, punch dough down and divide into 2 equal parts. Pat each part into a rectangle approximately 8½" wide. Shape into loaves and then place in loaf pans. Store in a warm place until it doubles in size. Before baking, brush outside with water and make diagonal slashes across the top with a sharp knife. Bake at 350° for 35 minutes or until golden brown.

Yield: 2 loaves

Variation:
Can add to dough raisins, nuts, sunflower seeds.

SOURDOUGH PANCAKES

1 cup whole wheat flour	1 cup SOURDOUGH STARTER
1½ tsp. BAKING POWDER	2/3 cup milk
1 egg, beaten	2 T. oil
2 T. honey	

Stir dry ingredients together. Beat egg; add other liquid ingredients. Pour liquid ingredients into dry ingredients. Mix by hand, only until moistened. Cook on a lightly greased griddle over medium high heat. Use 2 or 3 tablespoons of batter for each pancake. If you would like a thinner batter, add more milk.

Yield: 16 pancakes

SOURDOUGH OATMEAL MUFFINS

3/4 cup SOURDOUGH STARTER
1½ cups whole wheat flour
1 cup rolled oats
1 tsp. soda
1/4 cup honey

1 T. molasses, unsulfured
1 egg, slightly beaten
1/3 cup buttermilk
1/3 cup oil

Mix together the flour, oats and soda. Blend together the honey, molasses, egg, buttermilk and oil. Stir in the starter. Pour this mixture all at once into the flour mixture. Stir lightly to moisten ingredients. Batter will be lumpy. Grease muffin cups and fill 2/3 full. Bake at 375° for 30-35 minutes.

Yield: 12-15 muffins

COTTAGE CHEESE SOURDOUGH PAN ROLLS

1 T. active dry yeast
1/4 cup warm water (110°)
1 cup COTTAGE CHEESE
1 cup SOURDOUGH STARTER
1 egg
2 tsp. BAKING POWDER

1/4 tsp. soda
1 tsp. kelp
1 T. honey
4 cups whole wheat flour
2 T. butter

In a small bowl, dissolve the yeast in the warm water. In a blender, whirl the cottage cheese, starter and egg until smooth. In a large bowl, combine the baking powder, soda, kelp, honey and flour. With your fingers work in the butter until no large particles remain. Stir in the cottage cheese mixture and dissolved yeast. Turn dough out onto a floured board and knead until smooth, about 10 minutes; add flour as needed. Turn dough over in a greased bowl, cover, and let rise in a warm place until doubled, about 45 minutes. Punch down dough. Divide into 18 pieces and shape each into a ball. Arrange balls in 2 greased 8" round baking pans. Cover and let rise until puffy, about 20 minutes. Bake at 350° for 30-35 minutes, or until golden brown. Cool.

Yield: 1½ dozen

SOURDOUGH RYE BREAD

1 T. active dry yeast
1½ tsp. honey
1 cup warm water (about 110°)
2 tsp. oil
1 tsp. kelp
2 T. caraway seed

3/4 cup SOURDOUGH STARTER,
   at room temperature
1½ cups rye flour
2-2¼ cups whole wheat flour
Melted butter

Combine yeast, honey and water and let stand until bubbly, about 15 minutes. Stir in oil, kelp, caraway and starter. Mix in 1/2 cup rye flour and 1/2 cup whole wheat. Add the remaining 1 cup rye flour and beat well. Now mix in about 1 cup of whole wheat flour gradually. When dough becomes too stiff to mix, turn out onto a floured board and knead until smooth and elastic, about 10 minutes. Place in a greased bowl and turn over to grease all sides. Cover and let rise in a warm place until double in size, about 1 hour. Punch down and divide dough in half. Form into 2 smooth balls and place on a greased baking sheet. Should be shaped into a 9" round. Let rise in a warm place until double in size again. Brush tops lightly with melted butter. Bake at 375° for about 35 minutes or until well browned. Brush tops again with melted butter.

Yield: 2 loaves

MUFFINS

PEANUT BUTTER MUFFINS

1 egg
1¼ cups milk
1/3 cup oil
3/4 cup PEANUT BUTTER
4 T. unsulfured molasses
1 tsp. VANILLA EXTRACT
1 cup whole wheat flour

1/2 cup wheat germ
1 cup bran
1 cup chopped walnuts
2 tsp. BAKING POWDER
1/2 tsp. baking soda
1 cup raisins

Add the first six ingredients together and mix. Add all the other ingredients to it and mix only until moistened. Pour into greased muffin tins. Bake at 350° for 20 minutes.

Yield: 12 muffins

MUFFIN MIX

This is a mix that you can make ahead of time and store in the refrigerator and use whenever you want to make muffins. It will store for several weeks. It will separate during storage, so stir it gently to blend.

2½ cups whole wheat flour
2½ tsp. soda
3 cups rolled oats, uncooked
1 cup boiling water
1/2 cup butter, melted

1/3 cup honey
1/4 cup wheat germ
2 eggs, slightly beaten
2 cups buttermilk

Combine the flour, soda and set aside. In a large bowl, stir together the oats and boiling water; cool slightly. Stir in butter, honey, wheat germ, eggs, and buttermilk. Add flour mixture, stirring until just blended. To store, refrigerate in a tightly covered container for up to 4 weeks. To bake, stir batter down and spoon directly into greased muffin pan. Fill only 3/4 full. Bake in a 375° oven for 25 minutes, or until golden. Cool for about 5 minutes before removing from pan.

Yield: 2½ dozen

Variations:

Fruit and Nut Muffins: For each 1 cup muffin batter, stir in a total of 1/4 cup chopped nuts or shredded coconut and dried fruit (such as raisins, dates, prunes, apples). Spoon into muffin pan and bake as directed above.

Cheese Muffins: To 1 cup batter add 1/4 cup grated Cheddar cheese.

Applesauce Muffins: To 1 cup batter add 1/3 cup APPLESAUCE, 1/4 teaspoon cinnamon and 1/8 teaspoon nutmeg.

Carrot Date Muffins: To 1 cup batter add 1/4 cup grated carrots, 1/8 cup chopped dates and 1/8 teaspoon each allspice and cloves.

TWO GRAIN MUFFINS

1 well beaten egg
1/4 cup oil
1/4 cup honey
1 cup milk
1 tsp. VANILLA EXTRACT

1/2 cup whole wheat flour
1/2 cup soy flour
1 cup wheat germ
3 tsp. BAKING POWDER
1/2 cup raisins

Mix the egg, oil, honey, milk and vanilla together. Add all the other ingredients and mix lightly, only until moistened. Pour into greased muffin tin, 3/4 full and bake at 400° for 15 minutes.

Yield: 1 dozen

BUTTERMILK BRAN MUFFINS

2 cups bran
1 cup whole wheat flour
1½ tsp. BAKING POWDER
1/2 tsp. soda
1 cup sunflower seeds
1 cup raisins

1/4 cup sesame seeds
1 beaten egg
1 cup buttermilk
1/4 cup molasses, unsulfured
2 ripe bananas, mashed

Combine dry ingredients (the first 7 items) together in a bowl. Mix in a small bowl the egg, buttermilk, molasses, and bananas. Add the wet ingredients to the dry ones and stir only until all ingredients are moist. Fill greased muffin tins 3/4 full. Bake at 350° for 25 minutes.

Yield: 12 muffins

PUMPKIN MUFFINS

4 eggs
1/2 cup oil
1/3 cup honey
1/4 cup molasses, unsulfured
1½ cups pumpkin, cooked and
    mashed
2¼ cups whole wheat flour
1/2 cup bran
1/8 cup non-instant dry milk powder

3 tsp. BAKING POWDER
1/4 tsp. clove
1/2 tsp. nutmeg
1/2 tsp. cinnamon
1 tsp. grated orange rind
1 cup raisins
1/2 cup chopped pitted dates
1 cup chopped nuts

Beat together the eggs, oil, honey, molasses and pumpkin. Combine the flour, bran, dry milk, baking powder, cloves, nutmeg, cinnamon, orange rind, raisins, dates and nuts together. Then add the egg mixture to the dry ingredients and stir only until moistened. Pour into greased muffin tins. Fill 2/3 full. Bake at 375° for 20 minutes. Cool five minutes before removing from the pan.

Yield: 1½–2 dozen

BLUEBERRY MUFFINS

1 cup whole wheat pastry flour
1/2 cup whole wheat flour
2 tsp. BAKING POWDER
1/4 cup butter

1/4 cup honey
1 egg, beaten slightly
1/2 cup milk
1 cup fresh or frozen blueberries

Mix together the flours and baking powder. Cut butter into flour with a pastry cutter or 2 knives. In another bowl mix together the honey, egg, milk and blueberries. Then add the wet ingredients to the dry ingredients. Mix only until moist. DO NOT over stir. Place in greased muffin tin and bake 20 minutes at 375°.

Yield: 12 muffins

APPLE YOGURT MUFFINS

3 large apples, pared
2 cups whole wheat flour
1/4 cup honey
1½ tsp. BAKING POWDER
1/2 tsp. nutmeg
1 tsp. baking soda

1 tsp. cinnamon
1 cup plain YOGURT
1 egg, beaten
1/4 cup melted butter
2 tsp. grated lemon peel

Chop the apples into very small pieces and set aside. In a large bowl combine the flour, honey, baking powder, soda, nutmeg and cinnamon. In a small bowl stir yogurt until creamy, and stir in beaten egg. Add melted butter and grated lemon peel, mixing well. Pour all wet ingredients into flour mixture. Stir quickly until all the flour disappears. Gently fold in the apples, and spoon into muffin tins until 2/3 full. Bake 20 minutes at 400°. Serve warm.

Yield: 12-16 muffins

SPECIALTIES

PUMPERNICKEL BAGELS

2 T. dry yeast
1/4 cup lukewarm water (about 110°)
1 cup whole wheat flour
2 T. blackstrap molasses
1½ cups lukewarm water

1/4 cup oil
1/3 cup non-instant dry milk
    powder
3 cups rye flour
2 cups whole wheat flour

Dissolve yeast in 1/2 cup warm water. When bubbly, add 1 cup whole wheat flour and molasses. Beat vigorously about 100 strokes. Let rest in a warm spot for 15-20 minutes. Add water, oil, milk powder and rye flour. Knead mixture well, incorporating last 2 cups of whole wheat flour as needed to make a stiff dough. Let rest for an hour in a warm spot and shape into form. Place on cookie sheet and let rise about 20 minutes. Bake at 425° until brown, but not hard.

Yield: 20-25 bagels

WHOLE WHEAT BAGELS

1/2 cup warm water (110-115°)
3 T. active dry yeast
1½ cups very hot water
3 T. honey

1/4 cup oil
4 eggs
8 cups whole wheat flour
2 quarts water

Glaze:

1 egg   1 T. water

Mix together the 1/2 cup water and yeast. Let sit for 5 minutes. In another bowl combine the very hot water, honey and oil and stir until dissolved. Beat together the eggs and add this and the yeast combination into the liquid mixture and mix well. Add flour and stir until a stiff dough is formed. Knead well—about 10 minutes. Place in covered greased bowl and let rise until double in bulk. Punch down and divide into 30 balls. Holding each ball with both hands, poke your thumb through the center. With one thumb in the hole, work around perimeter, shaping like a doughnut, 3–3½" across. Allow to rise until double in size. Meanwhile bring 2 quarts of water to a boil. Drop bagels, about 4 at a time, into the boiling water. Boil for 3 minutes, remove and place on cookie sheet. Mix the glaze together and brush onto the bagels. Bake the bagels for 20 minutes at 425°, or until golden brown. Turn over half way through the baking process.

Yield: 30 bagels

Variations: To make different types of bagel use the above recipe but add different ingredients to the dough. For example:

Add 1/2 cup instant toasted onion to dough.

Add raisins or nuts to the dough after it has been punched down.

Add sesame seeds, poppyseeds, caraway seeds on top of glazed bagels before they are baked.

WHOLE WHEAT CRUMPETS

1 T. dry yeast
1/4 cup lukewarm water (about 110°)
1 tsp. honey

1¾ cups milk, room temperature
3½ cups whole wheat flour
1 tsp. kelp

Dissolve yeast in lukewarm water with the honey. Set aside. Mix milk with the flour and kelp in another bowl. When the yeast mixture bubbles, add it to the flour batter and beat very well. You will have a very thick batter or a very soft dough. Cover and let rise until double in bulk. Preheat an oiled griddle. Grease several tuna cans (with both ends removed) and set them on the griddle. Never let the griddle get more than medium hot (over 300°). With a ladle, fill the rings half full. As the muffins rise and brown on the griddle, remove the rings and turn the breads to complete the baking process. When both sides are light brown and firm, the muffins are ready. Cool slightly, then fork-split them. Good served with COTTAGE CHEESE, YOGURT, cream cheese, butter, TAHINI, jams, or cheese.

Yield: 8

WHOLE WHEAT ENGLISH MUFFINS

2 T. yeast
1-2/3 cups warm water (about 110°)
2 T. honey
1/2 cup non-instant dry milk
    powder

1/4 cup wheat germ
1/2 cup cracked wheat, or rolled
    oats
4 cups whole wheat flour
1/4 cup yellow cornmeal

Combine yeast and water and let stand 5 minutes. Stir in honey, dry milk, wheat germ, cracked wheat or rolled oats, and 2½ cups of the whole wheat flour. Beat with a mixer at medium speed for 5 minutes. Gradually add the rest of the flour either with a wooden spoon or heavy mixer. Knead dough for about 10 minutes. Place in a greased bowl, cover and let rise until double in bulk. Punch down and turn out on a board lightly sprinkled with cornmeal. Roll out dough to about 1/2'' thick. With a tuna can (with both ends removed) cut dough in rounds. Place muffins, cornmeal side up, about 1'' apart on a baking sheet. Cover and let rise until puffy, but not doubled; about 45-60 minutes. Preheat a griddle to about 275°. Lightly grease surface and bake muffins slowly until golden brown. It takes about 12-15 minutes. Cool. Refrigerate or freeze until needed; split muffins before freezing.

Yield: 1 dozen

SOURDOUGH WHOLE WHEAT ENGLISH MUFFINS

Follow the recipe above, using only 1 T. yeast, dissolved in 1-1/3 cups warm water. Add 1 cup SOURDOUGH STARTER (which is at room temperature) with honey and remaining ingredients. Finish as directed. Allow a little extra time for dough to rise.

QUICK MIX

Just as the name implies, it is quick. Just make up a batch of these dry ingredients and store in the refrigerator. When you want to make a number of different baked goods, such as biscuits, just take out the desired amount and add your liquid ingredients to it. No need to measure all of the dry ingredients each time you make a recipe.

4 cups whole wheat flour
3/4 cup wheat germ
1 cup soy flour

1/2 cup non-instant dry milk
    powder
4 T. BAKING POWDER

Add all of the ingredients together in a large bowl. Mix well. Now the mix is ready to be used in many different recipes. If not used right away, store in a glass container or plastic bag and place in the refrigerator or freezer. The use for this mixture is unlimited. Substitute it for flour in your favorite baking recipes. Only thing you need to do is omit the salt, baking powder and soda from the recipe. Depending on the recipe, you may find the batter too thin or too thick. Adjust the flour or liquid ingredients accordingly.

Yield: 6 cups

PANCAKES

2 cups QUICK MIX
2 eggs
1¾ cups buttermilk

2 T. oil
3 T. frozen apple juice concentrate
(unsweetened) or honey

Mix in a small bowl the eggs, buttermilk, oil and sweetener. Mix well together. Place in another bowl the Quick Mix and add the egg and milk mixture to it. Stir until all the ingredients are moistened. Spoon the mixture onto a hot griddle and cook until bubbles appear. Turn over and brown the other side.

Yield: 12 pancakes

NUT BREAD

2 T. molasses, unsulfured
1/3 cup honey
1/2 cup oil
1 egg

1 cup buttermilk
3 cups QUICK MIX
1 tsp. cinnamon
1 cup nuts, chopped

Mix the molasses, honey, oil, egg and buttermilk together in a bowl. Add the Quick Mix, cinnamon and chopped nuts and mix only until the dry ingredients are moistened. Bake at 350° for 1 hour.

Yield: 1 loaf

BISCUITS

1/3 cup oil
2/3 cup buttermilk
4 T. honey

2¼ cups QUICK MIX
Sesame seeds

Mix the oil, buttermilk and honey together and then add the Quick Mix to the mixture. Drop by tablespoon onto a greased cookie sheet and bake 15 minutes at 350°.

Yield: 1 dozen

SPICE COOKIES

2 eggs
2/3 cups oil
1/2 cup honey
2¼ cups QUICK MIX

1 tsp. cinnamon
1/2 tsp. cloves
1/2 tsp. nutmeg
1 cup GRANOLA

Beat together in a bowl the eggs, oil and honey. Add all the other ingredients and beat until well mixed. Drop onto a cookie sheet and bake at 350° for 10 minutes.

Yield: 3 dozen

CORNBREAD

2 cups cornmeal
1/2 cup whole wheat flour
3 tsp. BAKING POWDER
2 cups buttermilk

2 eggs
2 T. oil
3 T. honey

Sift dry ingredients into a large bowl. Beat liquid ingredients together well. Make a well in the center of the flour and pour liquid ingredients in. Stir only until blended. Bake in a greased 8" square baking dish for 25-30 minutes at 400°.

Yield: 16 squares

Variation: Mexican Cornbread:

1/2 cup chopped onions
2 T. jalapeno pepper, chopped

3/4 cup grated Cheddar cheese
1/2 cup kernel corn (optional)

Add all of the ingredients to the liquid mixture and then add to dry ingredients and proceed as directed.

BAKED SPICE DOUGHNUTS

2 cups whole wheat flour
3 tsp. BAKING POWDER
1/4 tsp. each nutmeg and cinnamon
1/4 cup butter
1/2 cup milk

2 T. honey
1 egg
Melted butter
Date sugar or GRANOLA

In a bowl mix together the flour, baking powder and spices. With a pastry cutter or 2 knives, cut in the 1/4 cup butter until particles are the size of small peas. Lightly beat together the milk, honey and egg with a fork. then stir into the dry ingredients just until moistened. Gather dough up into a ball and knead 8-10 times on a lightly floured board. Roll out dough 1/2" thick and cut out doughnuts and holes, using a floured 3" cutter. Place doughnuts and holes on an ungreased baking sheet. Bake at 425° until lightly browned, about 10-12 minutes. Immediately dip the tops in melted butter and then in the date sugar or granola.

Yield: 10 doughnuts

CROUTONS

Place bread in a 250-300° oven and warm until dry and crisp. Cut into 1" cubes. Toss the cubes with oil, garlic powder and different herbs that you would like, plus Parmesan cheese. Place back in the oven at 375° until golden brown and crisp, about 8 minutes. Cool and store until needed.

BREADSTICKS

Use half of the dough for FRENCH BREAD   1/4 cup sesame or poppy seeds

After the first rising with the bread, divide the dough into balls the size of a golf ball. Roll each ball into a stick about 1/2" x 6". Roll the sticks in the seeds. Place on a greased cookie sheet. Let them rise about 15 minutes. Place in a 350° oven and bake until golden brown, about 15 minutes.

Yield: 30 breadsticks

CORN TORTILLAS

1 cup stone ground cornmeal   2-2½ cups whole wheat flour
1 cup boiling water

Pour boiling water over cornmeal. Let sit 10 minutes or more. Add flour to the cornmeal mixture to make a kneadable dough. Knead 5-10 minutes. Let sit 5 minutes. Pinch off a piece of dough the size of a golf ball. Roll it out on a floured board to a more or less round shape about 4" in diameter. Cook on an unoiled hot griddle about 2 minutes on each side.

Yield: 12-15

FLOUR TORTILLA/CHAPATI

1 cup warm water   3 T. oil
3 cups whole wheat flour

Mix all of the ingredients together, adjusting the quantity of water to make a stiff dough. Knead the dough for 10 minutes on a lightly floured board until smooth and elastic. Gather into a ball and rub a small amount of oil on it. Wrap it in plastic and let it sit at least 12 hours. Divide the dough into 14 balls and roll each one out on a lightly floured surface. They should form circles about 7" in diameter. Heat a griddle on medium heat, but do not add any oil. Place one chapati onto griddle. It may blow up somewhat, just press down with light pressure from a spatula. When light brown spots appear turn over and cook the other side. Takes only a few minutes. Used as an accompaniment to curries and vegetable dishes. Use in Mexican dishes if you want a flour tortilla.

Yield: 14

PITA BREAD

2 T. yeast   5 cups whole wheat flour
2 cups warm water (105-115°)   Sesame seeds
1 T. honey   Cornmeal
3 T. oil

Dissolve yeast in warm water. In a large bowl, mix together the yeast mixture, honey, oil and 2½ cups flour until all ingredients are mixed well. Work in additional 2½ cups flour. Knead until firm and smooth (about 10 minutes). Place in a greased bowl and let rise in a warm place for 1 hour. The dough won't double but will get puffy. Divide dough into 16 pieces. On a floured board sprinkled with sesame seeds, roll each ball into a 5-6" circle, about 1/4" thick. Place on ungreased cookie sheet which has been sprinkled lightly with cornmeal. Let it sit and puff up for about 30 minutes. Bake in a 450° oven on lowest rack for 5-10 minutes until bread puffs up and starts to brown. When finished, remove from oven and cut in half and split open. Fill with favorite sandwich fillings. If not used right away, do not cut in half. Store in plastic bags, seal and freeze. Reheat before using.

Yield: 16

PANCAKES, WAFFLES AND CREPES

Pancakes and waffles have long been an American favorite for breakfast. But why wait to serve them just as a breakfast food? Try them as any meal of the day!

The basic ingredients for them are whole grains, milk, oil, eggs and a leavening agent. From this **CHAPTER 10** you can vary the recipes to suit your taste. Add different butters or toppings, or place fresh fruit and nuts in the batter. Arrange them differently on the plate, i.e., stacked with different layers of fruits or spreads between each layer, or roll them up after filling them with different fillings.

If you want to go fancy, try crepes. A very thin French pancake that is quick and easy to make as well as being delicious. The crepes can be filled with a number of different fillings, from seafood to fresh fruit. Then you can top them with any topping of your choice.

The waffle, pancake and crepe recipes in this section are wholesome, of high nutritional value and easy to prepare. Enjoy trying some of the different recipes.

HELPFUL HINTS

- Replace any of the liquid in the pancake or waffle recipe with an equal amount of YOGURT.

- To keep pancakes warm, stack them on aluminum foil and seal. Then place them in a warm oven until ready to use.

- Pancakes should only be turned once. Wait until bubbles occur on the top, then they are ready to flip.

- Use leftover pancakes by filling them with fish, chicken, eggs or spreads and folding them over. Just pop into the oven until they are reheated. If you want to serve them cold, just fill with fruits, nuts and cheeses.

- Add wheat germ to the batter to increase the nutritional value.
- Sprinkle nuts or seeds in the batter to give a crunchy taste to them.
- Freeze leftovers. When you want to eat them just pop them into a toaster for a few seconds.
- Crepes are inexpensive and a great buy for the money. Roll leftovers in them and serve as a meal.
- Vary the batter by using different flours, i.e., rye, soy, buckwheat, rice, oat and corn.
- Vary the liquids used in crepes by adding buttermilk, YOGURT, fruit juice.
- Fill the crepes with whatever you want, i.e., fruit, vegetables, fish, chicken. Top with different sauces such as TOMATO, CHEESE, CREAM SAUCE.
- After preparing the crepe batter let it rest for 40 minutes. The flour expands and absorbs all of the liquid and bubbles collapse, so there will be no air holes in the crepes.
- To see if the pan you are going to use for the pancakes, waffles or crepes is hot enough, sprinkle with some water and if it dances it is hot.
- Crepes freeze well. When you want to use them just defrost for 15 minutes.
- You can also freeze crepes that have been filled, baked or unbaked.

PANCAKES

BANANA PANCAKES

2 cups banana purée (3-4 bananas)
2½ cups milk
2 eggs
3 T. honey
4 cups whole wheat flour

3/4 cup soy flour
4 tsp. BAKING POWDER
1/2 tsp. baking soda
1/3 cup sunflower seeds

To make the banana purée, place the bananas in a blender and add just a little milk to help move the bananas around. Blend until smooth. Add the purée, eggs, milk and honey together and mix well. Add the rest of the ingredients and mix well. Bake on a hot griddle. Can serve topped with fruit syrup or my favorite is to top each pancake with a spoonful of YOGURT and pour over extra banana purée and then sprinkle with chopped nuts.

Yield: 28 medium-sized pancakes

BASIC PANCAKES

2 cups whole wheat pastry flour
1/2 cup wheat germ
1 tsp. BAKING POWDER
1 tsp. baking soda

1 T. frozen apple juice concentrate
   (unsweetened)
2 eggs
1-1/3 cups buttermilk
2 T. oil

Stir together the first five ingredients. Beat the eggs slightly and combine with buttermilk; then add to dry ingredients and stir briefly. Stir in oil with a few strokes. Pour in large spoonfuls onto a hot greased griddle. Cook over medium heat, turning once when bubbles come to the surface and pop.

Yield: Serves 4

Variations:

Blueberry Pancakes: Add 1 cup fresh or frozen blueberries and 1/2 cup sunflower seeds to the batter.

Peach Pancakes: Add 2 cups sliced fresh or frozen peaches and 1½ tsp. cinnamon to the batter and cook as directed.

Apple Pancakes: Add 1½ cups grated apples plus 1/2 tsp. cinnamon, 1/4 tsp. nutmeg and 1/3 cup soy grits.

PUMPKIN PANCAKES

1½ cups milk
1/2 cup plain YOGURT
2 eggs, well beaten
1 T. oil
1 T. honey
1 T. unsulfured molasses
2 cups whole wheat flour

1 T. soy grits (optional)
1 T. wheat germ
3 T. sunflower seeds, finely
   chopped
1½ cups pumpkin, cooked and
   mashed
1/4 tsp. nutmeg
1/2 tsp. cinnamon

Combine together the milk, yogurt, eggs, oil, honey and molasses. Gently stir in the flour, soy grits, wheat germ and sunflower seeds. Fold in the pumpkin, nutmeg and cinnamon. Stir until mixed. Spoon onto a hot greased griddle.

Yield: 10–16 pancakes

CORNMEAL GRIDDLE CAKES

1½ T. active dry yeast
1/4 cup warm water
1/4 cup molasses, unsulfured
2 eggs

1/2 cup milk
1 cup whole wheat flour
1 cup yellow cornmeal
3/4 cup milk

Combine in a large bowl the yeast and water and let sit for 5 minutes until the yeast softens. Beat in, mixing thoroughly, the molasses, 2 eggs and 1/2 cup milk. Add the flour and cornmeal, 1/2 cup at a time, beating until smooth. Blend in the milk. Cover and set aside for about 20 minutes, or store, tightly covered, in refrigerator overnight. When ready to prepare griddle cakes, heat the griddle and add a small amount of oil. Using about 1/4 cup batter for each griddle cake, pour onto hot griddle. Bake until bubbles form and break and it is lightly browned. Turn over for 1 minute longer. Serve immediately with butter and honey.

Yield: 10 large griddle cakes

TOFU PANCAKES

1½ cups milk
3 eggs
1 pound TOFU
1 T. oil
1 tsp. BAKING POWDER

1 T. honey
1 tsp. VANILLA EXTRACT
1/2 tsp. cinnamon
1 cup whole wheat flour

Place all of the ingredients in a blender except for the flour. Blend until smooth. Add the flour and blend again until well mixed. Let sit for 10 minutes and then spoon onto a greased hot griddle. Brown both sides and serve immediately with your favorite topping.

Yield: 8–10 pancakes

RICE PANCAKES

3 cups cooked brown rice
1/3 cup grated Parmesan cheese
1/4 cup grated onion

3 eggs. slightly beaten
1/2 tsp. vegetable seasoning

Combine all ingredients together. Spoon 1/4 cup portions onto greased griddle or heavy skillet. Flatten slightly. Cook until golden brown on both sides. Serve with applesauce or dollops of YOGURT.

Yield: 12 pancakes

POTATO PANCAKES

4 raw potatoes (about 3 cups grated)
1 T. soy grits
2-3 T. soy flour
2 eggs, lightly beaten

2 T. chopped parsley
1/4 cup onion, grated
1 tsp. vegetable seasoning
3 T. sesame seeds

Grate the potatoes and drain well by squeezing between the hands. Mix the potatoes with all of the ingredients except for the sesame seeds. Spoon onto a hot greased griddle and sprinkle with sesame seeds. Cook until browned. Serve with YOGURT, COTTAGE CHEESE or SOUR CREAM.

Yield: 4 servings

BUCKWHEAT PANCAKES

3/4 cup buckwheat flour
1/2 cup wheat germ
1/4 cup whole wheat flour
1¾ tsp. BAKING POWDER

2 eggs, lightly beaten
3 T. molasses, unsulfured
3 T. oil
Milk

Mix together the buckwheat flour, wheat germ, whole wheat flour and baking powder. In a separate bowl combine the eggs, molasses and oil. Add the liquid ingredients to the dry and add enough milk to make a batter that resembles thick heavy cream. Ladle batter onto a hot griddle and cook until brown on both sides.

Yield: 10 pancakes

WAFFLES

OATMEAL WAFFLES

1 cup rolled oats
1 cup wheat flakes
2 cups hot water
6 T. non-instant dry milk powder

2 eggs, beaten
2 T. oil
2 T. honey
2/3 cup sunflower seeds
2 tsp. BAKING POWDER

In a small bowl pour the hot water over the oats and wheat. Let them soften for a few minutes. Add all the rest of the ingredients and stir only until moistened. Spoon about 1/2 cup of the mixture into a hot waffle iron. This batter is thicker than usual so you'll have to spread it out to the corner. Bake until golden brown.

Yield: 6 waffles

WHOLE WHEAT WAFFLES

4 eggs, separated
1 cup milk
3 T. oil

2 tsp. BAKING POWDER
2 cups whole wheat pastry flour
1/2 cup sunflower seeds

Combine the egg yolks, milk and oil together. Stir together in a separate bowl the baking powder, flour and sunflower seeds. Add the milk mixture to the flour mixture and mix lightly. Beat the egg whites until stiff, but not dry. Fold the egg whites into the batter. Spoon mixture onto a hot waffle iron and bake until golden brown.

Yield: 7 waffles

Variations:

Decrease flour by 1/2 cup and add in place 1/2 cup wheat germ.

Fruit Waffles: Add 1 cup crushed or diced fruit, such as pineapple, apples, blueberries to name a few, to the batter before cooking the waffles.

Peanut Butter Waffles: Add 1/3 cup peanut butter to the milk mixture and proceed as directed.

Cheese Waffles: After folding in the egg whites, fold in 1/2 cup grated Cheddar cheese.

SPROUT WAFFLES

1/4 cup lukewarm water (110°)
2 T. dry active yeast
2 cups lukewarm milk (110°)
1/4 cup oil
1 T. unsulfured molasses

2 eggs, lightly beaten
1½ cups wheat sprouts, ground
1½ cups whole wheat flour
1/2 cup wheat germ

To prepare the sprouts, just place them in a blender and grind. No need to dry first. Dissolve the yeast in warm water and let stand in a warm place for 5 minutes. Add milk, oil, molasses, eggs and wheat sprouts. Blend in the flour and wheat germ and mix only until blended. Set the mixture in a warm place until it begins to rise, about 15 minutes. Spoon onto a hot greased waffle iron.

Yield: 4 waffles

CREPES

The basis of this elegant dish is simply flour, oil, milk and eggs. It makes a great main dish, or serve as a dessert, or breakfast pancake filled with fruit and topped with a sauce.

BASIC CREPE

1/2 cup whole wheat pastry flour
1 whole egg
1 egg yolk

3 T. oil
About 3/4 cup milk

Combine the flour, whole egg, egg yolk, oil and 4 tablespoons of milk in a small bowl. Beat the mixture until it is smooth. Add additional milk to give the batter the consistency of light cream. Cover and let sit in refrigerator for 30 minutes. When ready to cook the crepes, heat a medium-sized sauté pan (7"-10" diameter) over medium high heat. Dip a paper towel in oil and wipe out the hot pan. Ladle about 1/4 cup batter into pan. Tilt the pan to cover the bottom with a thin coating of batter. Brown the crepe on the underside and it should be dry on top. Turn over with a spatula and brown the other side. Place on a heatproof platter and keep warm in an oven set on low. You can stack crepes one on top of another.

Yield: 10-12 6" crepes

Variation:

Herb Crepes: Add 1 T. finely chopped fresh dill or chives and 2 T. finely chopped fresh parsley to the batter. Cook as described in basic recipe.

CORNMEAL CREPES

1 cup whole wheat pastry flour
1/2 cup yellow cornmeal
1 cup water

1/2 cup milk
3 eggs

Mix all of the ingredients together and place covered in refrigerator for 30 minutes. Blend again before using. This is a very thin batter. Follow cooking instructions in the Basic Crepe.

Yield: 20 8" crepes

TURKEY ALMONDINE CREPES

2 cups diced cooked turkey
1/2 cup diagonally sliced celery
1/4 cup minced green onion
1/2 tsp. vegetable seasoning

1/4 cup raw fresh peas
1/4 cup thinly sliced almonds
3/4 cup MAYONNAISE

Combine all ingredients, mixing well. Place some of the filling in each crepe and roll up. Place the rolled crepes in a baking dish and top with a cream sauce of your choice. Bake at 350° for 15-20 minutes.

Yield: Fills 8–10 crepes

CHICKEN CREPES

2 tsp. oil
1/2 cup finely chopped onion
1 egg
1½ cups cooked chopped chicken
1/2 cup chopped celery

1 tsp. tamari (soy sauce)
1/2 tsp. basil
1 T. chopped fresh parsley
1/2 cup chopped mushrooms
1 cup TOMATO SAUCE

Sauté the onion in oil until the onion is tender. In a bowl beat together the egg, chicken, celery, tamari, basil, parsley and mushrooms. Add the sautéed onion. Spread some of the filling in each crepe and roll up. Place in a baking dish and bake at 350° for 15 minutes. Serve topped with tomato sauce.

Yield: 8 8" crepes

SEAFOOD CREPES

1 cup flaked cooked crab meat,
   shrimp or fish
1/4 cup green onions, chopped
1/4 cup chopped celery

1/4 tsp. lemon juice
1/2 tsp. basil
MAYONNAISE

Mix all together and add just enough mayonnaise to hold filling together. Fill each crepe with the seafood and roll. Top with CHEESE SAUCE and bake in oven on a platter at 350° for 10 minutes.

Yield: 8 8" crepes

SPINACH AND MUSHROOM CREPES

10-12 cooked crepes

Filling:

1 pound fresh spinach, well-washed	4 egg yolks
3 T. oil	1/2 cup COTTAGE CHEESE
2 T. water	1/2 tsp. nutmeg
1 cup fresh mushrooms, chopped	1/2 tsp. finely chopped garlic
1 tsp. lemon juice	

Topping:

2 cups CHEESE SAUCE	2 T. freshly grated Parmesan cheese
2 T. whole wheat bread crumbs	

In a large pot, combine the spinach, 2 tablespoons oil and the water. Cook the spinach until it wilts, turning it occasionally, about 5 minutes. Drain the spinach and press it until it is completely dry. Chop it coarsely. Heat 1 tablespoon oil in a skillet and add mushrooms and lemon juice. Sauté for 2 minutes. Beat the egg yolks with the cottage cheese and add the spinach, mushrooms, nutmeg and garlic. Spread the filling in each crepe and roll up snugly. Place on a heatproof platter and spoon Cheese Sauce over the top. Sprinkle with breadcrumbs and grated cheese. Brown under the broiler for a minute.

Yield: 4-6 servings

AMBROSIA CREPES

1 cup COTTAGE CHEESE	2 peaches, sliced
1/2 cup chopped walnuts	2 small oranges, sectioned
1/2 cup flaked coconut, unsweetened	1/2 cup sliced strawberries
1/4 cup sesame seeds	YOGURT
1 banana, thinly sliced	ORANGE SAUCE

In a large bowl, combine the cheese, walnuts, coconut, sesame seeds and fruit. Place some of the filling on each crepe and then roll up. Top with yogurt and then pour Orange Sauce over top. If you want to serve them hot, place the crepes in a casserole dish and cover with sauce. Bake at 350° for 15 minutes. Remove and top with yogurt.

Yield: Fills 20 8" crepes

TOFU FRUIT CREPES

1/2 cup mashed TOFU   2 T. honey
1/2 cup COTTAGE CHEESE   1 tsp. VANILLA
1 cup strawberries or pineapple

Place all of the ingredients in a blender and blend until smooth and creamy. Fill each crepe with the filling. You can top the crepes with additional fruit and sunflower seeds.

Yield: Fills 10 8" crepes

CHEESE AND FRUIT CREPES

1 package (3 ounce) cream cheese,   2 T. honey
   softened   1/2 tsp. each cinnamon and
2 cups COTTAGE CHEESE   nutmeg
1 egg yolk   Fresh fruit

In a mixing bowl, combine the cheeses, egg yolk, honey and spices. Beat until smooth. Place some of this mixture in each crepe and then cover with sliced fresh fruit such as peaches, bananas, strawberries, blueberries. Roll up, place in casserole and heat in a 350° oven until it is warmed. Serve topped with additional fruit.

Yield: 4-6 servings

TOPPINGS FOR PANCAKES AND WAFFLES

1. APPLESAUCE

2. Molasses, spiced with cinnamon, nutmeg, allspice, clove or ginger

3. NUT BUTTERS

4. Cream cheese mixed with nuts and seeds

5. YOGURT, plain or mixed with fresh fruit

6. COTTAGE CHEESE with fruit and nuts mixed in

7. Make a mixture of honey, fruit juice and sesame seeds

8. Sliced pineapple and coconut shredded over a pineapple sauce

9. Any of the syrups and sauces listed in this section

10.   PEANUT BUTTER mixed with some honey

11.   HONEY BUTTER and BERRY BUTTER

12.   For a dinner pancake, fill with LENTIL EGG SALAD and top with CHEESE SAUCE. Or fill with other sandwich fillings and top with a sauce of your choice.

FRUIT SYRUP

2 cups fresh fruit (strawberries,
   berries, peaches, bananas)
1/2 cup apple juice
1 T. arrowroot powder

2 T. water
1 T. lemon juice
1 T. honey (optional)

Place the fresh fruit or combinations of fruit in a blender and add the apple juice. Blend until smooth. Pour this mixture into a saucepan and simmer for 5 minutes. Add arrowroot that has been mixed with the water, lemon juice and honey. Simmer for 2-3 minutes, until thick.

Yield: 2 cups

PINEAPPLE SYRUP

2 cups pineapple juice, unsweetened
1/2 cup apple juice, unsweetened

2 T. arrowroot powder
1/2 cup water

Heat together in a saucepan the two juices. Mix together the arrowroot and water and then add to the hot juices. Heat until thickened.

Yield: 2½ cups

ORANGE SAUCE

1/3 cup butter
2 T. honey

1/3 cup orange juice

Combine all together and heat to boiling, stirring constantly.

Yield: 1/2 cup

HONEY CREAM

1/2 cup butter
1/4 cup honey

1/2 cup plain YOGURT

Cream the butter until softened and add honey. Beat until well blended. Add the yogurt gradually and beat until smooth and fluffy. Chill and serve with waffles, pancakes or French toast.

Yield: About 1 cup

HONEY COCONUT SPREAD

3 T. melted butter   1/3-1/2 cup honey
3 T. unsweetened apple juice   1/2 cup unsweetened grated coconut

Combine all of the ingredients together and serve over pancakes or waffles.

Yield: 1 cup

HONEY YOGURT TOPPING

1 cup plain YOGURT   1 tsp. VANILLA EXTRACT
2 T. honey   1/3 cup chopped walnuts

Mix all ingredients together and stir until creamy. Serve over pancakes and waffles.

Yield: 1½ cups

APRICOT APPLE SPREAD

1 6-ounce can frozen apple juice   1 cup dried apricots, finely chopped
    concentrate, thawed   1/2 tsp. almond extract
1½ cups apple juice, unsweetened   1/4 tsp. cinnamon

In a saucepan combine the two apple juices and the apricots. Bring to a boil; reduce heat. Cover; simmer 25 minutes or until apricots are tender and most of the liquid is absorbed. Stir occasionally. Remove from heat and stir in the extract and cinnamon. Store in refrigerator. If it is too sweet, use water in place of the 1½ cups apple juice.

Yield: 2½ cups

BEVERAGES

This chapter suggest some alternatives to the soda pop dilemma by providing good-tasting and nutritious substitutes for those beverages that contain little or no food value.

Soda pop contains no food value at all!

It is full of calories, refined sugar, artificial colors and flavors, and a number of other chemicals. A lot of pop also contains caffeine which can cause an addiction to the drink. The ingredients found

CHAPTER 11

in these drinks tear down the wonderful human body that God created.

We need to drink beverages that will *build* our body, not tear it down.

The best substitutes for the sodas are fresh fruit and vegetable juices. Great drinks are easy to prepare. You can make anything from herb teas to milk shakes. Fresh fruit drinks are especially satisfying on a hot summer day, or a hot cider drink will warm your insides on a cold winter night. Whatever your desire, you will find some beverage ideas listed in this chapter. You can also create your own beverages by using the ideas that are listed here. Give it a try.

HELPFUL HINTS

- For a real flavor lift, mix grated lemon peel, finely chopped green onion, and YOGURT together to serve on top of chilled tomato juice.

- Have you tried Sun Tea? Take loose tea (place in a cheesecloth bag), or tea bags, and place it along with cold water in a big gallon jug. Put it in the sun. You will know the tea is ready by its color. Put it out in the morning and it is ready by evening.

- If you need ice cubes that are large, like for a punch, use nonstick muffin tins to freeze the water. The water freezes quickly and the ice pops out like magic.

- If you boil your water before making ice rings or ice cubes, they will freeze clear.

- Problems with ice melting in your punch bowl and diluting the punch: Make an extra batch of punch the day before and pour into your favorite mold. You may even want to add some slices of fresh fruit to the mold. Freeze and then place the mold into the punch bowl. When it melts you will have more punch, rather than water.

- Add a slice of lemon or lime to your glass of water. Adds a delightful flavor plus furnishes you with additional vitamin C.

- A juicer is an important piece of equipment to have in your kitchen. You can make many wonderful vegetable drinks that are so healthy for you.

- Do not drink with your meals. If you need some liquids, try just sipping on a glass of liquids. What happens when you drink with the meal is that it dilutes the digestive juices that are needed to digest your foods. You end up with digestion problems.

- Garnish your drinks with sprigs of parsley and mint. Use celery or carrot sticks. Place slices of oranges, lemons and limes into drinks. Add melon balls or pineapple sticks. There are many different foods you can use to give your drinks "eye appeal."

FRESH JUICES

There are so many flavorful fresh fruit and vegetable juices that are available for your use. Serve them ice cold to your family in place of soda pop. Listed below are some of the different types of juices you might enjoy.

Fruit		*Vegetable*
Apple	Grape	Tomato
Blackberry	Cranberry	Carrot
Strawberry	Cherry	Cucumber
Orange	Peach	Celery
Boysenberry	Pomegranate	Parsley
Pear	Prune	Potato
Plus any combination of the juices		Beet

LEMONADE

1/3 cup fresh squeezed lemon juice
    unstrained
4 cups water

1/4 cup apple juice (or to taste)
Fresh mint sprigs

Combine the water and lemon juice. Add apple juice to sweeten it. Refrigerate. Fill glasses with cold lemonade and place a sprig of fresh mint in each glass.

Yield: 8 servings

FRUIT PUNCH

1 quart (4 cups) boysenberry or
   cherry juice
4 cups apple cider

2 cups ice water
1/2 cup lemon juice

Combine all ingredients together and pour into a punch bowl. If you like a lot of bubbles in the punch, add sparkling cider instead of the apple cider, or add mineral water in place of the ice water. Make up a double batch and pour half of it into a ring mold and freeze. Place this in the punch bowl, along with lemon and lime slices.

Yield: 10 cups

Variation:
Instead of the boysenberry or cherry juice, use any fruit juice of your choice.

HOT CRANBERRY PUNCH

4 cups frozen cranberries
2 cinnamon sticks
8 whole cloves
Dash of nutmeg
1 tsp. whole allspice

2 cups water
1/2 cup water
4 cups apple cider
Honey to taste

Bring cranberries and spices to a boil in the 2 cups of water. Turn heat down, cover and simmer for about 12 minutes. Strain the mixture, pressing juice and as much pulp as possible through strainer. Discard skins and spices. Add 1/2 cup water and cider. Add honey to taste. Serve hot.

Yield: 8 cups

APPLE CIDER PUNCH

1 12-ounce can of frozen apple juice
   concentrate (unsweetened)

1 bottle (33 ounces) of mineral
   water
2 cups of water

Make sure all ingredients are ice cold. Pour all of them into a large serving bowl and mix with a spoon. Serve immediately as it will go flat if it sits too long.

Yield: 2 quarts

BUBBLING PINEAPPLE PUNCH

1 6-ounce can of frozen pineapple-
orange juice
1 cup pineapple juice

2 T. lemon juice
1 bottle mineral water, well chilled

Combine the pineapple-orange juice, pineapple juice and lemon juice. Chill well. When ready to serve, stir to blend and then pour about 1/4 cup of the mixture into glasses, and then fill with the mineral water.

Yield: 8 servings

Variation:
Instead of the mineral water use sparkling apple cider.

CRANAPPLE JUICE

1½ cups apple juice (unsweetened)   1/2 cup cranberries

Place the cranberries and 1 cup of the juice in a blender. Blend until berries are puréed, then add remaining juice and mix well. You can either strain out the cranberry bits or use the way it is.

Yield: 2 cups

CHRISTMAS CRANBERRY COCKTAIL

2½ cups apple cider
3/4 cup raw cranberries, fresh or
frozen

1 peeled banana
1/2 cup shelled sunflower seeds
1/2 cup strawberries, fresh or frozen

Blend all of the ingredients in the blender in the order given. Blend until smooth. Serve garnished with strawberries.

Yield: 4 servings

HOT CIDER

2 quarts apple cider
3 cups unsweetened pineapple juice
2-3 cups water
3 T. orange juice concentrate
2 T. lemon juice

1 stick cinnamon
1 tsp. whole cloves
1/2 tsp. whole allspice
1 small orange thinly sliced

Place all of the ingredients in a saucepan and bring to a simmer over low heat. Simmer for about 30 minutes. Before serving remove the spices and add a slice of orange to the cup.

Yield: 13 cups

HOT GRAPE JUICE

2 cups unsweetened grape juice
1 cup water
2 tsp. honey

1/4 tsp. cinnamon
Lemon slices

Combine ingredients in a small saucepan. Heat and serve topped with lemon slices.

Yield: 3 servings

ORANGE CRANBERRY DRINK

1 small orange, peeled and sliced
3/4 cup apple juice
1/3 cup water

1/4 cup frozen cranberries
1 T. honey
1 medium apple

Add all of the ingredients together and blend in a blender until smooth. Serve well chilled.

Yield: 2½ cups

HOT, MULLED PINEAPPLE JUICE

1 can (46-ounce) unsweetened
  pineapple juice
2 cups water
1 2"-piece cinnamon stick

1/8 tsp. nutmeg
1/8 tsp. allspice
5 whole cloves
Orange slices

Combine all ingredients in a medium-sized saucepan; bring to a boil over medium heat. Reduce heat; cover, and simmer for 20 minutes to blend flavors. Remove from heat and remove the cinnamon stick and cloves before serving.

Yield: 8 servings

TOMATO JUICE

1 quart skinned ripe tomatoes
1 large sprig parsley
1/4 cup cucumber, peeled and diced

2 tsp. chopped celery leaves
1 tsp. finely chopped scallion
1/4 tsp. oregano

Place the tomatoes in a blender, one at a time, and blend until smooth after each addition. Add the remaining ingredients and blend until smooth. Serve very cold.

Yield: 3 cups

HONEY EGGNOG

4 egg yolks
4 T. honey
2 cups milk

Nutmeg and cinnamon to taste
4 egg whites

In a bowl, beat the egg yolks until light. Beat in the honey, milk and seasonings. Whip egg whites until stiff, and fold in carefully. Chill. Serve with a dash of nutmeg on top.

Yield: 6 cups

CANTALOUPE COOLER

1½ pounds cantaloupe
2 eggs
1 T. honey

2 T. lime juice
1/4 cup milk
1/2 cup cracked ice

Remove rind and seeds from the cantaloupe and dice. Add the cantaloupe and eggs to a blender and blend until smooth. Add all of the other ingredients and whirl until smooth.

Yield: Serves 2

SPICY GOLDEN NOG

1½ cups peeled and sliced peaches
   or nectarines
2 eggs
2 T. honey

1/4 cup each orange juice and milk
2 T. lemon juice
1/8 tsp. ground cinnamon
1/2 cup cracked ice

Place all the ingredients into the blender and whirl until smooth.

Yield: Serves 2

BANANA SMOOTHIE

2 cups plain YOGURT
2 medium frozen bananas
1/2 cup apple juice

1/2 cup strawberries, fresh or
   frozen (unsweetened)
6 ice cubes, broken

Combine all the ingredients, except for the ice cubes, in a blender container. Whirl until smooth and thick.

Yield: 4 servings

Variation:
In place of the strawberries, use any diced fresh fruit of your choice.

SMOOTHIES, WITHOUT YOGURT

1 cup apple juice
3/4 cup water

1 banana, fresh or frozen
1/2 cup fruit of your choice

Some suggestions on different fruits to use are: papaya, peaches, nectarines, pears, pineapple and oranges. Place all of the ingredients in a blender and blend until smooth.

Yield: 2 servings

MILK SHAKE

2 cups milk
1 frozen banana
1/2 tsp. VANILLA EXTRACT

3/4 cup diced fruit of your choice
1 tsp. honey

Place all ingredients in the blender and blend for 30 seconds.

Yield: 2½ cups

Variations:
You can add honey ice cream and chopped nuts.

DATE AND PEANUT BUTTER SHAKE

2 cups milk
1 frozen banana
1/2 tsp. VANILLA EXTRACT

1/4 cup chopped dates
2 T. PEANUT BUTTER

Mix all together in a blender and blend until smooth and frothy.

Yield: 2 servings

CAROB MILK SHAKE

4 cups milk
1-2 T. molasses, unsulfured
1/2 cup non-instant dry milk
    powder

1/3 cup carob powder
1 frozen banana
1/4 cup nuts
1-2 T. wheat germ

Mix in a blender until smooth. If you would like you can add some honey ice cream.

Yield: 4 servings

LASSI

1 cup plain YOGURT
1 cup fresh fruit juice (pineapple, apple, etc.)
2 bananas

1/4 tsp. cinnamon or nutmeg
Honey to taste
Ice, crushed

Put all together in a blender and set at medium speed. Blend until smooth and ice is crushed thoroughly.

Yield: Serves 2

THE BOB TURNBULL SPECIAL PROTEIN DRINK

2 cups milk (soy or goat can be used)
1 egg
3 large T. HONEY VANILLA ICE CREAM
1 banana
1 T. PEANUT BUTTER

1 T. brewer's yeast
1 T. wheat germ oil or wheat germ
1 T. blackstrap molasses
3 T. protein powder
1 T. sunflower seeds

A word about the brewer's yeast: If you have not been using brewer's yeast in your diet, begin by adding only 1/2 teaspoon to the drink and then increase it as you become accustomed to it. Brewer's yeast is high in vitamin B and if you are deficient in it your stomach will bloat up if you take too much.

Place the milk, egg, ice cream, banana and peanut butter in the blender. Start blender and, with it running, add the rest of the ingredients, one at a time. Scrape the sides of the blender often. When well blended it is ready to serve.

Yield: 2 10-ounce servings

BANANA ORANGE FROSTY

2 ripe bananas, peeled and frozen
1 egg
1½ cups plain YOGURT

1/2 cup orange juice
1 T. wheat germ
1 tsp. VANILLA EXTRACT

Slice frozen bananas into blender container. Add remaining ingredients and blend.

Yield: 2 servings

PUMPKIN COOLER

1/2 cup pumpkin, cooked and mashed
4 cups chilled milk

2 T. honey
1 tsp. cinnamon

Combine the ingredients in a blender and mix well. Sprinkle with additional cinnamon when serving. It is a cool refreshing drink.

Yield: 4 servings

CAROB DRINK

2¼ cups milk
1-2 T. carob powder
1 banana

2 tsp. honey
1 tsp. VANILLA EXTRACT

Place all of the ingredients in a blender and blend well. If you want it hot just place it in a saucepan over low heat until warmed.

Yield: 2½ cups

SESAME MILK

1/2 cup sesame seeds
2 cups water

2 cups dates, soaked in water

In the blender blend the seeds until a powder. Add the dates and water and blend until all is mixed well. Refrigerate.

Yield: 3 cups

ALMOND MILK

1 cup almonds
3 T. chopped dates or raisins

4 cups water

Add almonds, dates or raisins and 1 cup water in a blender and blend until the almonds are all grated up. Add the rest of the water and blend well.

Yield: 4 cups

CASHEW MILK

1 cup cashews

3 cups water

Place 1 cup cashews and 1 cup water in the blender and blend well until the cashews are all ground up. Add the additional water and blend.

Yield: 3½ cups

DESSERTS

To me the most desirable desserts consist of fresh and dried fruits, seeds and nuts. They provide an abundance of nutrients, have no empty calories, and taste so natural and good. I mean, doesn't the following sound appetizing to you: Fresh picked, crunchy apples . . . bright red and sweet strawberries . . . a slice of melon in season . . . and a dish full of dried fruits, seeds and nuts?

For most of our lives we have been programmed to eat cakes, pies and cookies as desserts. It certainly would be hard to completely eliminate them. I have always enjoyed baking, and I still do, but I have changed my ingredients over the past years. The best thing to remember when making desserts for your family is to ask yourself, "Is this really healthy for them?" It will be if you're making delicious desserts from whole grains, unhydrogenated fats, and use alternatives for white and brown sugar, and corn syrup.

CHAPTER 12

In this chapter I use honey as one of the alternatives to white and brown sugar. Honey is one of nature's first and finest sweeteners. It is referred to in the Holy Bible 60 different times. For instance, John the Baptist lived off of locust and wild honey in Matthew 3:4. Kind David ate honey as recorded in 2 Samuel 17:29. And, of course, honey was used to describe the Promised Land in Exodus 3:8 and 17. Those are but a few verses.

Honey contains traces of minerals, vitamins and enzymes, and is assimilated in such a way in your body that your blood sugar level remains constant. Honey is made up of fructose and glucose. The fructose takes hours to be assimilated in the body. The glucose enters your system immediately. White sugar is made of sucrose that is rapidly assimilated into the blood stream. When this occurs the body alerts the pancreas to shoot out insulin to gobble up the excess sugar. Usually what happens is that the insulin gobbles up too much sugar and your blood sugar level drops. Then you end up craving still more sugar. It's a vicious circle and causes damage to your health.

Also, sugar does not contain any vitamins or minerals of its own. Every food needs those components so that the food can be metabolized properly. If the foods do not contain them then they have to rob the body's supply of nutrients. This is what happens with sugar which especially robs the body of vitamin B. Another vicious circle! These are just some of the reasons I have decided to remove white and brown sugars from our diets.

Try other sweeteners, too, besides honey. There are unsulfured molasses, fruit juices, date sugar (ground-up dates), sorghum, to name a few. Whatever alternatives you decide to use, remember this: Go Easy On The Sweeteners! Try to *decrease* them slowly in your diet. When baking with honey, decrease the amount you use each time by a teaspoon. A little sweetener is okay, but too much is bad for you—as stated in Proverbs 25:27.

Since all of us enjoy desserts—what are you waiting for?

HELPFUL HINTS

- To measure honey when baking: Measure the oil first and then the honey. It will slide out without a mess.

- Oatmeal browned in butter acts as a substitute for chopped nuts in cookies, cakes and pie crust.

- For a quick and tasty topping, if budget (or waistline) will not allow whipping cream, simply add one sliced banana to the white of an egg and beat until stiff. Then add a little honey and beat some more.

- Roll dried fruits and nuts in flour before adding to cakes or pies. This will prevent them from falling to the bottom.

- If your custard weeps, or liquid lines the bottom, this means that it was baked incorrectly or there was an imbalance in the recipe.

- Do not let a drop of water come in contact with your honey pot or it will sour.

- Decrease the amount of sweetener in your diet by a teaspoon each time. Before too long you will have made quite a decrease.

- To sour milk for use in recipes that call for buttermilk, place 2 tablespoons of cider vinegar or lemon juice in each cup of milk.

- Fill cake and cupcake pans only 2/3 full.

- Date sugar (dried ground dates) is a natural sweetener that can be used on top of fruits or cereals. It can be used any place brown sugar is called for. You need to dissolve it in some recipes before using. Do this by adding hot water and letting it sit for a few minutes.

- When adding honey to a whipped topping, or an airy dessert, warm some of it first to thin it.

- Raw honey may be used in place of sugar in recipes. You may have to decrease any liquids in the recipe and even increase the flour measurement.

- When using honey in your baked goods, reduce the oven temperature by 25° as honey makes food brown easily.

- Safflower oil is best used in the baking recipes as opposed to other oils as it is the mildest tasting of all the oils.

- To substitute honey for sugar in a recipe remember this: Substitute 1/2 cup honey for each cup of sugar. When using honey you will have to decrease the liquid by 1/4 cup. If there is no liquid to reduce, add 3–4 tablespoons of flour for each 1/2 cup of honey.

- Stir soy flour before measuring because it tends to pack in the container.

- An easy way to make a lattice top for a pie is to cut a circle of wax paper the size of the top of the pie. Weave the lattice onto it and then place all of it in the freezer or refrigerator. Chill until dough is firm. When firm, slide onto the pie.

- Cut drinking straws into short lengths and insert through slits in the pie crust. This will prevent juice from running over in the oven, and permit steam to escape.

- In making custard-type pies, bake at high temperatures for about 10 minutes to prevent a soggy crust. Then finish baking at a low temperature.

- If you need to precook the pie crust, place 2 cups of dried beans in a plastic roasting bag. Tie up the end and place this bag on top of the crust. This will help stop the crust from bubbling.

- Use a light hand with pastry. Roll the dough outward from the center in all directions to make a circle, lifting the rolling pin near the edges to avoid splitting the pastry or getting the edges too thin.

- Make sure the liquids used in making the pie crust are ice cold. Put an ice cube in the liquid and let it sit for 3 minutes before using. That makes for a lighter crust.

- Chill dough before rolling the pie crust. It will be easier to handle.

- Roll dough out between sheets of wax paper. You will not need to use much extra flour this way.

- For ease in placing pastry in pie plate, roll the pastry onto the rolling pin and then gently unroll the pastry over the pie plate.

- To freeze baked pie: Remove the pie from the oven when only slightly browned. It will finish browning when reheated for serving. Cool, then freeze without wrapping. Wrap when firm.

- To serve frozen baked pie: Partially thaw in original wrap at room temperature for 30 minutes. Unwrap and place on lower shelf at 375° for 30 minutes.

- Cookies located on the edges of a cookie sheet will brown more quickly.

- Soy grits uncooked may be substituted for all or part of the nuts in recipes.

- You can substitute 2 tablespoons of soy flour for 2 tablespoons of whole wheat flour in each cupful of flour.

- Test for doneness of cookies by touching lightly with fingers. If no print remains cookies are done.

- Soft cookies will stay moist in an airtight covered container. Add slice of apple or orange to help keep moist.

- Crisp cookies remain crisp if stored in a loosely covered container.

- Store only 1 type of cookie at a time in a container. Do not combine soft and crisp together as the crisp will become soft.

- You can grind leftover cookies into crumbs and use as toppings for desserts.

- Keep cookies fresh by adding tissue paper on the bottom of the cookie jar.

- To prevent drop cookies from spreading, chill dough first.

- For baking, use medium to large eggs. Extra large ones may cause cakes to fall when cooled.

- Make a couple extra batches of cookies and freeze the extra. They can keep for months if wrapped properly.

- Cakes made without baking powder or soda will not be as light and airy as traditional cakes. Just use more yeast or extra egg whites. Beat whites stiff and fold into batter just before you place it into the oven. Make sure it is a preheated oven.

- Try using a thread, instead of a knife, when cutting a cake that is still hot.

- To lessen the size of the "crack," typical of loaf cakes, let batter stand 20 minutes before baking.

- Cakes baked with honey will stay fresh longer than the traditional cakes.

- If a real light cake is desired, sift the bran out of the whole wheat flour. Be sure to save it for use in another recipe.

- Use sunflower seeds in place of more expensive nuts in your baking recipes.

- Add roasted soybeans to your mixed nuts. These are a great budget stretcher and are lower in calories.

- Buy nuts in bulk to save money, and insure freshness. Freeze the extras until needed.

- Add wheat germ to "enrich" any baked good.

- Use powdered milk to add protein and calcium to baked goods.

CAKES

DATE-HONEY CAKE

1½ cups dates
1½ tsp. baking soda
1½ cups boiling water
1 cup butter
1/8 cup molasses, unsulfured
1/2 cup honey
3 eggs, well-beaten

2 tsp. VANILLA EXTRACT
2 cups whole wheat pastry flour
1 tsp. nutmeg
1 tsp. cinnamon
1 cup walnuts, chopped
1/2 cup sunflower seeds

Put dates in a bowl along with baking soda and add boiling water. Stir until butter is melted. Cool. In another bowl, cream butter, honey and molasses. Add eggs and date mixture. Mix well. Add vanilla, flour, nutmeg and cinnamon. Fold in nuts and sunflower seeds. Pour into a greased bundt pan. Bake at 350° for 45 minutes. Frost with BUTTER FROSTING.

Yield: 1 bundt cake

CARROT CAKE

1½ cups oil
1/2 cup honey
1/4 cup molasses, unsulfured
3 eggs
3 cups whole wheat pastry flour
1 tsp. soda
1 tsp. each cinnamon and nutmeg

1/2 tsp. cloves, ground
2 cups grated, peeled carrots
1 10-ounce can crushed, unsweetened pineapple and juice
1½ cups unsweetened coconut flakes
1 cup walnuts, chopped
1 cup raisins

Cream together oil, honey, molasses and eggs. Add flour, soda, cinnamon, nutmeg, cloves, carrots, pineapple, pineapple juice, and coconut and mix well. Stir in raisins and walnuts. Pour into a greased bundt pan or two 9" cake pans. Bake in 325° oven for 50 minutes. Frost with CREAM CHEESE FROSTING.

Yield: 1 bundt or 9" cake

COFFEE CAKE

2 cups whole wheat pastry flour
2 tsp. BAKING POWDER
1/2 cup butter
1/4 cup honey
3 T. molasses, unsulfured

1 cup plain YOGURT
1 egg
1 tsp. VANILLA EXTRACT
1/4 cup raisins
1/4 cup sunflower seeds

Into the flour and baking powder cut butter, honey and molasses with a pastry blender until crumbly. Mix together the yogurt, vanilla and egg. Add the yogurt mixture to the flour mixture. Stir in raisins and sunflower seeds. Pour into a greased 8" square pan. Add NUTTY TOPPING and bake for 30 minutes at 325°.

Yield: 1 8" cake

APPLESAUCE SPICE CAKE

1 cup raisins
1 cup water
1 cup unsweetened APPLESAUCE
2 eggs, beaten
1/2 cup oil
2 cups whole wheat pastry flour

1 tsp. BAKING POWDER
1½ tsp. cinnamon
1/2 tsp. nutmeg
1/4 tsp. cloves
1 tsp. VANILLA EXTRACT
1/2 cup walnuts

Cook raisins in water until water is almost absorbed. Cool. Add applesauce, beaten eggs, 3 tablespoons of water that raisins were cooked in; mix. Add oil and mix well. Mix together flour, baking powder, spices. Stir into batter. Add vanilla and walnuts. Pour into an 8" square cake pan. Bake at 325° for 40–45 minutes. Choose from any of the many toppings.

Yield: 1 8" cake

PUMPKIN CAKE

1 cup honey
1/4 cup molasses, unsulfured
1 cup oil
2 cups mashed cooked pumpkin
4 eggs, lightly beaten
3 cups whole wheat pastry flour
2 T. cinnamon

3 tsp. BAKING POWDER
2 tsp. baking soda
2 tsp. almond flavoring
1 cup chopped nuts and/or sunflower seeds
1 cup raisins

Beat together honey, molasses, oil, pumpkin and eggs. Add all other ingredients and mix well. Pour into a greased 8" x 12" or two 9" cake pans. Bake at 350° for 40 minutes. Great topped with the 7 MINUTE or HONEY FROSTING.

Yield: 1 cake

CHEESE CAKE

Crust:

1/2 cup ground almonds
3/4 cup wheat germ
1/2 tsp. cinnamon

1 T. honey
1/4 cup butter, melted

Combine all of the ingredients together and press into the bottom of a 9" springform pan.

Batter:

1 pound cream cheese
8 ounces COTTAGE CHEESE
3 T. whole wheat flour
3/4 cup honey

4 eggs, separated
1/2 tsp. almond extract
2 T. lemon juice
1 tsp. grated lemon rind

Sieve the cottage cheese and whip with the cream cheese for 5 minutes. Add flour and honey and beat until light. Add egg yolks, one at a time. Add almond extract, lemon juice and rind. Beat egg whites until stiff, but not dry. Fold gently into cream cheese mixture. Pour into a prepared pan. Bake at 325° for about 1 hour. Turn heat off and leave cake in oven for 3/4 of an hour without opening the oven door. Cake should be lightly browned and puffed. Cake will crack as it cools.

Yield: Serves 12

MOTHER'S CAKE

Heat oven, get utensils and ingredients. Remove blocks and toy auto from table. Grease pan, crack nuts. Measure 2 cups flour, remove Jonathon's hands from flour, wash flour off him. Re-measure flour, put flour, salt, and baking powder in sifter. Get dust pan and brush up pieces of bowl Jonathon knocked on floor. Get another bowl, answer door bell. Return to kitchen. Remove Jonathon's hands from bowl. Wash Jonathon, grease another pan, answer telephone. Return to kitchen, find Jonathon. Remove one hammer from bowl. Take up greased pan and find layer of nut shells in it. Head for Jonathon, who flies, knocking bowl off table. Wash kitchen floor, table, walls, and dishes. Call bakery. Lie down!

Author Unknown

POUNDCAKE

1/2 cup butter, softened
3/4 cup mild-flavored honey
4 egg yolks
1/2 tsp. VANILLA EXTRACT

2 cups whole wheat pastry flour
2 tsp. BAKING POWDER
1/2 cup milk
4 egg whites, stiffly beaten

Beat butter until creamy. Gradually add honey in a steady stream, beat until fluffy. Add egg yolks and vanilla and beat until well blended. Stir together the dry ingredients. Alternately add the flour mixture and milk with the honey mixture. Beat egg whites until stiff and fold into mixture. Pour batter into a greased 8" square pan. Bake at 350° for 45 minutes. Cool. Cut cake in half, then slice crosswise. Wrap airtight and store at room temperature up to 8 days. Serve plain or top with yogurt, whipped cream, fruit. Try the various fillings and frostings of your choice.

Yield: 24 pieces

Variation:
In place of the milk, use buttermilk in the same proportion. Also add 1 teaspoon cinnamon, 1/2 teaspoon cloves and 1/4 teaspoon nutmeg.

CAROB CAKE

1/2 cup butter, softened
1/2 cup honey
6 egg yolks
2 tsp. VANILLA EXTRACT

1/3 cup milk
1¼ cups whole wheat pastry flour
1/2 cup carob, sifted
6 egg whites, stiffly beaten

Cream butter and honey until light. Add egg yolks, and vanilla. Mix well. Mix dry ingredients together and add alternating with milk. Fold in beaten egg whites. Turn into a greased 9" springform pan and bake for about 40 minutes in a 325° oven. Frost with CAROB ICING or any other icing of your choice.

Yield: 1 9" cake

GERMAN APPLE CAKE

2 eggs
3/4 cup oil
1/2 cup honey
2 cups whole wheat pastry flour
1 tsp. soda
1/2 tsp. BAKING POWDER

2 tsp. each cinnamon and nutmeg
1/2 tsp. cloves
4 cups diced, peeled apples
1/2 cup walnuts
1 cup raisins
1 tsp. VANILLA EXTRACT

Beat together until foamy, eggs, oil and honey. Add flour, soda, baking powder, cinnamon, nutmeg and cloves and mix well. Stir in apples, walnuts, raisins, and vanilla. Pour into a greased 9" x 13" inch pan. Bake 45 minutes at 350°. Frost with WHIPPED CREAM, Cream Cheese or SPICE ICING.

Yield: 1 9" x 13" cake

HOLIDAY FRUITCAKE

1¾ cups whole wheat flour
1 tsp. cinnamon
1/2 tsp. allspice
1/2 tsp. nutmeg
1/4 tsp. ground cloves
1/8 tsp. ground cardamon
1 cup honey-dipped pineapple
1 cup dried peaches and nectarines
  (combination)
1 cup pitted dates
1 cup dried apricots
1½ cups raisins

1/2 cup figs
1/2 cup whole wheat flour
1 cup walnuts
1 cup combination of cashews,
  pecans, Brazil nuts, and almonds
1 cup butter
1/2 cup honey
1/3 cup molasses, unsulfured
6 egg yolks
1 T. VANILLA EXTRACT
1/2 cup apple juice or cider
6 egg whites
Whole blanched almonds

Prepare two loaf tins, 9" x 5" x 3" size, by lining them with buttered parchment paper or brown wrapping paper. Let the paper extend above the long sides of the pan about 2". Combine 1¾ cups whole wheat flour with the spices. Cut all fruit into small pieces. Sprinkle and separate all fruit with 1/2 cup flour. Chop nuts coarsely and add to fruit. Preheat oven to 275°. Cream butter until soft. Beat in honey and molasses. Add egg yolks and vanilla and beat until fluffy. Add flour mixture and apple juice alternately to butter mixture, beating after each addition. Carefully fold in floured fruits and nuts. Beat egg whites until stiff, but not dry, and fold them carefully into batter. Turn batter into prepared pans. Lay whole blanched almonds on top of each loaf in desired design. Bake in preheated oven on middle rack for approximately 1½ hours. Cool for 30 minutes and remove from pan and paper. Wrap in several thicknesses of cheesecloth which have been drenched with apple juice, or cider. Then wrap in waxed paper and aluminum foil and store in refrigerator. Check moisture of the cake every week or so and redrench the cloth if needed. Let age for three weeks.

Yield: 2 loaves

CREAM PUFFS

1 cup water
1/2 cup oil
1 cup whole wheat flour

4 eggs
3 T. sesame seeds (optional)

Heat to boiling in saucepan, the water and oil. Stir in the flour and stir constantly over low heat until mixture leaves the pan and forms a ball. Remove from heat and cool about 2 minutes. Beat eggs in one at a time. Beat mixture until smooth and velvety. If used as appetizers, drop rounded teaspoon on ungreased baking sheet. If used as a dessert or as more of a meal, spoon batter into mounds, using 1/4 cup of dough for each. Bake at 275° for 30 minutes. Cool. Cut off top and scoop out center. Fill with chicken, seafood salad, CUSTARD FILLING with CAROB SYRUP on top, or fresh fruit and YOGURT.

Yield: 12 large size, 40 appetizer size

FROSTINGS AND FILLINGS

CAROB FROSTING

3 T. honey
1/3 cup non-instant dry milk
    powder

1/3 cup carob powder, sifted
1/4 cup YOGURT, plain
1 tsp. almond flavoring

Mix all together. If too thick, add water or more yogurt to thin.

Yield: Frosts 1 9"-cake

HONEY FROSTING (UNCOOKED)

1 egg white
1/8 tsp. cream of tartar

1/4 cup warm honey
1/2 tsp. almond extract

Beat egg white with mixer. Add cream of tartar and continue to beat. Pour honey in thin stream over egg white mixture. Add flavoring and continue to beat until fluffy and thick.

Yield: Frosts 1 9"-layer

BUTTER FROSTING

6 T. butter
1/3 cup honey

1/2 cup non-instant dry milk
    powder
1 tsp. VANILLA EXTRACT

Cream butter and honey together until smooth. Add milk powder a little at a time until the desired consistency is reached. Then mix in vanilla. If dry milk is at all lumpy, sift first before adding to mixture.

Yield: Frosts 9" layer cake

Variations:

Lemon Butter Frosting: Add 3 T. lemon juice and 2 T. grated lemon rind.

Carob Butter Frosting: Add 1/4 cup sifted carob powder and use only 1/4 cup dry milk powder.

7 MINUTE FROSTING

2 egg whites
1/2 cup honey

1/8 tsp. cream of tartar
1 tsp. VANILLA EXTRACT

In the top of a double boiler, combine all of the ingredients. Beat 1 minute with electric or rotary beater to combine ingredients. Cook over rapidly boiling water but don't let the water touch the top pot. Beat for about 7 minutes, until soft peaks form when beater is raised.

Yield: Frosts a 9" two-layer cake

ISLAND FROSTING

8 ounces softened cream cheese
1/4 cup honey
1 T. lemon juice + 1 tsp. grated
    lemon peel

1/2 cup drained, crushed pineapple
    (unsweetened)
1/4 cup shredded coconut
1/4 cup chopped nuts

Blend all of the ingredients together and spread on cooled cake or cupcakes.

Yield: Frosts a 9" two-layer cake

CREAM CHEESE FROSTING

1 8-ounce package of cream cheese
1/4 cup butter

3 T. honey
1 tsp. VANILLA EXTRACT

Cream all of the ingredients together. If it needs thinning, use milk or plain YOGURT.

Yield: Frosts 1 bundt or 9" cake

Variation:

Carob Cream Cheese Frosting: Add 1/4 cup sifted carob powder.

PEANUT BUTTER FROSTING

1/4 cup PEANUT BUTTER
2 T. oil
1/3 cup honey

1/4 cup warm milk
1 tsp. VANILLA EXTRACT

Blend all of the ingredients together in a blender until smooth.

Yield: Frosts 2 8"-layers

Variation:

Banana/Peanut Butter Frosting: Add one mashed banana.

SPICE ICING

1/3 cup honey
4 T. melted butter
1 cup non-instant dry milk powder
1½ tsp. cinnamon

1 tsp. allspice
1 tsp. carob powder
4 T. water
1 tsp. VANILLA EXTRACT

Mix all ingredients together until smooth.

Yield: Frosts 1 8''-cake

WHIPPED TOPPING

1/2 cup icy cold water
1 T. lemon juice
1/2 cup non-instant dry milk powder

1 T. honey
1/4 tsp. VANILLA EXTRACT

Pour the water and lemon juice into a chilled bowl. Sprinkle over the water the milk powder. Using chilled beater, beat until mixture stands in peaks when beater is slowly lifted upright. Beat in with final few strokes until blended with the honey and vanilla.

Yield: 2 cups

WHIPPED CREAM

2 yellow Delicious apples
Apple juice

1 tsp. lemon juice
1 cup ground raw cashews

Core, but do not peel, the apples. Cube and put in blender with just enough apple juice to start blender working. Add lemon juice. When puréed, gradually add cashews and continue to blend until smooth. Won't stand in peaks though. Use as you would whipped cream. Great on fruit, cakes.

Yield: 1 cup

Variation:

Another way to make whipped cream is by using TOFU. Use 4 ounces of tofu, 2 tablespoons honey and 1 tsp. vanilla. Blend all together well.

GRANOLA TOPPING

1 cup GRANOLA
1/2 cup wheat germ
1/2 cup melted butter

1/4 cup honey
1/2 tsp. cinnamon
1/4 tsp. nutmeg

Mix all together and sprinkle on top of desserts.

Yield: 1½ cups

CRUMBLY TOPPING

1/2 cup wheat germ
1 cup whole wheat flour
1 cup blender-ground oats
1/2 cup regular oats
1/4 cup oil
1/3 cup honey

1/4 cup molasses, unsulfured
1/2 cup finely chopped walnuts
1/4 cup sunflower seeds
1/4 cup sesame seeds
1 tsp. cinnamon
1 tsp. VANILLA EXTRACT

Mix all together. Can mix up an extra amount and store in refrigerator until needed. Use on pies, coffee cakes or other desserts.

Yield: 2½ cups

NUTTY TOPPING

1 cup oats
1 cup shredded coconut
3/4 cup chopped nuts

1/2 cup butter
1 T. VANILLA EXTRACT
1/4 cup honey

Mix all of the ingredients together. Place on either uncooked or cooked cake.

Yield: 2½ cups

CUSTARD FILLING

1/3 cup arrowroot powder
2/3 cup non-instant dry milk powder
1¾ cups water
1/3 cup honey

2 egg yolks, slightly beaten
1 T. lemon juice
1 tsp. VANILLA EXTRACT

In medium-sized saucepan, combine arrowroot and milk powder. Add 1/4 cup of water, stirring with a wooden spoon until free from lumps. Add remaining water and mix thoroughly. Add honey and place over medium heat. Stir constantly until custard thickens (10–12 minutes). Remove from heat. Add 2 tablespoons of hot mixture to egg yolks, mix well. Pour yolk mixture into custard, blending well. Return to heat and cook 3 minutes. Stir constantly. Remove from heat. Add lemon juice and vanilla. Cool before using.

Yield: 2 cups

DATE FILLING

3/4 cup dates, pitted and chopped
1/3 cup whole wheat flour
1 T. soy flour

3/4 cup YOGURT, plain
1 egg
1/4 cup molasses, unsulfured

Combine all ingredients in top of double boiler. Cook gently over hot water until thick. Cool.

Yield: 2¾ cups

RAISIN FILLING

1½ cups raisins
3/4 cup apple cider
1/4 cup molasses, unsulfured
2 T. whole wheat flour

1/2 tsp. cinnamon
1/8 tsp. cloves, ground
1 T. oil
1/2 tsp. lemon rind

Blend all together in a blender until smooth.

Yield: 2¾ cups

DECORATING IDEAS

1. Any frosting can be squeezed from a cake decorating bag.
2. For natural frosting or icing colorings, add a bit of cranberry juice for pink, carrot juice for yellow/orange, grape juice for a dark pink, crushed blueberries for blue.
3. Melt carob chips to use as "paint" to inscribe names and greetings with a clean water color brush on cakes, cookies.
4. Tint coconut shreds in unsweetened grape or cranberry juice.

PIES AND PIE CRUSTS

TOFU PINEAPPLE BANANA CHEESECAKE PIE

2 egg yolks
1/3 cup honey
2 T. lemon juice
1 tsp. lemon peel, grated
1 tsp. VANILLA EXTRACT

1/2 pound TOFU, drained and patted dry
2 medium-sized bananas
1 8-ounce can unsweetened crushed pineapple, drained
2 egg whites

Place the egg yolks, honey, lemon juice, lemon peel and vanilla in a blender and blend until well mixed. Add the tofu and bananas and continue blending until smooth. Remove from blender and place in a bowl. Stir into this mixture the crushed pineapple. In a separate bowl, beat the egg whites until they form soft peaks. Fold egg whites into the other mixture. Pour into a NUTTY or GRAHAM CRACKER CRUST. Bake at 350° for 1 hour. If you would like, sprinkle the top with unsweetened coconut flakes before you bake it.

Yield: 1 9"-pie

PUMPKIN or SQUASH PIE

1½ cups mashed cooked pumpkin or
   winter squash
1½ cups milk
2 beaten eggs
1/4 cup honey
1/4 cup molasses, unsulfured

1/2 tsp. each cinnamon, nutmeg,
   cloves
1/4 tsp. ginger
3/4 cup chopped walnuts
Recipe for FLAKY PIE CRUST—
   bottom crust

Blend together all ingredients. Pour into a 9" unbaked pie crust. Bake in 450°
oven for 15 minutes. Reduce to 350° for approximately 40 more minutes, or
until firmly set.

Yield: 1 9"-pie

PUMPKIN ICE CREAM PIE

Crust:

1½ cups ground pecans

2 T. butter

Mix pecans and butter together in a mixing bowl. Press into a 9" pie plate.
Bake for 10 minutes at 350°. Let crust cool before adding pumpkin filling.

Filling:

1 cup mashed cooked pumpkin
3 egg yolks, beaten
1/3 cup honey
1/8 cup molasses, unsulfured

1/2 tsp. cinnamon
1/4 tsp. each nutmeg, cloves
3 stiffly beaten egg whites
1 cup WHIPPED CREAM

Mix well together, the first 6 ingredients, fold in 3 stiffly beaten egg whites.
Whip 1 cup whipping cream until peaks form, and fold this into the pumpkin
mixture. Pour into cooled crust. Freeze for at least 2 hours before serving.

Yield: 1 9"-pie

LEMON MERINGUE PIE

6 T. arrowroot powder
3/4 cup honey
1½ cups boiling water
1 T. grated lemon rind
1/2 cup lemon juice
4 egg yolks, slightly beaten

4 egg whites
2 T. honey (softened by placing
   container in bowl of hot water)
1/2 tsp. VANILLA EXTRACT
1 recipe for OATMEAL CRUST or
   PRESSED PIE CRUST

Mix arrowroot and honey in top of double boiler. Add boiling water and
cook over direct heat until the mixture boils, stirring constantly. Set over hot
water, cover, and cook 20 minutes. Add lemon rind, lemon juice and beaten
egg yolks. Cook until thick, stirring constantly. Cool. Beat egg whites until
soft peaks form when beater is raised. Gradually beat in honey and vanilla.
Pile lemon filling into baked 9" pie shell and top with meringue. Bake 5 minutes in preheated 350° oven.

Yield: 1 9"-pie

PECAN PIE

3/4 cup molasses, unsulfured
1/2 cup honey
4 eggs, beaten
2 T. whole wheat flour
1/2 tsp. nutmeg

2 T. butter
1 T. lemon juice
1 cup pecans
1 recipe for WHOLE WHEAT
   PASTRY SHELL

Beat all the ingredients, except pecans, together. Stir in pecans. Pour into a 9" pie crust. Bake at 450° for 10 minutes and 350° for 30 minutes.

Yield: 1 9"-pie

BASIC CUSTARD PIE

3 eggs
3 cups milk
3 T. honey

1/4 tsp. VANILLA EXTRACT
1 recipe for WHEAT SPROUT
   CRUST

Blend all ingredients together. Turn into an unbaked piecrust. Sprinkle with nutmeg. Bake at 375° for 40 minutes.

Yield: 1 10"-pie

Variations:

1. Add 1 cup of any of the following: coconut, dates, raisins, figs or dried fruit (soaked in water for 30 seconds).

2. Sprinkle on top: sesame seeds, ground nuts, wheat germ, or cookie crumbs.

APPLE PIE

1 recipe for FLAKY PIE CRUST

Slice:

7 cups peeled apples, Gravenstein, Rome

In a saucepan combine the following:

2/3 cup unfiltered, unsweetened
   apple juice
1 T. arrowroot powder
1 T. honey

1 T. molasses, unsulfured
1 tsp. cinnamon
1/2 tsp. nutmeg and cloves

Cook over medium heat until thickened. Pour over apples and mix well. Pour into an uncooked pie crust and dot with butter. Add top pie crust or CRUM-BLY TOPPING. Bake at 350° for 45–50 minutes.

Yield: 1 9"-pie

CHERRY PIE

5 T. arrowroot powder
1 tsp. cinnamon
1/2-3/4 cup honey
1/2 tsp. almond extract
1 cup apple or cherry juice
   (unsweetened)

3½ cups pitted unsweetened pie
   cherries
1 T. butter
1 recipe for FLAKY PIE
   CRUST

Mix arrowroot with cinnamon. Mix honey and fruit juice together. Then combine with arrowroot mixture in a saucepan. Cook over medium heat until mixture is thick and clear. Stir often. Remove from heat and stir in extract and cherries. Pour into a 9" uncooked pie crust. Dot with butter and add top crust. Make sure you add slits on the top. Bake at 425° for 45 minutes.

Yield: 1 9"-pie

STRAWBERRY PIE

1 pie crust recipe (bottom only)
5 cups strawberries
3 T. arrowroot powder
1/2 cup honey

1/2 cup boiling water
3 tsp. lemon juice
WHIPPED TOPPING
Sunflower seeds

Mash some of the berries to make 1 cup. Place the arrowroot, crushed berries and honey in a small saucepan. Add the boiling water and cook over medium heat until thickened and clear. Be sure to stir frequently. Remove from heat and add the lemon juice. Cool. Place the rest of the whole berries in the pie shell and pour the cooled sauce over the top. Mix in well to coat the berries. Chill and serve with the topping and sunflower seeds.

Yield: 1 8"-pie

BERRY PIE

5 cups berries
1/4 cup honey
3 T. flour
1 T. lemon juice

1/2 tsp. each cinnamon and nutmeg
2 T. butter
1 FLAKY PIE CRUST recipe

In a large bowl, blend all ingredients, except butter. Pour into an unbaked 9" pie crust. Dot with butter and cover with crisscross strips of pastry dough or a full top crust. Seal and flute edge. Slit crust in several places if using a top crust. Bake in a 400° oven for 50 minutes or until fruit is tender and top is golden.

Yield: 1 9"-pie

PEACH OR NECTARINE PIE

5 cups sliced peaches, peeled or
   nectarines, unpeeled
1 whole peach or nectarine, pitted
   and peeled
1 T. lemon juice
3 T. flour

1 tsp. cinnamon
1/4 tsp. nutmeg
1 T. butter
1/8 cup honey
1/2 cup chopped walnuts

Place whole fruit into blender along with lemon juice, flour, cinnamon, nutmeg, butter and honey. Blend this to a liquid. Arrange sliced fruit in unbaked pie crust. Pour liquid over peaches and all walnuts. Bake at 425° for 15 minutes and then 350° for 20 minutes.

Yield: 1 9"-pie

PEANUT BUTTER ICE CREAM PIE

1 quart HONEY VANILLA ICE
   CREAM, slightly softened
3/4 cup chunky PEANUT BUTTER
3/4 cup crushed peanuts (unsalted)

1½ T. VANILLA EXTRACT
1 10" GRAHAM CRACKER
   CRUST
WHIPPED CREAM

Combine ice cream, peanut butter, 1/2 cup peanuts and vanilla in large bowl and mix well. Turn into crust and sprinkle with remaining peanuts. Freeze. Decorate with whipped cream.

Yield: 1 10"-pie

FROZEN STRAWBERRY PIE

2 cups plain YOGURT
2 cups strawberry-flavored yogurt
   (sweetened with honey)

2 cups strawberries (sliced)
1 cup WHIPPED CREAM

Mix together the 2 yogurts and sliced strawberries. Whip the cream until stiff and fold into the yogurt mixture. Pour into baked 9" pie crust. Cover and place in freezer until it becomes frozen.

Yield: 1 9"-pie

PINEAPPLE CHIFFON PIE

20-ounce can crushed pineapple
(unsweetened)
1 T. unflavored gelatin
1/4 cup honey
3 beaten egg yolks
1½ cups COTTAGE CHEESE

4 ounces drained TOFU or cream
cheese
1/4 cup lemon juice
3 egg whites, beaten to soft peaks
1 OATMEAL CRUST recipe

Drain pineapple, reserving 1/2 cup of the juice. Set pineapple aside. In a saucepan combine the gelatin, honey, egg yolks and reserved juice. Cook and stir until just slightly thickened. Chill until partially set. In a medium-sized bowl, combine the cottage cheese, tofu and lemon juice. Beat well. Gradually add the gelatin mixture, beating until smooth. Fold in reserved pineapple. Beat the egg whites to soft peaks, fold into pineapple mixture. Turn into a 13" x 9" x 2" pan that has been lined with a baked Oatmeal Crust. Refrigerate for 1 hour.

Yield: 1 pie

FLAKY PIE CRUST

3 cups whole wheat pastry flour
1/2 cup oil
1 egg

1 T. cider vinegar
5 T. ice water

Mix oil, egg, vinegar and water together. Place the flour in a medium-size bowl. Make an indentation in the center of the flour and pour in the liquid ingredients. Mix with a fork until it forms a soft ball. Divide dough in half and roll each out between wax paper. Place into a 9" pie pan. Add filling and then place on the top crust. Make sure you make slits to allow steam to escape. If a baked pie crust is needed, bake for 7 minutes in 350° oven.

Yield: Top and bottom crust

OATMEAL CRUST

1 cup blender-ground oats
1/2 cup whole wheat pastry flour
1/4 cup shredded coconut
1/2 cup wheat germ
1 T. sesame seeds

1/4 cup honey
1/4 cup oil
1 tsp. cinnamon
Apple juice, unsweetened

Mix all together and add just enough apple juice to make a workable dough. Press into a pie pan and bake at 375° for 12 minutes. Cool and then add filling.

Yield: 1 10" bottom crust

PRESSED PIE CRUST

3/4 cup whole wheat pastry flour
3/4 cup rolled oats
1/4 cup roasted sesame seeds

1 T. honey
1/4-1/2 cup oil
1/4 cup apple juice or cider

Combine flour and oats in mixing bowl. Add sesame seeds and honey. Add oil slowly, rubbing it in with your hands or cutting it in, until it looks like bread crumbs. Put a handful of the mixture in the palm of your hand, make a fist and open your hand. If mixture sticks together, then the amount of oil is sufficient. Moisten with a little bit of juice and press into a 9" pie pan. Bake for 10 minutes at 375°.

Yield: 1 9" bottom crust

WHEAT SPROUT CRUST

Spread 1 cup of 2-day-old wheat sprouts on bottom of 10" pie pan. Pour in filling and bake. Best with custard-type pie.

Yield: 1 10" bottom crust

SPICY PIE CRUST

Sift together

1 cup whole wheat pastry flour
2 T. honey
1/4 tsp. cinnamon

1/8 tsp. cloves
1/8 tsp. pumpkin pie spice

Cut in

1/3 cup cold butter

Sprinkle over mixture, 1 tablespoon at a time

2-3 T. orange juice

Toss lightly with a fork only until mixture is moist enough to hold together in a ball. Roll out between 2 layers of wax paper. Fit into a 9" pie pan. For a baked pie crust, bake at 350° for 12 minutes.

Yield: 1 9" bottom crust

WHOLE WHEAT PASTRY SHELL

1 cup whole wheat pastry flour
1 T. wheat germ

1/4 cup oil
2 T. cold milk

Add wheat germ and flour together. Add oil and milk; mix with fork into a dough. Roll between 2 pieces of wax paper. Peel off top paper. Turn pastry into a 9" pie pan. Remove top paper.

Yield: 1 9" bottom crust

GRAHAM CRACKER CRUST

2 cups GRAHAM CRACKERS
1/4 cup melted butter
4 T. honey

1/4 tsp. nutmeg
1/4 cup ground almonds
1/4 tsp. cinnamon

Mix all of the ingredients together. Press firmly into sides and bottom of pie pan. If baked pie crust is needed, bake 7 minutes at 350°.

Yield: 1 9" bottom crust

NUTTY CRUST

1/2 cup ground almonds
3/4 cup wheat germ
1/2 tsp. cinnamon

1 T. honey
1/4 cup butter, melted

Combine all of the ingredients together. It will be crumbly. Press into bottom of 9" pie pan. If baked pie crust is needed, bake 10 minutes in a 350° oven.

Yield: 1 9" bottom crust

RICE CRUST

1½ cups cooked, brown rice
2 T. butter
1 egg beaten
1/4 cup Parmesan cheese, grated

Juice of 1 lemon
1 T. fresh parsley, chopped
1/4 cup toasted sesame seeds

Mix all together and pat into a 10" pie pan. Bake 10 minutes at 350°. Great for dinner pies.

Yield: 1 10" bottom crust

CHEESE CRUST

1 cup whole wheat pastry flour
1/4 tsp. dry mustard
1 cup grated Cheddar cheese

1/4 cup oil
1/4 cup ice water

Mix the ingredients together and add just enough water to hold dough together. Roll out, place in 10" pie pan and bake 5 minutes at 375° before adding filling.

Yield: 1 10" bottom crust

COOKIES

OATMEAL/MOLASSES COOKIES

3/4 cup butter
1/4 cup molasses, unsulfured
1/4 cup honey
1 egg
1/4 cup water
1 tsp. VANILLA EXTRACT
1 cup whole wheat flour

1/2 tsp. soda
1 tsp. cinnamon
1 tsp. nutmeg
1/2 tsp. cloves
1 cup raisins
1 cup nuts
3 cups oats

Cream together butter, molasses and honey. Add egg, water and vanilla. Mix well. Mix in all the rest of the ingredients but add only 2 cups of the oats. Roll into teaspoon size balls and roll in the extra 1 cup of oats. Place on greased baking sheet. Bake at 350° for 10 minutes.

Yield: 5 dozen

PEANUT BUTTER COOKIES

1/2 cup oil
1/4 cup honey
3 T. molasses, unsulfured
3/4 cup PEANUT BUTTER
1 egg

1 tsp. VANILLA EXTRACT
1½ cups whole wheat flour
1½ tsp. orange juice or water
1 tsp. BAKING POWDER
3/4 cup chopped peanuts

Mix oil, honey, molasses and peanut butter together. Add egg and vanilla. Mix in flour and baking powder, alternately with juice or water. Add peanuts. Shape into small balls and flatten with a fork dipped in flour. Bake on greased cookie sheet at 350° for 10 minutes.

Yield: 4 dozen

VANILLA WAFERS

1 cup whole wheat flour
1-1/8 tsp. BAKING POWDER
1/2 cup butter

1/4 cup honey
1 beaten egg yolk
3 T. cold water

In a bowl combine the flour and baking powder. In another bowl cream together the butter and honey. Add the egg yolk and mix well. Add the water and liquid ingredients to the flour and mix. With a teaspoon drop mixture onto a greased cookie sheet. Press flat with palm of hand or a floured glass. Bake at 350° for 8–10 minutes.

Yield: 2 dozen

FUDGE BROWNIES

1/4 cup oil
1/4 cup butter
1 T. molasses, unsulfured
1/2 cup honey
4 eggs
2/3 cup sifted carob powder

1 tsp. VANILLA EXTRACT
1/4 cup soy flour
3/4 cup whole wheat pastry flour
1 cup chopped walnuts
1/2 cup raisins

Beat first 4 ingredients together until fluffy. Add eggs one at a time and mix until well blended. Add rest of ingredients and mix well. Pour into a greased 8" square pan. Bake at 350° for 30 minutes. Cool and cut into squares. Serve plain or frost with any of the CAROB FROSTINGS.

Yield: 1 dozen

NUT-FRUIT BARS

3 T. honey
1/2 cup oil
2 cups pitted dates, finely chopped
2/3 cup walnuts, chopped
1/2 cup sesame seeds
1/4 cup sunflower seeds

1/2 cup dried coconut flakes, unsweetened
2/3 cup milk
1 tsp. almond extract
2 cups whole wheat flour
2 cups oat flour

Blend all of the ingredients together, in the order given. Add only enough oat flour to make a dough of a consistency that will hold together. Turn the dough into 2 greased 8" pans, and press firmly until smooth. Bake at 375° for 20-25 minutes.

Yield: 2½ dozen bars

SLICE AND BAKE SPICE COOKIES

1/2 cup oil
1/3 cup honey
1 egg, beaten
Rind of 1 lemon, grated
1¾ cups whole wheat flour

2 T. wheat germ
1/2 tsp. cinnamon
1/2 tsp. nutmeg
1/4 tsp. allspice, ground

Beat oil and honey together until smooth and creamy. Beat in egg and grated lemon. Add flour, wheat germ and spices and stir until smooth. Shape into 2 logs, each about 8" long. Wrap and refrigerate at least 1 hour. When ready to bake, slice dough into rounds about 1/4" thick. Place on ungreased sheet and bake in 350° oven for 10-12 minutes.

Yield: 4 dozen

Variation:

Almond Cookies: Add 1 tsp. almond extract and 3/4 cup ground almonds to the original dough.

CARROT GEMS

1/2 cup boiling water
1/2 cup raisins
1/2 cup honey
1/2 cup oil
1 egg

1 tsp. lemon juice
1/2 cup finely grated carrots
1-2/3 cups whole wheat flour
2 tsp. BAKING POWDER

Pour boiling water over raisins. Soak for 5 minutes, then drain. Beat together honey, oil, egg, and lemon juice. Stir in carrots and drained raisins. Add flour and baking powder and blend well. Drop by teaspoon onto greased cookie sheet. Bake at 350° for 8–12 minutes.

Yield: 4 dozen

ENERGY COOKIES

1 cup vegetable oil
1½ cups honey
4 beaten eggs
1 T. VANILLA EXTRACT
2½ cups whole wheat flour
1/2 cup non-instant dry milk powder
1/2 cup carob powder

1 T. BAKING POWDER
1/3 cup bran flakes
1/3 cup wheat germ
1 cup chopped macadamia nuts,
    pecans or walnuts
1 cup sesame seeds
1½ cups dates, chopped

Mix first 4 ingredients together until blended. Sift the next 6 ingredients together and add to the first 4. Add the last of the ingredients together and mix until well blended. Drop by teaspoonfuls onto a greased cookie sheet. Bake for 10 minutes at 325°.

Yield: 5 dozen

CONGLOMERATION COOKIES

1/4 cup oil
1/4 cup molasses, unsulfured
1/4 cup honey
2 eggs
1¼ cups whole wheat flour
1-1/3 cups rolled oats
1/2 cup coconut flakes, unsweetened
1/4 cup non-instant dry milk powder

1 tsp. cinnamon
1 tsp. nutmeg
1/2 tsp. cloves
1/4 tsp. powdered ginger
2/3 cup raisins
2/3 cup CAROB CHIPS
1/4 cup peanuts
1/3 cup sunflower seeds
1/4 cup sesame seeds

Beat eggs in a bowl, add molasses, honey and oil and mix well. Add all of the rest of the ingredients and combine until dry mixture is moistened. If too dry add a little liquid milk until dough is of drop cookie consistency. Drop teaspoonfuls onto greased cookie sheet. Bake at 350° for 10 minutes.

Yield: 5 dozen

YUMMY HONEY COOKIES

1/2 cup oil
1/2 cup honey
2 eggs
2 cups oatmeal
1¼ tsp. soda
2/3 cup wheat germ

2 tsp. VANILLA EXTRACT
1/2 tsp. each cloves, nutmeg, ginger
2 tsp. cinnamon
1¼ cups whole wheat flour
1 cup raisins
1 cup walnuts or sunflower seeds

Cream together oil, honey and eggs. Add oatmeal, soda, wheat germ, vanilla and spices and mix. Add flour, a little at a time. Then stir in the nuts and raisins. Drop by the teaspoon onto greased baking sheet. Bake at 350° for 8-10 minutes.

Yield: 5 dozen

FIG NEWTONS

1/2 cup butter
1/2 cup honey
1/4 cup molasses, unsulfured
2 eggs

1 tsp. VANILLA EXTRACT
2¾ cups whole wheat pastry flour
1/4 tsp. soda
1/2 tsp. each cinnamon, nutmeg

Cream together until fluffy the butter, honey, and molasses. Beat in eggs and vanilla. Add the flour, soda and spices. Add more flour if needed to make dough pliable to knead for a few minutes. Refrigerate for at least 1 hour.

Fig Filling:

4 cups figs
2½ cups water

3 T. lemon juice
3/4 cups walnuts

Combine all of the above in a saucepan and heat until thick. Add nuts and cool. Roll refrigerated dough out until about 1/8" thick and cut into 3"-wide strips. Add filling down each strip then pull over one side and then the other and seal. Cut into 1" pieces. Place on greased baking sheet. Bake for 10 minutes at 350°.

Yield: 3 dozen

FIG PICK UP BARS

2 cups figs, chopped
1/2 cup ground raisins
1/4 cup sunflower seeds
1/2 cup fresh orange juice

1/4 cup carob powder
1/4 cup wheat germ
1/2 cup shredded coconut

Mix well together all ingredients, except coconut. Press firmly into a metal ice cube tray. Chill thoroughly. Cut into bars and roll in coconut. Keep tightly covered with plastic wrap.

Yield: 10 bars

CAROB CHIP COOKIES

1/2 cup oil
1/2 cup honey
2 eggs
2-1/3 cups whole wheat flour
2 tsp. BAKING POWDER

1 cup walnuts, chopped
1 tsp. VANILLA EXTRACT
1 cup CAROB CHIPS
1 cup raisins (optional)

In a large mixing bowl, mix oil and honey. Add eggs and mix well. Stir in flour, baking powder, nuts, vanilla, carob chips, and optional raisins. Mix well. Chill dough. Drop by the teaspoonfuls onto a greased baking sheet. Bake at 350° for 10 minutes.

Yield: 4 dozen

GRANOLA BARS

1 cup shredded coconut
2 cups rolled oats
2 cups barley flakes
1 cup rye flakes
1/2 cup wheat germ
1/2 cup whole wheat flour
1/2 cup sesame seeds
1/2 cup sunflower seeds
1/2 cup chopped, raw almonds

1 cup raw cashews
1/2 cup flaked bran
1 cup chopped dates
1½ cups raisins
1/4 cup non-instant dry milk
   powder
1½ cups honey or part honey/
   molasses
2/3 cup oil

In a large bowl, mix together all the dry ingredients. Heat honey and oil in a saucepan. Pour over dry ingredients and stir until well-coated. Spread and pack into large cake pans. You want them at least 1/2" thick. Oil the pan first. Bake at 275° for 45 minutes to 1 hour. Bars will be soft. Cut into squares while still warm. Store in covered container.

Yield: 30 bars

GINGERSNAPS

2½ cups whole wheat flour
1½ tsp. baking soda
1 tsp. ground ginger
1/2 tsp. ground cinnamon
1/2 tsp. ground cloves

3/4 cup butter, softened
1/3 cup honey
1 egg
1/2 cup molasses, unsulfured
Sesame seeds

Measure flour, baking soda, ginger, cinnamon and cloves onto wax paper. Beat butter, honey and egg in a large bowl with an electric mixer until light and fluffy. Add molasses, blending thoroughly. Stir in flour mixture. Shape dough between palms of hands, a level tablespoon at a time, into balls. Roll in sesame seeds. Bake at 350° for 8 minutes.

Yield: 4 dozen

ZUCCHINI COOKIES

1/2 cup butter or oil
1/2 cup honey
1 egg
1/2 tsp. VANILLA EXTRACT
1 cup zucchini, peeled and grated
2 cups whole wheat pastry flour

1 tsp. soda
1 tsp. cinnamon
1/2 tsp. cloves
1 cup chopped nuts
1 cup raisins

Cream together the first 4 ingredients. Add zucchini. Stir in the remaining ingredients. Chill dough for 1 hour. Drop by the teaspoonfuls onto a greased cookie sheet. Bake 12-15 minutes at 350°.

Yield: 3 dozen

FROSTED ALMOND SQUARES

Dough:

1/2 cup butter
1/4 cup honey
1/2 tsp. almond flavoring
2 eggs

1½ cups whole wheat pastry flour
1 tsp. BAKING POWDER
1 cup sliced unblanched almonds

Cream together butter, honey and almond flavoring. Add eggs, one at a time. Mix in flour and baking powder. Spread into greased 8" square pan. Sprinkle with almonds.

Topping:

2 egg whites
1/2 tsp. almond flavoring

1 T. honey
1/2 cup coconut

Beat egg whites until stiff. Add honey and flavoring. Fold in coconut. Spread evenly over almond-topped dough. Bake 40 minutes at 325°. Cut into squares while warm. This makes a good holiday cookie.

Yield: 16 squares

SPRITZ COOKIES

1 cup butter
1 T. liquid soy lecithin
1 tsp. almond flavoring

1/4 cup honey
2 egg yolks
2½ cups whole wheat pastry flour

Cream butter, lecithin and flavoring until soft. Gradually add the honey and mix until fluffy. Thoroughly beat in 2 egg yolks, one at a time. Add flour in halves, blending well after each addition. Fill a cookie press about 2/3 full with dough. Press out into desired designs. Can decorate with different seeds and nuts or color with the vegetable dyes listed in the cake decorating section. You can also purchase them at your local health food store. Bake at 350° for 12 minutes.

Yield: 6 dozen

ALMOND ROCA COOKIES

Dough:

1 cup butter	1 tsp. VANILLA EXTRACT
1/3 cup honey	1 beaten egg yolk
3 T. molasses, unsulfured	2 cups whole wheat flour

Cream together all of the above ingredients. Spread into a greased 8" x 12" pan. Bake at 350° for 25 minutes. Cool.

Topping:

16 ounces CAROB CHIPS	1½ cup chopped walnuts
2 T. YOGURT, plain	

Melt the carob chips and yogurt over a double boiler. Water should not touch top pan. Spread the melted carob over the cooled cookie dough. Sprinkle with nuts and cut into squares while warm. A good holiday cookie.

Yield: 36 cookies

THUMBPRINT COOKIES

1/2 cup butter	1 cup whole wheat flour
1/3 cup honey	1½ cups chopped walnuts
1 egg, separated	Jam—raspberry, strawberry, or
1/2 tsp. almond flavoring	blackberry (honey sweetened)

Cream together butter, honey, egg yolk and almond flavoring. Add flour and mix well. Roll dough into balls. Beat the egg white slightly with fork. Dip balls in egg white and roll in nuts. Press thumb gently into center to make a small well. Bake on greased cookie sheet for 10–12 minutes at 350°. Cool and fill with jam. Good cookie to serve during the holidays.

Yield: 3 dozen

WHOLE WHEAT CUT OUT COOKIES

1/2 cup butter	2½ cups whole wheat flour
2/3 cup honey	1½ tsp. BAKING POWDER
2 beaten eggs	1/2 tsp. nutmeg
1 tsp. almond extract	

Cream together honey and butter. Add eggs and flavoring. Mix in flour, baking powder and nutmeg. Refrigerate dough for 1 hour. Roll dough out onto lightly floured board, 1/4" thick. Cut with favorite cookie cutters. Bake at 350° for 10–12 minutes. Frost if desired with BUTTER FROSTING.

Yield: 3 dozen

PUDDINGS AND CUSTARDS

VANILLA PUDDING

1/4 cup honey
3 T. arrowroot powder
2 cups milk

3 well-beaten eggs
2 tsp. VANILLA EXTRACT
1 T. lemon juice

Mix together the honey and arrowroot in the top of a double boiler over medium heat. Add the milk gradually and cook for about 2 minutes. Take a small amount of the mixture out and mix with the eggs then add this mixture back to the double boiler. Cook, stirring frequently, for about 3 minutes or until mixture is thickened. Remove from the heat and add the vanilla and lemon juice. Chill and serve garnished with chopped nuts and shredded coconut.

Yield: Serves 4

Variations:

Carob Pudding: Add 3-4 tablespoons of sifted carob powder along with the milk in the double boiler.

Banana Pudding: Add 3-4 mashed bananas along with the honey and arrowroot.

CEREAL PUDDING

1 cup cooked cereal (leftovers work
   great)
2 T. arrowroot powder
1/3 cup honey
3 cups milk

1 T. butter
3 eggs, well beaten
1½ tsp. VANILLA EXTRACT
1/2 cup chopped dates or raisins
1/3 cup chopped nuts

Mix together the cooked cereal, arrowroot and honey. Place the milk in a saucepan and bring to a boil over medium heat. Stir the cereal mixture in vigorously. When it is well blended, remove from the heat and stir in the remaining ingredients. Serve topped with YOGURT.

Yield: 4 servings

CAROB PEANUT BUTTER PUDDING

1/4 cup honey	1½ cups milk
1 T. butter	3 eggs, beaten
1/2 cup PEANUT BUTTER	1/4 tsp. almond extract
4 T. sifted carob powder	

Combine the honey, butter, peanut butter and carob in the top of a double boiler. Heat and stir until mixture is smooth. Add the milk and heat until hot. Stir frequently. Remove some of the hot mixture and add it to the eggs, then stir the eggs back into the hot mixture. Cook, stirring constantly, until it thickens. It will take about 5-7 minutes. Remove from the heat and add the extract. Chill for several hours. Serve topped with YOGURT and chopped nuts.

Yield: Serves 4

RICE PUDDING

2 cups cooked brown rice	1 T. lemon juice
1 cup raisins	3 T. unsweetened frozen apple juice
1/2 cup sunflower seeds	concentrate
1/4 cup chopped walnuts	1/2 tsp. each nutmeg and cinnamon
2 cups milk	2 eggs, beaten

Add all the ingredients together in a large bowl and mix well. Pour into a 2 quart casserole dish. Bake at 325° for 30-40 minutes.

Yield: 6 servings

FRUITED RICE PUDDING WITH COCONUT

2 cups cooked brown rice	3/4 cup chopped, pitted dates
2 cups milk	1/2 cup dried apricots, quartered
1/2 cup honey	3 T. melted butter
3 tart apples	3 eggs, separated
1/4 tsp. grated lemon peel	2/3 cup shredded coconut,
3 T. lemon juice	unsweetened

In a large bowl, mix together the rice, milk and 1/4 cup honey. Peel and finely chop apples; stir into rice mixture along with the lemon peel and juice, dates, apricots and butter. Beat egg yolks lightly and stir into pudding. In another bowl beat the egg whites until soft peaks form. Continue beating as you pour in the last 1/4 cup of honey. Fold the egg whites into the rice mixture and pour into a greased 3 quart baking dish. Sprinkle the coconut on top. Bake, uncovered, at 350° for about 40-45 minutes, or until a knife inserted near the edge comes out clean. Serve warm with cream, if desired.

Yield: 8-10 servings

CAROB CREAM

1 T. unflavored gelatin
1 T. honey
3 egg yolks, slightly beaten
2 cups milk

4 T. carob powder, sifted
1 tsp. **VANILLA EXTRACT**
3 egg whites
3 T. honey

Mix the gelatin and honey together in a saucepan. Add the egg yolks and mix well. Add 1 cup milk and carob powder and place over low heat. Cook about 8 minutes, until the gelatin dissolves. Remove from the heat and add the other cup of milk and vanilla. Chill this mixture until slightly firm. Beat the egg whites until stiff peaks form. Gradually add the honey in a steady stream. Fold this egg white mixture into the pudding. Pour into a mold or individual molds and chill for several hours until firm. When firm remove from the mold and serve. It will look like it has two layers.

Yield: 6 servings

BAKED CUSTARD

4 cups milk
3 egg yolks
2 whole eggs

1½ tsp. **VANILLA EXTRACT**
1/3–1/2 cup honey
Nutmeg

Place all of the ingredients except the nutmeg in a blender and blend well. Pour into an ungreased 2 quart baking dish or individual custard cups and sprinkle with nutmeg. Place the baking dish into another pan that contains water. Bake at 300° for 30-40 minutes or until firm.

Yield: 6 servings

Variations:

Fruit Custard: Place sliced fresh peaches, pears or pineapple on the bottom of the baking dish and then pour custard over the fruit. Cook as directed.

Date-Almond Custard: Mix into custard 1/2 cup chopped dates and 1/4 cup soy grits. Use almond extract in place of the vanilla.

PUMPKIN CUSTARD

2 cups **COTTAGE CHEESE**
2 cups cooked pumpkin
4 eggs
1/4 cup honey

1 T. molasses, unsulfured
1/2 ripe banana
1/4 tsp. pumpkin pie seasoning

Place all the ingredients in an electric blender and blend until smooth. Pour into six oiled custard cups. Sprinkle with nutmeg. Place cups in a pan of hot water and bake until custard is firm or until a knife inserted comes out clean. Bake at 350° for about 30 minutes.

Yield: 6 servings

SWEET POTATO CUSTARD

1 cup finely grated sweet potato	1/4 tsp. cinnamon
2 ripe bananas	1/4 tsp. VANILLA EXTRACT
1/2 cup apple juice, unsweetened	

Mash the bananas until creamy and mix with the sweet potato. Blend all ingredients together until smooth. Serve cold in custard dishes.

Yield: Serves 2

PEANUT BUTTER FONDUE

1 cup PEANUT BUTTER	1/3 cup honey
1 cup light cream	1 tsp. VANILLA EXTRACT
apple wedges	whole strawberries
peach quarters	raisins
pear quarters	pitted dates
banana chunks	flaked coconut and/or wheat germ

Place peanut butter in fondue pot. Gradually stir in cream, vanilla and honey. Place over low heat, stirring constantly until mixture starts to boil. Keep warm on table while serving. Dip fruit into fondue pot. Coat with coconut and/or wheat germ.

DESSERT SAUCES

CARAMEL SAUCE

4 T. arrowroot powder	1/4 cup butter
2 cups apple juice (unsweetened)	1 tsp. almond extract
1 cup molasses, unsulfured	

In a saucepan dissolve arrowroot in 3 tablespoons juice; add remaining juice, molasses and butter. Place over medium heat until it thickens and turns clear. Stir frequently. Remove from heat and add extract.

Yield: 2½ cups

LEMON SAUCE

1 cup boiling water
1/4 cup honey
1 T. arrowroot powder dissolved in
   1 T. water

2 T. butter
3 T. lemon juice
1/2 tsp. nutmeg

In a small saucepan mix honey, water and arrowroot. Cook for 3 minutes, stirring constantly. Add butter, lemon juice and nutmeg. Simmer a few minutes more until thick.

Yield: 1 cup

CAROB SYRUP

1/3 cup carob, sifted
1/3 cup honey
2 T. butter
1 tsp. arrowroot powder mixed
   with 2 tsp. hot water

2/3 cup hot water
1 T. lemon juice
1/2 tsp. VANILLA EXTRACT

In a small saucepan, combine carob, honey, butter and arrowroot. Add water and bring to a boil, stirring constantly. Boil slowly for 5 minutes. Remove from heat and cool. Add vanilla and lemon juice. Serve hot or cold over cake, ice cream.

Yield: 1 cup

FROZEN DESSERTS

ICE CREAM

The ice cream you buy at the store is so full of chemicals that it is very unhealthy for you. For instance the flavoring used for vanilla—Piperonal—is a de-lousing chemical. Banana flavoring is called amyl acetate and is a solvent for oil paint. Besides having the chemicals in it, it is usually full of white sugar. You do not need to feed your family those things when making homemade ice cream is so easy. You can use either a machine or just freeze it in the freezer. I will explain both methods.

Churn freezers: There are old-fashioned hand-cranked freezers and electric ones. Both types have a center canister, either metal or plastic, with a paddle inside called a "dasher." As you, or the motor, cranks, the dasher moves around whipping the ice cream. Layers of cracked ice and rock salt are surrounding the bucket. The reason you use the rock salt is salted ice melts at lower temperatures than unsalted ice.

Small electric freezers: There are two kinds—one that goes right into your freezer, and the other that works on the counter. The freezer model uses the refrigerator's cold air to make the ice cream, instead of salt and ice. They are battery operated or plugged into an outlet outside the refrigerator. You do need a freezer that freezes well though. The counter type model uses regular table salt, trays of ice cubes and water to produce soft ice cream in 20-50 minutes. It works the same as the large electric models but it just uses ingredients that are more freely available.

No machine method: Put the ice cream mixture right into an ice cube tray, minus the divider. Cover with foil and freeze. When the top and sides are frozen, but the middle is still soft, take the mixture out of the freezer and beat it. This breaks up the frozen lumps and ice crystals. It also redistributes any nuts or fruits that have settled to the bottom.

Adding fruit and nuts to the ice cream: Fruits and nuts can be added to the mix when it is just beginning to harden in the freezer can—when it is getting hard to turn. To flavor a gallon of ice cream, add 5 cups of fruit. Purée the fruit or chop in very fine pieces. If you are using fresh fruit you may want to dribble honey over it and let it sit for a few hours to help bring out the juice. You may also want to roast the nuts slightly before adding to the mixture as the flavor will stand out more.

Hints:

1. If you get the ice cream mixture very cold before freezing, the results will be creamier.

2. Do not fill the machine canister more than 3/4 full of ice cream mixture, for when ice cream freezes it expands.

3. Do not skimp on flavoring or sweetener. After freezing, flavor can get dull.

4. Do not store ice cream in the machine cannister. Instead place it in plastic containers, filling to 1/2" of the top. Cover with foil or plastic and place the top on it. This helps prevent ice crystals and preserves the flavor.

5. Do not store for more than 1 month. Be sure to store it at 0°.

6. Allow ice cream to soften slightly before serving.

7. The packing ratio for rock salt to ice is 6-8 cups cracked ice to each cup of coarse rock salt.

8. If a recipe calls for light cream you can use half and half. If it calls for very heavy cream, you want whipping cream.

TREATS YOU CAN ADD TO THE ICE CREAM

Vary amounts to taste, but 1/4 cup seems to work well for the 1 quart recipes.

- Toasted coconut
- Toasted nuts—walnuts, almonds, pistachios, filberts, sunflower seeds, Brazil nuts, cashews, pumpkin seeds
- Orange rind—1 T.
- Lemon rind—2 T.
- MARSHMALLOWS
- Crushed PEANUT BRITTLE
- CAROB SYRUP
- PEANUT BUTTER
- Frozen fruit, puréed
- APPLESAUCE
- Cookie crumbs
- Jam mixed in at the beginning or swirled in after cranking
- Spices—1 or 2 tsp, cinnamon, nutmeg, cardamon, ground cloves, ginger
- Dried fruits

FRENCH VANILLA ICE CREAM

6 eggs
1/2 cup honey

8 cups light cream
4 tsp. VANILLA EXTRACT

Separate the eggs and beat the yolks until smooth. Add the honey to the yolks and beat until well blended. Beat the egg whites until smooth and stir into the egg yolk mixture. Add the cream. Place this over top of a double boiler and cook until thick, about 15 minutes. Make sure you stir continuously. Remove from heat and stir in vanilla. Pour into freezer can and follow the directions that are on your ice cream churner.

Yield: 4 quarts

HONEY VANILLA ICE CREAM

2 cups milk
2 cups light cream
7 T. honey
1 T. unflavored gelatin

1/4 cup water
3 eggs, separated
1 tsp. VANILLA EXTRACT

Combine the milk and cream in the top of a double boiler. Add honey and heat the mixture. Sprinkle the gelatin over the 1/4 cup of water and let soak for a few minutes. Then add the gelatin to the hot milk mixture. Beat the egg yolk and add a little of the milk mixture. When this is mixed then add back to the hot mixture in the double boiler. Cook until mixture coats spoon, stirring constantly. Remove from heat and stir in the vanilla. Pour into refrigerator trays. Cover and place in the refrigerator. After it is frozen around the edges, but soft in the center, add the egg whites that have been stiffly beaten. Replace in freezer and continue to freeze. Stir periodically so it will have a creamy consistency.

Yield: 8-10 servings

Variations:

Carob Ice Cream: Add 1/4 cup sifted carob powder to the milk before it goes onto the heat.

Carob Mint Ice Cream: Add to the Carob Ice Cream 1/4 tsp. mint extract.

Date Ice Cream: To the 2 cups milk, add 3 cups dates and soak overnight. Remove dates in the morning, chop and add to the mixture.

STRAWBERRY HONEY ICE CREAM

2 eggs, separated
3/4 cup honey, warmed

1 pint whipping cream
1 pint strawberries, puréed

Beat the egg yolks and mix with the honey. Whip the cream and combine with the puréed strawberries. Add this mixture to the egg and honey mixture. Blend well. Pour into freezing trays and cover. Freeze for about 1 hour. Remove from freezer and fold in the egg whites which have been beaten until stiff. Return to the freezer. Beat the mixture every 30 minutes during the freezing process to insure a smooth ice cream.

Yield: 3 cups

STRAWBERRY BANANA ICE

5 cups strawberries, mashed
2 bananas, mashed
2 T. frozen apple juice concentrate

1 T. unflavored gelatin + 1/4 cup
   cold water
3/4 cup boiling water

Mash both the fresh strawberries and bananas. Add the apple juice and stir to mix. Soak the gelatin in 1/4 cup of cold water, then dissolve it in the 3/4 cup boiling water. Cool, add the strawberries and bananas and place in a freezer tray. Freeze until mushy and then remove and beat. Replace in freezer and during the freezing process beat several times.

Yield: Serves 6

FRESH PEACH ICE CREAM

2 cups crushed fresh peaches
1/2 cup honey
1 tsp. almond extract
2 T. whole wheat flour

2 eggs. slightly beaten
1½ cups milk
2 tsp. VANILLA EXTRACT
2 cups heavy cream

Mix the peaches with 3 tablespoons of the honey. Add the almond extract. Mix the remaining honey and flour in a pan. Blend in the eggs and one quarter of the milk. Add the remaining milk and cook over low heat until the mixture coats a metal spoon, stirring constantly. Remove from heat and cool. Add the vanilla and cream. Pour into 2-quart can of an ice cream freezer and place the can in the freezer tub. Cover with the lid, put on the gear case and adjust until the handle turns easily. Pack with one part rock salt to eight parts crushed ice. Turn the crank until the mixture is half frozen (when you feel resistance). Add the crushed peaches. Pack the tub with additional salt and ice and turn the crank fairly rapidly until too hard to turn, at which point the mixture will have frozen. Remove the gear case, lid and dasher. Cover the can with aluminum foil, replace the lid and stop up the hole in the top of the lid. Drain the water from the tub and pack with one part salt to four parts ice. Let stand 2 hours.

Yield: 1½ quarts

Variation:

In freezer trays: After all of the ingredients, except for the peaches, have been mixed, pour into freezer trays and freeze until the mixture is frozen 1/2" around the edge. Remove from the trays and beat vigorously until smooth and fluffy. Fold in the peaches, return to the trays and freeze until firm.

PINEAPPLE SHERBET

2 cups unsweetened pineapple juice
1/4 cup honey
2 T. lemon juice
1 T. unflavored gelatin

1½ cups unsweetened, crushed
pineapple drained
2 egg whites

In a saucepan combine the pineapple juice, honey and lemon juice. Sprinkle gelatin over the juice and blend together. Place over medium heat and stir until gelatin is dissolved. Remove from heat and cool the mixture. Stir in the crushed pineapple. Pour into freezer trays and place in freezer. When it is mushy remove and add unbeaten egg whites. Beat until mixture is fluffy but still thick. Return to freezer and freeze. In about 1 hour take it out again and beat. Then return to freezer to harden.

Yield: 6 servings

POPSICLES

1 (6-ounce) can frozen orange, apple
or pineapple juice concentrate
1 (6-ounce) can water

1 pint HONEY VANILLA ICE
CREAM softened or
plain YOGURT
Popsicle sticks and cups

Whirl all of the ingredients together in a blender. Pour into molds, insert sticks and freeze.

Yield: 10 cups

CREAMSICLES

1 cup heavy cream
2 fresh, ripe peaches, sliced and
pitted

1 tsp. honey
Popsicle sticks and cups

Whip cream in a blender for 30–45 seconds. Add peaches and honey. Whirl until smooth. Pour into molds, insert sticks and freeze.

Yield: 10 cups

FRUITSICLES

Pour undiluted fruit juice into ice cube trays. When half frozen, insert clean popsicle sticks. Continue freezing. Juices to use:

grape
cherry
orange
pineapple

strawberry
pear
apple
blackberry

FROZEN DATE DESSERT

2 cups dates, cut up
1 cup water

2 cups light cream
Dash of cinnamon and nutmeg

Soak the dates in the water for a couple of hours. Place the light cream, dates and liquid, and spices in a blender and blend until smooth. Turn mixture into 6 freezer-proof custard cups and freeze. Will taste just like ice cream.

Yield: 6 servings

HOLIDAY STOCKING DESSERT

4 T. unflavored gelatin
1 T. honey
2 cups boiling water
2 cups (1 pint) HONEY VANILLA
  ICE CREAM, softened

3-4 cups frozen raspberries,
  partially thawed
1 banana
1 tsp. VANILLA EXTRACT
1/3 cup flaked coconut
WHIPPED CREAM

In a large bowl, mix gelatin with honey; add boiling water and stir until gelatin is completely dissolved. Place raspberries and banana in blender and blend until crushed. With wire whip or rotary beater, blend in ice cream, raspberry/banana mixture and vanilla. Let stand until mixture is slightly thickened, about 1 minute; fold in coconut. Turn into 11" x 7" baking pan and chill until firm. Unmold onto flat serving platter. To form stocking, cut out piece 2½" wide and 7¼" down length of mold. Larger L-shaped piece which remains will be stocking. Cut smaller piece into 4" x 2½" and use to extend top of stocking; use remainder to extend toe. Garnish with whipped cream and top, if desired, with added coconut.

Yield: Serves 6-8

FRUIT DESSERTS

FRUIT COBBLER

Filling:

5 cups sliced fresh fruit
1/2 cup honey
1 T. lemon juice
1 T. whole wheat flour
Spices and flavorings
     Apple: 1 tsp. cinnamon; 1 tsp. nutmeg
     Peaches: 1/2 tsp each cinnamon and nutmeg; 1/2 tsp almond extract
     Pears: 1 tsp. nutmeg; 1/2 tsp. ginger
     Rhubarb: 1 tsp. cinnamon; 1/2 tsp. cloves

Mix together in a bowl the fruit, honey, lemon juice, flour, spice and flavorings. Spread all over the bottom of a greased 8" square baking dish. Drop the topping in spoonfuls all over the top of the fruit. Bake at 375° for 30 minutes, or until the fruit is tender.

Topping:

1 cup whole wheat flour
2 T. soy flour
1/4 cup wheat germ
1 T. BAKING POWDER

1 egg, beaten
1/2 cup milk
1 T. oil
2 T. honey

Mix the flours, wheat germ and baking powder together. In another bowl combine the egg, milk, oil and honey and then add to the flour mixture. Mix only until moistened.

Yield: 9 servings

BERRY COBBLER

5 cups berries
1/2 cup honey
2 T. arrowroot powder

1 T. oil
1 T. lemon juice

Place the berries, honey and arrowroot in a saucepan and stir over medium heat until thickened and clear. Remove from heat and stir in the oil and lemon juice. Pour into a greased 8" square baking dish. Add the topping used for the fruit cobbler. Bake in a 350° oven for 15-20 minutes.

Yield: 9 servings

APPLE CRISP

6-7 baking apples
2 T. lemon juice
1 T. whole wheat flour
1/4 cup raisins
1/3 cup chopped nuts

1 tsp. cinnamon
1 tsp. nutmeg
1/2 cup unsweetened apple juice
2-2½ cups CRUMBLY TOPPING

Peel, core and slice apples. Place the apples in a bowl and add the lemon juice, flour, raisins, nuts, cinnamon and nutmeg. Toss together thoroughly. Place in a baking dish and pour apple juice over fruit and then top with the Crumbly Topping. Bake in a 350° oven for 30 minutes, or until apples are tender. Serve topped with YOGURT or a whipped topping.

Yield: 6-8 servings

Variation:

Peach Crisp: In place of apples use 7-8 peaches. Add 1 tablespoon whole wheat flour to the peach mixture and remove the raisins. Follow the rest of the directions for the crisp.

FRUIT PARFAIT

2 cups fruit or fruits of your choice
20 VANILLA WAFERS or
   GRAHAM CRACKERS

2 cups WHIPPED CREAM
1/4 cup GRANOLA TOPPING

Cut the fruit in small pieces. Place the wafers or graham crackers in a blender and blend until fine crumbs. Prepare the whipped topping. Spoon into 4 individual sherbet or parfait glasses a layer of crumbs. On top of the crumbs spoon in a layer of fruit and then a layer of whipped topping. Repeat layers ending with the whipped topping. Sprinkle top of each glass with some granola topping. Serve immediately or refrigerate until serving time.

Yield: 4 servings

PAPAYA SURPRISE

1 whole papaya
2 oranges, peeled and cut
1 cup fresh pineapple chunks

2 bananas, slightly mashed[4]
1/2 cup chopped walnuts
Grated coconut flakes, unsweetened

Slice papaya in half and remove seeds. Mix the oranges, pineapples, bananas and walnuts together. Heap the mixture into the center of each papaya half. Sprinkle with fresh grated coconut.

Yield: 2 servings

STUFFED PEARS

4 Bartlett pears
2 T. lemon juice
8 ounces cream cheese
3 tsp. honey

1/4 cup chopped pecans
1/4 cup raisins
Pecan halves as garnish

Core pears from the top and leave peel on around the outside. Scoop out all seeds. Coat inside of pear with lemon juice. Beat cream cheese with 2 tablespoons lemon juice; mix in the honey, pecans and raisins. Stuff cheese mixture into pears. Garnish stuffed pears with pecan halves. Serve immediately or wrap in plastic and refrigerate.

Yield: 4 servings

BANANAS WITH RAISIN-WALNUT SAUCE

4 T. butter
1 T. honey
2 T. lemon juice

4 bananas, peeled
1/2 cup raisins
1/2 cup walnuts

In a large skillet melt the butter; add honey and lemon juice. Peel bananas, cut in half lengthwise, and add to skillet. Cook, turning once, 1 or 2 minutes on each side. Add raisins and walnuts. Remove from heat and ready to serve.

Yield: 5 servings

BAKED APPLES

6 large baking apples
1/4 cup walnuts, chopped
1/4 cup raisins
3 T. sunflower seeds
1 cup water

1/4 cup honey
2 tsp. cinnamon
1/2 tsp. nutmeg
1 T. lemon juice

Wash and core the apples. Place in a shallow baking dish and fill each apple cavity with a mixture of walnuts, raisins and sunflower seeds. Place the water, honey, cinnamon and nutmeg in a saucepan and bring to a boil. Reduce heat and simmer for 4 minutes. Remove from the heat and stir in the lemon juice. Pour this syrup over the apples. Bake in a 350° oven for 30–35 minutes or until apples are tender. Baste periodically with the syrup. Can serve topped with YOGURT.

Yield: 6 servings

BANANA DELIGHT

4 ripe bananas
1 T. lemon juice
1 T. honey

2 cups fresh berries (raspberries, strawberries, blueberries)
Sunflower seeds and nuts

Mash the bananas with a fork or in a blender. Add the lemon juice and honey. Fold in the berries. Put in a parfait or dessert dish. Sprinkle with sunflower seeds and nuts. Could also add a dollop of WHIPPED CREAM.

Yield: 2 servings

APPLESAUCE

3 medium sized apples (about 1 pound)
1/3-1/2 cup unsweetened apple juice

2 T. lemon juice
1/2 tsp. cinnamon
1/2 tsp. nutmeg

Wash, peel, and core apples. Place in a saucepan, add apple juice, lemon juice. Cover pan and simmer for 5-10 minutes, until tender. Remove from heat and add cinnamon and nutmeg.

Yield: 2 cups

GRAPE FINGER JELLO

1 (12 ounce) can frozen grape juice concentrate

3-4 T. unflavored gelatin
1½ cups water

Soften gelatin in grape juice. Boil water, add juice/gelatin mixture and stir until gelatin dissolves. Remove from the heat, pour into a lightly greased 9" x 13" pan and chill. Cut into squares when firm.

Yield: 30 pieces

Variation: Use other juice concentrates.

FRUIT LEATHER

Fruit leather is puréed fruit dried on a heavy plastic wrap. It is nutritious and delicious. Eat it just like candy.

Any fruit can be used. Select ripe or overripe fruit such as apples, apricots, bananas, berries, grapes, peaches, pears to just name a few. Remove pits or seeds from the fruits. Seeds of berries and grapes need not be removed. You need not peel the fruit unless you would like to.

Cut fruit into chunks and place in a blender to purée. For yellow or light colored fruits, add 1 tablespoon lemon or lime juice. Add honey for sweetness if desired and any other spices.

Line a cookie sheet with a heavy plastic wrap. Be sure cookie sheet has an edge to avoid spillage. Pour the purée onto the sheet about 1/4" deep. Distribute evenly by tilting the tray. Do not use a spatula or knife to smooth the fruit.

Drying time depends on the method used. Sun drying takes from 2-3 days, depending on temperature and humidity. Bring inside each night between drying days. To oven dry the leather: set oven at lowest setting. Leave the door ajar and it will take 4-5 hours to dry.

To test for doneness, lift the plastic wrap from a corner of the leather. If it peels readily, and the leather is sticky to the touch, it is dry. Now just roll the leather in waxed paper and store in plastic bags. You can store for years in the freezer, for months in the refrigerator, and at room temperature for a couple of months.

Here are two fruit leather ideas:

BANANA-PEANUT BUTTER LEATHER

3 cups ripe bananas   1 tsp. VANILLA EXTRACT
1 cup chunky PEANUT BUTTER

Blend all ingredients together until puréed. Follow the directions for preparing the basic fruit leather.

SPICED APPLE LEATHER

8 medium apples, peeled, cored and   1/4 tsp. cinnamon
    cut into chunks   1/8 tsp. cloves
1/4 cup honey   1/2 cup walnuts, chopped
2 T. lemon juice

Place all the ingredients except the walnuts, in a blender and blend until it is a purée. Stir in walnuts. Spread onto prepared trays and dry as in basic leather recipe.

APPLE STRUDEL

Strudel Pastry:

2 cups whole wheat pastry flour
1/4 cup oil
1 T. lemon juice

2 egg whites
2/3-1 cup luke warm apple juice
Oil

Place the flour in a mixing bowl. Make a well in the center of the flour and cut in oil. Add lemon juice and egg whites and work these ingredients into the dough, gradually adding apple juice until a very soft, sticky dough is formed. Knead on a lightly floured surface until smooth and elastic, about 10 minutes. Place dough in an oiled bowl and set in a warm place for 10-15 minutes. Cover your table with a pastry cloth or a clean, old tablecloth large enough to drape over the sides. Rub flour into the cloth. Place dough on the cloth. Sprinkle with flour and roll out in a rectangular form about 1/4" thick. Brush the surface with oil. Cover your hands with flour and place them under the dough (palms down), make a fist and stretch the dough out from the center toward the edges, until it is as thin as possible. If it starts to dry out or break in areas, brush those areas with oil. Allow dough to rest 5-10 minutes. Trim edges. Brush surface once more with oil.

Filling:

1 cup raisins
Apple juice
3 cups chopped apples, unpeeled

3/4 cup chopped walnuts
1/2 cup sunflower seeds
3-4 T. TAHINI or NUT BUTTER

Soak raisins in apple juice until soft. Drain juice. Add to the raisins the apples, nuts, sunflower seeds and tahini. Mix well. Spread the surface of the dough with the filling leaving a 1" border on all edges. Carefully roll up pastry, starting with the long side, as you would a jelly roll. Flip the dough onto a well-greased baking sheet. Bake at 350° for 45-50 minutes. When it is finished cooking, and while it is still hot, brush with the glaze.

Glaze:

2 cups water
3/4 cup honey
1/2 tsp. cinnamon

1/4 cup butter
3/4 cup chopped walnuts

Combine the water, honey and cinnamon. Bring to a boil and then simmer for 10 minutes. Add the butter and stir to melt. Stir in the nuts. Pour over strudel.

Yield: Serves 6-8

CANDY

HONEY DATE BALLS

1 cup finely chopped dates
1/2 cup honey
4 T. butter
2 eggs

2 cups GRANOLA
1/2 cup chopped nuts or sunflower
 seeds
Flaked coconut

Beat eggs and stir in chopped dates and honey. Melt butter in a heavy pan. Stir mixture of eggs, dates and honey into melted butter. Over medium to low heat, cook for 10 minutes, stirring constantly. Remove from heat and stir in granola and chopped nuts. When cool enough to handle, but still warm, form into 1" balls and roll in coconut. Store in airtight container.

Yield: 6-7 dozen balls

SEEDS AND NUTS CLUSTERS

1/3 cup warm water
2 T. sweet butter
1/3-1/2 cup non-instant dry milk
 powder
1/3 cup carob powder

2 rounded T. lecithin granules
1 T. honey
1 tsp. VANILLA EXTRACT
1 cup shelled peanuts
1 cup raisins

In a blender, mix together the water, butter, milk powder, carob, lecithin granules, honey and vanilla, briefly, until smooth. Put the peanuts and raisins into a large mixing bowl and pour the carob mixture over them. Mix very well, until all the nuts and raisins are covered. If the mixture is too runny, add more powdered milk. Very lightly grease a large baking sheet and spoon out into clumps. Starting in a cold oven, bake clusters on a middle rack until the tops barely begin to dry—10-15 minutes at 300°. Remove, and put aside for a couple of hours, until they are dry enough to handle.

Yield: 25 clusters

BUTTERSCOTCH CHEWS

1/2 cup honey

2 T. butter

Put honey and butter into a small pot and simmer about 12 minutes. Pour into a very lightly buttered soup bowl and allow to cool until it can be handled. Spoon out teaspoonfuls of the candy and shape them between the palms of your hands. Let them cool and set. Wrap in wax paper for storage.

Yield: 16 chews

PEANUT BUTTER SESAME EGGS

3/4 cup PEANUT BUTTER
1/2 cup honey
1 tsp. VANILLA EXTRACT
3/4 cup non-instant dry milk powder
1 cup rolled oats

1/4 cup sesame seeds
1/4 cup boiling water (as needed)
1/4 cup nuts
1/2 cup raisins or sunflower seeds
   (optional)

In a medium-sized bowl, combine peanut butter, honey and vanilla, blend thoroughly. Mix in milk powder and oatmeal. Gradually add to peanut butter mixture—use hands if necessary. Blend in sesame seeds. Add boiling water to mixture, blending well. Roll into balls and roll in chopped nuts, raisins or sunflower seeds. Refrigerate. Great treat for Easter or anytime.

Yield: 15-20

FUDGE

1/2 cup honey
1 cup PEANUT BUTTER,
   crunchy or smooth

1/2 cup carob powder, sifted
Sesame seeds, sunflower seeds,
   walnuts, raisins

Heat honey and peanut butter together over low heat in a saucepan. When heated, 1-2 minutes, remove from heat and stir in carob powder. Add also seeds and nuts (the amount to your liking) and stir quickly. Turn into a greased 8" square pan. Chill for 2 hours before you cut into squares.

Yield: 25 pieces

HOMEMADE CAROB CHIPS

1/2 cup coconut oil
1 cup honey
1 T. liquid lecithin
2 tsp. VANILLA EXTRACT

3/4-1 cup carob powder
1/2 cup soy milk powder
2/3 cup non-instant dry milk
   powder

Melt first 4 ingredients in top of double boiler, until blended together. In a large bowl, sift together dry ingredients twice for thorough mixing. Pour liquid mixture into dry mixture and mix and stir until all lumps are out. It will pull away from sides of bowl. Spread 1/4" thin on oiled cookie sheet. Refrigerate and when hard break into pieces. Must be refrigerated.

FRUIT AND NUT BARS

1 cup raisins	1 cup walnuts
1 cup figs	1 cup almonds
1 cup dates	1 cup coconut

Grind all the ingredients, except coconut. Mix together and knead the ground mixture on 1 layer of the coconut. Shape into balls, bars or triangles and decorate with whole walnuts.

STUFFED DATES

20-25 pitted dates   1/2 cup shredded coconut
                          Peanut butter fondant:
    1/3 cup honey   1/2 cup non-instant dry milk
    1/3 cup peanut butter   powder

Mix together and chill until firm enough to handle.

Make the peanut butter fondant into small rolls and insert in the seed cavity of the dates. Dates are then rolled into shredded coconut.

Variations:

1. Mixture of cream cheese or COTTAGE CHEESE, chopped nuts and seeds.

2. Mixture of YOGURT, fruit juice, nuts and raisins.

HONEY CRACKER JACKS

1/3 cup honey	8 cups popped POPCORN
1/3 cup butter	1 cup peanuts
1/4 cup molasses, unsulfured	

Heat honey, butter and molasses in saucepan over medium heat. Heat until well blended. Cool slightly. Pour over popcorn and peanut mixture. Stir until coated and then pour into a baking pan in a thin layer. Cookie sheet works well. Bake in 325° oven for 10 minutes. Be sure to keep a close eye on it or it could burn. Cool and break into pieces. Store in an airtight container. When serving it to the kids add a little prize within—just like the old-time cracker jacks.

Yield: 8 cups

JAWBREAKERS

Freeze green grapes, red sweet cherries and melon balls. Suck on these for a treat. Delicious. Make a large batch and freeze for future use.

HONEY-SESAME CANDY

1 pound (about 3-1/8 cups) sesame
    seeds
1 cup chopped almonds, or flaked
    coconut
3/4 cup honey
1/8 cup molasses, unsulfured

1/4 cup water
1 tsp. VANILLA EXTRACT
Optional: 1/2 cup coarsely chopped
    almonds, walnuts, or coconut;
    or additional whole sesame
    seeds

Spread the sesame seeds evenly over two 10" x 15" rimmed baking pans. Bake for 15 minutes in a 350° oven. Cool. In a blender, whirl the seeds, 1 cup at a time, until it is the texture of cornmeal. Turn into a 5-quart bowl and stir well to break up large lumps. Mix in the 1 cup chopped nuts or coconut. In a 2-quart pan, combine the honey, molasses, water. Bring to a boil, stirring, until everything is dissolved. Reduce heat to medium and continue to cook, without stirring, until a candy thermometer registers 250°. Remove from heat, and immediately start pouring slowly over the sesame mixture, stirring until thoroughly moistened. Stir in vanilla. Let sit for 20 minutes. Divide mixture in half; squeeze and press each half into a ball. On a board, roll one portion at a time to make a log about 1½" in diameter. If desired, you can roll the log over the 1/2 cup of chopped nuts or seeds. Wrap in plastic and store in refrigerator. Can last up to 2 weeks. Slice into 1/2" thick rounds.

Yield: 2 logs, 14" long

Variation:

Carob Honey-Sesame Log: Add 2 T. carob powder to the honey mixture before bringing it to a boil.

SESAME CRISPS

2 cups sesame seeds, roasted lightly
1/2 cup chopped nuts
1/2 cup honey

1/4 cup molasses, unsulfured
3/4 tsp. cinnamon
1 tsp. VANILLA EXTRACT

In a 12" fry pan, combine the honey, molasses and cinnamon. Bring mixture to a boil over medium heat, stirring constantly; cook for 2 minutes. Remove pan from heat and immediately stir in vanilla, seeds and nuts. Turn into a buttered 9" x 13" baking dish. With a large buttered spoon, press candy firmly and evenly over bottom. Cool at room temperature about 15 minutes, then lift out of pan. Use a large knife to cut candy into 1" x 2" rectangles. Wrap in plastic and store at room temperature.

Yield: 48 bars

Variation:

Instead of nuts you can use sunflower seeds or pumpkin seeds. You can also add 1/2 cup unsweetened coconut.

PEANUT BRITTLE

2 cups honey
4 T. butter

1/2-1 cup peanuts, cashew halves
or pecan halves

Put honey and butter into saucepan rinsed with cold water. Bring to boil at 234° (use candy thermometer), or until the mixture holds together when dropped into cold water. Beat until it begins to lose its gloss. Add nuts, pour into well-buttered glass pan or break into bits before it hardens completely.

OLD-FASHIONED TAFFY

2 cups unsulfured molasses
2 tsp. apple cider vinegar

2 T. butter

Combine molasses and vinegar in a stainless steel 1½ quart saucepan. Cook slowly until temperature reaches 270° (use a candy thermometer), stirring constantly. Remove from heat. Add butter and stir until mixture stops foaming. Pour onto a shallow buttered dish or platter. Let cool until you can handle it. Divide into 4 sections or more—you'll need 3 people to help you. Pull until light in color, and twist into a rope shape. Let stand until hardened, then break into small pieces with the blunt end of a knife.

BANANA TREATS

4 ripe bananas
1 cup plain YOGURT, sweetened
   with apple juice

1 cup mixture of chopped peanuts,
sesame seeds, and walnuts

Peel bananas and cut in half. Place a popsicle stick in one end. Roll banana in yogurt and then into nut mixture. Place into freezer. Great treat for all ages. Tastes just like ice cream.

Yield: 8 treats

BANANA BON BONS

2 ripe bananas
1 cup CAROB SYRUP

1/2 cup chopped walnuts or
peanuts

Cut each banana into 8 smaller pieces. Dip banana into carob syrup and then roll in the nuts. Place on plastic wrap on platter. Freeze until firm. Then wrap and store in container in freezer. Serve frozen.

Yield: 16 pieces

BANANA-PEANUT BUTTER SURPRISES

3 ripe bananas
3/4 cup PEANUT BUTTER
1/4 cup orange, pineapple, or apple
   juice

1/2 cup chopped peanuts
1/2 cup unsweetened coconut

Peel bananas and slice in half lengthwise. Spread each half with peanut butter. Press together. Brush the outside with the juice. Roll bananas in the mixture of peanuts and coconut. Cut into 1" pieces.

Yield: 15 pieces

PEANUT BUTTER CUPS

2 cups CAROB CHIPS
1 cup PEANUT BUTTER
1 cup rolled oats

1/2 cup soy grits
1/2 cup GRANOLA
1/2 cup chopped walnuts

Heat the carob chips and peanut butter in the top of a double boiler. Heat until melted and smooth. Remove from heat and stir in the rest of the ingredients. Press into 1-ounce paper nut cups and refrigerate.

Yield: 2-3 dozen

HONEY MARSHMALLOWS

1 T. plain gelatin
1/4 cup cold water

1 tsp. VANILLA EXTRACT
1 cup warm honey

Soak gelatin in bowl with cold water for about 1 minute. Place the bowl over another bowl of warm water so the gelatin can dissolve. When dissolved, add the vanilla and warm honey and beat with a mixer at high speed for 10-15 minutes, or until thick and light. Pour into a greased 9" square pan. Let it sit at room temperature for 1½ days. Dip knife into cold water to slice. You can serve them plain or roll in coconut.

Yield: 2-3 dozen

DAIRY

Cheese is one of the most nutritious and versatile foods. Because it is an excellent source of many important nutrients in the diet, and because it is a well-liked food, cheese is used freely by many in preparing nutritious meals.

With the wide variety of flavors, colors and consistencies to choose from, natural, unprocessed cheeses are suitable for any meal of the day, from appetizers to desserts, and between meal snacks as well. Cheese adds that special something to foods.

Cheese contains many of the nutrients found in milk, especially calcium, phosphorus, vitamins A and B_1. A meal in itself, 3 ounces of cheese contains as much protein as 3 large eggs, two cups of milk, or 3 ounces of meat, poultry or fish.

Eggs are an excellent food, considered by scientists **CHAPTER 13** to be the "perfect" food—meaning eggs have all of the protein in near perfect proportion. Scientists use the egg as a standard of measurement for protein value in other foods. It is rated high on the nutrition scale, being rich in protein, and also supplying iron and vitamins A and B_2. Talking about eggs always brings up the subject of cholesterol. Many people stay away from eggs because of the cholesterol in them. Besides containing cholesterol, eggs also contain an ingredient called lecithin. This is the factor that works hand in hand with cholesterol to help keep the cholesterol broken up. So the egg has its own built-in ammunition to deal with cholesterol. But be sure to use eggs that have been fertilized (most eggs nowadays are not) because the lecithin is contained in the rooster's sperm. If you are concerned about cholesterol, the foods you should stay away from are the refined flours, sugars, and hydrogenated fats.

Yogurt is a rich source of protein, calcium and B vitamins at an inexpensive price. It costs you just pennies if you make your own yogurt. It also contains what is termed "friendly bacteria." These bacteria are needed in your system to help fight off the *bad* bacteria in your intestinal tract.

There are so many and varied ways to use dairy products effectively and inexpensively, all of which furnish your body with the protein it needs. In this chapter I show you some of these ways.

HELPFUL HINTS

- Eggs should be refrigerated at all times or they will lose their freshness.
- Store eggs in refrigerator with large ends up.
- Brown and white eggs are of the same nutritional quality.
- If egg whites do not beat up properly, there may be a trace of egg yolk in them; or, the beaters may not be absolutely clean and dry; or, there may be moisture or grease in the bowl.
- Egg whites are stiff when they stand in glossy peaks, look wet and shiny and cling tightly to the whip or beater when it is help upright.
- A soufflé may not rise and also may be grainy in the center if the egg whites are beaten until dry rather than just stiff.
- When you are finished cooking eggs, such as scrambled eggs, rinse the skillet in cold, rather than hot water. It will be easier to clean later.
- Egg whites can be frozen up to 1 year.
- Egg yolk can be covered with water while stored in the refrigerator. Keeps fresh for several days.
- Vinegar added to the water that soft or hard-cooked eggs are cooked in will help prevent eggs from oozing out of the shell if it cracks.
- Have eggs at room temperature when making a soufflé.
- Eggs straight from the farm (fresh ones) will not hard cook very well. When peeling them the white comes off completely with the shell. Let them sit for at least a week or use them in other dishes. When the time is up they hard cook better.
- Eggs are a protein food that needs to be cooked over a low temperature to retain their tenderness and nutritional value.
- Fertile eggs are eggs laid by a hen that has been fertilized by a rooster. (Most of your laying hens today never come in contact with a rooster.) These eggs have a higher nutritional value. They also contain lecithin which is acquired from the rooster's sperm.
- Leftover egg yolks: Two egg yolks will replace one whole egg in thickening power. Use them to re-enrich scrambled eggs, fried rice, breads, cakes, cookies, sauces or custards. Gently hard cook unbroken egg yolks in small amount of water. Grate over salads, sauces or vegetables. Mix one egg yolk with 1 tablespoon water and brush over rolls and breads before baking.
- Leftover egg whites: Use 1 or 2 whites with several whole eggs in omelets or scrambled eggs. Beat 1 or 2 extra whites until stiff and fold into waffle or cake batter which yields a lighter and higher product.
- Cooking with raw eggs: Best if they are just taken out of the refrigerator. They separate better and thicken MAYONNAISE or HOLLANDAISE sauce faster.

- Poach eggs in water flavored with tarragon vinegar for a subtle, delicate taste.

- 2 large eggs equal 1/2 cup. 3 medium-sized eggs equal 1/2 cup. 2 medium eggs equal 1/3 cup. 3 large eggs equal 2/3 cups.

- When beating egg whites do not tap beater on bowl of egg whites. The jarring will cause the whites to lose a great deal of their fluffiness. Tap on your hand.

- Make a good meringue by using a glass bowl not an aluminum one. Beat at low speed and gradually speed up. Do not turn the bowl while beating.

- For baking, use medium to large size eggs. Extra large ones may cause cake to fall when cooled.

- To tell if an egg is hard cooked or not, spin it. If it spins around and around, it is hard cooked. If it wobbles and will not spin, it is raw.

- When soft or hard cooking eggs, poke a tiny pin hole in the end of the egg. This will help prevent it from cracking.

- A fresh egg sinks when placed in cold water. Inside, the yolk is firm and the white thick.

- Never wash eggs before refrigerating them. The full coating on the shell helps retain the freshness.

- You can fight inflation by remembering this when shopping for eggs: If a smaller sized egg is less than 7 cents a dozen over the larger sized eggs, then the larger sized eggs are a better buy.

- Having difficulty separating eggs? Break the egg into a funnel over a small glass. The yolk remains in the funnel while the white will pass through.

- To keep egg yolks from crumbling when slicing hard-cooked eggs, wet the knife before cutting.

- Bread crumbs added to scrambled eggs will improve the flavor and make larger helpings possible.

- If your cheese dries out, just grate it and place it in an airtight container in the refrigerator and use in your cooking. If cheese develops mold, scrape it off and use the remaining part as usual.

- Most cheese that is orange (Cheddar) has been dyed. Undyed Cheddar is white. We need to get artificial colors out of our diet, so look for the un-dyed in your stores.

- Many varieties of cheese can be successfully frozen in small pieces. Among the varieties are: Brick, Cheddar, Edam, Swiss, Muenster, Mozzarella and Camambert.

- When you use cheese as an ingredient do not overcook it. If heated too long or at too high a temperature, it gets stringy.

- 1/4 pound cheese equals 1 cup grated.

- Whey (left from making cottage cheese) should be used. It contains valuable minerals and B vitamins.

- To keep cheese such as Swiss, Cheddar or hard Italian types, wrap in waxed paper, seal in a plastic container, and freeze.

- Wipe your grater with oil before grating cheese. It keeps the cheese from sticking and makes the grater easier to clean.

- To make cheese last longer, wrap in moistened cheesecloth and then place in refrigerator.

- Store cottage cheese containers upside down. It will last twice as long.

- Buy Parmesan cheese in bulk and grate off it when you need some. It is more flavorful plus it is less expensive than the pregrated cheese.

- Serve cheeses at room temperature.

- Cheeses with wax trims must have the wax trimmed before using.

- A proper cheese knife looks somewhat like a scimitar with two points on the end. Thus you can cut the cheese and use the points on the end to pick up the cheese. If you do not have this type of knife you can use dinner knives, steak knives and even butter spreaders.

- To soften butter quickly, place a warm bowl over the butter.

- There is no difference between unsalted and sweet butter. Sweet butter can be either salted or unsalted.

- To make a skillet handle ovenproof, cover it with foil.

- Heat milk slowly and stir constantly to prevent its separating and forming a skin on top.

- When baking in a glass container, be sure to lower the cooking temperature by 25°.

- Do not pour the filling into the pie shell for a quiche until just before cooking. This will prevent a soggy crust.

- To seal the crust and prevent it from soaking up the custard mixture and becoming soggy when making quiche, brush bottom with egg whites, egg yolks or Dijon mustard.

EGGS

THE EGGS YOU BUY

Grade AA: Excellent for table use. When broken, the white covers only a small area. The yolk will stand high and there is a large amount of thick white hugging the yolk and a small amount of thin white at the very edge. When hard cooked, the yolk will be centered. When fried, the yolk is round; the white is high and thick around the yolk.

Grade A: Good for table use. When broken, the white spreads over a larger area. Yolk will stand high and a large amount of thick white hugging the yolk and a small amount of thin white at the very edge. When hard cooked, the yolk is slightly off center. When fried, the yolk is round; the white is more spread out.

Grade B: Fair for table use. Good used in cooking and baking. When broken, the white spreads out wide; the yolk is somewhat flat. There is a medium amount of thick white around the yolk, but it looks flat. There is also a medium amount of thin white. When hard cooked, the yolk is far off center. When fried, the yolk looks flat; the white spreads widely and is thin.

Grade C: Alright for cooking and baking. When broken, the white covers a large area and is thin. The yolk is very flat and easily broken. When hard cooked, the yolk is far off center. When fried, the white is thin and spreads easily over a large area; the yolk is flat.

How to test your eggs for freshness: Open the carton and put an egg in your hand. The egg should feel heavy. Now shake it gently. The contents should not shake inside. If they do, it is old. To explain how this works: The egg shell is porous which allows some of the watery substance to evaporate and permits air to be absorbed. The older the egg the less solid the material inside and the more room for the contents to move around. So shake that egg.

SOFT COOKED EGGS

Cover eggs with water to 1" above them. Do not use eggs with cracked shells. Bring rapidly to a boil and then remove from heat. Cover and let stand for 3-5 minutes.

HARD COOKED EGGS

Follow instructions for Soft Cooked Eggs, letting eggs stand 20 minutes. When finished, run under cold water immediately. This will make the shell come off more easily.

EGG AND CHEESE CASSEROLE

6-8 hard-cooked eggs, coarsely
    chopped
3/4 cup finely chopped celery
1/3 cup finely chopped green pepper
1/3 cup chopped pecans
2 T. finely chopped fresh parsley
1 tsp. grated onion

1 tsp. vegetable seasoning
1/4 tsp. kelp
2/3 cup MAYONNAISE
1 cup shredded Cheddar cheese
3/4 cup coarsely chopped
    TORTILLA CHIPS

Combine the first 9 ingredients in a large bowl, tossing lightly until well mixed. Spoon mixture into a 1½ quart casserole dish. Sprinkle the top with the cheese and chips. Bake at 375° for 25 minutes, or until mixture is thoroughly heated.

Yield: 4 servings

EGG CUTLETS

4 hard-cooked eggs
1 cup WHITE SAUCE
1 tsp. tamari (soy sauce)
1/3 cup wheat germ
1/2 cup chopped celery
TOMATO SAUCE

1/4 cup shredded cheese
1 egg, slightly beaten
1 T. water
1/2 cup fine dry bread crumbs,
    whole wheat

Dice the eggs and combine with the sauce, tamari, wheat germ, celery and cheese. Chill in refrigerator for an hour or longer. Then pat into cutlet-shaped patties. Dip in a mixture of the egg and water. Coat well in the bread crumbs. Sauté in a skillet until evenly browned. Serve topped with the Tomato Sauce.

Yield: 6 servings

BAKED EGGS

4 eggs
4 T. milk or cream

Vegetable seasoning
1 tsp. butter

Butter 4 individual casseroles or heat-resistant custard cups. Break, one at a time, each egg into one of the dishes. Top each egg with 1 tablespoon of milk or cream and season each one. Then place a 1/4 teaspoon butter on each egg. Bake uncovered in a 325° oven for 15-20 minutes. Whites should be firm and the yolks still soft.

Yield: 4 servings

Variations:

Tomato Baked Eggs: Line a small casserole dish with 1 tomato slice. Break the eggs over top and add the milk, seasoning and butter. Cook as directed.

Chicken Cheese Bake: Line a small casserole dish with slices of Swiss or Muenster cheese. Sprinkle on top 1/2 cup chopped cooked chicken. Break the eggs over top and proceed as directed.

POACHED EGGS

For a poached egg that is covered with the white, bring 2" of lightly vinegared water to a simmer. Make a whirlpool by stirring the water rapidly and drop in the egg. Simmer, uncovered, 2-3 minutes or until the white is firm but yolks are soft. Remove egg with a slotted spoon, drain well and serve at once. Or, to prepare ahead, put the cooked eggs in a bowl of cold water and refrigerate. Rewarm by simmering for a minute. Serve the eggs over toasted bread or ENGLISH MUFFINS; or serve over vegetables. Top with a cream sauce or HOLLANDAISE SAUCE.

HOW TO SCRAMBLE EGGS

Break eggs into a bowl. Add milk as follows: For creamy scrambled eggs, add 1 tablespoon milk for each egg; for dry scrambled eggs, add 1/2 tablespoon milk for each egg. Season. Pour into a heated skillet and reduce heat. When the eggs have set slightly, stir constantly with a fork. Should be soft and creamy. Do not overcook. You can add so many different herbs to the eggs to give many different flavors. Try adding grated cheese, or add vegetables that have been lightly sautéed, and then cook right along with the eggs.

FRENCH OMELET

4 eggs
4 T. milk or water

1/4 tsp. vegetable seasoning
1½ tsp. butter

Beat eggs until light and fluffy. Add the milk and vegetable seasoning. Heat the butter in a small skillet or omelet pan. Add the eggs to the skillet. Cook over low heat, without stirring, until edges set. Then lift the edges with a spatula or fork to allow the uncooked egg to run underneath. Continue until the omelet is firm, but moist. Place the filling in the omelet and then fold the omelet in half. Tilt the pan down and roll the omelet out of the pan onto the serving plate.

Yield: Serves 1

PUFFY OMELET

3 T. milk
1/2 tsp. vegetable seasoning
4 egg yolks

4 egg whites
2 tsp. butter

Add the milk and seasoning to the egg yolk. Beat until thick and lemon colored. Beat egg whites until stiff but not dry. Fold the egg whites gently into the egg yolks. Heat the butter in an ovenproof skillet until it sizzles. Pour in the omelet mixture and cook without stirring until it is lightly brown on the bottom. Now put the skillet under the broiler and broil until the top is lightly browned. Gently put the filling in the omelet and fold over. Slide out onto a serving plate and serve at once.

Yield: Serves 1

Variation:

Cheese Omelet: 1 cup shredded Cheddar cheese placed on omelet before it goes into the oven.

TOSTADA OMELET

3 T. oil	1 cup shredded Cheddar cheese
3 CORN TORTILLAS, cut in eighths	2-4 T. diced green chilies
8 eggs	1½ cups shredded lettuce
1/4 cup water	1 large tomato, diced
3 T. SALSA sauce	GUACAMOLE
1/2 tsp vegetable seasoning	1/2 cup SOUR CREAM or
1 cup shredded Jack cheese	YOGURT
	Green onions for garnish

In an ovenproof skillet, over medium heat, cook the tortillas (cut up) in the oil for 1 minute. Remove from the pan. Mix together the eggs, water, salsa and seasoning. Add the tortillas. Pour into the ovenproof skillet and cook lifting the edges so the uncooked portion can flow underneath. Cook until the eggs are set. Remove from heat. Combine the cheeses and chilies; sprinkle over the omelet. (Do not fold over.) Broil top of omelet just until cheese melts. Top with the lettuce, tomato, guacamole, sour cream or yogurt and green onions. Cut into wedges.

Yield: Serves 4

FILLINGS FOR OMELETS

Fruit filling: Slice bananas, apples and strawberries. Chop nuts coarsely. Place both in the omelet just before it is folded over. Top with additional sliced fruit and YOGURT.

Herb filling: Combine 1/2 cup slivered fresh spinach, 1/4 cup coarsely chopped parsley, 1 tablespoon each dill, chives and basil. Add this mixture to the egg batter just before going into the pan.

Vegetable filling: Sauté 1/4 cup chopped onion and 1/2 teaspoon minced garlic in 1 tablespoon butter until golden. Add 1/2 cup diced peeled eggplant and 1 small diced tomato. Simmer for 5 minutes and season with vegetable seasoning.

Potato onion filling: Cook in a skillet with 2 tablespoons oil, 1/4 cup finely diced new potato and 1/4 cup diced onion. Cook until the potatoes are soft to the bite but only slightly browned. Place this mixture and 1/4 cup chopped walnuts in the omelet before it is folded over.

Artichoke filling: Slice 6 artichoke hearts and 1 onion. Sauté both in oil until heated through. Place in omelet and fold top over.

Jam or jelly filling: Just before folding the omelet in half, spread with 1/3–1/2 cup of your favorite honey-sweetened jam or jelly.

FRITTATA

A frittata is simply a flat omelet—Mediterranean style. Cook the egg mixture in a skillet without stirring or lifting, add the topping and then slip the whole thing under the broiler for browning. It is a terrific way to get 4 or more main course servings from one omelet. It is just as great cold as it is served hot.

6 eggs	Vegetable seasoning to taste
1/4 cup milk	Butter

Beat the eggs with the milk and vegetable seasoning. Heat the butter in an 8" ovenproof skillet and add eggs. Cook without stirring until they are golden brown on the underside. Push whatever filling you choose into the uncooked top of the frittata. Put the skillet under the broiler and broil until top surface is brown and firm. Cut into wedges and serve either hot or cold.

Yield: Serves 4

Fillings:

Zucchini and onion: Sauté 1 small onion, chopped, and 1 cup of diced zucchini for 5 minutes in 1 tablespoon oil.

Potato cheese: Sauté in 1 tablespoon oil, 1/4 cup finely diced new potatoes and 1/4 cup diced onion. Cook, stirring over low heat about 10 minutes, until potatoes are soft to the bite but only slightly browned. Place on top of the frittata before it goes into the oven. When it comes out add shredded Swiss cheese (3 tablespoons), 1 tablespoon chopped fresh parsley, 1/4 cup chopped walnuts and a mound of SOUR CREAM or YOGURT placed on top.

HUEVOS RANCHEROS

1 T. oil	2 cups puréed tomatoes
1/4 cup minced onion	1 cup shredded Cheddar cheese
1 clove garlic, crushed	4 eggs
1 can (4 ounce) green chilies, chopped	Vegetable seasoning to taste
	Chopped fresh parsley
1/2 tsp. oregano	Avocado slices as garnish
1/4 cup TOMATO SAUCE	

Heat oil in skillet and sauté onion and garlic until transparent. Add chilies, (reserve 1 whole one), oregano, tomato sauce, and tomato purée. Cook until flavors are well blended, about 5 minutes. Place the sauce in a small casserole dish. Add the cheese and place in the oven until almost melted. Break the 4 eggs into the casserole dish, on top of the sauce and cheese. Season with vegetable seasoning. Bake at 350° until eggs are set, about 12 minutes. Sprinkle with chopped parsley. Garnish with the reserved chili cut into strips and avocado wedges.

FLORENTINE CREPE CUPS

1½ cups shredded Cheddar cheese
3 T. whole wheat flour
3 eggs. slightly beaten
2/3 cups MAYONNAISE
2 cups spinach, chopped finely
1/3 cup mushrooms

1 tsp. tamari (soy sauce)
1/2 tsp. vegetable seasoning
1/8 tsp. kelp
12 8"-CREPES
Parsley as garnish

Toss the cheese with the flour, add remaining ingredients; mix well. Fit the crepes into greased muffin pan; fill with the egg and cheese mixture. Bake at 350° for 40 minutes or until set. Garnish with fresh parsley.

Yield: 6 servings

MIXED VEGETABLE SOUFFLÉ

1/4 cup butter
1/4 cup whole wheat flour
3/4 tsp. vegetable seasoning
3 T. diced onion
Dash red pepper
1/4 tsp. thyme
1½ cups milk

5 egg yolks
2 cups shredded Cheddar cheese
2 T. grated Parmesan cheese
1-1/3 cups finely diced assorted
    vegetables
6 egg whites

Extend height of 2-quart soufflé dish by wrapping a 5"-wide double thickness foil strip around outside so it stands about 3" above rim, fastening with masking tape. Melt butter in a saucepan over low heat and stir in flour, vegetable seasoning, onion, pepper and thyme. Blend well. Slowly add the milk, blend until thickened. Blend a small amount of the hot mixture into the egg yolks and then add back to the saucepan. Stir for 1 minute. Add cheeses and stir until melted. Remove from heat and fold in the vegetables. Cool. Beat egg whites until soft peaks form. Combine 1/3 of the egg whites with the cheese mixture. Gently fold in the remaining whites until blended. Do not over stir. Pour into the greased soufflé dish. Bake at 350° for 50 minutes. Serve immediately.

Yield: 6 servings

Variation:

Cheese Souffle: Use the recipe for the Mixed Vegetable Soufflé but just omit the vegetables.

SPINACH SOUFFLÉ

1/4 cup butter
1/3 cup whole wheat flour
2 T. minced onion
1 tsp. dried vegetable broth
1/2 tsp. dry mustard
1/2 tsp. ITALIAN HERBS
1¼ cups milk

2 cups spinach, steamed and
  chopped
1½ cups Cheddar cheese
1/4 cup grated Parmesan cheese
6 eggs, separated
3/4 tsp. cream of tartar

In a medium saucepan melt the butter and add the flour, onion, vegetable broth, mustard and herbs. Cook, stirring constantly, over medium-high heat until mixture is smooth and bubbly. Stir in milk all at once. Cook, stirring constantly, until mixture boils and thickens. Remove from heat. Stir in the spinach and cheeses. In a large bowl beat the egg whites and cream of tartar at high speed until stiff but not dry. In a small mixing bowl beat egg yolks slightly. Blend a little of hot spinach mixture into yolks. Stir yolk mixture into hot spinach mixture. Gently but thoroughly fold yolk mixture into whites. Pour into a greased soufflé dish and bake at 350° for 25-35 minutes until delicately browned and knife inserted near center comes out clean. Serve immediately.

Yield: 6 servings

QUICHE

1 medium onion finely chopped
1 cup chopped raw spinach
Oil
1½ cups shredded Swiss cheese
5 mushrooms, sliced
1 cup broccoli flowerets

4 eggs
1½ cups milk
1/4 tsp. dry mustard
1 tsp. tamari (soy sauce)
3 tsp. Dijon mustard
FLAKY PIE CRUST, bottom only

Cook onion and spinach in small amount of oil in frying pan until onion is limp. Spread a small amount of the Dijon mustard (save the rest for later) on a partially baked 10" pie crust. Then sprinkle the cheese on the crust. Next add mushrooms, onion and spinach mixture, and broccoli. Beat together the last 5 ingredients and pour over mixture in pie crust. Bake for one hour in 350° oven or until knife inserted into quiche comes out clean.

Yield: Serves 4

Variations:

Seafood Quiche: To the milk mixture add 3/4 cup cooked crab or shrimp.

Chicken Quiche: Layer on top of the broccoli 1/2 cup raw peas and 1 cup diced cooked chicken.

Tostada Quiche: Do not add the broccoli but instead layer 2-3 chopped chili peppers. Add to the milk mixture 1 cup cooked kidney or pinto beans. Cook as directed. When it is ready to be served pile some shredded lettuce in the center of the quiche. On top of that, place sliced tomatoes and then on top of that, a spoonful of GUACAMOLE.

FRESH VEGETABLE QUICHE

4 or 5 slices whole wheat bread,
  toasted
2 T. oil
1 medium onion, sliced
1 clove garlic, minced
5 cups mixed fresh vegetables cut in
  pieces, including broccoli,
  cauliflower and carrots

2 T. water
3 eggs
1/2 cup COTTAGE CHEESE
1/2 tsp. vegetable seasoning
1/2 tsp. each thyme, marjoram and
  basil
1/2 cup grated Swiss cheese
1/4 cup Parmesan cheese

Grease an 8" or 9" square pan and line the bottom with the bread slices. Heat oil in a large saucepan then sauté the onion and garlic until tender but not browned. Add the rest of the vegetables. Stir continuously while lightly tossing, for about 2 minutes. Add 2 tablespoons water, cover and steam for 5 minutes. Meanwhile, beat eggs in a small bowl. Add the cottage cheese, vegetable seasoning and herbs and mix well. Spread the mixed vegetables over bread slices. Pour egg mixture evenly over vegetables. Sprinkle with the Swiss cheese and Parmesan cheese. Bake at 325° for 35–40 minutes or until set.

Yield: Serves 4

CHEESE

BAKED CHEESE FONDUE

3 cups whole wheat bread cubes
1 T. melted butter
1 tsp. poppy seed
2 cups milk
3 T. grated onion
3 cups shredded Cheddar cheese
1/2 tsp. vegetable seasoning

1/4 tsp. kelp
1/2 tsp. dry mustard
1/4 tsp. paprika
Dash of tamari (soy sauce)
4 egg yolks, well beaten
4 egg whites

Toss 1 cup of the bread cubes with the butter and poppy seeds. Set cubes aside. Scald the milk and then pour into a large mixing bowl. Add to it the onion, cheese and the 2 cups of uncoated bread cubes. Add the vegetable seasoning, kelp, mustard, paprika and tamari. Mix lightly but thoroughly until cheese is melted. Add gradually, stirring constantly the egg yolks. Beat the whites until stiff. Gently fold the egg whites into the cheese mixture. Pour into a buttered 2-quart casserole dish. Top with the poppy seed coated bread cubes. Set the casserole in a baking dish that contains water 1" deep. Bake at 375° for 45–50 minutes. Serve immediately.

Yield: 6 servings

CHEESE LUNCHEON DISH

6 slices of whole wheat bread
1 cup Cheddar cheese, shredded
3 eggs
1¼ cups milk

1/4 tsp. vegetable seasoning
1/4 tsp. dry mustard
Dash of kelp

Remove the crusts from the bread. Arrange 3 slices in bottom of a shallow baking dish. Fit them in so bottom of dish is entirely covered. Cover the bread with the cheese. Top with remaining bread slices. Beat the eggs together with the milk, seasoning, mustard and kelp. Pour over the bread and cheese. Bake in a 325° oven for 40 minutes or until puffed and browned.

Yield: 2 servings

CHEESE BALL

3 cups grated Cheddar cheese
2 ounces crumbled Blue cheese
1 8-ounce package softened cream
   cheese

4 T. butter
1 T. minced green onion
1 tsp. tamari (soy sauce)
1/2-3/4 cup finely chopped walnuts

Combine all the ingredients together and then shape into a ball. Roll in the walnuts and coat well. Refrigerate until firm and then wrap in plastic. This cheese ball can also be frozen.

Yield: 1 cheese ball

MUSHROOM AND CHEESE PUFF

1 pound fresh mushrooms
4 T. oil
1/2 cup chopped onion (1 medium)
6 eggs, separated
1½ cups grated Cheddar cheese

3 T. grated Parmesan cheese
2 T. whole wheat flour
1 tsp. vegetable seasoning
1/8 tsp. kelp

Rinse, pat dry and slice the mushrooms. In an ovenproof skillet, heat 2 table-spoons of the oil and add the onions and the mushrooms. Sauté until golden, about 5 minutes. Take out 1/4 cup to sprinkle on top of the puff. Spread to evenly coat the bottom of the skillet. Set aside. Add to the egg yolk, the cheeses, flour, vegetable seasoning and kelp. Beat whites until stiff peaks form when beaters are raised. Fold whites into cheese mixture. Spread on top of mushrooms and onion in skillet. Top with reserved sautéed mushrooms and onions. Bake until puffy and firm, about 20 minutes.

Yield: 4-6 servings

CHEESE LUNCHEON PIE

2 eggs
2 cups COTTAGE CHEESE
2 cups hot mashed potatoes (3 medium potatoes)
3/4 cup plain YOGURT
1/4 cup finely chopped onion

1/4 cup chopped celery
2 T. chopped pimiento
1 tsp. vegetable seasoning
1/2 tsp. oregano
2 T. butter
Pastry for 1 crust pie, unbaked

Beat the 2 eggs until thick. Blend into the eggs the cottage cheese, potatoes, yogurt, onion, celery, pimiento, seasoning and oregano. Turn into the pie shell, spreading evenly. Dot surface with the butter. Bake at 350° about 1½ hours or until lightly browned. Serve hot or cold along with a crisp green salad.

Yield: 8 servings

 ## ITALIAN STYLE CHEESE EGG PIE

1 can (7 ounce) tuna
2 cups Mozzarella cheese
1 tomato
6 eggs
1/4 cup milk

1/4 tsp. vegetable seasoning
1/4 tsp. kelp
1/2 tsp. basil
1/2 tsp. oregano
Pastry for 1 crust pie, unbaked

Flake the tuna and set aside. Prepare the cheese by shredding it. Dice the tomato. In a large bowl mix together the eggs, milk, seasoning, kelp, basil and oregano. Add the tuna, cheese and tomato. Turn into an unbaked pie shell. Bake at 425° 35-40 minutes or until pie is lightly browned. Cut pie into wedges and serve at once.

Yield: 6 servings

MACARONI AND CHEESE

3 T. oil
2 T. diced onion
1/3 cup chopped green pepper
3 T. whole wheat flour
1/4 cup chopped fresh parsley
2 cups milk
1 tsp. dry mustard
1½ tsp. vegetable seasoning

2 T. plain YOGURT
1 tsp. tamari (soy sauce)
1½ cups shredded Cheddar cheese
1/4 cup Parmesan cheese
4 cups whole wheat macaroni, cooked
1 cup chopped tomatoes
1/4 cup whole wheat bread crumbs
1/4 cup rolled oats

Place the oil, onion and green pepper in a saucepan and sauté for 3 minutes. Add the flour and parsley, stirring well. Slowly pour in the milk and then add the mustard and vegetable seasoning. Stir. As it starts to thicken add the yogurt and tamari. Cook only until thickened. Remove from heat and add the cheeses. Mix well. Place the cooked macaroni and tomatoes in a 2½ quart casserole dish. Pour the sauce over the mixture in the casserole and stir until mixed. Sprinkle on top a mixture of bread crumbs and oats. Bake in a 350° oven for 20 minutes. Serve hot.

Yield: Serves 6

COTTAGE CHEESE

1 gallon milk (certified raw; or
    homogenized, whole or skim)

1/2 cup buttermilk or lemon juice
    or vinegar

Place the milk and buttermilk, lemon juice or vinegar in a large glass bowl. Mix thoroughly and cover loosely with cheesecloth. You want the mixture to breathe or you will end up with a musty odor. Allow to stand for 12-18 hours in a warm place (75-80°). When the milk has clabbered or thickened (whey and curd have separated) you need to cut the curd to allow more whey to separate out. Cut into 2" strips with a knife and then slice crosswise to get 2" squares. Now place bowl in a large pot with a few inches of water and place over low heat. Heat the milk to 115°. Keep it at that temperature for 1/2 hour, stirring gently periodically. Pour into a cheesecloth-lined strainer and allow to drain. Rinse with water carefully. When curds are dry, remove from cheesecloth and add a little milk. Refrigerate and use the cottage cheese as desired. Also save the liquid that drained from the cottage cheese. That is called whey and is full of minerals and B vitamins. Add the whey to soups, beverages, or casseroles; cook rice in it or add it to a sauce.

Yield: 1½ pounds

SOUR CREAM

1 pint sweet cream

2 T. lemon juice

Add the lemon juice to the sweet cream and place in a glass bowl. Mix, cover bowl and set in a warm place until it thickens.

Yield: 1 pint

MOCK SOUR CREAM

1 cup COTTAGE CHEESE
1 cup buttermilk

4 tsp. lemon juice

Place all of the ingredients in a blender and blend until smooth. Use as you would sour cream on baked potatoes, on fresh fruit, salads or fish.

Yield: 2 cups

Variation:

Blend 1 cup COTTAGE CHEESE, 1/4 cup plain YOGURT, 1 tablespoon lemon juice, 2 tablespoons oil, 1/4 cup buttermilk, 1/4 teaspoon tarragon, 1 tablespoon cider vinegar and 1 tablespoon chopped chives or green onions in a blender until smooth and creamy. Use on baked potatoes.

YOGURT

WHAT YOU WILL NEED TO START

Milk: You can use any type of milk. Homogenized or low-fat, raw, goat, soy, pasteurized, or non-instant dry milk. On the low-fat milk make sure no thickening or bodying agents are added. Do not use condensed or evaporated milks.

Starter: For your first batch you should begin with a *starter* that is sold in the freeze-dried form in your local health food store. After you make your first batch you can save a couple of tablespoons to use as a starter for the next batch. If you're unable to find the starter, then use plain, unflavored yogurt from fresh commercial yogurt. Just make sure the yogurt has not been pasteurized after the addition of the culture as the culture will not be an active one.

Equipment: You'll need a saucepan to cook the milk in; a candy thermometer that will register temperatures of 110° to 180°; a yogurt maker or a quart jar, plus a big kettle and a bath towel.

Hints: Incubation time for the yogurt will vary. Such factors as the temperature the culture was maintained, the kind of milk, the type of equipment used and even the weather outside has an influence. If whey develops on top of the yogurt, that is an indication that it has incubated too long. There is nothing wrong with the yogurt, just stir it back in, but it will be a little runny. The yogurt can keep up to a week in the refrigerator. If incubated too long it will also develop a tart flavor. Make sure all equipment that comes in contact with the milk is dishwasher clean or scalded to prevent any bacterial action that could interfere with the action of the yogurt starter. Your starter must always be fresh. Even if you use yogurt from your last batch, make sure the yogurt is not over a week old.

WHY YOGURT DOES NOT FORM

1. Milk was not heated sufficiently to kill existing bacteria.
2. Milk may have been too hot (above 120°) or too cold (below 90°) when the starter was added. 115° is optimal.
3. The starter was not mixed thoroughly into the cooled milk.
4. The milk or the starter mixture may have been too old.
5. The milk-and-starter mixture may have been disturbed, shaken, or otherwise vibrated during incubation.

6. The milk may have been contaminated by residues of medication that have been given to the cows for disease. The medication would kill off the culture.

7. Fresh raw milk was not boiled.

YOGURT RECIPE

4 cups milk   3 T. yogurt starter
1/2 cup non-instant dry milk powder

First, make sure all your equipment is very clean. Pour the 4 cups of milk into a saucepan and heat to scalding, 180°, but do not let it boil. Remove from the heat and let it cool until it is lukewarm, 110°. When cooled, stir in the non-instant dry milk. This will help make a thicker yogurt. Then stir in the yogurt culture. Pour into your yogurt maker and proceed as directed by the manufacturer's instructions on the maker. If you do not have a maker, you can make one with just a few items. Pour the milk into a quart jar. Place the lid on the jar and place the jar into a large kettle (one large enough so the jar can stand upright with the kettle lid on). Pour water that is 115° into the kettle up to 1'' of the top of the yogurt jar. Place the lid on the kettle and wrap a towel all around the kettle to keep the heat in. Allow to sit for 5-8 hours. The water needs to be checked periodically to make sure it stays at about that temperature. If you are using the freeze-dried culture the yogurt may take a little longer to become firm. After the time period is up you will have yogurt. Remember to save 3 tablespoons from this batch to act as a starter for your next batch.

                                                        Yield: 1 quart
Variation:

Fruit Yogurt: Add any types of puréed fruit and fruit slices. Plus you can add some fresh fruit juices as sweeteners or use honey if desired.

HOW TO USE YOGURT

There are so many uses for yogurt that I want to list some of the *different* ways yogurt can be fixed, and also some of the different uses for the yogurt.

1. Substitute for buttermilk and sour cream in recipes.

2. Dab it on baked potatoes or apples.

3. Spoon over vegetables that are cooked.

4. Combine with fresh fruit for a dessert.

5. Use as a digestive aid.

6. Add chunks of Roquefort cheese and make a salad dressing.

7. Use as a sunburn cream.

8. Make a SMOOTHIE with it by adding fresh fruit and fruit juice, and blend in a blender.

9. Eat to calm frazzled nerves.

10. Whip with egg whites for a dessert topping.

11. Add oatmeal and honey (warmed) to it and use as a facial. Leave on for about 15 minutes.

12. Feed to babies as an antidote for diarrhea.

13. Eat to restore friendly bacteria killed by antibiotics.

14. Take for relief from a gassy, bloated feeling.

15. Add chopped nuts and seeds.

16. Flavor it with cinnamon, nutmeg, cloves, molasses, honey, carob, vanilla or almond, to name just a few.

17. Use instead of aspirin for relief from migraine headaches.

18. Eat to prevent food poisoning when visiting foreign countries.

19. Apply to skin to bleach out freckles.

20. Use in cole slaw.

21. Place between layer of cake, wrap and freeze. Take out of the freezer and frost with your favorite frosting.

22. Stir in GRANOLA or cookie crumbs as a special treat.

YOGURT CHEESE

To make the cheese, pour thick, cold yogurt into a clean moist cloth (like cheesecloth). Tie the top of the cloth and hang the bag where it can drain for 4-6 hours. Place a container under the bag to catch the whey. The whey is very nutritional, so do not toss out. (Use it in beverages, in salad dressings, soups or use in your baking in place of milk.) Place the bag in a colander set in a drip pan; cover, and let refrigerate overnight. In the morning remove it from the bag and store airtight in the refrigerator for up to a week. Each quart of yogurt makes 1½ cups cheese. Add honey and cinnamon and use it as a spread on breakfast bread, muffins or waffles. Try it with fresh fruit or use it to make spreads, dressings or dips. Below and on the next page are some suggestions on what to make from the cheese:

Mustard Spread: To the cheese add 1 tablespoon Dijon mustard and 1 clove garlic minced. Good in sandwiches.

Herb Garlic Dip: Use on crackers or with fresh vegetables. To the cheese add 1 teaspoon each finely chopped parsley and green onion, 1/2 teaspoon each basil and thyme, and 1 small clove garlic.

Pineapple Topping: Use on cakes, fruit salads, crepe fillings. Add 1 can (8 ounces) crushed unsweetened pineapple. Sweeten to taste with honey. Thin with milk or fruit juice if needed.

Herb Dressing: Use on green salads, hot and cold vegetables. Make herb dip and add 1½ tablespoons lemon juice. Thin with milk or water.

Swiss Cheese: Use with fresh fruit and tea breads. To the cheese add about 2 tablespoons frozen orange juice concentrate or apple juice; honey to taste, 3 tablespoons finely chopped nuts.

YOGURT AVOCADO DIP

1/2 cup plain YOGURT
1 large avocado
3 T. lemon juice

1/4 tsp. garlic powder
1/4 tsp. vegetable seasoning
2 tsp. finely chopped green onion

Mash avocado and add all the other ingredients and mix well. Serve with fresh vegetables.

Yield: 1 cup

GREEN GODDESS DRESSING

1 soft, ripe avocado
1 cup plain YOGURT
1 T. chopped fresh parsley
2 tsp. onion, minced

1/4 cup MAYONNAISE
1/2 tsp. vegetable seasoning
1/4 tsp. garlic powder
Milk to thin

Put all ingredients except for the milk in a mixing bowl. Blend ingredients with wire whip. If it needs thinning, add milk. Mix thoroughly.

Yield: 2 cups

YOGURT WHEAT GERM ROLLS

1 cup warm YOGURT (110°)
1 T. dry active yeast
1/4 cup butter
1 tsp. kelp
3 T. blackstrap molasses

1 egg
3/4 cup wheat germ
2½ cups whole wheat flour
1/3 cup non-instant dry milk
    powder

Place the yeast in the yogurt and let sit for a few minutes. Add the butter, kelp, molasses, egg and wheat germ to it and stir quickly. Add the flour and milk powder and combine well. Beat for 10 minutes with an electric mixer or 200 strokes by hand. Cover bowl, and put in a warm place until it doubles in size (about 1 hour). Shape into rolls and bake at 350° for 20 minutes.

Yield: 20 2" rolls

YOGURT POPSICLE

2 cups YOGURT, plain
2 tsp. VANILLA EXTRACT

6 ounces frozen orange juice
1 orange, peeled and chopped

Mix all of the ingredients together until smooth. Pour into popsicle molds or paper cups and insert ice cream sticks. Freeze until firm.

Yield: 2½ cups

YOGURT CHEESE PIE

1 8-ounce package cream cheese,
  softened
1/3 cup honey
3 eggs
2 tsp. VANILLA EXTRACT

2 cups plain YOGURT
2 cups raspberries or any other fruit
1 GRAHAM CRACKER PIE
  CRUST, baked

In a large bowl combine the cream cheese and the honey. Beat until well combined. Mix in the eggs, one at a time. Then add the vanilla and combine well. Using low speed, blend in the yogurt. Stir in the fresh fruit. Pour this mixture into the prepared pie crust. Bake at 350° for 40 minutes, or until dry when lightly touched. Cool, then chill at least 4 hours or as long as over-night. To serve, cut in wedges and top with additional fresh fruit if desired.

Yield: 8 servings

YOGURT SHERBET

1 T. unflavored gelatin
1 T. lemon juice
2 T. water
1 cup strawberries, blueberries,
  raspberries, peaches or nectarines

1 cup crushed pineapple, packed in
  its own liquid, drained
1 cup plain YOGURT

Soften gelatin in lemon juice and water on top of a double boiler. Heat over hot water until gelatin dissolves. Remove from heat and add the fruits and yogurt. Beat until fluffy and freeze. When mixture is frozen solid, remove from freezer and allow to sit at room temperature for about 1 hour or until it can be broken up. Beat with electric beater until creamy but still quite thick. Serve immediately.

Yield: 4 servings

VANILLA FROZEN YOGURT

1 T. unflavored gelatin	3 cups plain YOGURT
1/2 cup milk	1/3 cup honey
2 whole eggs, separated	2 T. VANILLA EXTRACT

Combine the gelatin and milk and let stand about 5 minutes. Now place in the top of a double boiler and stir over simmering water until gelatin completely dissolves. Cool about 5 minutes. Beat the egg yolks lightly and beat in the yogurt and all but 2 tablespoons of the honey. Blend until smooth. Beat in the gelatin and vanilla. Beat the egg whites until soft peaks form, then gradually beat in the remaining 2 tablespoons of honey. Beat until firm. Fold this into the yogurt mixture. If it needs more sweetener add some now. (After it is frozen it will taste a little sweeter.) Turn yogurt mixture into a 2 quart or larger ice cream freezer. Assemble the freezer according to manufacturer's directions, using about 4 parts ice to 1 part rock salt. Remove the dasher when it becomes difficult to mix. Transfer to another container and place in your freezer.

Yield: 1¼ quarts

Variations:

Fresh Berry Yogurt: Rinse about 1 pint berries and whirl in the blender until coarsely crushed (you need 1½ cups crushed berries). Add 1/4 cup apple juice and let stand until juices form, then spoon off and reserve 1/2 cup juice. Follow the recipe for Vanilla Frozen Yogurt, except substitute the 1/2 cup berry juice for the milk to dissolve gelatin. Omit 2 tablespoons of honey and the vanilla. Instead add 2 tablespoons lemon juice, the berries and any remaining juices to the yogurt mixture. Add the 2 tablespoons honey to the egg whites as directed above.

Fresh Peach, Nectarine or Apricot Yogurt: Remove pits from peeled ripe peaches or unpeeled nectarines or apricots. Whirl fruit in the blender until coarsely crushed (you will need about 1½ cups). To the crushed fruit add 1/4 cup honey and 2 tablespoons lemon juice. Let stand until juices form, then spoon off and reserve 1/2 cup juice. Follow recipe for Vanilla Frozen Yogurt, except substitute the 1/2 cup fruit juice for milk to dissolve the gelatin. Substitute 1/8-1/4 teaspoon almond extract for the vanilla. After mixture is frozen, stir in 1/2 cup toasted almonds.

Date and Almond Yogurt: Follow recipe for Vanilla Frozen Yogurt, except substitute 1/2 cup fresh orange juice for the milk to dissolve the gelatin. Without cooling gelatin mixture, pour it over 1 cup finely chopped dates; stir until evenly mixed. Omit vanilla and add 1/2 teaspoon each grated orange peel and cinnamon and 1/4 teaspoon cloves to the yogurt mixture. After mixture is frozen, stir in 1/2 cup toasted, chopped almonds

Freezer Made Frozen Yogurt: You can make soft frozen yogurt without an ice cream freezer, but it will not be as fine textured. Pour chilled mixture into a 9" square pan; freeze mixture, stirring several times so that yogurt freezes evenly, about 3 hours. Break frozen mixture into chunks in a large chilled bowl. Beat with electric mixer until smooth.

FROZEN LEMON YOGURT SOUFFLE

3 cups plain YOGURT
1/2 cup honey to taste
Juice and finely grated rind of
  2 lemons

1 tsp. VANILLA EXTRACT
2 egg whites
Pinch of cream of tartar
1/2 cup whipping cream

Beat the honey into the yogurt. Add to the yogurt the lemon rind and juice and vanilla; stir well. Add the egg whites and cream of tartar together and beat until stiff. Whip cream until stiff also. Gently fold egg whites and then whipped cream into the yogurt mixture. Pour into a freezer container, cover and freeze.

Yield: 4 cups

YUMMY BANANA FROZEN YOGURT

1 T. unflavored gelatin
1/2 cup water
2 large ripe bananas
2 cups plain YOGURT

1/4 cup honey
1 tsp. VANILLA EXTRACT
1/8 tsp. cinnamon

Combine gelatin and water to soften. Place on the stove and heat slowly until gelatin dissolves. Mash bananas. Combine together the bananas, yogurt, honey, vanilla and cinnamon in a blender. Whirl until well blended. Continuing to whirl, pour in the gelatin and blend until well blended. Pour into a bowl and freeze 1-2 hours until partially frozen. Stir once or twice. Beat until smooth. Return to freezer for 30 minutes. For a smoother consistency, beat again. Spoon into sherbet dishes and serve.

Yield: 4-6 servings

KEFIR

Kefir is a cultured milk that is heavy like buttermilk. It is one of the oldest of the fermented milk drinks. This drink is very popular in Russia, Europe and the Middle East. Its nutritional properties are similar to yogurt, but it does differ in that it has an added bacillus. It also does not have to be heated like yogurt so you are able to use raw milk as the base. Kefir helps with digestion in that it stimulates the flow of saliva and the digestive juices. Frequently it can be tolerated by persons who are allergic to cow's milk. Kefir is quite easy to make as the only items you need are the milk, culture and storage container. You just place the culture in the milk and then add the milk to the containers and let set at room temperature for 1-2 days. It is then ready to drink. If you would like, you can blend it in a blender with some fresh fruit to give you a Kefir fruit shake. To continue making the kefir you need to save a few teaspoons of it each time to use as a culture for your next batch. To get started you need to buy a kefir culture. A freeze-dried culture can be ordered through the mail from: The International Yogurt Company, 628 North Doheny Drive, Los Angeles, California 90069.

POTPOURRI

This chapter is a combination of foods that accompany the *main* foods in a meal. These accompaniments should be as nutritious as the rest of the foods in your diet. What I find so frequently, though, is that these foods are disregarded or just passed over. I want to show you how to make these foods a vital part of your life.

There will be a number of recipes for sauces and butters that can complement your foods, and can turn even a dull dish into a tasty one. They can be used served with the main dish or even over vegetables, grains and noodles. Just remember you want them to complement, not overpower the dish.

I have a section on homemade honey-sweetened jams and fruit butters. These items are usually so laden with white sugar that they are very unhealthy for you. You do not need to cut these delights out of your diet, but what you do need to do is change over to honey-sweetened preserves that are really tasty.

CHAPTER 14

In this chapter you are also going to be shown how to make your own vanilla extract and baking powder. Plus you will be shown how to use herbs and spices to help "spice" up your foods.

Do not overlook this chapter as it could be a *fun* part of your diet and meal planning.

HELPFUL HINTS

- When making butter sauces always use real butter. Its taste and smoothness are essential to a great sauce.

- Heat butter over low heat when melting, otherwise it will scorch.

- Add a pair of whole cloves to the teapot and discover a delicious flavor.

- Try a dash of mace and discover the delight of spinach.

- To prevent a skin from forming on a sauce, dot the surface with softened butter. Or place a piece of plastic wrap over the top of the sauce to keep the air out.

- Try herbed butter or oregano butter on roast corn or broiled potatoes.

- If your jam does not jell, just use it as a syrup on pancakes and waffles.

- When using honey in making preserves, use a mild tasting one. Strong tasting ones may mask the fruit flavor.

- When making jams and jellies, wash and sterilize the jar and keep it warm until used. Never boil the seal as it may ruin the rubber sealing edge. Just place the seal in the water after it has boiled, and the other items have been removed.

- In your kettle of jelly or jam add a pat of butter to help keep the foam down. You can save up to 1/2 cup of jelly or jam by doing this.

- Food in jars that have not sealed when preserving may be reheated and spooned into hot sterilized jars and reprocessed.

- Do not readjust the band after the jar has been removed from the water bath. It could break the seal.

- After cooling the jars of preserves for 10 hours you can remove the bands if the seal "took."

- Use the preserves over pancakes and waffles. Use as a filler between layers of cakes. Place on top of ice cream and YOGURT. Use on crackers and bread.

- Use leftover sauces by adding to soups and casseroles or mix vegetables into it and serve as a vegetable dish. Use it as a spread on a sandwich.

- Many of the butters can be made in a blender.

- Add 1/4 teaspoon each of thyme, basil, parsley, and chives to 1 pound of cooked buttered noodles for a delicious taste.

- To clean your blender put a little soapy warm water in it and turn it on. Cleans it quickly.

- To clean burned pots, put water and baking soda in it and bring to a boil. Then simmer for 45 minutes. Helps to loosen the burned particles.

- A bay leaf in your flour, cornmeal, rice or other staples will ward off weevils and leave absolutely no taste.

- When a sauce is made ahead of time, it is best to reheat it in a double boiler. This will prevent sticking and scorching from occurring. Cover it to prevent the formation of a skin on it.

- Butter sauces should be light and rich. You do not want the added herbs to overpower it. They should just lend a subtle taste to the butter.

- Uses for the butters: With crackers as a snack, on vegetables, spread on sandwiches, served with fish, chicken.

- To remove odor after cleaning the oven, place orange peelings on the rack in the oven and turn to 350°. Let it sit for a short while.

- For a candlelight dinner, put candles in the refrigerator a few hours before using them and you will not have a problem with dripping wax.

SAUCES

BASIC WHITE SAUCE

2 T. oil
2 T. whole wheat flour

Choice of herbs: Thyme, parsley, oregano, vegetable seasoning, to taste
1 cup milk

In a skillet add oil, flour and herbs. Stir flour until it browns. Gradually add milk, stirring until it thickens.

Yield: 1½ cups

Variations:

Brown Sauce: Toast flour in a dry skillet before adding the oil.

Mushroom-Onion Sauce: Sauté 3 T. chopped onions and 1/4 cup sliced mushrooms in oil before adding flour.

Thick White Sauce: Follow directions above, using 3 T. of flour and butter.

Sauce Velouté: Substitute chicken or fish broth for milk and proceed as for white sauce.

Cheese Sauce: To the white sauce add 1/2 cup grated Cheddar cheese or 1/2 cup Swiss cheese (grated) and 1 T. Parmesan; 1/4 tsp. dry mustard.

HERB SAUCE

2 T. chopped scallions
2 T. oil
2 T. chopped chives
2 T. chopped fresh tarragon leaves
3 T. chopped fresh parsley

1/2 pound mushrooms, sliced
3 T. oil
Vegetable seasoning to taste
1/2 cup chicken broth
1 T. honey

Sauté scallions in oil until soft. Remove pan from heat, add chives, tarragon, parsley. Sauté mushrooms in 3 T. oil, quickly season, add the herbs and scallions, chicken broth, simmer for 5 minutes, stir in honey and simmer 2 more minutes. Good on chicken and broiled fish.

Yield: 1 cup

HOLLANDAISE SAUCE

3 egg yolks
1 T. hot water
2 T. lemon juice

1/2 cup butter
1/4 tsp. vegetable seasoning

Heat water in bottom of double boiler, keeping level low enough so it will not touch the upper pot. Do not let water boil. Place egg yolks in top of double boiler and add the hot water. With a wire whisk beat the water and yolks until mixture is light. Add lemon juice and mix in well. Cut butter into thirds. Add 1/3 butter to egg yolk mixture and beat until butter is completely melted. Repeat with another 1/3 of butter. Repeat with remaining butter, beating until mixture thickens and is heated through. Remove from heat. Stir in vegetable seasoning. If sauce curdles: Place a teaspoon of lemon juice and a tablespoon of curdled sauce in bowl. Beat with whisk until creamy and thickened. Then gradually beat in remaining sauce, a tablespoon at a time, making sure each addition has thickened before adding the next.

Yield: 3/4 cup

Variation:

Quick Hollandaise Sauce: Heat 1/2 cup butter to bubbling, but do not brown. Place 3 egg yolks, 2 tablespoons lemon juice, 1/4 tsp. vegetable seasoning and a pinch of cayenne in a blender. Turn on low and add hot butter gradually. Blend about 15 seconds or until thick and smooth.

AVOCADO HOLLANDAISE

4 eggs
1/2 cup lemon juice
1 cup butter, melted

2 avocados, halved and peeled
Dash of vegetable seasoning
Dash of red pepper

Blend eggs with lemon juice in blender until lemon colored. Slowly add hot butter while blender is whirling at low speed. Blend in avocados and seasoning. Chill 30 minutes. Serve as sauce for poached eggs, eggs Benedict or as a vegetable dip.

Yield: 3 cups

CHILI SAUCE

2 onions, finely chopped
1 clove garlic, minced
2 T. oil
1½ cups canned green chilies,
   rinsed, seeded and chopped

5 ripe tomatoes, peeled and
   chopped
Pinch of oregano
1 tsp. vegetable seasoning
1/4 tsp. cumin

Sauté onions and garlic in the oil until transparent and limp. Add chopped chilies and tomatoes, oregano, vegetable seasoning and cumin. Cook over low heat, stirring occasionally, until mixture thickens.

Yield: 4 cups

TOMATO SAUCE

7 large tomatoes
1 (6 ounce) can tomato paste
1 T. oil
1 large sized onion, chopped
2 cloves garlic, minced
1/2 cup green pepper, chopped

1 T. fresh parsley, chopped
1 tsp. oregano
1/2 tsp. thyme
1/2 tsp. basil
1/8 tsp. marjoram
1 tsp. vegetable seasoning

Place the tomatoes in a pot of boiling water for 10 seconds. Remove tomatoes and peel the skin off the tomatoes. Blend the tomatoes and tomato paste in the blender until smooth. Sauté in oil the onion, garlic and green pepper. Cook for about 3 minutes. Place the tomato mixture in a saucepan along with the sautéed vegetables and all the other ingredients. Simmer, uncovered for 1 hour. Cool and refrigerate for 1 day before using; this helps to mellow the flavor.

Yield: 2 cups

Variations:

Spaghetti Sauce: Sauté with the other vegetables 1/2 cup mushrooms, 2 stalks celery and tops, chopped. Add to the other herbs 1/4 teaspoon rosemary. Cook as in the Tomato Sauce.

Enchilada Sauce: Sauté with the other vegetables 2 or 3 seeded and chopped chili peppers or jalapenos. In place of the herbs (thyme, basil and marjoram) add 2 teaspoons chili powder and 1 teaspoon cumin.

QUICK BÉARNAISE

1 T. white wine vinegar
1 T. tarragon vinegar
2 tsp. chopped tarragon
2 tsp. chopped onion or shallots
1/2 cup butter

3 egg yolks
2 T. lemon juice
1/4 tsp. vegetable seasoning
Pinch of cayenne pepper

Combine the two vinegars, tarragon and onion in a skillet. Bring to a boil and cook rapidly until almost all the liquid disappears. In a small saucepan heat the butter to bubbling, but do not brown. Place the egg yolks, lemon juice, vegetable seasoning and cayenne in the container of a blender. Cover the container and flick the motor off and on at high speed. Remove the cover, turn the motor on high and gradually add the hot butter. Add the herb mixture, cover and blend on high speed 4 seconds.

Yield: 3/4–1 cup

EGG SAUCE

4 hard-cooked eggs
2 T. oil
2 T. whole wheat flour

2 cups milk
1/2 tsp. vegetable seasoning
1 tsp. Dijon mustard

Peel eggs and separate the yolk and the white. Chop the whites fine and mash the yolks with a fork. In a small saucepan over low heat, mix together the oil and flour. Gradually add the milk and stir until smooth. Add the seasoning and mustard. Cook for about 15 minutes, stirring frequently. Remove from heat and add the whites and yolk. Serve over fish, CREPES, or vegetable loaves.

Yield: 2 cups

SWEET AND SOUR SAUCE

1 cup CHICKEN STOCK, strained
1/4 cup honey
1/8 tsp. ground ginger
2 T. butter
1/3 cup unsweetened pineapple juice
4 T. lemon juice

2 T. tamari (soy sauce)
2 T. arrowroot powder
3 T. water
1½ cups pineapple chunks
1/4 cup slivered almonds, toasted

Combine the stock, honey, ginger, butter, pineapple juice, lemon juice and tamari in a saucepan and stir. Mix the arrowroot with the water and drizzle into mixture in the saucepan, stirring constantly. Bring to a boil. Reduce to simmer and cook, stirring constantly, until sauce thickens. Add pineapple chunks and continue cooking, stirring as needed, until sauce is nice and clear. Add almonds before serving.

Yield: 2 cups

SALSA

2 large tomatoes, chopped
1-2 green chilies, rinsed, seeded and
  chopped
1 large onion, finely chopped
3 T. chopped parsley

2 tsp. minced garlic
1 tsp. kelp
1/8 tsp. each cumin, chili powder
Juice of 1 lemon
1 T. olive oil

Combine all ingredients and mix thoroughly. Chill before serving.

Yield: 3 cups

KETCHUP

2 quarts peeled tomatoes, quartered
1/2 cup cider vinegar
1 clove garlic, minced
1 tsp. oregano
1/2 tsp. mustard powder

1/4 tsp. cumin
1/2 tsp. nutmeg
1 tsp. honey
1 T. arrowroot powder dissolved
   in 1 T. of water

Place tomatoes in a saucepan, mash and cook until they are soft. Then place the tomatoes in a blender and purée them. Return them to the saucepan, add the remaining ingredients and simmer for 30 minutes or until it thickens.

Yield: 1 quart

BARBECUE SAUCE

1 cup tomato purée
1 large tomato
2 T. oil
1/4 cup cider vinegar

1/8 tsp. cayenne
3 T. honey
1 medium onion, sliced
1/2 green pepper, sliced

Mix all of the ingredients together in a blender until smooth. Use as a basting sauce on your chicken, fish or anything else you want to barbecue. Keep sauce refrigerated.

Yield: 2 cups

DILL SAUCE

3 T. oil
2 sprigs dill
1 T. chives

1 tsp. dill seeds
1 tsp. kelp
Juice and rind of 1 lemon

Blend all together. Serve over fish and vegetables.

Yield: 1/4 cup

CUCUMBER SAUCE

2 cucumbers, in chunks
1 onion, sliced
1/4 cup YOGURT, plain
1 tsp. cider vinegar
1/4 tsp. celery seeds, ground

1 T. fresh parsley, chopped
1 T. dill
1 tsp. mint
1 tsp. kelp

Blend all ingredients. Chill. Serve with cold fish.

Yield: 3/4 cup

POTATO DILL SAUCE

1/2 onion, chopped
2 T. oil
2 cups VEGETABLE STOCK
4 potatoes, peeled and cubed
2 tsp. dill

2 T. fresh chopped parsley
1 clove fresh garlic, minced
1½ tsp. vegetable seasoning
1/4 tsp. kelp

Sauté the onion in the oil. Add the stock, potatoes and dill. Cook until potatoes are tender. Place those ingredients into a blender and purée until smooth. Add all the other ingredients and mix well. Good served over green beans, broccoli and Brussels sprouts.

Yield: 3 cups

ORIENTAL SAUCE

1/4 cup tamari (soy sauce)
1/4 cup oil
2 T. KETCHUP

1 T. cider vinegar
2 cloves garlic, crushed

Mix all ingredients together in a bowl. Chill well.

Yield: 1 cup

MUSHROOM GRAVY

1½ cups sliced mushrooms
3 T. chopped onion
1/4 cup oil
1/4 cup whole wheat flour
2 cups CHICKEN or VEGETABLE
STOCK

1/2 tsp. each oregano, basil and
vegetable seasoning
1/4 tsp. each garlic powder and
thyme

Sauté in oil the mushrooms and onions until onions are tender. Add the flour and stir until brown. Add the stock and herbs and continue to stir until mixture is thickened.

Yield: 2 cups

HORSERADISH SAUCE

1 cup plain YOGURT
1/4 tsp. vegetable seasoning

2 T. grated lemon peel
2 T. prepared horseradish

Combine all ingredients in a small bowl. Refrigerate and serve well chilled.

Yield: 1 cup

TERIYAKI SAUCE

1/2 cup tamari (soy sauce)
1/2 cup water
1 T. honey

1 clove garlic, crushed
Medium piece fresh ginger, grated

Mix all the ingredients and use as a marinade.

Yield: 1 cup

Variation:

Thick Teriyaki Sauce: Place the Teriyaki Sauce in a pan, add 1 tablespoon arrowroot powder dissolved in 2 tablespoons water. Heat and stir constantly until the sauce thickens. Serve on vegetables and in casseroles.

SWEET AND SOUR MUSTARD SAUCE

1 cup BASIC WHITE SAUCE
2 tsp. mustard powder

1 tsp. honey
1½ tsp. vinegar

Dissolve mustard in vinegar. Stir all the ingredients together and heat.

Yield: 1 cup

PESTO SAUCE

Pesto is a sauce using fresh basil, Parmesan cheese and olive oil. It has many uses; for instance, use it to flavor vinaigrette dressing or spaghetti sauce; stir it into soups; blend it with butter to melt over chicken, fish or vegetables; or use in a MAYONNAISE for a dip. It will keep about a week in the refrigerator. Just stir it up before using it. You can freeze it by placing it into ice cube trays, and once frozen, store in plastic bags. When you use it in soups, sauces, or other dishes that require cooking, stir it in during the last few minutes. If fresh basil is not available you can substitute 1/2 cup dry basil leaves and 1½ cups fresh parsley for 2 cups of fresh basil.

2 cups packed basil leaves
1 cup freshly grated Parmesan cheese

2 large cloves garlic, peeled
1/2 cup olive oil

In a blender combine the basil, Parmesan cheese and garlic. Whirl at high speed until smooth. With motor running, gradually pour in oil and whirl until well mixed. Cover and refrigerate up to one week, or freeze as directed.

Yield: 1-1/3 cups

TARTAR SAUCE

1 cup MAYONNAISE or YOGURT
2 T. chopped fresh parsley
2 T. finely chopped pickle
2 T. finely chopped onion
1 tsp. horseradish

1 tsp. lemon juice
1/8 tsp. tamari (soy sauce)
1/8 tsp. vegetable seasoning
Dash liquid hot pepper sauce

Combine all ingredients together and mix well. Good served with fish or burgers.

Yield: 1½ cups.

BUTTERS

HERB BUTTER

1/2 cup butter
1 clove garlic, minced
2 T. chopped fresh parsley

1 T. chopped chives
1 T. chopped fresh tarragon
1 tsp. vegetable seasoning

Cream all of the ingredients together until smooth. Use on bread, vegetables, fish or chicken.

Yield: 2/3 cup

MUSTARD HERB BUTTER

1/2 cup butter
2 T. prepared MUSTARD

1 T. chopped chives or green onion
1 T. chopped fresh parsley

Cream butter. Beat in mustard, then stir in chopped herbs.

Yield: 2/3 cup

GARLIC BUTTER

1/2 cup butter

1 clove garlic, minced

Beat melted butter and garlic together. Do not be tempted to add more garlic. Butter sauces should be light and rich, with just enough spicing to add a subtle flavor. Place on FRENCH BREAD and then heat the bread. Or use as a butter with seafood or chicken.

Yield: 1/2 cup

CHEESE BUTTER

1/2 cup butter, softened
1/4 cup cream cheese
1/4 cup Roquefort cheese

1 T. chives, minced
1 tsp. celery seeds, crushed
1 T. soy flour

Blend all together. Use with crackers, bread or vegetables.

Yield: 1 cup

CURRY BUTTER

1/2 cup butter
1/2 tsp. CURRY POWDER

1/4 tsp. dry mustard
1/8 tsp. cayenne

Cream all of the ingredients together. Use on sandwiches, on cooked vegetables or spread on crackers as an appetizer.

Yield: 1/2 cup

PARMESAN BUTTER

1/2 cup butter   1/2 cup grated Parmesan cheese

Melt butter and cheese together over a low heat. Use poured over freshly popped POPCORN. Can also be served over vegetables or pasta.

Yield: 2/3 cup

LEMON BUTTER

1/2 cup butter, softened
2 T. lemon juice

Rind of 1 lemon, grated

Blend all together. Use with fish or fowl.

Yield: 3/4 cup

DILL BUTTER

1/2 cup butter, softened
1 sprig fresh dill, minced
1/2 tsp. dill seed, crushed

1 tsp. lemon juice
1 T. fresh parsley, minced

Blend all together. Use with fish, potatoes or other vegetables.

Yield: 3/4 cup

BERRY BUTTER

1/2 cup butter, softened
3 T. fresh berries, crushed

1 tsp. lemon juice
1 sprig mint, minced

Blend together. Use on quick breads.

Yield: 1/2 cup

FILBERT BUTTER SAUCE

1/2 cup butter
1/3 cup chopped filberts or pecans

2 tsp. minced chives
1 tsp. lemon juice

Combine melted butter with nuts, chives and lemon juice, while stirring over low heat. Filbert sauce can be used as a baste when baking fish or as a garnish, or both. Good with perch, cod or turbot.

Yield: 1 cup

SEED AND NUT BUTTER

1 cup sunflower seeds
1 cup sesame seeds
2 cups nuts (almond, cashew, Brazil)

Oil
Honey to taste

Place the seeds and nuts in a blender and grind until fine. While the blender is whirling, add just enough oil to have it all hold together. Do not add too much or it will turn out runny. Add honey to taste. Blend thoroughly. Use on sandwiches or crackers. Great on slices of banana and apples. Basically use as you would PEANUT BUTTER.

Yield: 2 cups

HONEY BUTTER

1 cup butter, softened

3 T. honey

Beat the butter and honey together until well blended. Place into a storage container and refrigerate until needed. Use on pancakes, waffles, cornbread.

Yield: 1 cup

ENRICHED BUTTER

In this butter you are adding oil which is a good source of essential fatty acids (which the butter is lacking) and lecithin. Lecithin works hand in hand in our bodies with cholesterol to keep the cholesterol broken up. This spread is used in place of margarine which happens to be one of the most processed foods. It is sometimes said that eating margarine is just like eating plastic. With the addition of oil this butter becomes more spreadable so you need a lot less of it. It just seems to stretch that cube of butter a lot farther.

1/2 cup butter   1 tsp. liquid lecithin
1/2 cup oil

Place all of the ingredients in the blender and blend until smooth. Place in a storage container and store in the refrigerator. Use as you would margarine and butter.

Yield: 1½ cups

HERBS

GENERAL HINTS FOR FLAVORING WITH HERBS AND SPICES

1.   Store herbs in driest, coolest, darkest place in the kitchen. Be sure to date the containers so you will know how long you have had them.

2.   Fresh garlic usually loses its full strength after 6 months. Always store this herb in a container with a loose-fitting lid.

3.   Following are herbs that can be stored up to 1 year at full flavor (but after that they lose their potency): basil, bay, caraway, chives, coriander, dill, fennel, marjoram, mint, oregano, parsley, savory, shallots and tarragon.

4.   Some herbs that can be stored up to 2 years at full flavor: nutmeg (whole), peppercorns, rosemary, sage and thyme.

5.   Use a small amount of one or more herbs to enhance the flavor of the food. You should not be able to recognize a definite herb flavor. Try 1/2 teaspoon per pint for liquid food or for 1 pound of fish and chicken.

6.   Each herb has a characteristic oil which gives its flavor or fragrance to food. Chop very fine if using fresh herbs so more of the herb's oils can escape.

7.   Heat releases the oil of the herbs quickly. Cold does not.

8. In cold juices, cheese, etc., herbs should be presoaked, or added several hours before serving. In hot soups or stews, herbs are added about 30 minutes before cooking ends.

9. The dried herbs are more concentrated in flavor than the fresh ones. One tablespoon dried equals 3 tablespoons fresh.

10. Herbs left too long in any dish will develop strong flavors.

HOW TO FLAVOR WITH HERBS AND SPICES

Herbs are added to foods to give flavor in two ways:

1. Chopped fine and added to food directly.

2. Herb bouquets, which are mixtures, should be tied in a cloth bag and removed before food is served.

HERBS, SEEDS, SEASONINGS—THEIR MANY USES

1.	Allspice:	Similar to cinnamon and cloves. Used with carrots, squash, fish, rice and baked goods like pies, cookies, cakes.
2.	Anise:	Has a licorice taste—mentioned in the Bible in Matthew 23:23. Use in salad dressing, cookies, soups, breads, desserts.
3.	Basil:	Used with cauliflower, cucumbers, soups, stews, cheese, vegetables, eggs, sauces, tomatoes, rice.
4.	Bay Leaf:	Used in flour to keep bugs out. Soups, stews, potatoes, eggplant, chicken, and fish.
5.	Caraway Seeds:	Cakes, puddings, cookies, rye and black breads, salads, cottage cheese.
6.	Cardamon:	Interchangeable with cinnamon. Use in Danish pastry, curry dishes, squash, desserts.
7.	Cayenne:	Is red pepper to be used sparingly with tomato juice, eggs, soups, onions, spinach, zucchini and seafood.
8.	Celery Seeds:	Salads, soups, stuffing, potatoes, zucchini, carrots and fish.
9.	Chervil:	Similar to the Biblical myrrh and is fragant. Use in fish, soups, stews, eggs, salads, and sauces.
10.	Chili Pepper:	Used in Mexican dishes, chili, soups, cheese and egg dishes.
11.	Chives:	Of the onion family. Used with cheese, eggs, fish, stews, potatoes, soups, butter.

12. Cinnamon: Written about in Exodus 30:23 and Proverbs 7:17. Used in sweet potatoes, squash, desserts, beverages, cereals, and puddings.

13. Cloves: Cider, cakes, cookies, breads, fruit dishes, onions, carrots, squash, sweet potatoes.

14. Coriander: Bread, cakes, sweets, curries, casseroles and mushrooms. Read about it in Exodus 16:31 and Numbers 11:7.

15. Cumin: Curries, chili, Mexican dishes, sauces, tomato based dishes, bean dishes. In the Bible in Isaiah 28:25, 27, Matthew 23:23.

16. Curry Powder: Used widely in India. Mixture of pepper, ginger, garlic and coriander. Cream soups, potato salad, eggs, rice or grain dishes.

17. Dill: Cheese, salads, sauces, pickles, dressings, soups, fish, cucumber, green beans, cabbage, carrots.

18. Fennel: Has a licorice taste. Fish, pickles, cabbage, eggplant, salads, soups, desserts.

19. Garlic: A member of the onion family. Mentioned in Numbers 11:5. Italian dishes, soups, stews, casseroles, sauces for poultry and fish, dressings, grain dishes, vegetables.

20. Ginger: A spicy root from tropical Asia. Use in Chinese cooking, bakery items, carrots, peas, fruits, sweet potatoes.

21. Lemon Balm: Used where a lemon flavor is needed. Fruit cups, beverage, salads, teas, garnishes.

22. Mace: Fruit of nutmeg tree. Carrot cake, spice cake, cookies, smoothies, pudding, broccoli, cabbage, eggs.

23. Sweet Marjoram: Spaghetti sauce, poultry, soups, stews, dressings, carrots, corn, turnips, mushrooms, sweet potatoes.

24. Mint: Vegetables, soups, jellies, fruits, desserts, peas, carrots, tea. Look for it in the Bible in Matthew 23:23.

25. Mustard: Mentioned in Matthew 13:31-32, and Luke 13:19. Curries, salads, dressings, potato salad, cheese dishes, cucumber.

26. Nutmeg: Desserts, soufflés, quiches, carrots, beets, applesauce, eggs, squash, Brussel sprouts.

27. Oregano: Part of the mint family. Italian cooking, vegetables, soup, stews, good with tomato based dishes, broccoli, cucumbers, poultry dishes.

28.	Paprika:	Eggs, potatoes, fish, casseroles, salads.
29.	Parsley:	It is mild. Can be used in potatoes, fish, sauces, casseroles, loaves, salads, egg dishes.
30.	Poppy Seeds:	Salad dressings, cakes, breads, carrots, parsnips, cabbage, potatoes.
31.	Rosemary:	Chicken, soups, fruit salads, potatoes, eggs, split peas, green peas, beans, corn.
32.	Sage:	From the mint family. Stuffing, rice dishes, egg dishes, poultry, vegetables.
33.	Savory:	Also from the mint family and has a slight peppery taste. Cabbage, Brussel sprouts, green beans, soups, grain dishes, potatoes.
34.	Sesame Seeds:	Breads, cakes, pastries, loaves, salads, granola, casseroles.
35.	Sorrel:	Sour tasting leaves used in salads and vegetables.
36.	Tarragon:	Sauces, egg dishes, cheese dishes, poultry, broccoli, vinegar, cauliflower, stew, tomatoes, asparagus. Often called the "King" of the herbs.
37.	Thyme:	Part of the mint family. Poultry, soups, cheese dishes, peas, onions, eggplant, green beans, eggs, cauliflower, carrots.
38.	Turmeric:	Mayonnaise, corn, curries, cream sauces.

HERB BOUQUET MIXTURES
GENERAL RECIPE

Mix equal parts (1 tablespoon) of each dried herb desired. Blend the mixture well and store in tightly covered jars. One teaspoon of the mixture will flavor about 2 cups liquid. Place the teaspoon mixture in a cheesecloth bag and tie the end. Remove the bag before serving food.

Suggested Mixtures for Herb Bouquets:

1. For eggs and chicken fishes: Tarragon, chervil, basil, chives, savory.

2. For vegetables: Chervil, basil, summer savory, chives, sweet marjoram.

3. For fish: Marjoram, thyme, basil, sage, fennel.

4. For soups and stews: Parsley, thyme, basil, sweet marjoram, celery, rosemary, savory.

Make up your own herb mixtures and place them in a bottle:

1. Mexican Herbs

    5 parts basil
    4 parts oregano
    4 parts cumin
    3 parts chili powder
    1/2 part ground coriander

2. Italian Herbs

    4 parts marjoram
    4 parts oregano
    4 parts basil
    2 parts rosemary
    2 parts thyme

CHILI POWDER

2 tsp. cumin
1/4 tsp. cayenne
1/4 tsp. sage

1/4 tsp. oregano
1/4 tsp. allspice

Mix all together and store in a jar with a tight-fitting lid.

CURRY POWDER

2 ounces coriander seed
1 tsp. cumin seed
2 ounces tumeric
1 tsp. cardamon seed

1 tsp. ground ginger
Dash red chili pepper
1 tsp. fenugreek
1 tsp. dill seed

Pound and grind together in pestle with a mortar until fine. Store in a jar with a tight-fitting lid.

STUFFING SEASONING

1/2 cup dried celery
1/2 cup sage
1/2 cup parsley flakes

1/4 cup dried thyme
1/4 cup savory
1/4 cup marjoram

Mix all together and store in an airtight container. Use 2 tablespoons per 4 cups bread crumbs in your stuffing recipe.

HERB MIXTURE

2 T. dry parsley flakes	1/2 tsp. onion powder
1 tsp. paprika	1/2 tsp. sweet basil
1/2 tsp. tumeric	1/2 tsp. thyme
1 T. dill weed	1/2 tsp. marjoram
1/2 tsp. garlic powder	1/2 tsp. dry mustard
1/2 tsp. tarragon (crushed)	1 T. oregano
1/2 tsp. ground celery seed	

Combine all ingredients. Mix thoroughly. Store in an airtight container and shake well before using in dips, salad dressings or vegetable dishes.

DRYING AND STORING HERBS

For drying, herbs should be gathered when they contain the maximum amount of their oil. Flowers in Summer, leaves and bark in Spring, roots in Spring and Fall.

Clean carefully before drying.

1. **OVEN DRYING:**   Put herbs on a baking sheet. Set oven at 150°. Stir often, and leave several hours until all moisture is removed and herbs are crisp.

2. **INDOOR DRYING:**   Spread herbs on a screen and keep in a warm room or attic until dry.

STORING: When herbs are crisp and dry, crush, rub together or leave whole. Put into jars, cover tightly, and label.

3. **SCREEN DRYING:**   Cover a small meshed screen with cheesecloth and place the herbs on the cheesecloth. Cover with another piece of cheesecloth. Suspend the mesh above the ground in your house. This permits air circulation. Will take about 2–3 weeks.

4. **DRY BY HANGING:** Group herbs in small bunches and tie the ends with string. Suspend upside down from a nail. To prevent dust from accumulating on them, tie a perforated paper bag around them.

JAMS

STRAWBERRY JAM

6 cups strawberries, crushed
1 box powdered pectin

2 cups honey
1/4 cup lemon juice

Place the fruit and the pectin in a large kettle, stir well. Place over high heat; bring to a boil, stirring constantly to avoid scorching. Add the honey and lemon juice; mix well. Continue stirring and bring to full rolling boil (one that you can not stir down). Boil hard exactly 4 minutes. Remove from heat. Spoon off foam. Ladle into hot, sterilized jars (1/4" from top) and seal. Process for 15 minutes in a boiling water bath.

Yield: 7½ pints

BLACKBERRY JAM

5½ cups blackberries, crushed
1 box powdered pectin

1-1/3 cups honey

Place the crushed blackberries and pectin in a large kettle, stir well. Place over high heat; bring to a boil. Stir constantly to prevent scorching. Add the honey and bring to a full rolling boil. Boil hard for 4 minutes. Remove from the heat. Spoon off foam. Ladle into hot, sterilized jars (1/4" from top) and seal. Process for 15 minutes in a boiling water bath.

Yield: 9 6-ounce jars

HONEY PEACH JAM

4 cups prepared fruit, about 3 pounds
    fully-ripe peaches
3 T. lemon juice

2 cups honey
1 tsp. cinnamon
1 box powdered pectin

Wash, peel and pit peaches. Chop and coarsely grind to measure 4 cups, and blend with the lemon juice. Place in a large kettle and bring to a full rolling boil; add the honey and cinnamon and boil for 1 minute. Make sure you stir constantly. Remove from the heat; stir in the pectin. Return to the heat and bring to full rolling boil; boil hard 1 minute, stirring. Remove from the heat. Skim off foam and alternately stir and skim 5 minutes to cool slightly and prevent fruit from floating. Ladle into hot, sterilized glasses. Seal. Process in a boiling water bath for 10 minutes.

Yield: 12 6-ounce jars

APRICOT HONEY FREEZER JAM

3 cups prepared fruit, 2½ pounds,
    fully-ripe apricots
1/4 cup lemon juice

1 box powdered pectin
2 cups honey

Wash, pit and coarsely grind apricots. Measure fruit and lemon juice into a 2-quart bowl. Stir well. Slowly add the pectin and stir vigorously. Let stand 30 minutes, stirring occasionally. Add honey and mix well. Ladle into washed and scalded 1/2-1 pint freezer containers, leaving 1/2" head space. Cover and store in the freezer. Can keep in the refrigerator when opened for 2-3 weeks.

Yield: 5 1/2 pints

Variation:

Strawberry Freezer Jam: In place of the apricots, use strawberries in the same proportion.

FRUIT BUTTERS

APPLE BUTTER

9-10 tart cooking apples, peeled,
    cored and sliced (about 3 pounds)
1 cup apple juice or cider
1/4 cup lemon juice

1/2 tsp. allspice
1 tsp. cinnamon
1/4 tsp. cloves
1¼ cups honey or to taste

Combine apple slices and apple and lemon juices in a heavy kettle. Cover and cook over medium heat until apples are mushy, about 15 minutes. Place the contents in a blender and blend well. Return the apples to the kettle and add the allspice, cinnamon and cloves. Cook and stir frequently over medium heat, about 30-40 minutes or until mixture is thick. Remove from the heat and add the honey to taste. The amount of honey varies depending on the sweetness of the apples you are using. Pour into hot sterilized jars to 1/4" of top. Seal. Process in a boiling water bath for 12 minutes.

Yield: 6 8-ounce jars

Variation:

To freeze butter: Spoon cooled apple butter into freezer containers or jars to within 1" of top. Cover and freeze.

APRICOT PINEAPPLE HONEY BUTTER

4 pounds apricots
1 can (20-ounce) unsweetened
    crushed pineapple (including juice)

1 tsp. grated orange peel
1/4 cup lemon juice
2½ cups honey

Wash the apricots and cut in halves and remove pits. Whirl apricots (a portion at a time) in a blender until smooth to make 7 cups purée. Also whirl, separately, the pineapple and its juice until smooth. Place in a large kettle the apricot and pineapple purée. Add the orange peel, lemon juice and honey. Simmer purée mixture, uncovered, stirring more frequently as it thickens. Cook about 2 hours. Add more honey if needed. Store in refrigerator.

Yield: 8 cups

PEAR-GINGER HONEY BUTTER

4 pounds Bartlett pears (about 8
    large pears)
1/4 cup lemon juice

3/4 tsp. ginger, ground
1½ tsp. grated lemon peel
1 cup honey

Wash, quarter, and core the pears. In a large kettle, combine fruit and lemon juice. Simmer, covered, stirring occasionally, until fruit is soft. It will take about 30 minutes. Whirl mixture in a blender (a portion at a time) until smooth, to give you 2 quarts purée. Return the purée to the kettle and add the ginger, lemon peel and honey. Simmer, uncovered, stirring more frequently as it thickens, about 1½-2 hours. Add more honey if desired. Refrigerate up to 3 months. If so desired, freeze. Follow the instructions given with APPLE BUTTER.

Yield: 10 cups

PAPAYA BUTTER

3 large ripe papayas
1/4 cup lime juice

1 tsp. grated lime peel
1 cup honey

Remove peel and seeds from the papayas; cut in small chunks. Add the lime juice. Whirl papaya and the juice in a blender until smooth; then pour purée into a large kettle. Stir in the lime peel and the honey. Bring to a simmer and cook, uncovered, stirring until mixture thickens. Let cool. Store in refrigerator up to 3 weeks or freeze in freezer containers.

Yield: 2 pints

NECTARINE OR PEACH HONEY BUTTER

5 pounds unpeeled nectarines or   1 tsp. grated orange peel
   peeled peaches   2¼ cups honey
1/2 cup orange juice

Remove pits and slice the fruit. Whirl fruit (a portion at a time) in a blender until smooth to make 2 quarts purée. Pour purée into a 5-quart kettle. Stir in the orange juice, orange peel and honey. Simmer, uncovered, stirring more frequently as it thickens, about 2-2½ hours. Taste; add up to 1/4 cup more honey if desired. Refrigerate up to 3 months. If you would like to freeze, follow instructions listed with APPLE BUTTER.

Yield: 6 cups

STRAWBERRY HONEY BUTTER

12 cups strawberries (5-6 baskets)   1 tsp. grated lemon peel
2 T. lemon juice   2¼ cups honey

Wash the strawberries and remove stems. Whirl berries (a portion at a time) in a blender until smooth to make 2 quarts purée. Pour purée into a large kettle. Stir in the lemon juice, peel and honey. Simmer, uncovered, stirring more frequently as it thickens. Simmer for about 2½-3 hours. If you need more honey, add up to 1/4 cup extra. Refrigerate up to 3 months. If you would like to freeze, follow instructions listed with APPLE BUTTER.

Yield: 5 cups

SPECIAL HELPS

BAKING POWDER—LOW SODIUM

2 cups arrowroot powder   1 cup potassium bicarbonate
2 cups cream of tartar

The potassium bicarbonate is available at your local drugstore. Ask the pharmacist. Mix all of the ingredients together and store in an airtight container. Use in the same proportions as you would the other baking powder.

Yield: 5 cups

VANILLA EXTRACT

1 large whole vanilla bean
1/4 cup boiling water
1/2 tsp. liquid lecithin

1 T. honey
1 T. vegetable oil

Cut vanilla bean into small pieces, place in small mixing bowl. Pour boiling water over the bean pieces, cover bowl, allow to steep overnight. Next morning: Blend bean and water in electric blender. Add lecithin, honey and oil. Blend again. Pour into storage containers, cap tightly. Store in refrigerator. Shake before using. Use as you would commercial vanilla.

PECTIN

Pectin is used with fruits that lack their own natural pectin and will not gel. Peaches, strawberries, pears, cherries, pineapple and most berries lack their own pectin. Pectin can also be added to other fruits in order to cut down on cooking time necessary to form a gel. Jellies made with pectin require less fruit than the cooked-down type to make the same amount of finished product.

In making the pectin you will use apples and water. Wash apples and cut into small pieces without peeling. Place in a kettle and add 1 pint of water for each pound of apples. Boil for 15 minutes. Pour the apples into a single thickness of cheesecloth that is lining a colander. Catch all of the free-running juice as this is homemade pectin. Do not squeeze the pulp. Return to the kettle and add the same amount of water as before. Cook over a low heat simmering for 15 minutes. Let it stand for 10 minutes and then strain it again through the cheesecloth. Allow the pulp to cool and squeeze out all the juice by pressing it in the cheesecloth. Add this to the other juice acquired earlier. Now you have pectin. You can use it immediately or store it for future use. If you are going to store it, pour into hot, sterilized jars and place in a boiling water bath for 5 minutes. You can also freeze this mixture if you would like. Add 1 cup fruit pectin for each cup of fruit. Use as you would commercial pectin.

CITRUS PEEL POWDER

Select citrus fruits that have not been artificially colored, gassed, waxed nor sprayed with insecticides. Best to get the natural organic citrus. Wash and dry fruit and then peel citrus. Remove the white membrane from the rind. Cut into small slices. Place on a cookie sheet and place in the sun to dry. You may want to place a thin layer of cheesecloth over the top if you have a lot of bugs around. When thoroughly dry, place in a blender and grind until it is a powder. You can make it either fine or coarse, depending on your own preference. Store in tightly covered jars and label. Keeps indefinitely. Use in breads, pancakes, frostings, desserts, cookies, spreads. It is also a neat gift idea. Give a friend a jar plus some bread that you used the powdered peels in.

HONEYED CITRUS PEEL

Select the same type of citrus as listed in the CITRUS PEEL POWDER. Remove the white membrane from the peel and slice into strips. Soak the strips in a mixture of water and honey until they become soft and pliable. There should be more honey than water. Drain slices and spread on wax paper. Let set for 2–3 days until they dry. Store and refrigerate. Can be used in a number of different dessert recipes.

MUSTARD

Mustard is made from seeds ground to various degrees of fineness. You can use an electric blender, but a nut grinder is better suited for the proper grinding. This mustard will be coarser than the store-bought type which is ground to a flour. Mustard can be either hot or cool. The difference is due to the temperature of the liquid mixed with the seed. Heat inhibits the flavor and produces sweet mustard. Store in a tightly covered container. Flavor deteriorates after a week or two, so make up only a small amount.

HERB MUSTARD

2 T. mustard seed   1 T. oil
1 tsp. chervil, parsley and tarragon   1 T. cider vinegar

Grind together the mustard seed, chervil, parsley and tarragon. Add the oil and vinegar. Mix into a paste and allow to sit for 1 hour before using.

HOT MUSTARD

1/2 cup ground mustard   1 T. molasses, unsulfured
3 T. cold water   3 T. vinegar
1/4 tsp. each allspice, cayenne and
    vegetable seasoning

Mix the mustard and water together and allow to sit for 15 minutes. Mix in all the other ingredients and stir into a paste.

LIST OF NATURAL FOODS

Agar-Agar—It is a gelatin that comes from the seaweed. It is a good source of minerals. It is used like gelatin in molded foods or can be used in place of pectin. It comes in flakes, powder or stick form. For 1¾ cups liquid use 1 tablespoon flakes, or 1½ teaspoons powdered, or 7'' from the stick.

Arrowroot Powder—Comes from the root of a tropical plant that is high in minerals. It is a natural thickening agent. Use in place of cornstarch and white flour.

Baking Powder—Use low-sodium baking powder as it is free from both sodium compounds and aluminum compounds. Available in your local health food stores or make your own (see Chapter 14).

Brewer's Yeast—Also called nutritional yeast. It is a nonleavening yeast that is a rich source of vitamin B and protein. To increase the nutritional value of your foods add a small amount to soups, salads, bean and grain dishes, and even your desserts. A lot of times it is added to beverages such as was used in the BOB TURNBULL SPECIAL PROTEIN DRINK. Some brands do not taste very good, so experiment until you find one that suits your taste.

APPENDIX A

Brown Rice Flour—Brown rice ground up very fine. Has a sweet flavor. Use alone as the only flour in cookie recipes or combine with whole wheat in breads.

Butter—Use unsalted or lightly salted. If available, try getting butter made from raw milk.

Carob Powder—Also called St. John's Bread as it has been said it sustained John the Baptist in the wilderness. It is powder ground from the carob pod, which comes from a tree of the locust family. Toasted, carob powder strongly resembles chocolate, but it has none of chocolate's undesirable features. Carob is low in fat and starch, rich in minerals, vitamins and natural sugars. It is also called carob flour. To use as a substitute in a recipe, use 3 tablespoons carob plus 2 tablespoons of water for 1 square of chocolate.

Cheese—Do not use processed cheese spreads or cheese foods. Use aged, hard, undyed cheeses. If available use raw milk cheese.

Date Sugar—Made from dried ground dates. It is a natural sweetener and can be used as you would brown sugar. Try it sprinkled on cereals, desserts, granola or fruit salads. It has to dissolve, though, to be a part of your recipe.

Dried Fruits—Sundried, unsulfured fruits. A lot of dried fruit has been treated with sulfur dioxide. If the package does not say *un*sulfured most likely it has been sulfur treated. You can soften the dried fruit just by soaking in water.

Eggs—Try to get fresh ones available from local farmers. If available use fertile eggs.

Extracts or Flavorings—Make sure your extracts are pure and natural, without sugars and artificial colors. Try making your own vanilla (see Chapter 14).

Gelatin—Plain, unflavored and unsweetened gelatin is used.

Graham Flour—A whole wheat flour with some of the bran removed.

Honey—Raw, uncooked and unfiltered honey is used. The type of honey is up to you as there are so many different flavors. A mild tasting one is best for baking purposes. If it crystalizes, just place the jar in a pan of hot water and it will liquefy.

Juices—The juices used, such as apple, pineapple and orange, are all unsweetened natural juices.

Kelp—A seaweed available in powdered form. Use as seasoning in place of salt. Good source of iodine, calcium and protein.

Oat Flour—Oats give baked goods a natural sweetness. Place rolled oats in a blender and blend until it becomes a fine powder.

Milk—You can use raw, any types of pasteurized milk (whole, low-fat, non-fat), reconstituted powder milk, soy or goat milk in the recipes throughout this book.

Millet Flour—Ground millet, which is a whole grain.

Molasses, Blackstrap—Made from the sugar cane. It has a very strong flavor so you may want to keep the amount used in your baking small.

Molasses, Unsulfured—A sweet dark sugar cane syrup that is 100% pure. I use it a lot in my baking along with honey. It gives my baked items a special rich flavor.

Non-instant Dry Milk Powder—Used frequently in the powdered form in the book. It has twice the nutritive value as the instant variety. It is a very fine powder and is difficult to dissolve by just stirring. Best to place it in the blender with water and run the blender on low until it is blended. To reconstitute it takes 2/3 cup non-instant dry milk per quart. The instant dry milk takes 1-1/3 cups per quart. You save money by using the non-instant.

Nuts—Nuts are a good source of protein, unsaturated fats, and a number of different vitamins and minerals. A lot of different nuts are mentioned in the Bible; for instance, almonds, hazel and chestnuts. There are many other nuts that are good to eat—Brazil, cashews, macadamia, peanuts, pecan, walnuts, piñon. Use them all in their raw, unsalted form.

Oil—Use unrefined oils in your diet. Those are the ones that have not gone through the refining, bleaching and deodorizing that refined oils have been through. Unrefined oils contain all the nutrients that the food it was extracted from contains. It also contains unsaturated fatty acids, lecithin, and vitamin E which are lacking in refined oils. There is a wide variety of unrefined oils that can be used. For example:

Corn—Used in baking but has too strong a flavor to be used in salad dressings.

Safflower—A mild taste and can be used for overall cooking such as sautéing, salad dressings, baking. Use in place of Crisco and lard.

Sesame and **Sunflower**—Good for sautéing and stir-frying. Also for baking and salad dressings.

Olive—Good in Italian, Greek and Mediterranean cooking. Use also for salad dressings.

Peanut and **Soy**—Have strong flavors and best used for sautéing.

You can substitute the oils for solid fats in your recipes. Just substitute equal amounts. You will have to increase dry ingredients though.

Peanut Butter—In the recipes that call for it, use freshly ground peanut butter. It is easy to make your own (see Chapter 2). The commercial kind contains sugar, salt, preservatives, and they have been hydrogenated. If there is not a layer of oil on the top of the peanut butter when you buy it, it means it has been hydrogenated. Pass it up for an unhydrogenated one.

Peanut Flour—Made from ground peanuts. Add along with other flour in your baked goods. The foods will be dark and heavy with the addition of this flour.

Potato Flour—Use as a thickening agent. Substitute for whole wheat flour.

Rye Flour—Made from finely ground whole grain rye. Should be mixed with whole wheat when baking because rye tends to be heavy by itself.

Seeds—In Genesis 1:29 God gave Man every herb bearing seed as his meat. There are many varieties of seeds and they all are a good source of protein, vitamin B and many different minerals, and unsaturated fatty acids. Try pumpkin, sesame seeds, sunflower seeds, chia seeds. Use them in their raw, unsalted form.

Sorghum Syrup—It is made from a grain similar to corn. It is a natural sweetener that is somewhere between molasses and honey, similar to brown sugar. Use as you would honey or brown sugar.

Soy Grits—Made from coarsely cracked soybeans. Use in place of soybean in your recipes as they do not take as long to cook. Also act as a substitute for nuts in baked goods as they are real crunchy.

Soy Flour—Made from soybeans ground very fine. Good source of protein. Substitute it for part of the whole wheat flour in your baked goods. For each cup of flour you can replace 2 tablespoons whole wheat with 2 tablespoons soy flour. Soy flour browns easily, so be sure to turn the temperature on the oven down 25°.

Soy Lecithin—Comes either in liquid or granular form. It is a natural emulsifier that gives a smooth texture to baked goods. Use a teaspoon or up to a tablespoon in your baked goods.

Sunflower Seed Meal—Sunflower seeds coarsely ground.

Tamari (soy sauce)—This is naturally fermented soy sauce made from wheat, soybeans, water and salt. It is aged in wood for 2 years. It contains vitamins, minerals, natural sugars and protein. Good seasoning for vegetables, soups, sauces and grains.

Triticale Flour—Comes from the grain that is a cross between rye and wheat. It is low in gluten so has to be mixed with whole wheat when using it for baking.

Vegetable Seasoning—A mixture of natural herbs and vegetables in a powdered form. I use a brand named "Vegit" but there are many other brands available at your local health food stores. I use it as a substitute for salt and it is found in many of my recipes.

Vinegar—Use apple cider vinegar that has been aged in wood and has also been made from unsprayed apples.

Whole Wheat Flour—Stone ground whole wheat is superior to the kind that is ground with steel rollers as the heat generated by the friction of the grains against the blades destroys a lot of the vitamins. It is a hard wheat and can be used for any of your baking needs. Because the germ is still in the flour it can spoil easily. It is best to grind your own in a flour grinder. But if you are unable to, you should buy only a small amount and make sure you keep it refrigerated. It can also be frozen to keep it fresh.

Whole Wheat Pastry Flour—This flour is made from a soft wheat. It is a lighter flour and can be used in pastries, cookies and cakes. This flour will help make them light. It should not be used in recipes calling for yeast as the gluten content is very low.

EXPLANATION OF COOKING TERMS

Al dente—An Italian term for not-quite-tender pasta.

Au Gratin—Topped with bread crumbs (or shredded cheese) and browned.

Bake—To cook by dry heat, usually in the oven, covered or uncovered. When applied to meats and vegetables, this is called roasting.

Baste—Spoon liquid over cooking food to add flavor and moisture. Or use baster.

Beat—To make mixture smooth by adding air with a brisk whipping or stirring motion using an electric mixer or a spoon.

Bisque—A thick cream soup containing game or fish. Also puréed vegetables.

Blanch—To remove skins from vegetables, fruits or nuts by letting them stand in boiling water until skins peel off easily. On occasion it is necessary to drain off the first water and add more boiling water. **APPENDIX B**

Blend—To completely mix two or more ingredients until smooth and uniform.

Boil—To cook in liquid at boiling temperature (212° at sea level) where bubbles rise to the surface and break. For a full rolling boil, bubbles form rapidly throughout the mixture.

Braise—To cook slowly with a small amount of liquid in tightly covered pan in oven or on top of range.

Bread—To coat with bread crumbs before cooking.

Broil—To cook directly over an open fire or grill, or under a flame or heating unit.

Chill—To place in the refrigerator to reduce temperature.

Chop—To cut into small pieces about the size of peas with a chopper, knife or blender.

Clean Garlic—Separate into cloves and remove thin, papery outer skin.

Coat—To roll various foods in flour, sugar, crumbs, nuts, etc., until all the sides are evenly covered; or, to dip first into slightly beaten egg or milk, then cover with whatever coating is called for in your recipe.

Combine—To mix all the ingredients.

Cool—To remove from heat and let stand at room temperature.

Cream—To beat with electric mixer, or spoon, until mixture is soft and smooth. When applied to blending butter and honey, mixture is beaten until fluffy and light.

Croissant—Flaky, crescent-shaped roll.

Crouton—A smallish cube of dry, toasted bread served on top of salad or soup.

Cube—To cut a solid into little cubes from about 1/2" to 1".

Cut In—(a) To break up food into pieces with a knife or scissors. (b) To combine butter with dry ingredients by working together with two knives, used scissor fashion, or with pastry blender. (Usually applied to pastry making.)

Dice—To cut food into smaller than 1/2" cubes of uniform size and shape.

Dissolve—To make a liquid and a dry substance go into solution.

Dredge—To coat food with some dry ingredient such as seasoned flour.

Dust—To sprinkle a food, or coat lightly with flour.

Fillet—A strip of lean meat or of fish without bone.

Fine Herbs—A mixture of finely chopped herbs; for example, chives, parsley, tarragon, etc.

Flake—To break lightly into small pieces.

Flute Edge of Pastry—Press index finger on edge of pastry, then pinch pastry with thumb and index finger of other hand. Lift fingers and repeat procedure to flute entire edge.

Fold—To add ingredients gently to a mixture. Using a spatula, cut down through mixture. Go across bottom of bowl and up and over, close to surface. Turn bowl frequently for even distribution.

Fricassee—A dish usually containing browned chicken cooked in a seasoned sauce or broth.

Full, Rolling Boil—The point at which the liquid rises in the pan, then tumbles into waves that can not be stirred down. It usually occurs, for example, in cooking jams and jellies.

Garnish—To decorate any foods. For example, nuts, olives and parsley are called garnishes when used to give a finish to a recipe.

Gnocchi—An Italian dumpling often made with potatoes.

Grate—To rub on a grater that separates the food into very fine particles.

Grind—To put food through a chopper. Choppers usually have two or three blades. Use a blade with smaller holes to grind foods fine and one with larger holes for coarse chopping or grinding.

Grind Nuts—To put nuts through a medium blade of food chopper or blender.

Julienne—Matchlike pieces of meat, vegetables or fruit.

Linguine—An Italian word that pertains to a narrow, flat pasta about 1/8'' wide.

Knead—To work and press dough hard with the heels of your hands so the dough becomes elastic and stretched.

Manicotti—A thin, rectangular-shaped pasta stuffed with ricotta cheese mixture.

Marinate—To let food stand in acid, such as lemon juice, wine, tomato juice, or in an oil-acid mixture like French dressing. Acts as a tenderizer. Steps up flavor.

Melt—To heat solid food until it becomes liquid.

Mince—To chop food in very small pieces, but finer than chopped.

Mix—To combine ingredients, usually by stirring, until evenly distributed.

Mornay—A cheese-flavored white sauce.

Panbroil—To cook uncovered on hot surface, removing fat as it accumulates.

Parboil—To cook food in a boiling liquid until partially done. This is usually a preliminary step to further cooking. Beans, for example, are parboiled then later baked.

Pare—To cut away coverings of fruits and vegetables.

Peel—To slip off or strip outer coverings of some fruits and vegetables.

Pilaf—A rice dish with poultry or meat and vegetables, or raisins and spices. Cooked in oil, then steamed and seasoned.

Poach—To cook in hot liquid, being careful that food holds its shape while cooking.

Polenta—Thick cornmeal mush, often served with sauce, stew or gravy. May be cooked firm and sliced, or cooked just until consistency of mashed potatoes.

Precook—To cook food partially or completely before final cooking or reheating.

Preheat—To heat oven to stated temperature before using.

Purée—To press vegetables or fruits through a sieve, or food mill, or blend in an electric blender until food is pulpy. Sauces, vegetables and soups are often puréed.

Ratatouille—A stew of eggplant, green pepper, tomatoes, and squash, seasoned with garlic and other condiments. Sometimes meat is added. Serve either hot or cold.

Reduce Liquid—To continue cooking the liquid until the amount is sufficiently decreased, thus concentrating flavor and sometimes thickening the original fluid.

Roux—A mixture of flour and fat that is cooked, sometimes until the flour browns, and is used to thicken sauces and soups.

Sauté—To cook foods until golden and tender, in a small amount of oil on top of range.

Scald—To bring to a temperature just below the boiling point where tiny bubbles form at the edge of the pan.

Scallop—To bake food, usually in a casserole, with sauce or other liquid. Crumbs are often sprinkled on top.

Score—To cut narrow slits or grooves partway through the outer surface of food.

Shallot—A small, pear-shaped, reddish onion.

Shirr—To break eggs into a dish with crumbs or cream, then bake.

Shred—To rub on a shredder to form small, long narrow pieces.

Sieve—To force through sieve or food mill.

Sift—To put one or more dry ingredients through a sieve or sifter.

Simmer—To cook in liquid over low heat at a temperature of 185°-210° where bubbles form at a slow rate and burst before reaching the surface.

Sliver—To cut or split into long, thin strips, with a knife on a cutting board.

Soft Peaks—To beat egg whites or whipping cream until peaks are formed when beaters are lifted, but tips curl over.

Soufflé—A light, fluffy baked dish containing a sauce with egg yolks, a flavoring mixture and beaten egg whites which cause the mixture to puff during baking.

Steam—To cook in steam with or without pressure. A small amount of boiling water is used, more water being added during steaming process if necessary.

Steep—To allow a substance to stand in a very hot liquid in order to extract color and flavor.

Sterilize—To heat in boiling water or steam for at least 20 minutes, until living organisms are destroyed.

Stiff Peaks—To beat egg whites until peaks stand up straight when beaters are lifted, but are still moist and glossy.

Stir—To mix ingredients with a circular motion until well blended.

Toss—To tumble ingredients lightly with a lifting motion.

Vermicelli—Pasta shaped into long thin strings thinner than regular spaghetti

Vinaigrette—A seasoned vinegar and oil sauce.

Whip—To rapidly beat eggs, heavy cream, etc., in order to incorporate air and expand volume.

HOW TO SUBSTITUTE

RECIPE REPLACEMENTS OR SUBSTITUTIONS

Foods to Omit	Replacements	Special Instructions
Baking powder with aluminate	Low-sodium BAKING POWDER	Use in same proportions
	Active dry yeast	Need to dissolve in warm liquid. Other ingredients need to be at room temperature.
	Eggs	1 egg can be used for 1/2 tsp. baking powder.
Bread crumbs, white bread or crushed cornflakes	Whole grain bread crumbs or wheat germ can be used.	
Buttermilk—1 cup	YOGURT	
	Whole milk	Add 1 T. vinegar or lemon juice and let sit for 5 minutes.
Cereals, boxed	GRANOLA or whole grain cereals	
Cheese, processed or spreads	Aged, hard, undyed cheese	

APPENDIX C

Foods to Omit	Replacements	Special Instructions
Chocolate	Carob powder	3 T. carob plus 2 T. water will equal 1 square of chocolate.
Cocoa	Carob powder	Use equal amounts.
Chocolate chips	CAROB CHIPS	Equal proportions
Coffee and black teas	Herb teas Cereal grain beverages Postum	
Cream Cheese	YOGURT CHEESE	
Flour, white, unbleached all purpose	Whole wheat flour or other whole grain flours	Need to add more liquids.
Cake flour	Whole wheat pastry flour	Need to add more liquids.
Jams and jellies	FRUIT BUTTERS with honey JAMS and JELLIES sweetened with honey	
Jello—sweetened gelatin powder, artificially flavored	Unsweetened and unflavored gelatin Agar-agar	Equal amounts
Milk—1 cup	Soy, nut, goat and raw milk	Use in equal amounts.
	Non-instant dry milk powder	4 T. powder plus 1 cup water
	YOGURT	Equal amounts

Foods to Omit	Replacements	Special Instructions
Nuts, roasted and salted	Raw and unsalted	Roast peanuts at home by placing them in a 250° oven for 15 minutes—it takes away the raw taste. Use all other nuts raw.
Pancake syrup	Honey Molasses FRUIT SYRUP	
Pasta, white flour	WHOLE WHEAT PASTA Vegetable pasta Soy pasta	
Rice, white or instant	Brown rice Bulgur wheat Buckwheat groats	
Salt	Tamari Kelp Vegetable seasoning Herbs	To taste. Use equal proportions for all the rest.
Shortening Shortening or margarine—1 cup	Butter Unrefined oils	Equal amounts 7/8 cup oil for each cup. Need to increase dry ingredients also.
Soda pop	Unsweetened fresh juices SMOOTHIES	
Sour cream	YOGURT COTTAGE CHEESE	Place in blender and blend until smooth.

Foods to Omit	Replacements	Special Instructions
Sugar, white—1 cup	1/2 cup honey	For each 1/2 cup honey used decrease liquid by 1/4 cup. If no liquid, increase flour by 1/4 cup. Decrease oven temperature by 25°.
	Unsulfured molasses	
	Fruit juices	Use in smaller amounts.
	Sorghum	
Brown—1 cup	Date sugar	Use 3/4 cup date sugar.
Thickeners		
Cornstarch—1 T.	Arrowroot powder	Use 3 tsp. arrowroot.
White flour—1 T.	Arrowroot powder	Use 1/2 T. arrowroot
	Whole wheat flour	Equal amounts
Vanilla, and other artificial and synthetic flavors	VANILLA, pure Pure natural flavors No artificial dyes or flavors	
Vegetables, canned	Fresh vegetables	
Vinegar, distilled	Apple cider vinegar	Use equal amounts.
Worchestershire, 3 T.	Tamari (soy sauce)	Use 4 T. tamari

HELP FOR SHOPPER—LIST OF EQUIVALENTS

Item	Unit	Equivalent
Almonds		
Unshelled, whole	1 pound	1¾ cups nutmeat
Unblanched, whole	1 pound	3 cups nutmeat
Unblanched, ground	1 pound	2-2/3 cups nutmeat
Almond extract	1/4 tsp.	1 tsp. ground almonds
Apples		
Whole	1 pound, unpared	3 cups pared, sliced
Whole, for drying	10 apples	1 pound dried
Apricots	1 pound	3¼ cups dried
Arrowroot powder	1½ tsp.	1 T. flour
	2 tsp.	1 T. cornstarch
Baking powder	1 tsp.	1/4 tsp. baking soda plus 1/2 cup buttermilk or YOGURT
	1 tsp.	1/4 tsp. baking soda plus 1/4 cup molasses
Bananas	3-4 medium sized (1 pound)	1¾-2 cups mashed 2 cups sliced
Bay leaf	1/4 tsp.	1 whole bay leaf
Beans, dried	1 cup	2½-3 cups cooked
Blue cheese	4 ounces	1 cup crumbled
Brazil nuts, whole	1 pound	3¼ cups nutmeat
Bread crumbs, dry	1/2 cup	1 slice bread
Brown rice, uncooked	1 cup	3 cups cooked
Butter 1 stick	4 ounces	8 T. or 1/2 cup
4 sticks	1 pound	2 cups

Item	Unit	Equivalent
Buttermilk	1 cup	1 cup YOGURT 1 cup sweet milk and 1 T. vinegar (let stand 5 minutes)
Cabbage	1 head (1 pound)	4½ cups shredded
Carob powder	3 T. plus 2 T. water	1 square (1 ounce) chocolate
Carrots	1 pound (6-8 medium)	3 cups shredded
Celery	1 medium bunch	4½ cups diced or chopped
Cheese	1 pound	4 cups grated
Cottage cheese	1 pound	2 cups
Cracker crumbs	3/4 cup	1 cup bread crumbs
Cream cheese	8 ounces	1 cup
Cream, heavy	1/2 pint (1 cup)	2 cups whipped
Dates	1 pound	2 cups chopped
Eggs		
Large	5	1 cup approximately
Medium	6	1 cup approximately
Small	7	1 cup approximately
Egg yolks	12-14	1 cup
Egg whites	8-10	1 cup
Figs	1 pound	2¾-3 cups chopped
Flour, all-purpose white	4 cups 1 cup	3½ cups cracked wheat 1 cup cornmeal or 1¼ cups rye flour or 7/8 cup gluten flour or 1 cup whole wheat flour

Item	Unit	Equivalent
Garlic	1 clove	1/8 tsp. powder
Green onion with tops	1 bunch (7 medium)	1/2 cup sliced
Green pepper	1 large (6 ounces)	1 cup diced
Herbs, dried	1 T.	3 T. fresh herbs
Lemon and lime Rind	1 medium 1 tsp. grated rind 1 medium	3 T. juice 1/2 tsp. lemon extract 1½–2 T. grated
Macaroni	1 cup uncooked	2¼ cups cooked
Milk Whole Skim	 1 quart 1 cup	 1 quart skim milk plus 3 T. cream 1/3 cup instant dry milk plus 3/4 cup water
Noodles	3 cups uncooked	3 cups cooked
Oatmeal	1 cup uncooked	1¾ cups cooked
Onion	1 medium	1/2 cup chopped
Oranges	1 medium	1/4–1/3 cup juice 1/2 cup diced or sectioned
Peaches	1 medium	1/2 cup sliced
Pear	1 medium	1/2 cup sliced
Pecans Whole	 1 pound	 3¾ cups chopped 4½ cups halved
Potatoes	1 pound (3 medium)	2 cups pared and sliced 2 cups cubed 1¾ cups mashed

Item	Unit	Equivalent
Raisins	1 pound	2¾ cups
Rolled oats	1 pound	8 cups cooked
Spaghetti	8 ounces	4 cups cooked
Spinach	1 pound (4 cups)	1½ cups cooked
Strawberries	1 quart	4 cups sliced
Tomatoes	1 cup canned	1-1/3 cups chopped fresh, simmered
	1 pound (4 small)	1½ cups cooked
Walnuts In shell Shelled	 1 pound 1 pound	 1-2/3 cups nutmeat 4 cups nutmeat
Wheat germ	12 ounces	3 cups
Yeast, compressed	1 cake (3/5 ounce)	1 pkg. active dry yeast
Yeast, active dry	1 package	1 T.
Yogurt	1 cup	1 cup buttermilk

WEIGHTS AND MEASUREMENTS

Dash or pinch . . . . Less than 1/8 teaspoon
1 teaspoon . . . . 1/3 tablespoon
1 tablespoon . . . . 3 teaspoons
3 teaspoons . . . . 1 tablespoon (1/2 fluid ounce)
2 tablespoons . . . . 1/8 cup (1 fluid ounce)
4 tablespoons . . . . 1/4 cup (2 fluid ounces)
5-1/3 tablespoons . . . . 1/3 cup (2-2/3 fluid ounces)
8 tablespoons . . . . 1/2 cup (4 fluid ounces)
10 tablespoons + 2 teaspoons . . . . 2/3 cup (5-1/3 fluid ounces)
12 tablespoons . . . . 3/4 cup (6 fluid ounces)
14 tablespoons . . . . 7/8 cup (7 fluid ounces)
16 tablespoons . . . . 1 cup (8 fluid ounces)
1/8 cup . . . . 2 tablespoons
1/4 cup . . . . 4 tablespoons
3/8 cup . . . . 1/4 cup + 2 tablespoons
5/8 cup . . . . 1/2 cup + 2 tablespoons

APPENDIX D

7/8 cup . . . . 3/4 cup + 2 tablespoons
1 cup . . . . 1/2 pint (8 fluid ounces)
2 cups . . . . 1 pint (16 fluid ounces)
1 quart . . . . 4 cups (2 pints)
4 quarts . . . . 1 gallon
8 quarts . . . . 1 peck
4 pecks . . . . 1 bushel
1 pound . . . . 16 ounces (dry measure)

APPROXIMATE CAN SIZES

Can Size	Weight	Contents
6 ounce	6 ounces	3/4 cup
8 ounce	8 ounces	1 cup
No. 1	11 ounces	1-1/3 cups
12 ounce	12 ounces	1½ cups
No. 303	16 ounces	2 cups
No. 2	20 ounces	2½ cups
No. 2½	28 ounces	3½ cups
No. 3	33 ounces	4 cups

CONVERTING REGULAR COOKING TIME TO CROCK POT TIME

Cooking Time in Recipe	Crock Pot Cooking Time
15–30 minutes	1½–2½ hours on high (300°-340°) or 4–8 hours on low (190°-240°)
35–45 minutes	3–4 hours on high (300°-340°) or 6–10 hours on low (190°-240°)
50 minutes to 3 hours	4–6 hours on high (300°-340°) or 8–18 hours on low (190°-240°)

RECOMMENDED READING LIST

There are so many excellent cookbooks on the market today that have been very beneficial to me. Following are some of the several cookbooks, listed in alphabetical order, that I feel you might enjoy adding to your cookbook library.

Cheese Making At Home, Don Radke, New York: Doubleday and Co., 1974.
Demonstrates how to make many different cheeses at home.

Complete Sprouting Cookbook, The, Karen Cross Whyte, San Francisco: Troubador Press, 1973.
Shows what to sprout, how to do it and how to use sprouts in many recipes.

Deaf Smith Country Cookbook, The, Marjorie Winn Ford, New York: Macmillan Publishing Co., 1973.
An excellent health food cookbook covering many areas of your diet.

Diet For A Small Planet, Frances Moore Lappé, New York: Ballantine Books, Inc., 1971.
Shows the principles, along with recipes, of meatless cookery.

Putting It Up With Honey, Susan Geiskopt, Ashland, Oregon: Quicksilver Productions, 1979.
The whys and hows of preserving with honey are answered in this book.

APPENDIX E

Recipes For a Small Planet, Ellen Buchman Ewald, New York: Ballantine Books, Inc., 1973.
High protein vegetarian cookery.

Simpler Life Cookbook, The, Frank Ford, Fort Worth, Texas: Harvest Press, 1974.
Good nutritional based recipes.

Soybean Cookbook, The, Dorothea Van Gundy Jones, New York: Arco Publishing Co., 1963.
    Demonstrates many recipes using all the soybean products.

Stocking Up, Revised, Emmaus, Pennsylvania: Rodale Press, 1977.
    How to preserve the foods you grow naturally.

Tofu Goes West, Gary Landgrebe, Palo Alto: Fresh Press, 1978.
    Many different recipes showing all the different ways tofu can be used.

MEET THE AUTHOR

Yvonne Turnbull

APPENDIX F

Yvonne (Gourlie) Turnbull was born and raised in Everett, Washington. She graduated from Everett High School and then attended Washington State College in Pullman where she received a BS Degree in Psychology. During her collegiate days she became quite interested in nutrition and since then has avidly pursued an extensive research and study program in nutrition for over 10 years. She is currently working on a Double Masters in both Nutrition and Home Economics.

While working in a travel agency in Honolulu, Hawaii, she met and married "The Chaplain of Waikiki Beach," the Rev. Dr. Bob Turnbull. They currently live on the Mainland and work together as a team ministry in conducting a variety of seminars.

Yvonne is currently the Nutritionist for "The 700 Club," a nationally syndicated TV talk show, over the Christian Broadcasting Network.

To contact Yvonne, write:

Yvonne Turnbull
"The 700 Club"
CBN Center
Virginia Beach, VA 23463

INDEX

NOTES

NOTES

NOTES

NOTES

NOTES

NOTES

NOTES

NOTES